WRITING
AND
DIFFERENCE

Translated, with
an Introduction and
Additional Notes,
by ALAN BASS

The University
of
Chicago Press

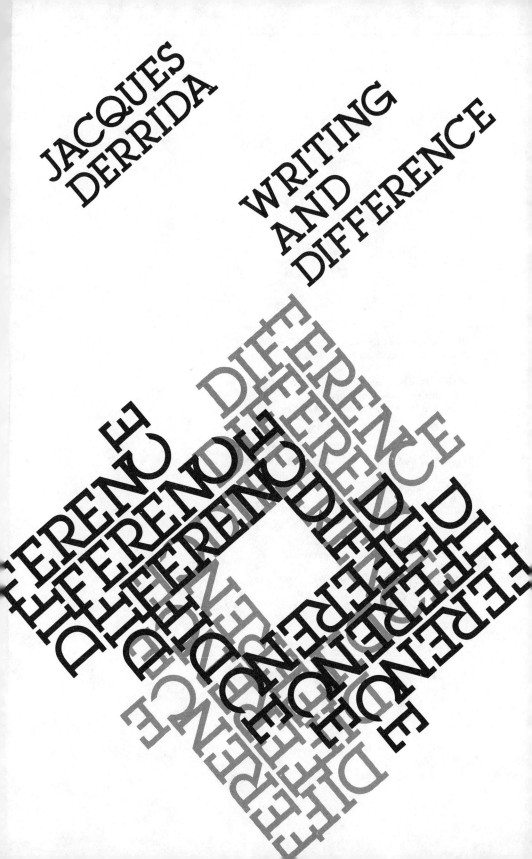

The University of Chicago Press, Chicago 60637
Routledge & Kegan Paul Ltd, London and Henley

89   7

Library of Congress Cataloging in Publication Data

Derrida, Jacques.
 Writing and difference.

 Translation of L'écriture et la différence.
 Includes bibliographical references.
 1. Philosophy—Addresses, essays, lectures.
I. Title
B2430.D482E5 1978 100 77-25933
ISBN 0-226-14328-7
  0-226-14329-5 (paper)

Le tout sans nouveauté
qu'un espacement
de la lecture

Mallarmé,
Preface to *Un Coup de dés*

Contents

"Par la date de ces textes, nous voudrions marquer qu'à l'instant, pour les relier, de les relire, nous ne pouvons nous tenir à égale distance de chacun d'eux. Ce qui reste ici le *déplacement d'une question* forme certes un *système*. Par quelque *couture* interprétative, nous aurions su après-coup le dessiner. Nous n'en avons rien laissé paraître que le pointillé, y ménageant ou y abandonnant ces blancs sans lesquels aucun texte jamais ne se propose comme tel. Si *texte* veut dire *tissu,* tous ces essais en ont obstinément défini la couture comme *faufilure*. (Décembre 1966.)" This note originally appeared appended to the bibliography of *L'écriture et la différence,* a collection of Derrida's essays written between 1959 and 1967 and published as a volume in the latter year. A glance at the list of sources (p. 341 below) will show that although Derrida has arranged the essays in order of their original publication, the essay that occupies the approximate middle of the volume was actually written in 1959, and therefore precedes the others. Before translating the note—in fact one of the most difficult passages in the book to translate—let us look at what Derrida said about the chronology of his works up to 1967 in an interview with Henri Ronse published in *Lettres françaises,* 6–12 December 1967 and entitled "Implications." (This interview, along with two others, has been collected in a small volume entitled *Positions,* Paris: Editions de Minuit, 1972.) Hopefully this discussion of chronology will serve to orient the reading of *Writing and Difference,* and to clarify why the essay that is in many respects the first one—" 'Genesis and Structure' and Phenomenology"—occupies the middle of the volume.

The year 1967 marks Derrida's emergence as a major figure in contemporary French thought. *La voix et le phénomène* (translated by David Allison as *Speech and Phenomena,* Evanston: Northwestern University Press, 1973), a work devoted to analyzing Husserl's ideas about the sign, and *De la grammatologie* (translated by Gayatri Spivak as *Of Grammatology,* Baltimore: Johns Hopkins University Press, 1976), devoted mainly to Rousseau's "Essay on the Origin on Languages" seen in the light of the history of the idea of the sign, both appeared in 1967, along with *L'écriture et la différence.* In response to Ronse's question about how to read these three books published one on the heels of the other, Derrida first says that *De la grammatologie* can be considered a bipartite work in the middle of which one could insert *L'écriture et la différence.* By implication, this would make the first half of *De la grammatologie*—in which Derrida demonstrates the system of ideas which from ancient to modern times has regulated the notion of the sign—the preface to *L'écriture et la différence.* It would be useful to keep this in mind while reading *L'écriture et la différence,* for while there are many references throughout the essays to the history of the notion of the sign, these references are nowhere in this volume as fully explicated as they are in the first half of *De la grammatologie.* Derrida explicitly states that the insertion of *L'écriture et la différence* into *De la grammatologie* would make the second half of the latter, devoted to Rousseau, the twelfth essay of *L'écriture et la différence.* Inversely, Derrida goes on to say, *De la grammatologie* can be inserted into the middle of *L'écriture et la différence,* for the first six essays collected in the latter work preceded *en fait et en droit* (*de facto* and *de jure*—a favorite expression of Derrida's) the publication, in two issues of *Critique* (December 1965 and January 1966), of the long essay which was further elaborated into the first part of *De la grammatologie*—our preface by implication to *L'écriture et la différence.* The last five essays of *L'écriture et la différence,* Derrida states, are situated or engaged in "l'ouverture grammatologique," the grammatological opening (*Positions,* p. 12). According to Derrida's statements a bit later in the interview, this "grammatological opening," whose theoretical matrix is elaborated in the first half of *De la grammatologie*—which, to restate, systematizes the ideas about the sign, writing and metaphysics which are scattered throughout *L'écriture et la différence*—can be defined as the "deconstruction" of philosophy by examining in the most faithful, rigorous way the "structured genealogy" of all of philosophy's concepts; and to do so in order to determine what issues the history of philosophy has hidden, forbidden, or repressed. The first step of this deconstruction of philosophy, which attempts to locate that which is *present* nowhere in philosophy, i.e., that which philosophy must hide in order to remain philosophy, is precisely the examination of the notion of *presence* as undertaken by Heidegger. Heidegger, says Derrida, recognized in the notion of presence the "destiny of philosophy," and the reference to the Heideggerean deconstruction of presence is a constant throughout Derrida's works. (Indeed, the reader unfamiliar with Heidegger may well be mystified by Derrida's frequent references to the notion of presence as the central target in the deconstruction of philosophy.) The *gramma*tological (from the Greek *gramma* meaning letter or writing) opening consists in the examination of the treatment of *writing* by philosophy, as a "particularly revelatory symptom" (*Positions,* p. 15) both of how the notion of presence functions in philosophy and of what this notion serves to repress. Derrida arrived at this position through a close scrutiny of the philosophical genealogy of linguistics, especially the philosophical treatment of the sign. From Plato to Heidegger himself, Derrida demonstrates, there is a persistent exclusion of the notion of writing from the philosophical definition of the sign. Since this exclusion can always be shown to be made in the name of *presence*—the sign allegedly being most present in spoken discourse—Derrida uses it as a "symptom" which reveals the workings of the "repressive" logic of presence, which determines Western philosophy as such.

Derrida's division of *L'écriture et la différence* into two parts, then, serves to remind the reader that between the sixth and seventh essays a "theoretical matrix" was elaborated whose principles are to some extent derived from the first six essays and are more systematically put to work in the last five. However, I would like to propose another division of the book, a division between the fifth ("'Genesis' and Structure' and Phenomenology") and sixth essays. My reason for placing the division at this point stems from what Derrida says about *La voix et le phénomène,* the other work published in 1967; like this latter work "'Genesis and Structure' and Phenomenology" is devoted to Husserl. In a "classical philosophical architecture," Derrida says of the three books published in 1967, *La voix et le phénomène* would have to be read first, for in it is posed, at a point which he calls "decisive," the "question of the voice and of phonetic writing in its relationships to the entire history of the West, such as it may be represented in the history of metaphysics, and in the most modern, critical and vigilant form of metaphysics: Husserl's transcendental phenomenology" (*Positions,* p. 13). Thus *La voix et le phénomène* could be bound to either *De la grammatologie* or *L'écriture et la différence,* Derrida says, as a long note.

Where would it be appended to *L'écriture et la différence*? In the same paragraph of the interview Derrida refers to another of his essays on Husserl, his introduction to his own translation of Husserl's *The Origin of Geometry,* published in 1962. He says that the introduction to *The Origin of Geometry* is the counterpart of *La voix et le phénomène,* for the "problematic of writing was already in place [in the former], as such, and bound to the irreducible structure of [the verb]'*différer*' [to differ and to defer, or, grossly put, difference in space and in time] in its relationships to consciousness, presence, science, history and the history of science, the disappearance or deferral of the origin, etc.'' (p. 13). Derrida might have said that this problematic was already in place in 1959, for a passage from '' 'Genesis and Structure' and Phenomenology'' poses the question of writing, again in relation to *The Origin of Geometry,* in the same terms employed in the 1967 interview, i.e., in terms of *writing and difference:* ''Reason, Husserl says, is the *logos* which is produced in history. It traverses Being with itself in sight, in order to appear to itself, that is, to state itself and hear itself as *logos* . . . . It emerges from itself in order to take hold of itself within itself, in the 'living present' of its self-presence. In emerging from itself, [*logos* as] hearing oneself speak constitutes itself as the history of reason through the detour of *writing. Thus it differs from itself in order to reappropriate itself. The Origin of Geometry* describes the necessity of this exposition of reason in a worldly inscription. An exposition indispensable to the constitution of truth . . . but which is also the danger to meaning from what is outside the sign [i.e., is neither the acoustic material used as the signifier, nor the signified concept the sign refers to]. In the moment of writing, the sign can always 'empty' itself . . . .'' If *La voix et le phénomène,* then, is the counterpart to the introduction to *The Origin of Geometry,* and if it can be attached to *L'écriture et la différence* as a long note, it seems that this would be the place to do so, for here the general conditions for a deconstruction of metaphysics based on the notions of writing and difference, and first arrived at through a reading of how the notion of the sign functions in Husserlian phenomenology, are explicitly stated. This would make *La voix et le phénomène* the sixth essay of a hypothetical twelve in *L'écriture et la différence,* but in the form of a long footnote attached to the middle of the volume.

   Chronologically, of course, Derrida's division of *L'écriture et la différence* is more reasonable than the one I am proposing. I offer this division, again, to help orient the reader who comes to *Writing and Difference* knowing only that Derrida is very difficult to read. Indeed, without some foreknowledge of (1) the attempt already begun by Derrida in 1959, but not presented until approximately the middle of this volume, to expand the deconstruction of metaphysics via a reading of Husserl's treatment of the sign; a reading which always pushes toward a moment of irreducible difference conceived not only as the danger to the doctrines of truth and meaning which are governed by presence, but also as an inevitable danger in the form of writing which allows truth and meaning to present themselves; and (2) the constant reference to Heidegger's analyses of the notion of presence, the first five essays of *Writing and Difference* might be incomprehensible. This is not to gainsay Derrida's statement that the last five essays only are ''engaged in the grammatological opening.'' These last five essays *do* follow Derrida's original publication (in *Critique*) of a systematic theoretical matrix for a deconstruction of metaphysics along the lines first laid out in the analyses of Husserl; this is why *La voix et le phénomène* comes first. Therefore, without setting aside the specific, individual contents of the first five essays, one must also be alerted to their developing systematicity, a systematicity whose guiding thread is embedded in the passage just cited from " 'Genesis and Structure' and Phenomenology.'' The best way to follow this thread is to pay close attention to Derrida's demonstrations—less and less elliptical as one continues through *Writing and Difference*—of how philosophically "traditional" some of the most "modern" concepts of criticism and philosophy are, for example in the references to Kant and Leibniz in the analysis of literary formalism in the first essay, "Force and Signification.''

The conclusion of this brief discussion of chronology with the metaphor of following a thread through a text brings us to the translation of the note originally appended to the list of sources in *L'écriture et la différence*. The translation is impossible without commentary, which will be placed in brackets: "By means of the dates of these texts, we would like to indicate [*marquer:* to mark] that in order to bind them together [*relier:* to put between covers the pages forming a work, originally by sewing], in rereading them [*relire: relier* and *relire* are anagrams], we cannot maintain an equal distance from each of them. What remains here the *displacement of a question* certainly forms a *system*. With some interpretive *sewing* [*couture*] we could have sketched this system afterward [*après-coup;* in German *nachträglich*. Cf. "Freud and the Scene of Writing" for the analysis of this notion.] We have only permitted isolated points [*le pointillé:* originally a means of engraving by points] of the system to appear, deploying or abandoning in it those blank spaces [*blancs:* Derrida's analysis of Mallarmé, which was to be written in 1969, focuses on the role of the *blanc* in the text; see also the epigraph to this volume which refers to Mallarmé's notion of *espacement:* "the whole without novelty except a spacing of reading.'' For the analysis of the *blanc* and *espacement* see "La double séance" in *La dissémination*, Paris: Seuil, 1972] without which no text is proposed as such. If *text* [*texte*] means *cloth* [*tissu:* the word *texte* is derived from the Latin *textus*, meaning cloth (*tissu*), and from *texere*, to weave (*tisser*); in English we have *text* and *textile*. Derrida comments on this derivation at the outset of *La pharmacie de Platon* also in *La dissémination*.], all these essays have obstinately defined sewing [*couture*] as *basting* [*faufilure:* the *faux*, "false," in *fau-filure*, or "false stringing," is actually an alteration of the earlier form of the word, *farfiler* or *fourfiler*, from the Latin *fors*, meaning outside. Thus basting is sewing on the outside which does not bind the textile tightly.] (December 1966.)''

The essays of *Writing and Difference*, then, are less "bound" than "basted" together. In turn, each essay is "basted" to the material of the other texts it analyzes, for, as he has stated, Derrida's writing is "entirely consumed in the reading of other texts.'' If one reads *Writing and Difference* only in order to extract from it a system of deconstruction—which has been our focus so far—one would overlook the persistent import of *Writing and Difference*. To repeat Derrida's terms, these essays always affirm that the "texture" of texts makes any assemblage of them a "basted" one, i.e., permits only the kind of fore-sewing that emphasizes the necessary spaces between even the finest stitching. In practical terms, I would suggest a "basted," well-spaced reading of *Writing and Difference*. Instead of reading through the book as a unified, well-sewn volume, one could follow both its arguments and its design in a way that would make them more comprehensible by choosing any of the essays to start with, and by reading the major works it refers to. (I have provided all possible references to English translations of the works in question.) Derrida is difficult to read not only by virtue of his style, but also because he seriously wishes to challenge the ideas that govern the way we read. His texts are more easily grasped if we read them in the way he implicitly suggests—which is not always the way we are used to reading.

The question arises—and it is a serious one—whether these essays can be read in a language other than French. It is no exaggeration to say that most of the crucial passages of *L'écriture et la différence* require the same kind of commentary as was just given for a bibliographical note. Some of the difficulties can be resolved by warning the reader that Derrida often refers back to his own works, and anticipates others, without explicitly saying so; some of these instances have been annotated. This difficulty, however, is compounded by frequent use of the terminology of classical philosophy, again without explicit explanation or reference. I will indicate below *some* of the terms that appear most frequently in *Writing and Difference;* throughout the text I have annotated translations that presented problems for specific essays, and have also provided some references not provided by Derrida to works under discussion without specifically being cited. More important, however, are the general issues raised by the question of translatability. Derrida always writes with close attention to the resonances and punning humor of etymology. Occasionally, when the Greek and Latin inheritances of English and French coincide, this aspect of Derrida's style can be captured; more often it requires the kind of laborious annotation (impossible in a volume of this size) provided above. The translator, constantly aware of what he is sacrificing, is often tempted to use a language that is a compromise between English as we know it and English as he would like it to be in order to capture as much of the original text as possible. This compromise English, however, is usually comprehensible only to those who read the translation along with the original. Moreover, despite Derrida's often dense and elliptical style, he certainly does not write a compromise French. It has been my experience that however syntactically complex or lexically rich, there is no sentence in this book that is not perfectly comprehensible in French—with patience. Therefore, I have chosen to try to translate into English as we know it. Sometimes this has meant breaking up and rearranging some very long sentences. At other times it has been possible to respect the original syntax and to maintain some very long, complex sentences. Some etymological word play has been lost, some has been annotated, and some translated.

These empirical difficulties of translation are, of course, tied to the question of the sign itself. Can *any* translation be made to signify the same thing as the original text? How crucial is the play of the signifiers—etymological play, stylistic play—to what is signified by the text? Derrida has addressed himself to this question in the second interview in *Positions* (entitled "Semiologie et Grammatologie"). The crux of the question is the inherited concept that the sign consists of a signifier and a signified, that is, of a sensible (i.e., relating to the senses, most often hearing) part which is the vehicle to its intelligible part (its meaning). Derrida states that the history of metaphysics has never ceased to impose upon semiology (the science of signs) the search for a "transcendental signified," that is, a concept independent of language (p. 30). However, even if the inherited opposition between signifier and signified can be shown to be programmed by the metaphysical desire for a transcendental, other-worldly meaning (that is often derived from the theological model of the presence of God), this does not mean that the opposition between signifier and signified can simply be abandoned as an historical delusion. Derrida states: "That this opposition or difference cannot be radical and absolute does not prevent it from functioning, and even from being indispensable within certain limits—very wide limits. For example, no translation would be possible without it. And in fact the theme of a transcendental signified was constituted within the horizon of an absolutely pure, transparent and unequivocal translatability. Within the limits to which it is possible, or at least *appears* possible, translation practices the difference between signified and signifier. But if this difference is never pure, translation is no more so; and for the notion of translation we would have to substitute a notion of *transformation:* a regulated transformation of one language by another, of one text by another. We will never have, and in fact have never had, any 'transfer' of pure signifieds—from one language to another, or within one language—which would be left virgin and intact by the signifying instrument or 'vehicle' " (*Positions,* p. 31).

The translator, then, must be sure that he has understood the syntax and lexicon of the original text in order to let his own language carry out the work of transformation. Again, this is best facilitated by obeying the strictures of his language, for a precipitate bending of it into unaccustomed forms may be indicative more of his own miscomprehension than of difficulties in the original text. In this respect, the translator's position is analogous to that of the psychoanalyst who attempts to translate the manifest language of dreams into a latent language. To do so, the analyst must first be sure that he has understood the manifest language. As Derrida says in note 3 of "Cogito and the History of Madness," "The latent content of a dream (and of any conduct or consciousness in general) communicates with the manifest content only through the unity of a language; a language which the analyst, then, must speak as well as possible." The discussion of terms offered below, and the translator's footnotes in the text, are an attempt to provide a guide to the "manifest" language of *Writing and Difference*. Like the analyst, however, the reader must let his attention float, and be satisfied with a partial understanding of a given essay on any particular reading. As the manifest language begins to become more familiar, the persistence of the *latent* content—what Derrida has called "the *unconscious* of philosophical opposition" (*Positions,* p. 60, note 6; my italics)—will become a surer guide, a more salient thread in the weave of these texts.

Derrida's terms. Wherever Derrida uses *différance* as a neologism I have left it untranslated. Its meanings are too multiple to be explained here fully, but we may note briefly that the word combines in neither the active nor the passive voice the coincidence of meanings in the verb *différer:* to differ (in space) and to defer (to put off in time, to postpone presence). Thus, it does not function simply either as *différence* (difference) or as *différance* in the usual sense (deferral), and plays on both meanings at once. Derrida's 1968 lecture "La différance" (reprinted in *Marges,* Paris: Editions de Minuit, 1972) is indispensable here. Throughout *Writing and Difference* Derrida links the concept of *différance* to his play on the words *totalitarian* and *solicitation.* He sees structuralism as a form of philosophical totalitarianism, i.e., as an attempt to account for the totality of a phenomenon by reduction of it to a formula that governs it *totally.* Derrida submits the violent, totalitarian structural project to the counterviolence of *solicitation,* which derives from the Latin *sollicitare,* meaning to shake the totality (from *sollus,* "all," and *ciere,* "to move, to shake"). Every totality, he shows, can be *totally shaken,* that is, can be shown to be founded on that which it excludes, that which would be in *excess* for a reductive analysis of any kind. (The English *solicit* should be read in this etymological sense wherever it appears.) This etymological metaphor covering a philosophical-political violence is also implied in the notion of *archia* (*archie* in French; also a neologism). *Archia* derives from the Greek *archē,* which combines the senses of a founding, original principle and of a government by one controlling principle. (Hence, for example, the etymological link between *arche*ology and mon*archy.*) Philosophy is founded on the principle of the *archia,* on regulation by *true, original* principles; the deconstruction of philosophy reveals the differential excess which makes the *archia* possible. This excess is often posed as an *aporia,* the Greek word for a seemingly insoluble logical difficulty: once a system has been "shaken" by following its totalizing logic to its final consequences, one finds an excess which cannot be construed within the rules of logic, for the excess can only be conceived as *neither* this *nor* that, or both at the same time—a departure from all rules of logic. *Différance* often functions as an *aporia:* it is difference in neither time nor space and makes both possible.

Ousia and *parousia* are the Greek words for being governed by presence; *parousia* also contains the sense of reappropriation of presence in a second coming of Christ. *Epekeina tes ousias* is the Platonic term for the beyond of being; Derrida has often used this concept as a stepping-stone in his deconstructions. *Signified* and *signifier* have been explained above. Derrida also consistently plays on the derivation of *sens* (meaning or sense; *Sinn* in German) which includes both a supposedly intelligible, rational *sense* (a signified meaning) and a vehicle dependent on the *senses* for its expression (the signifier). Further, in French *sens* also means direction; to lose meaning is to lose direction, to be lost, to feel that one is in a labyrinth. I have inflected the translation of *sens* to conform to its play of meanings wherever possible.

Heidegger's terms. While the concept of Being belongs to the entire metaphysical tradition, its translation into English has become particularly difficult since Heidegger's analyses of it. German and French share the advantage that their infinitives meaning *to be (sein, être)* can also be used as substantives that mean Being in general. Further, in each language the present participle of the infinitive *(seiend, étant)* can also be used as a substantive meaning particular *beings.* No such advantage exists in English, and since Heidegger is always concerned with the distinction between *Sein (être,* Being in general) and *Seiendes (étant,* beings) the correct translation of these substantives becomes the first problem for any consideration of Heidegger in English. (The verb forms present no difficulties: *sein* and *être* as infinitives become *to be,* and the gerunds *seiend* and *étant* become *being.*) I have followed the practice of John Macquarrie and Edward Robinson in their translation of *Being and Time* (New York: Harper and Row, 1962) and have translated the substantive (derived from the infinitive) *Sein (être)* as "Being" (with a capital initial) wherever it appears in this volume. However I have modified their translation of *Seiendes (étant)*—the substantive from the present participle—as "entity" or "entities," and have translated it as "being" or "beings." Macquarrie and Robinson, in fact, state that "there is much to be said" for this translation (*Being and Time,* p. 22, note 1). I feel that it is preferable to "entity" not only because, as they state, "in recent British and American philosophy the term 'entity' has been used more generally to apply to anything whatsoever, no matter what its ontological status" (ibid.), but also because "entity" derives from *ens,* the Latin present participle for the verb *to be, esse.* No one has been more attentive than Heidegger to the difficulties caused by the translation of Greek thought into Latin. The Latin inheritance of "entity" continues the tradition of these difficulties. Once more, we face the problem of the *transformation* of one language by another. There is one major exception to the translation of *étant* by "being," and this is in *Violence and Metaphysics,* Derrida's essay on Emmanuel Levinas. The major work by Levinas under consideration in this essay, *Totalité et Infini,* has been translated into English. Since much of this work is concerned with Heidegger, I have maintained the translation of *étant* as "existent"—the solution chosen by Alphonso Lingis, the translator of *Totality and Infinity*—in all citations from this work. This translation is particularly problematical in that it tends to confuse the distinction (in terms of *Being and Time*) between the *existential,* ontological status of Being, and the ontical status of being. The reader is requested to read "being" for "existent" wherever the latter appears.

This brings us to another term, one from Heidegger's later thought—that of *difference.* From the existential analytic of *Dasein*—man's Being—in *Being and Time,* Heidegger moved to a contemplation of the *difference* between beings and Being in his later works. He calls this the *ontico-ontological difference,* and this idea itself is submitted to powerful scrutiny in his *Identity and Difference.* The title of this work alone should bring it to the attention of the serious reader of *Writing and Difference;* in the introduction to "Freud and the Scene of Writing" Derrida gives a brief indication of the importance of *Identity and Difference* to *Writing and Difference* when he speaks of *"différance* and identity," *"différance* as the pre-opening of the ontico-ontological difference." From *Identity and Difference* also comes the term *onto-theology* which characterizes Western metaphysics as such. Very roughly put, Heidegger analyzes the contradictions of the logic of presence which is forced to conceive Being as the most general attribute of existence (*onto-*), and as the "highest," most specific attribute of God (*theo-*). *Logos* is the true verb: the *spoken* discourse in which the notion of truth governed by this onto-theo-*logy* of presence is revealed. Also from *Identity and Difference,* among other places in Heidegger, comes the concept of difference as it is inscribed in the "ontological double genitive," i.e., the necessary fluctuation of the subjective and objective cases in order to speak of Being, which always means the Being *of beings* and the beings *of Being.*

From *Kant and the Problem of Metaphysics,* the work which immediately follows *Being and Time,* comes the term "auto-affection," which Derrida uses often, and which I have discussed briefly in note 25 of " 'Genesis and Structure' and Phenomenology." Briefly here too, "auto-affection" refers to the classical notion of time as a self-produced, infinite chain of present moments that also, as scrutinized by Kant and Heidegger, causes some problems for the traditional opposition of senses and intellect: does time belong to the sensible or the intelligible? From Heidegger's extended confrontation with Nietzsche's doctrine of the will comes the concept of voluntarism. Throughout *Writing and Difference* "voluntarism" must be read in its etymological sense of "doctrine of the will," deriving as it does from the Latin *voluntas* (whence our "volition"). The French *vouloir,* to want, maintains its etymological resonances in more striking fashion

than do any of its English equivalents; Derrida plays on these resonances especially in connection with *vouloir dire,* which means either "meaning" or "to
mean," but has a strong connotation of "the will to say." The concluding
paragraphs of "Cogito and the History of Madness" develop this point.

Husserl's terms. The most important terms from Husserl are the linked concepts
of bracketing, *epoché,* and the phenomenological reduction. These are carefully
explained in sections 31, 32, and 33 of *Ideas* (translated by W. R. Boyce Gibson,
New York: Macmillan, 1962). Husserl, following Descartes's attempt to find
absolutely certain truths by putting everything into doubt, proposes to put between brackets (or parentheses) "the general thesis which belongs to the essence
of the natural standpoint." This phenomenological "abstention" (*epoché*) prohibits the use of any "judgment that concerns spatio-temporal existence" (*Ideas,*
p. 100). "Pure consciousness" becomes accessible through this transcendental
epoché, which Husserl therefore speaks of as *the* phenomenological reduction.
The relationship of this "pure consciousness" to "pure essences" is governed
by *intentionality,* for all consciousness is consciousness *of* something, although
again it is not a question of a relationship to a psychological event (experience) or
to a real object. Sensory experience, the relationship to *hylé* (matter) contains
nothing intentional for Husserl; it is intentional *morphé* (form, shape) which
bestows meaning on sensory experience. The opposition of *hylé* to *morphé*
(matter to form) leads Husserl to divide "phenomenological being" into its
hyletic and *noetic* (intentionally meaningful; from the Greek *nous,* meaning mind
or spirit) sides. The pure form of the *noesis* is in *noema,* which Husserl construes
as the immanent meaning of perception, judgment, appreciation, etc. in the
"pure," i.e., phenomenologically reduced, form of these experiences themselves. As much of *Ideas* is concerned with the theory of noetic-noematic
structures, the reader will appreciate the inadequacy of these remarks.

Hegel's terms. The most important term from Hegel, *Aufhebung,* is untranslatable due to its double meaning of conservation and negation. (The various
attempts to translate *Aufhebung* into English seem inadequate.) The reader is
referred to Derrida's discussion of the term in "Violence and Metaphysics,"
section III, first subsection ("Of the Original Polemic), B, and to the translator's
notes in "From Restricted to General Economy," where other terms from Hegel
are discussed. The Hegelian figure of the "unhappy consciousness" is discussed
in note 23 of *Violence and Metaphysics,* but there is also an important discussion
of it at the beginning of "Cogito and the History of Madness." The unhappy
consciousness, for Hegel, is always divided against itself; its historical figure is
Abraham, the prototype of the "Jewish" consciousness for which there is an
intrinsic conflict between God and nature. In many ways the theme of the unhappy consciousness runs throughout *Writing and Difference.* "Violence and

Metaphysics'' is epigraphically submitted to the conflict between the Greek—
"happy," at one with nature—and the Hebraic—unhappy—consciousnesses.
Like all inherited oppositions, this one too is programmed by the logic of
presence which demands a choice between the terms, or a resolution of the
conflict. Derrida pushes the unhappy consciousness to its logical limits in order
to bring it to the point where the division within it becomes irreducible. This
occurs most importantly in the two essays devoted to Jabès, whose poetry inter-
rogates the meaning of the Jewish, divided consciousness. This interrogation
becomes particularly poignant for Derrida in its ties to the Jewish, unhappy
consciousness as the experience of the (people of the) Book and Writing, for, as
discussed above, these are the inherited concepts which are Derrida's central
targets. Derrida has closed each of the essays on Jabès with the name of one of
Jabès's imaginary rabbis: Rida and Derissa. In this way he alerts us to the
"latent," philosophically "unconscious" impact of *Writing and Difference:* an
expanded concept of difference through the examination of writing. Derrida's
rebus-like play on his own name across this volume reminds us how unlike the
Book this one is.

All Greek terms have been transliterated. Unless the English translation of a
French or German text is specifically referred to, citations of texts in these
languages are of my own translation. I owe a debt of thanks to Professor Richard
Macksey of the Johns Hopkins University for the assistance he offered me at the
outset of this project, and for his generous permission to revise his own fine
translation of "Structure, Sign and Play in the Discourse of the Human Sciences." Most of the translation of this essay belongs to Professor Macksey. I
consulted Jeffrey Mehlman's translation of "Freud and the Scene of Writing,"
which appeared in *Yale French Studies,* no. 48 (1972). And I have also profited
greatly from the careful scholarship of Rodolphe Gasché's German translation of
L'écriture et la différence (Die Schrift und Die Differenz, Frankfurt: Suhrkamp
Verlag, 1972).

ALAN BASS
New York City
April 1977

WRITING
AND
DIFFERENCE

One

Force and Signification

It might be that we are all tattooed savages since Sophocles. But there is more to Art than the straightness of lines and the perfection of surfaces. Plasticity of style is not as large as the entire idea . . . . We have too many things and not enough forms. (Flaubert, *Préface à la vie d'écrivain*)

If it recedes one day, leaving behind its works and signs on the shores of our civilization, the structuralist invasion might become a question for the historian of ideas, or perhaps even an object. But the historian would be deceived if he came to this pass: by the very act of considering the structuralist invasion as an object he would forget its meaning and would forget that what is at stake, first of all, is an adventure of vision, a conversion of the way of putting questions to any object posed before us, to historical objects—his own—in particular. And, unexpectedly among these, the literary object.

By way of analogy: the fact that universal thought, in all its domains, by all its pathways and despite all differences, should be receiving a formidable impulse from an anxiety about language—which can only be an anxiety of language, within language itself—is a strangely concerted development; and it is the nature of this development not to be able to display itself in its entirety as a spectacle for the historian, if, by chance, he were to attempt to recognize in it the sign of an epoch, the fashion of a season, or the symptom of a crisis. Whatever the poverty of our knowledge in this respect, it is certain that the question of the sign is itself more or less, or in any event something other, than a sign of the times. To dream of reducing it to a sign of the times is to dream of violence. Especially when this question, an unexpectedly

3

historical one, approaches the point at which the simple significative nature of language appears rather uncertain, partial, or inessential. It will be granted readily that the analogy between the structuralist obsession and the anxiety of language is not a chance one. Therefore, it will never be possible, through some second- or third-hand reflection, to make the structuralism of the twentieth century (and particularly the structuralism of literary criticism, which has eagerly joined the trend) undertake the mission that a structuralist critic has assigned to himself for the nineteenth century: to contribute to a "future history of imagination and affectivity."[1] Nor will it be possible to reduce the fascination inherent in the notion of structure to a phenomenon of fashion,[2] except by reconsidering and taking seriously the meanings of imagination, affectivity, and fashion—doubtless the more urgent task. In any event, if some aspect of structuralism belongs to the domains of imagination, affectivity, or fashion, in the popular sense of these words, this aspect will never be the essential one. The structuralist stance, as well as our own attitudes assumed before or within language, are not only moments of history. They are an astonishment rather, by language as the origin of history. By historicity itself. And also, when confronted by the possibility of speech and always already within it, the finally acknowledged repetition of a surprise finally extended to the dimensions of world culture—a surprise incomparable to any other, a surprise responsible for the activation of what is called Western thought, the thought whose destiny is to extend its domains while the boundaries of the West are drawn back. By virtue of its innermost intention, and like all questions about language, structuralism escapes the classical history of ideas which already supposes structuralism's possibility, for the latter naively belongs to the province of language and propounds itself within it.

Nevertheless, by virtue of an irreducible region of irreflection and spontaneity within it, by virtue of the essential shadow of the undeclared, the structuralist phenomenon will deserve examination by the historian of ideas. For better or for worse. Everything within this phenomenon that does not in itself transparently belong to the question of the sign will merit this scrutiny; as will everything within it that is methodologically effective, thereby possessing the kind of infallibility now ascribed to sleepwalkers and formerly attributed to instinct, which was said to be as certain as it was blind. It is not a lesser province of the social science called history to have a privileged concern, in the acts and institutions of man, with the immense region of somnambulism, the *almost-everything* which is not the pure waking state, the sterile and silent acidity of the question itself, the *almost-nothing*.[3]

Since we take nourishment from the fecundity of structuralism, it is too soon to dispel our dream. We must muse upon what it *might* signify from within it. In the future it will be interpreted, perhaps, as a relaxation, if not a lapse, of the attention given to *force,* which is the tension of force itself. *Form* fascinates when one no longer has the force to understand force from within itself. That is,

to create. This is why literary criticism is structuralist in every age, in its essence
and destiny. Criticism has not always known this, but understands it now, and
thus is in the process of thinking itself in its own concept, system and method.
Criticism henceforth knows itself separated from force, occasionally avenging
itself on force by gravely and profoundly proving that separation is the condition
of the work, and not only of the discourse on the work.[4] Thus is explained the
low note, the melancholy pathos that can be perceived behind the triumphant
cries of technical ingenuity or mathematical subtlety that sometimes accompany
certain so-called "structural" analyses. Like melancholy for Gide, these
analyses are possible only after a certain defeat of force and within the movement
of diminished ardor. Which makes the structural consciousness consciousness in
general, as a conceptualization of the past, I mean of facts in general. A reflection of the accomplished, the constituted, the *constructed*. Historical, eschatalogical, and crepuscular by its very situation.

But within structure there is not only form, relation, and configuration. There
is also interdependency and a totality which is always concrete. In literary criticism, the structural "perspective" is, according to Jean-Pierre Richard's expression, "interrogative and totalitarian."[5] The force of our weakness is that impotence separates, disengages, and emancipates. Henceforth, the totality is more
clearly perceived, the panorama and the panoramagram are possible. The
panoramagram, the very image of the structuralist instrument, was invented in
1824, as Littré states, in order "to obtain immediately, on a flat surface, the
development of depth vision of objects on the horizon." Thanks to a more or less
openly acknowledged schematization and spatialization, one can glance over the
field divested of its forces more freely or diagrammatically. Or one can glance
over the totality divested of its forces, even if it is the totality of form and
meaning, for what is in question, in this case, is meaning rethought as form; and
structure is the *formal* unity of form and meaning. It will be said that this
neutralization of meaning by form is the author's responsibility before being the
critic's, and to a certain extent—but it is just this extent which is in question—
this is correct. In any event, the project of a conceptualization of totality is more
easily stated today, and such a project in and of itself escapes the *determined*
totalities of classical history. For it is the project of exceeding them. Thus, the
relief and design of structures appears more clearly when content, which is the
living energy of meaning, is neutralized. Somewhat like the architecture of an
uninhabited or deserted city, reduced to its skeleton by some catastrophe of
nature or art. A city no longer inhabited, not simply left behind, but haunted by
meaning and culture. This state of being haunted, which keeps the city from
returning to nature, is perhaps the general mode of the presence or absence of the
thing itself in pure language. The pure language that would be housed in pure
literature, the object of pure literary criticism. Thus it is in no way paradoxical
that the structuralist consciousness is a catastrophic consciousness, simultane-

ously destroyed and destructive, *destructuring,* as is all consciousness, or at least the moment of decadence, which is the period proper to all movement of consciousness. Structure is perceived through the incidence of menace, at the moment when imminent danger concentrates our vision on the keystone of an institution, the stone which encapsulates both the possibility and the fragility of its existence. Structure then can be *methodically* threatened in order to be comprehended more clearly and to reveal not only its supports but also that secret place in which it is neither construction nor ruin but lability. This operation is called (from the Latin) *soliciting.* In other words, *shaking* in a way related to the *whole* (from *sollus,* in archaic Latin "the whole," and from *citare,* "to put in motion"). The structuralist solicitude and solicitation give themselves only the illusion of technical liberty when they become methodical. In truth, they reproduce, in the register of method, a solicitude and solicitation of Being, a historico-metaphysical threatening of foundations. It is during the epochs of historical dislocation, when we are expelled from the *site,* that this structuralist passion, which is simultaneously a frenzy of experimentation and a proliferation of schematizations, develops for itself. The baroque would only be one example of it. Has not a "structural poetics" "founded on a rhetoric"[6] been mentioned in relation to the baroque? But has not a "burst structure" also been spoken of, a "rent poem whose structure appears as it bursts apart"?[7]

The liberty that this critical (in all the senses of this word)[8] disengagement assures us of, therefore, is a solicitude for and an opening into totality. But what does this opening hide? And hide, not by virtue of what it leaves aside and out of sight, but by virtue of its very power to illuminate. One continually asks oneself this question in reading Jean Rousset's fine book: *Forme et Signification: Essais sur les structures littéraires de Corneille à Claudel.*[9] Our question is not a reaction against what others have called "ingenuity" and what seems to us, except in a few instances, to be something more and something better. Confronted by this series of brilliant and penetrating exercises intended to illustrate a method, it is rather a question of unburdening ourselves of a mute anxiety, and of doing so at the point at which this anxiety is not only ours, the reader's, but also seems to conform, beneath the language, operations, and greatest achievements of this book, to the anxiety of the author himself.

Rousset certainly acknowledges kinships and affiliations: Bachelard, Poulet, Raymond, Picon, Starobinski, Richard, etc. However, despite the familial air, the many borrowings and numerous respectful acknowledgments, *Forme et Signification* seems to us, in many respects, a solitary attempt.

In the first place, this is due to a *deliberate* difference. Rousset does not isolate himself within this difference, keeping his distance; rather, he scrupulously examines a community of intentions by bringing to the surface enigmas hidden beneath values that are today accepted and respected—modern values they may be, but values already traditional enough to have become the commonplaces of criticism, making them, therefore, open to reflection and suspicion. Rousset presents his theses in a remarkable methodological introduction that, along with the introduction to *l'Univers imaginaire de Mallarmé,* should become an important part of the discourse on method in literary criticism. In multiplying his introductory references Rousset does not muddle his discourse but, on the contrary, weaves a net that tightens its originality.

For example: that in the literary fact language is one with meaning, that form belongs to the content of the work; that, according to the expression of Gaeton Picon, "for modern art, the work is not expression but creation"[10]—these are propositions that gain unanimous acceptance only by means of a highly equivocal notion of form or expression. The same goes for the notion of *imagination,* the power of mediation or synthesis between meaning and literality, the common root of the universal and the particular—as of all other similarly dissociated couples—the obscure origin of these structural frameworks and of the empathy between "form and content" which makes possible both the work and the access to its unity. For Kant, the imagination was already in itself an "art," was art itself, which originally did not distinguish between truth and beauty; and despite all the differences, Kant speaks of the same imagination in the *Critique of Pure Reason* and the *Critique of Judgment* as does Rousset. It is art, certainly, but a "hidden art"[11] that cannot be "revealed to the eyes."[12] "Now since the reduction of a representation of the imagination to concepts is equivalent to giving its exponents, the aesthetic idea may be called an *inexponible* representation of the imagination (in its free play)."[13] Imagination is the freedom that reveals itself only in its works. These works do not exist *within* nature, but neither do they inhabit a world *other* than ours. "The imagination (as a productive faculty of cognition) is a powerful agent for creating, as it were, a second nature out of the material supplied to it by actual nature."[14] This is why intelligence is not necessarily the essential faculty of the critic when he sets out to encounter imagination and beauty; "in what we call beautiful, intelligence is at the service of the imagination, and the latter is not at the service of intelligence."[15] For "the freedom of the imagination consists precisely in the fact that it schematizes without a concept."[16] This enigmatic origin of the work as a structure and indissociable unity—and as an object for structuralist criticism—is, according to Kant, "the first thing to which we must pay attention"[17] According to Rousset also. From his first page on, he links "the nature of the literary fact," always insufficiently examined, to the "role in art of imagination, that fundamental activity" about which "uncertainties and oppositions abound." This notion of an imagination that produces metaphor—that is, everything in language except to verb *to be*—remains for critics what certain philosophers today call a naively utilized *operative concept.* To surmount this technical ingenuousness is to reflect the operative concept as a *thematic concept.* This seems to be one of Rousset's projects.

To grasp the operation of creative imagination at the greatest possible proximity to it, one must turn oneself toward the invisible interior of poetic freedom.
One must be separated from oneself in order to be reunited with the blind origin
of the work in its darkness. This experience of conversion, which founds the
literary act (writing or reading), is such that the very words "separation" and
"exile," which always designate the interiority of a breaking-off with the world
and a making of one's way within it, cannot directly manifest the experience;
they can only indicate it through a metaphor whose genealogy itself would
deserve all of our efforts.[18] For in question here is a departure from the world
toward a place which is neither a *non-place* nor an *other* world, neither a utopia
nor an alibi, the creation of "a universe to be added to the universe," according
to an expression of Focillon's cited by Rousset (*Forme et Signification,* p. 11).
This universe articulates only that which is in excess of everything, the essential
nothing on whose basis everything can appear and be produced within language;
and the voice of Maurice Blanchot reminds us, with the *insistence* of profundity,
that this excess is the very possibility of writing and of literary *inspiration* in
general. Only *pure absence*—not the absence of this or that, but the absence of
everything in which all presence is announced—can *inspire,* in other words, can
work, and then make one work. The pure book naturally turns toward the eastern
edge of this absence which, beyond or within the prodigiousness of all wealth, is
its first and proper content. The pure book, the book itself, by virtue of what is
most irreplaceable within it, must be the "book about nothing" that Flaubert
dreamed of—a gray, negative dream, the origin of the total Book that haunted
other imaginations. This emptiness as the situation of literature must be acknowledged by the critic as that which constitutes the specificity of his object, as that
around which he always speaks. Or rather, his proper object—since nothing is
not an object—is the way in which this nothing *itself* is determined by disappearing. It is the transition to the determination of the work as the disguising of its
origin. But the origin is possible and conceivable only in disguise. Rousset shows
us the extent to which spirits as diverse as Delacroix, Balzac, Flaubert, Valéry,
Proust, T. S. Eliot, Virginia Woolf, and many others had a sure consciousness of
this. A sure and certain consciousness, although in principle not a clear and
distinct one, as there is not intuition of a thing involved.[19] To these voices should
be added that of Antonin Artaud, who was less roundabout: "I made my debut in
literature by writing books in order to say that I could write nothing at all. My
thoughts, when I had something to say or write, were that which was furthest
from me. I never had any ideas, and two short books, each seventy pages long,
are about this profound, inveterate, endemic absence of any idea. These books
are *l'Ombilic des limbes* and *le Pèse-nerfs.*"[20] The consciousness of having
something to say as the consciousness of nothing: this is not the poorest, but the
most oppressed of consciousnesses. It is the consciousness of nothing, upon
which all consciousness of something enriches itself, takes on meaning and

shape. And upon whose basis all speech can be brought forth. For the thought of the thing as *what* it *is* has already been confused with the experience of pure speech; and this experience has been confused with experience *itself*. Now, does not pure speech require inscription [21] somewhat in the manner that the Leibnizian essence requires existence and pushes on toward the world, like power toward the act? If the anguish of writing is not and must not be a *determined* pathos, it is because this anguish is not an empirical modification or state of the writer, but is the responsibility of *angustia:* [22] the necessarily restricted passageway of speech against which all possible meanings push each other, preventing each other's emergence. Preventing, but calling upon each other, provoking each other too, unforeseeably and as if despite oneself, in a kind of autonomous overassemblage of meanings, a power of pure equivocality that makes the creativity of the classical God appear all too poor. Speaking frightens me because, by never saying enough, I also say too much. And if the necessity of becoming breath or speech restricts meaning—and our responsibility for it—writing restricts and constrains speech further still. [23] Writing is the anguish of the Hebraic *ruah,* [24] experienced in solitude by human responsibility; experienced by Jeremiah subjected to God's dictation ("Take thee a roll of a book, and write therein all the words that I have spoken unto thee"), or by Baruch transcribing Jeremiah's dictation (Jeremiah 36:2,4); or further, within the properly human moment of *pneumatology,* the science of *pneuma, spiritus,* or *logos* which was divided into three parts: the divine, the angelical and the human. It is the moment at which we must *decide* whether we will engrave what we hear. And whether engraving preserves or betrays speech. God, the God of Leibniz, since we have just spoken of him, did not know the anguish of the choice between various possibilities: he conceived possible choices in action and disposed of them as such in his Understanding or Logos; and, in any event, the narrowness of a passageway that is *Will* favors the "best" choice. And each existence continues to "express" the totality of the Universe. There is, therefore, no tragedy of the book. There is only one Book, and this same Book is distributed throughout all books. In the *Theodicy,* Theodorus, who "had become able to confront the divine radiancy of the daughter of Jupiter," is led by her to the "palace of the fates;" in this palace "Jupiter, having surveyed them before the beginning of the existing world, classified the possibilities into worlds, and chose the best of all. He comes sometimes to visit these places, to enjoy the pleasure of recapitulating things and of renewing his own choice, which cannot fail to please him." After being told all this by Pallas, Theodorus is led into a hall which "was a world." "There was a great volume of writings in this hall: Theodorus could not refrain from asking what that meant. It is the history of this world which we are now visiting, the Goddess told him; it is the book of its fates. You have seen a number on the forehead of Sextus. Look in this book for the place which it indicates. Theodorus looked for it, and found there the history of Sextus in a form more ample than the outline he had seen. Put your finger on any line you please, Pallas said to him, and you will see represented actually in all its detail that which the line broadly indicates. He obeyed, and he saw coming into view all the characteristics of a portion of the life of that Sextus."[25]

To write is not only to conceive the Leibnizian book as an impossible possibility. Impossible possibility, the limit explicitly named by Mallarmé. To Verlaine: "I will go even further and say: the Book, for I am convinced that there is only One, and that it has [unwittingly] been attempted by every writer, even by Geniuses."[26] " . . . revealing that, in general, all books contain the amalgamation of a certain number of age-old truths; that actually there is only one book on earth, that it is the law of the earth, the earth's true Bible. The difference between individual works is simply the difference between individual interpretations of one true and established text, which are proposed in a mighty gathering of those ages we call civilized or literary."[27] To write is not only to know that the Book does not exist and that forever there are books, against which the meaning of a world not conceived by an absolute subject is shattered, before it has even become a unique meaning; nor is it only to know that the non-written and the non-read cannot be relegated to the status of having no basis by the obliging negativity of some dialectic, making us deplore the absence of the Book from under the burden of "too many texts!" It is not only to have lost the theological certainty of seeing every page bind itself into the unique text of the truth, the "book of reason" as the journal in which accounts (*rationes*) and experiences consigned for Memory was formerly called,[28] the genealogical anthology, the Book of Reason this time, the infinite manuscript read by a God who, in a more or less deferred way, is said to have given us use of his pen. This lost certainty, this absence of divine writing, that is to say, first of all, the absence of the Jewish God (who himself writes, when necessary), does not solely and vaguely define something like "modernity." As the absence and haunting of the divine sign, it regulates all modern criticism and aesthetics. There is nothing astonishing about this. "Consciously or not," says Georges Canguilhem, "the idea that man has of his poetic power corresponds to the idea he has about the creation of the world, and to the solution he gives to the problem of the radical origin of things. If the notion of creation is equivocal, ontological and aesthetic, it is not so by chance or confusion."[29] To write is not only to know that through writing, through the extremities of style, the best will not necessarily transpire, as Leibniz thought it did in divine creation, nor will the transition to what transpires always be *willful,* nor will that which is noted down always infinitely *express* the universe, resembling and reassembling it.[30] It is also to be incapable of making meaning absolutely precede writing: it is thus to lower meaning while simultaneously elevating inscription. The eternal fraternity of theological optimism and of pessimism: nothing is more reassuring, but nothing is more despairing, more destructive of our books than the Leibnizian Book. On what could books in general live, what would they be if they were not alone, so alone, infinite, isolated worlds? To write is to know that what has not yet been produced within literality has no other dwelling place, does not await us as prescription in some *topos ouranios,* or some divine understanding. Meaning must await being said or written in order to inhabit itself, and in order to become, by differing from itself, what it is: meaning. This is what Husserl teaches us to think in *The Origin of Geometry.* The literary act thus recovers its true power at its source. In a fragment of a book he intended to devote to *The Origin of Truth,* Merleau-Ponty wrote: "Communication in literature is not the simple appeal on the part of the writer to meanings which would be part of an a priori of the mind; rather, communication arouses these meanings in the mind through enticement and a kind of oblique action. The writer's thought does not control his language from without; the writer is himself a kind of new idiom, constructing itself."[31] "My own words take me by surprise and teach me what I think,"[32] he said elsewhere.

It is because writing is *inaugural,* in the fresh sense of the word, that it is dangerous and anguishing. It does not know where it is going, no knowledge can keep it from the essential precipitation toward the meaning that it constitutes and that is, primarily, its future. However, it is capricious only through cowardice. There is thus no insurance against the risk of writing. Writing is an initial and graceless recourse for the writer, even if he is not an atheist but, rather, a writer. Did Saint John Chrysostom speak of the writer? "It were indeed meet for us not at all to require the aid of the written Word, but to exhibit a life so pure, that the grace of the spirit should be instead of books to our souls, and that as these are inscribed with ink, even so should our hearts be with the Spirit. But, since we have utterly put away from us this grace, come let us at any rate embrace the second best course."[33] But, all faith or theological assurance aside, is not the experience of *secondarity* tied to the strange redoubling by means of which constituted—written—meaning presents itself as prerequisitely and simultaneously *read:* and does not meaning present itself as such at the point at which the other is found, the other who maintains both the vigil and the back-and-forth motion, the work, that comes between writing and reading, making this work irreducible? Meaning is neither before nor after the act. Is not that which is called God, that which imprints every human course and recourse with its secondarity, the passageway of deferred reciprocity between reading and writing? or the absolute witness to the dialogue in which what one sets out to write has already been read, and what one sets out to say is already a response, the third party as the transparency of meaning? Simultaneously part of creation and the Father of Logos. The circularity and traditionality of Logos. The strange labor of conversion and adventure in which grace can only be that which is missing.

Thus, the notion of an Idea or "interior design" as simply anterior to a work which would supposedly be the expression of it, is a prejudice: a prejudice of the traditional criticism called *idealist.* It is not by chance that this theory—or , one could now say, this theology—flowered during the Renaissance. Rousset, like so many others past or present, certainly speaks out against this "Platonism" or "Neo-Platonism." But he does not forget that if creation by means of "the form rich in ideas" (Valéry) is not the purely transparent expression of this form, it is nevertheless, simultaneously, revelation. If creation were not revelation, what would happen to the finitude of the writer and to the solitude of his hand abandoned by God? Divine creativity, in this case, would be reappropriated by a hypocritical humanism. If writing is *inaugural* it is not so because it creates, but because of a certain absolute freedom of speech, because of the freedom to bring forth the already-there as a sign of the freedom to augur. A freedom of response which acknowledges as its only horizon the world as history and the speech which can only say: Being has always already begun. To create is to reveal, says Rousset, who does not turn his back on classical criticism. He comprehends it, rather, and enters into dialogue with it: "Prerequisite secret and unmasking of this secret by the work: a reconciliation of ancient and modern aesthetics can be observed, in a certain way, in the possible correspondence of the preexisting secret to the Idea of the Renaissance thinkers stripped of all Neo-Platonism."

This revelatory power of true literary language as poetry is indeed the access to free speech, speech unburdened of its signalizing functions by the word "Being" (and this, perhaps, is what is aimed at beneath the notion of the "primitive word" or the "theme-word," *Leitwort,* of Buber).[34] It is when that which is written is *deceased* as a sign-signal that it is born as language; for then it says what is, thereby referring only to itself, a sign without signification, a game or pure functioning, since it ceased to be *utilized* as natural, biological, or technical information, or as the transition from one existent to another, from a signifier to a signified. And, paradoxically, inscription alone—although it is far from always doing so—has the power of poetry, in other words has the power to arouse speech from its slumber as sign. By enregistering speech, inscription has as its essential objective, and indeed takes this fatal risk, the emancipation of meaning—as concerns any actual field of perception—from the natural predicament in which everything refers to the disposition of a contingent situation. This is why writing will never be simple "voice-painting" (Voltaire). It creates meaning by enregistering it, by entrusting it to an engraving, a groove, a relief, to a surface whose essential characteristic is to be infinitely transmissible. Not that this characteristic is always desired, nor has it always been; and writing as the origin of pure historicity, pure traditionality, is only the *telos* of a history of writing whose philosophy is always to come. Whether this project of an infinite tradition is realized or not, it must be acknowledged and respected in its sense as a project. That it can always fail is the mark of its pure finitude and its pure historicity. If the play of meaning can overflow signification (signalization), which is always enveloped within the regional limits of nature, life and the soul, this overflow is the moment of the attempt-to-write. The attempt-to-write cannot be understood on the basis of voluntarism. The will to write is not an ulterior determination of a primal will. On the contrary, the will to write reawakens the willful sense of the will: freedom, break with the domain of empirical history, a break whose aim is reconciliation with the hidden essence of the empirical, with pure historicity. The will and the attempt to write are not the desire to write, for it is a question here not of affectivity but of freedom and duty. In its relationship to Being, the attempt-to-write poses itself as the only way out of affectivity. A way out that can only be aimed at, and without the certainty that deliverance is possible or that it is outside affectivity. To be affected is to be finite: to write could still be to deceive finitude, and to reach Being—a kind of Being which could neither be, nor affect me by *itself*—from without existence. To write would be to attempt to forget difference: to forget writing in the presence of so-called living and pure speech.[35]

In the extent to which the literary act proceeds from this attempt-to-write, it is indeed the acknowledgment of pure language, the responsibility confronting the vocation of "pure" speech which, once understood, constitutes the writer as such. Heidegger says of pure speech that it cannot "be conceived in the rigor of its essence" on the basis of its "character-as-sign" (*Zeichencharakter*), "nor even perhaps of its character-as-signification" (*Bedeutungscharakter*).[36]

Does not one thus run the risk of identifying the work with original writing in general? Of dissolving the notion of art and the value of "beauty" by which literature is currently distinguished from the letter in general? But perhaps by removing the specificity of beauty from aesthetic values, beauty is, on the contrary, liberated? Is there a specificity of beauty, and would beauty gain from this effort?

Rousset believes so. And the structuralism proper to Jean Rousset is defined, at least theoretically, against the temptation to overlook this specificity (the temptation that would be Poulet's, for example, since he "has little interest in art"),[37] putting Rousset close to Leo Spitzer and Marcel Raymond in his scrupulousness about the formal autonomy of the work—an "independent, absolute organism that is self-sufficient" (*Forme et Signification* p. xx). "The work is a totality and always gains from being experienced as such" (p. xxi). But here again, Rousset's position depends upon a delicate balance. Always attentive to the unified foundations of dissociation, he circumvents the "objectivist" danger denounced by Poulet by giving a definition of structure that is not purely objective or formal; or circumvents the "objectivist" danger denounced by Poulet by giving a definition of structure that is not purely objective or formal; or circumvents it by at least not in principle dissociating form from intention, or from the very act of the writer: "I will call 'structures' these formal constants, these liaisons that betray a mental universe reinvented by each artist according to his needs" (p. xii). Structure is then the unity of a form and a meaning. It is true that in some places the form of the work, or the form as the work, is treated *as if* it had no origin, as if, again, in the masterpiece—and Rousset is interested only in masterpieces—the wellbeing of the work was without history. Without an intrinsic history. It is here that structuralism seems quite vulnerable, and it is here that, by virtue of one whole aspect of his attempt—which is far from covering it entirely—Rousset too runs the risk of conventional Platonism. By keeping to the legitimate intention of protecting the *internal* truth and meaning of the work from historicism, biographism or psychologism (which, moreover, always lurk near the expression "mental universe"), one risks losing any attentiveness to the internal historicity of the work itself, in its relationship to a subjective origin that is not simply psychological or mental. If one takes care to confine classical literary history to its role as an "indispensable" "auxiliary," as "prologomenon and restraint" (p. xii, n. 16), one risks overlooking another history, more difficult to conceive: the history of the meaning of the work itself, of its *operation*. This history of the work is not only its *past,* the eve or the sleep in which it precedes itself in an author's intentions, but is also the impossibility of its ever being *present,* of its ever being summarized by some absolute simultaneity or instantaneousness. This is why, as we will verify, there is no *space* of the work, if by space we mean *presence* and *synopsis*. And, further on, we will see what the consequences of this can be for the tasks of criticism. It seems, for the moment, that if "literary history" (even when its techniques and its "philosophy" are renewed by "Marxism," "Freudianism," etc.) is only a restraint on the internal criticism of the work, then the structuralist moment of this criticism has the counterpart role of being the restraint on an internal geneticism, in which value and meaning are reconstituted and reawakened in their proper historicity and temporality. These latter can no longer be *objects* without becoming absurdities, and the structure proper to them must escape all classical categories.

Certainly, Rousset's avowed plan is to avoid this stasis of form, the stasis of a form whose completion appears to liberate it from work, from imagination and from the origin through which alone it can continue to signify. Thus, when he distinguishes his task from that of Jean-Pierre Richard,[38] Rousset aims directly at this totality of thing and act, form and intention, entelechy and becoming, the totality that is the literary fact as a concrete form: "Is it possible to embrace simultaneously imagination and morphology, to experience and to comprehend them in a simultaneous act? This is what I would like to attempt, although well persuaded that this undertaking, before being unitary, will often have to make itself *alternative* [my italics]. But the end in sight is indeed the simultaneous comprehension of a homogenous reality in a unifying operation" (p. xxii).

But condemned or resigned to alternation, the critic, in acknowledging it, is also liberated and acquitted by it. And it is here that Rousset's difference is no longer *deliberate*. His personality, his *style* will affirm themselves not through a methodological decision but through the play of the critic's spontaneity within the freedom of the "alternative." This spontaneity will, in fact, unbalance an alternation construed by Rousset as a theoretical norm. A practiced inflection that also provides the style of criticism—here Rousset's—with its structural form. This latter, Claude Lévi-Strauss remarks about social models and Rousset about structural motifs in a literary work, "escapes creative will and clear consciousness" (p. xv). What then is the imbalance of this preference? What is the preponderance that is more actualized than acknowledged? It seems to be *double*.

II

> There are lines which are monsters.... A line by itself has no meaning; a second one is necessary to give expression to meaning. Important law. (Delacroix)
>
> Valley is a common female dream symbol. (Freud)

On the one hand, structure becomes the object itself, the literary thing itself. It is no longer what it almost universally was before: either a heuristic instrument, a method of reading, a characteristic particularly revelatory of content, or a system of objective relations, independent of content and terminology; or, most often, both at once, for the fecundity of structure did not exclude, but, on the contrary, rather implied that relational configuration exists within the literary object. A structural realism has always been practiced, more or less explicitly. But never has structure been the exclusive *term*—in the double sense of the word—of critical description. It was always a *means* or relationship for reading or writing, for assembling significations, recognizing themes, ordering constants and correspondences.

Here, structure, the framework of construction, morphological correlation, becomes *in fact and despite his theoretical intention* the critic's sole preoccupation. His sole or almost sole preoccupation. No longer a method within the *ordo cognescendi,* no longer a relationship in the *ordo essendi,* but the very being of the work. We are concerned with an ultrastructuralism.

On the other hand (and consequently), structure as the literary thing is this time taken, or at least practiced, *literally.* Now, stricto sensu, the notion of structure refers only to space, geometric or morphological space, the order of forms and sites. Structure is first the structure of an organic or artificial work, the internal unity of an assemblage, a *construction;* a work is governed by a unifying principle, the *architecture* that is built and made visible in a location. "Superbes monuments de l'orgueil des humains, / Pyramides, tombeaux, dont la noble structure / a temoigné que l'art, par l'adresse des mains / Et l'assidu travail peut vaincre la nature" ("Splendid monuments of human pride, pyramids, tombs, whose noble structure Bears witness that art, through the skill of hands and hard work, can vanquish nature''—Scarron). Only metaphorically was this *topo-graphical* literality displaced in the direction of its Aristotelean and *topical* signification (the theory of commonplaces in language and the manipulation of motifs or arguments.) In the seventeenth century they spoke of ''the choice and arrangement of words, the *structure* and harmony of the composition, the modest grandeur of the thoughts.''[39] Or further: ''In bad *structure* there is always something to be added, or diminished, or changed, not simply as concerns the topic, but also the words.''[40]

How is this history of metaphor possible? Does the fact that language can determine things only by spatializing them suffice to explain that, in return, language must spatialize itself as soon as it designates and reflects upon itself? This question can be asked in general about all language and all metaphors. But here it takes on a particular urgency.

Hence, for as long as the metaphorical sense of the notion of structure is not acknowledged *as such,* that is to say interrogated and even destroyed as concerns its figurative quality so that the nonspatiality or original spatiality designated by it may be revived, one runs the risk, through a kind of sliding as unnoticed as it is *efficacious,* of confusing meaning with its geometric, morphological, or, in the best of cases, cinematic model. One risks being interested in the figure itself to the detriment of the play going on within it metaphorically. (Here, we are taking the word ''figure'' in its geometric as well as rhetorical sense. In Rousset's style, figures of rhetoric are always the figures of a geometry distinguished by its suppleness.)

Now, despite his stated propositions, and although he calls structure the union of formal structure and intention, Rousset, in his analyses, grants an absolute privilege to spatial models, mathematical functions, lines, and forms. Many examples could be cited in which the essence of his descriptions is reduced to this. Doubtless, he acknowledges the interdependency of space and time (*Forme et Signification,* p. xiv.). But, in fact, time itself is always reduced. To a *dimension* in the best of cases. It is only the element in which a form or a curve can be displayed. It is always in league with a line or design, always extended in space, level. It calls for measurement. Now, even if one does not follow Claude Lévi-Strauss when he asserts that there ''is no necessary connection between measure and *structure,*''[41] one must acknowledge that for certain kinds of structures—those of literary ideality in particular—this connection is excluded in principle.

The geometric or morphological elements of *Forme et Signification* are corrected only by a kind of mechanism, never by energetics. Mutatis mutandis, one might be tempted to make the same reproach to Rousset, and through him to the best literary formalism, as Leibniz made to Descartes: that of having explained everything in nature with figures and movements, and of ignoring force by confusing it with the quantity of movement. Now, in the sphere of language and writing, which, more than the body, ''corresponds to the soul,'' ''the ideas of

size, figure and motion are not so distinctive as is imagined, and . . . stand for
something imaginary relative to our perceptions."[42]

This geometry is only metaphorical, it will be said. Certainly. But metaphor is
never innocent. It orients research and fixes results. When the spatial model is hit
upon, when it functions, critical reflection rests within it. In fact, and even if
criticism does not admit this to be so.

One example among many others.

At the beginning of the essay entitled *"Polyeucte,* or the Ring and the Helix,"
the author prudently warns us that if he insists upon "schemas that might appear
excessively geometrical, it is because Corneille, more than any other, practiced
symmetry." Moreover, "this geometry is not cultivated for itself," for "in the
great plays it is a means subordinated to the ends of passion" (p. 7).

But what, in fact, does this essay yield? Only the geometry of a theater which
is, however, one of "mad passion, heroic enthusiasm" (p. 7). Not only does the
geometric structure of *Polyeucte* mobilize all the resources and attention of the
author, but an entire teleology of Corneille's progress is coordinated to it. Everything transpires as if, until 1643, Corneille had only gotten a glimpse of, or
anticipated the design of, *Polyeucte,* which was still in the shadows and which
would eventually coincide with the Corneillean design itself, thereby taking on
the dignity of an entelechy toward which everything would be in motion. Corneille's work and development are put into perspective and interpreted teleologi-
cally on the basis of what is considered its destination, its final structure. *Before
Polyeucte,* everything is but a sketch in which only what is missing is due
consideration, those elements which are still shapeless and lacking as concerns
the perfection to come, or which only foretell this perfection. "There were
several years between *La galerie du palais* and *Polyeucte.* Corneille looks for and
finds himself. I will not here trace the details of his progress, in which *Le Cid* and
Cinna show him inventing his own structure" (p. 9). After *Polyeucte?* It is never
mentioned. Similarly, among the works prior to it, only *La galerie du palais* and
Le Cid are taken into account, and these plays are examined, in the style of
preformationism, only as structural prefigurations of *Polyeucte.*

Thus, in *La galerie du palais* the inconctancy of Célidée separates her from her
lover. Tired of her inconstancy (but why?), she draws near him again, while he,
in turn, feigns inconstancy. They thus separate, to be united at the end of the play,
which is outlined as follows: "Initial accord, separation, median reunification
that fails, second separation symmetrical to the first, final conjunction. The
destination is a return to the point of departure after a circuit in the form of a
crossed ring" (p. 8). What is singular is the crossed ring, for the destination as
return to the point of departure is of the commonest devices. Proust himself . . . (cf. p. 144).

The framework is analogous in *Le Cid:* "The ring-like movement with a median crossing is maintained" (p. 9). But here a new signification intervenes, one

that panorography immediately transcribes in a new dimension. In effect, "at each step along the way, the lovers develop and grow, not only each one for himself, but through the other and for the other, according to a *very Corneillean* [my italics] law of progressively discovered interdependence; their union is made stronger and deeper by the very ruptures that should have destroyed it. Here, the phases of distanciation are no longer phases of separation and inconstancy, but tests of fidelity" (p. 9). The difference between *La galerie du palais* and *Le Cid*, one could be led to believe, is no longer in the design and movement of presences (distance-proximity), but in the *quality* and inner intensity of the experiences (tests of fidelity, manner of being for the other, force of rupture, etc.). And it could be thought that by virtue of the very enrichment of the play, the structural metaphor will now be incapable of grasping the play's quality and intensity, and that the work of forces will no longer be translated into a difference of form.

In believing so one would underestimate the resources of the critic. The dimension of *height* will now complete the analogical equipment. What is gained in the tension of sentiments (quality of fidelity, way of being-for-the-other, etc.) is gained in terms of *elevation;* for values, as we know, mount scalewise, and the Good is most high. The union of the lovers is deepened by an "aspiration toward the highest" (p. 9). *Altus:* the deep is the high. The ring, which remains, has become an "ascending spiral" and "helical ascent." And the horizontal flatness of *La galerie* was only an appearance still hiding the essential: the ascending movement. *Le Cid* only begins to reveal it: "Also the destination (in *Le Cid*), even if it apparently leads back to the initial conjunction, is not at all a return to the point of departure; the situation has changed, for the characters have been elevated. *This is the essential* [my italics]: the *Corneillean movement* is a movement of violent elevation . . ." (but where has this violence and the force of movement, which is more than its quantity or direction, been spoken of?) " . . . of aspiration toward the highest; joined to the crossing of two rings, it now traces an ascending spiral, helical ascent. This formal combination will receive all the richness of its signification in *Polyeucte*" (p. 9). The structure thus was a receptive one, waiting, like a girl in love, ready for its future meaning to marry and fecundate it.

We would be convinced if beauty, which is value and force, were subject to regulation and schematization. Must it be shown once more that this is without sense? Thus, if *Le Cid* is beautiful, it is so by virtue of that within it which surpasses schemes and understanding. Thus, one does not speak of *Le Cid* itself, if it is beautiful, in terms of rings, spirals, and helices. If the movement of these lines is not *Le Cid*, neither will it become *Polyeucte* as it perfects itself still further. It is not the *truth of Le Cid* or *of Polyeucte*. Nor is it the psychological truth of passion, faith, duty, etc., but, it will be said, it is this truth according to Corneille; not according to Pierre Corneille, whose biography and psychology do not interest us here: the "movement toward the highest," the greatest specificity

of the schema, is none other than the *Corneillean movement* (p. 1). The progress
indicated by *Le Cid,* which also aspires to the heights of *Polyeucte* is a "progress
in the Corneillean meaning" (ibid.). It would be helpful here to reproduce the
analysis of *Polyeucte,* [43] in which the schema reaches its greatest perfection and
greatest internal complication; and does so with a mastery such that one wonders
whether the credit is due Corneille or Rousset. We said above that the latter was
too Cartesian and not Leibnizian enough. Let us be more precise. He is also
Leibnizian: he seems to think that, confronted with a literary work, one should
always be able to find a line, no matter how complex, that accounts for the unity,
the totality of its movement, and all the points it must traverse.

In the *Discourse on Metaphysics,* Leibniz writes, in effect: "Because, let us
suppose for example that someone jots down a quantity of points upon a sheet of
paper helter skelter, as do those who exercise the ridiculous art of Geomancy;
now I say that it is possible to find a geometrical line whose concept shall be
uniform and constant, that is, in accordance with a certain formula, and which
line at the same time shall pass through all of those points, and in the same order
in which the hand jotted them down; also if a continuous line be traced, which is
now straight, now circular, and now of any other description, it is possible to find
a mental equivalent, a formula or an equation common to all the points of this
line by virtue of which formula the changes in the direction of the line must
occur. There is no instance of a fact whose contour does not form part of a
geometric line and which can not be traced entire by a certain mathematical
motion." [44]

But Leibniz was speaking of divine creation and intelligence: "I use these
comparisons to picture a certain imperfect resemblance to the divine wisdom . . . . I do not pretend at all to explain thus the great mystery upon which
depends the whole universe." [45] As concerns qualities, forces and values, and
also as concerns nondivine works read by finite minds, this confidence in
mathematical-spatial *representation* seems to be (on the scale of an entire civilization, for we are no longer dealing with the question of Rousset's language, but
with the totality of our language and its credence) *analogous* to the confidence
placed by Canaque artists[46] in the level representation of depth. A confidence
that the structural ethnographer analyzes, moreover, with more prudence and less
abandon than formerly.

Our intention here is not, through the simple motions of balancing, equilibra-
tion or overturning, to oppose duration to space, quality to quantity, force to
form, the depth of meaning or value to the surface of figures. Quite to the
contrary. To counter this simple alternative, to counter the simple choice of one
of the terms or one of the series against the other, we maintain that it is necessary
to seek new concepts and new models, an *economy* escaping this system of
metaphysical oppositions. This economy would not be an energetics of pure,
shapeless force. The differences examined *simultaneously* would be differences

of site[47] and differences of force. If we appear to oppose one series to the other, it is because from within the classical system we wish to make apparent the noncritical privilege naively granted to the other series by a certain structuralism. Our discourse irreducibly belongs to the system of metaphysical oppositions. The break with this structure of belonging can be announced only through a *certain* organization, a certain *strategic* arrangement which, within the field of metaphysical opposition, uses the strengths of the field to turn its own stratagems against it, producing a force of dislocation that spreads itself throughout the entire system, fissuring it in every direction and thoroughly *delimiting* it.[48]

Assuming that, in order to avoid "abstractionism," one fixes upon—as Rousset does at least theoretically—the union of form and meaning, one then would have to say that the aspiration toward the highest, in the "final leap which will unite them . . . in God," etc., the passionate, qualitative, intensive, etc., aspiration, finds *its* form in the spiraling movement. But to say further that this union—which, moreover authorizes *every* metaphor of elevation—is *difference itself,* Corneille's own idiom—is this to say much? And if this were the essential aspect of "Corneillean movement," where would Corneille be? Why is there more beauty in *Polyeucte* than in "an ascending movement of two rings"? The force of the work, the force of genius, the force, too, of that which engenders in general is precisely that which resists geometrical metaphorization and is the proper object of literary criticism. In another sense than Poulet's, Rousset sometimes seems to have "little interest in art."

Unless Rousset considers every line, every spatial form (but every form is spatial) beautiful a priori, unless he deems, as did a certain medieval theology (Considérans in particular), that form is transcendentally beautiful, since it is and makes things be, and that Being is Beautiful; these were truths for this theology to the extent that monsters themselves, as it was said, were beautiful, in that they exist through line or form, which bear witness to the order of the created universe and reflect divine light. *Formosus* means beautiful.

Will Buffon not say too, in his *Supplement to Natural History* (vol. XI, p. 417): "Most monsters are such with symmetry, the disarray of the parts seeming to have been arranged in orderly fashion?"

Now, Rousset does not seem to posit, in his theoretical Introduction, that every form is beautiful, but only the form that is aligned with meaning, the form that can be understood because it is, above all, in league with meaning. Why then, once more, this geometer's privilege? Assuming, in the last analysis, that beauty lets itself be espoused or exhausted by the geometer, is he not, in the case of the sublime—and Corneille is said to be sublime—forced to commit an act of violence?

Further, for the sake of determining an essential "Corneillean movement," does one not lose what counts? Everything that defies a geometrical-mechanical framework—and not only the pieces which cannot be constrained by curves and helices, not only force and quality, which are meaning itself, but also *duration,* that which is pure qualitative heterogeneity within movement—is reduced to the appearance of the inessential for the sake of this essentialism or teleological structuralism. Rousset understands theatrical or novelistic movement as Aristotle understood movement in general: transition to the act, which itself is the repose of the desired form. Everything transpires as if everything within the dynamics of Corneillean meaning, and within each of Corneille's plays, came to life with the aim of final peace, the peace of the structural *energeia: Polyeucte.* Outside this peace, before and after it, movement, in its pure duration, in the labor of its organization, can itself be only sketch or debris. Or even debauch, a fault or sin as compared to *Polyeucte,* the "first impeccable success." Under the word "impeccable," Rousset notes: "*Cinna* still sins in this respect" (p. 12).

Preformationism, teleologism, reduction of force, value and duration—these are as one with geometrism, creating structure. This is the *actual* structure which governs, to one degree or another, all the essays in this book. Everything which, in the first Marivaux, does not announce the schema of the "double register" (narration and look at the narration) is "a series of youthful novelistic exercises" by which "he prepares not only the novels of maturity, but also his dramatic works" (p. 47). "The *true* Marivaux is still *almost* absent from it" (my italics). "From our perspective, there is only one fact to retain . . ." (ibid.). There follows an analysis and a citation upon which is concluded: "This outline of a dialogue above the heads of the characters, through a broken-off narration in which the presence and the absence of the author alternate, is the outline of the veritable Marivaux . . . . Thus is sketched, in a first and rudimentary form, the properly Marivauldian combination of spectacle and spectator, perceived and perceiver. We will see it perfect itself" (p. 48).

The difficulties accumulate, as do our reservations, when Rousset specifies that this "permanent structure of Marivaux's,"[49] although invisible or latent in the works of his youth, "belongs," as the "willful dissolution of novelistic illusion," to the "burlesque tradition" (p. 50; cf. also p. 60). Marivaux's originality, which "retains" from this tradition only "the free construction of a narration which simultaneously shows the work of the author and the author's reflection on his work," is then "critical consciousness' (p. 51). Marivaux's idiom is not to be found in the structure described but in the intention that animates a traditional form and creates a new structure. The truth of the general structure thus restored does not *describe* the Marivauldian organism along its own lines. And less so its force.

Yet: "The structural fact thus described—the double register—appears as a constant . . . . *At the same time* [my italics] it corresponds to the knowledge that Marivauldian man has of himself: a 'heart' without vision, caught in the field of a consciousness which itself is only vision" (p. 64). But how can a "structural fact," traditional during this era (assuming that as it is defined, it is determined and original enough to belong to an era) "correspond" to the consciousness of "Marivauldian man"? Does the structure correspond to Marivaux's most singu-lar intention? Is Marivaux not, rather, a *good example*—and it would have to be demonstrated why he is a *good* example—of a literary structure of the times and, through it, an example of a structure of the era itself? Are there not here a thousand unresolved methodological problems that are the prerequisites for a *single* structural study, a monograph on an author or a work?

If *geometrism* is especially apparent in the essays on Corneille and Marivaux, preformationism triumphs à propos of Proust and Claudel. And this time in a form that is more organicist than topographical. It is here too, that prefor-mationism is most fruitful and convincing. First, because it permits the mastering of a richer subject matter, penetrated more from within. (May we be permitted to remark that we feel that what is best about this book is not due to its method, but to the quality of the attention given to its objects?) Further, because Proust's and Claudel's aesthetics are profoundly aligned with Rousset's.

For Proust himself—and the demonstration given leaves no doubt on this subject, if one still had any—the demands of structure were constant and con-scious, manifesting themselves through marvels of (neither true nor false) sym-metry, recurrence, circularity, light thrown backward, superimposition (without adequation) of the first and the last, etc. Teleology here is not a product of the critic's projection, but is the author's own theme. The implication of the end in the beginning, the strange relationships between the subject who writes the book and the subject of this book, between the consciousness of the narrator and that of the hero—all this recalls the style of becoming and the dialectic of the "we" in the *Phenomenology of the Mind*.[50] We are indeed concerned with the phenomenology of a mind here: "One can discern still more reasons for the importance attached by Proust to this circular form of a novel whose end returns to its beginning. In the final pages one sees the hero and the narrator unite too, after a long march during which each sought after the other, sometimes very close to each other, sometimes very far apart; they coincide at the moment of resolution, which is the instant when the hero becomes the narrator, that is, the author of his own history. The narrator is the hero revealed to himself, is the person that the hero, throughout his history, desires to be but never can be; he now takes the place of this hero and will be able to set himself to the task of edifying the work which has ended, and first to the task of writing *Combray*, which is the origin of the narrator as well as of the hero. The end of the book makes its existence possible and comprehensible. The novel is conceived such that its end engenders its beginning" (p. 144). Proust's aesthetics and critical method are, ultimately, not outside his work but are the very heart of his creation: "Proust will make this aesthetic into the real subject of his work" (p. 135). As in Hegel, the philosophical, critical, reflective consciousness is not only contained in the scrutiny given to the operations and works of history. What is first in question is the history of this consciousness *itself*. It would not be deceptive to say that this aesthetic, as a concept of the work in general, exactly overlaps Rousset's. And this aesthetic is indeed, if I may say so, a practiced preformationism: "The *last chapter* of the last volume," Proust notes, "was written immediately after the *first chapter* of the first volume. Everything in between was written afterward."

By preformationism we indeed mean preformationism: the well-known biological doctrine, opposed to epigenesis, according to which the totality of hereditary characteristics is enveloped in the germ, and is already in action in reduced dimensions that nevertheless respect the forms and proportions of the future adult. A theory of *encasement* was at the center of preformationism which today makes us smile. But what are we smiling at? At the adult in miniature, doubtless, but also at the attributing of something more than finality to natural life— providence in action and art conscious of its works. But when one is concerned with an art that does not imitate nature, when the artist is a man, and when it is consciousness that engenders, preformationism no longer makes us smile. *Logos spermatikos* is in its proper element, is no longer an export, for it is an anthropomorphic concept. For example: after having brought to light the necessity of *repetition* in Proustian composition, Rousset writes: "Whatever one thinks of the device which introduces *Un amour de Swann,* it is quickly forgotten, so tight and organic is the liaison that connects the part to the whole. Once one has finished reading the *Recherche,* one perceives that the episode is not at all isolable; without it, the ensemble would be unintelligible. *Un amour de Swann* is a novel within a novel, a painting within a painting . . . , it brings to mind, not the stories within stories that so many seventeenth- or eighteenth-century novelists encase in their narratives, but rather the inner stories that can be read the *Vie de Marianne,* in Balzac or Gide. At one of the entryways to his novel, Proust places a small convex mirror which reflects the novel in abbreviated form" (p. 146). The metaphor and operation of encasement impose themselves, even if they are finally replaced by a finer, more adequate image which, at bottom, signifies the same relationship of implication. A reflecting and representative kind of implication, this time.

It is for these same reasons that Rousset's aesthetic is aligned with Claudel's. Moreover, Proust's aesthetic is defined at the beginning of the essay on Claudel. And the affinities are evident, above and beyond all the differences. These affinities are assembled in the theme of "structural monotony": " 'And thinking once more about the monotony of Vinteuil's works, I explained to Albertine that great writers have created only a single work, or rather have refracted the same beauty that they bring to the world through diverse elements' " (p. 171). Claudel: " '*Le soulier de satin* is *Tête d'or* in another form. It summarizes both *Tête d'or* and *Partage de midi.* It is even the conclusion of *Partage de midi* . . . ' " " 'A poet does hardly anything but develop a preestablished plan' " (p. 172).

This aesthetic which neutralizes duration and force as the *difference* between the acorn and the oak, is not autonomously Proust's or Claudel's. It translates a metaphysics. Proust also calls "time in its pure state" the "atemporal" or the "eternal." The truth of time is not temporal. Analogously (analogously only), time as irreversible succession, is, according to Claudel, only the phenomenon, the epidermis, the surface image of the essential truth of the universe as it is conceived and created by God. This truth is absolute *simultaneity*. Like God, Claudel, the creator and composer, "has a taste for things that exist together" (*Art poétique*).[51]

This metaphysical intention, in the last resort, validates, through a series of mediations, the entire essay on Proust and all the analyses devoted to the "fundamental scene of Claudel's theater" (p. 183), the "pure state of the Claudelian structure" (p. 177) found in *Partage de midi,* and to the totality of this theater in which, as Claudel himself says, "time is manipulated like an accordion, for our pleasure" such that "hours last and days are passed over" (p. 181).

We will not, of course, examine in and of themselves this metaphysics or theology of temporality. That the aesthetics they govern can be legitimately and fruitfully applied to the reading of Proust or Claudel is evident, for these are *their* aesthetics, daughter (or mother) of *their* metaphysics. It is also readily demonstrable that what is in question is the metaphysics implicit in all structuralism, or in every structuralist proposition. In particular, a structuralist reading, by its own activity, always presupposes and appeals to the theological simultaneity of the book, and considers itself deprived of the essential when this simultaneity is not accessible. Rousset: "In any event, reading, which is developed in duration, will have to make the work simultaneously present in all its parts in order to be global. . . . Similar to a 'painting in movement,' the book is revealed only in successive fragments. The task of the demanding reader consists in overturning this natural tendency of the book, so that it may present itself in its entirety to the mind's scrutiny. The only complete reading is the one which transforms the book into a simultaneous network of reciprocal relationships: it is then that surprises emerge" (p. xiii). (What surprises? How can simultaneity hold surprises in store? Rather, it neutralizes the surprises of nonsimultaneity. Surprises emerge from the dialogue between the simultaneous and the nonsimultaneous. Which suffices to say that structural simultaneity *itself* serves to reassure.) Jean-Pierre Richard: "The difficulty of every structural account resides in that it must describe sequentially, successively, that which in fact exists all at once, simultaneously" (*L'univers imaginaire de Mallarmé,* p. 28). Thus, Rousset invokes the difficulty of gaining access to the simultaneity which is truth within reading, and Richard the difficulty of accounting for it within writing. In both cases, simultaneity is the myth of a total reading or description, promoted to the status of a regulatory ideal. The search for the simultaneous explains the capacity to be fascinated by the spatial image: is space not "the order of coexistences" (Leibniz)? But by saying "simultaneity" instead of space, one attempts to *concentrate* time instead of *forgetting* it. "Duration thus takes on the illusory form of a homogenous milieu, and the union between these two terms, space and duration, is simultaneity, which could be defined as the intersection of time with space."[52] In this demand for the flat and the horizontal, what is intolerable for structuralism is indeed the richness implied by the volume, every element of signification that cannot be spread out into the simultaneity of a form. But is it by chance that the book is, first and foremost, volume?[53] And that the meaning of meaning (in the general sense of meaning and not in the sense of signalization) is infinite implication, the indefinite referral of signifier to signifier? And that its force is a certain pure and infinite equivocality which gives signified meaning no respite, no rest, but engages it in its own *economy* so that it always signifies again and differs? Except in the *Livre irréalisé* by Mallarmé, that which is written is never identical to itself.

Unrealized: this does not mean that Mallarmé did not succeed in realizing a Book which would be at one with itself—he simply did not want to. He unrealized the unity of the Book by making the categories in which it was supposed to be securely conceptualized tremble: while speaking of an "identification with itself" of the Book, he underlines that the Book is at once "the same and other," as it is "made up of itself." It lends itself not only to a "double interpretation," but through it, says Mallarmé, "I sow, so to speak, this entire double volume here and there ten times."[54]

Does one have the right to constitute this metaphysics or aesthetics so well adapted to Proust and Claudel as the general method of structuralism?[55] This, however, is precisely what Rousset does, in the extent to which, as we have at least tried to demonstrate, he decides that everything not intelligible in the light of a "preestablished" teleological framework, and not visible in its simultaneity, is reducible to the inconsequentiality of accident or dross. Even in the essays devoted to Proust and Claudel, the essays guided by the most comprehensive structure, Rousset must decide to consider as "genetic accidents" "each episode, each character" whose "eventual independence" from the "central theme" or "general organization of the work" is noticeable (p. 164); he must accept the confrontation of the "true Proust" with the "Novelist" to whom, moreover, he can sometimes "do wrong," just as the true Proust, according to Rousset, is also capable of missing the "truth" of love, etc. (p. 166). In the same way that "the true Baudelaire is perhaps only in the *Balcon,* and all of Flaubert is in *Madame Bovary*" (p. xix), the true Proust is not simultaneously everywhere. Rousset must also conclude that the characters of *l'Otage* are severed not by "circumstance," but, "to express it better," by the "demands of the Claudelian framework" (p.179); he must deploy marvels of subtlety to demonstrate that in *Le soulier de satin* Claudel does not "repudiate himself" and does not "renounce" his "constant framework" (p. 183).

What is most serious is that this "ultrastructuralist" method, as we have called it, seems to contradict, in certain respects, the most precious and original intention of structuralism. In the biological and linguistic fields where it first appeared, structuralism above all insists upon preserving the coherence and completion of each totality at its own level. In a given configuration, it first prohibits the consideration of that which is incomplete or missing, everything that would make the configuration appear to be a blind anticipation of, or mysterious deviation from, an orthogenesis whose own conceptual basis would have to be a *telos* or an ideal norm. To be a structuralist is first to concentrate on the organization of meaning, on the autonomy and idiosyncratic balance, the completion of each moment, each form; and it is to refuse to relegate everything that is not comprehensible as an ideal type to the status of aberrational accident. The pathological itself is not the simple absence of structure. It is organized. It cannot be understood as the deficiency, defect, or decomposition of a beautiful, ideal totality. It is not the simple undoing of *telos*.

It is true that the rejection of finalism is a rule, a methodological norm, that structuralism can apply only with difficulty. The rejection of finalism is a vow of infidelity to *telos* which the actual effort can never adhere to. Structuralism lives within and on the difference between its promise and its practice. Whether biology, linguistics, or literature is in question, how can an organized totality be perceived without reference to its end, or without presuming to know its end, at least? And if meaning is meaningful only within a totality, could it come forth if the totality were not animated by the anticipation of an end, or by an intentionality which, moreover, does not necessarily and primarily belong to a consciousness? If there are structures, they are possible only on the basis of the fundamental structure which permits totality to open and overflow itself such that it *takes on meaning* by anticipating a *telos* which here must be understood in its most indeterminate form. This opening is certainly that which liberates time and genesis (even coincides with them), but it is also that which risks enclosing progression toward the future—becoming—by giving it form. That which risks stifling force under form.

It may be acknowledged, then, that in the rereading to which we are invited by Rousset, light is menaced from within by that which also metaphysically menaces every structuralism: the possibility of concealing meaning through the very act of uncovering it. *To comprehend* the structure of a becoming, the form of a force, is to lose meaning by finding it. The meaning of becoming and of force, by virtue of their pure, intrinsic characteristics, is the repose of the beginning and the end, the peacefulness of a spectacle, horizon or face.[56] Within this peace and repose the character of becoming and of force is disturbed by meaning itself. The meaning of meaning is Apollonian by virtue of everything within it that can be seen.[57]

To say that force is the origin of the phenomenon is to say nothing. By its very

articulation force becomes a phenomenon. Hegel demonstrated convincingly that
the explication of a phenomenon by a force is a tautology.[58] But in saying this,
one must refer to language's peculiar inability to emerge from itself in order to
articulate its origin, and not to the *thought* of force. Force is the other of language
without which language would not be what it is.

In order to respect this strange movement within language, in order not to
reduce it in turn, we would have to attempt a return to the metaphor of darkness
and light (of self-revelation and self-concealment), the founding metaphor of
Western philosophy as metaphysics. The founding metaphor not only because it
is a photological one—and in this respect the entire history of our philosophy is a
photology, the name given to a history of, or treatise on, light—but because it is
a metaphor. Metaphor in general, the passage from one existent to another, or
from one signified meaning to another, authorized by the initial *submission* of
Being to the existent, the *analogical* displacement of Being, is the essential
weight which anchors discourse in metaphysics, irremediably repressing discourse into its metaphysical state.[59] This is a fate which it would be foolish to
term a regrettable and provisional accident of "history"—a slip, a mistake of
thought occurring *within* history (*in historia*). *In historiam*, it is the fall of
thought into philosophy which gets history under way. Which suffices to say that
the metaphor of the "fall" deserves its quotation marks. In this heliocentric
metaphysics, force, ceding its place to *eidos* (i.e., the form which is visible for
the metaphorical eye), has already been separated from itself in acoustics.[60] How
can force or weakness be understood in terms of light and dark?

That modern structuralism has grown and developed within a more or less
direct and avowed dependence upon phenomenology suffices to make it a trib-
utary of the most purely traditional stream of Western philosophy, which, above
and beyond its anti-Platonism, leads Husserl back to Plato. Now, one would seek
in vain a concept in phenomenology which would permit the conceptualization of
intensity or force. The conceptualization not only of direction but of power, not
only the *in* but the *tension* of intentionality. All value is first constituted by a
theoretical subject. Nothing is gained or lost except in terms of clarity and
nonclarity, obviousness, presence or absence for a consciousness, coming to
awareness or loss of consciousness. Diaphanousness is the supreme value; as is
univocity. Hence the difficulties in thinking the genesis and pure temporality of
the transcendental ego, of accounting for the successful or unsuccessful incarnation of *telos,* and the mysterious failures called crises. And when, in certain
places, Husserl ceases to consider the phenomena of crisis and the failure of *telos*
as "accidents of genesis," or as the *inessential* (*Unwesen*), it is in order to
demonstrate that forgetting is eidetically dictated, and is necessary, under the
rubric of "sedimentation," for the development of truth. For the revealing and
illumination of truth. But why these forces and failures of consciousness? And
why the force of weakness which dissimulates in the very act by which it reveals?

If this "dialectic" of force and weakness is the finitude of thought itself in its relationship to Being, it can only be articulated in the language of form, through images of shadow and light. For force is not darkness, and it is not hidden under a form for which it would serve as substance, matter, or crypt. Force cannot be conceived on the basis of an oppositional couple, that is, on the basis of the complicity between phenomenology and occultism. Nor can it be conceived, from within phenomenology, as the *fact* opposed to *meaning*.

Emanicipation from this language must be attempted. But not as an *attempt* at emancipation from it, for this is impossible unless we forget *our* history. Rather, as the dream of emancipation. Nor as emancipation from it, which would be meaningless and would deprive us of the light of meaning. Rather, as resistance to it, as far as is possible. In any event, we must not abandon ourselves to this language with the abandon which today characterizes the worst exhilaration of the most nuanced structural formalism.

Criticism, if it is called upon to enter into explication and exchange with literary writing, some day will not have to wait for this resistance first to be organized into a "philosophy" which would govern some methodology of aesthetics whose principles criticism would receive. For philosophy, during its history, has been determined as the reflection of poetic inauguration. Conceived apart, it is the twilight of forces, that is, the sun-splashed morning in which images, forms, and phenomena speak; it is the morning of ideas and idols in which the relief of forces becomes repose, its depth flattened in the light as it stretches itself into horizontality. But the enterprise is hopeless if one muses on the fact that literary criticism has already been determined, knowingly or not, voluntarily or not, as the philosophy of literature. As such—that is to say, until it has purposely opened the strategic operation we spoke of above, which cannot simply be conceived under the authority of structuralism—criticism will have neither the means nor, more particularly, the motive for renouncing eurythmics, geometry, the privilege given to vision, the Apollonian ecstasy which "acts above all as a force stimulating the eye, so that it acquires the power of vision."[61] It will not be able to exceed itself to the point of embracing both force and the movement which displaces lines, nor to the point of embracing force as movement, as desire, for itself, and not as the accident or epiphany of lines. To the point of embracing it as writing.

Hence the nostalgia, the melancholy, the fallen Dionysianism of which we spoke at the outset. Are we mistaken in perceiving it beneath the praise of structural and Claudelian "monotony" which closes *Forme et Signification*?

We should conclude, but the debate is interminable. The divergence, the *difference* between Dionysus and Apollo, between ardor and structure, cannot be erased in history, for it is not *in* history. It too, in an unexpected sense, is an original structure: the opening of history, historicity itself. *Difference* does not simply belong either to history or to structure. If we must say, along with

Schelling, that "all is but Dionysus," we must know—and this is to write—that, like pure force, Dionysus is worked by difference. He sees and lets himself be seen. And tears out (his) eyes. For all eternity, he has had a relationship to his exterior, to visible form, to structure, as he does to his death. This is how he appears (to himself).

"Not enough forms . . . ," said Flaubert. How is he to be understood? Does he wish to celebrate the other of form? the "too many things" which exceed and resist form? In praise of Dionysus? One is certain that this is not so. Flaubert, on the contrary, is sighing, "Alas! not enough forms." A religion of the work as form. Moreover, the things for which we do not have enough forms are already phantoms of energy, "ideas" "larger than the plasticity of style." In question is a point against Leconte de Lisle, an affectionate point, for Flaubert "likes that fellow a lot."[62]

Nietzsche was not fooled: "Flaubert, a new edition of Pascal, but as an artist with this instinctive belief at heart: 'Flaubert est toujours haïssable, l'homme n'est rien, l'oeuvre est tout.'"[63]

We would have to choose then, between writing and dance.

Nietzsche recommends a dance of the pen in vain: " . . . dancing with the feet, with ideas, with words, and need I add that one must also be able to dance with the pen—that one must learn how to write?"[64] Flaubert was aware, and he was right, that writing cannot be thoroughly Dionysiac. "One can only think and write sitting down," he said. Joyous anger of Nietzsche: "Here I have got you, you nihilist! A sedentary life is the real sin against the Holy Spirit. Only those thoughts that come when you are walking have any value."[65]

But Nietzsche was certain that the writer would never be upright; that writing is first and always something over which one bends. Better still when letters are no longer figures of fire in the heavens.

Nietzsche was certain, but Zarathustra was positive: "Here do I sit and wait, old broken tables around me and also new half tables. When cometh mine hour?—The hour of my descent, of my down-going."[66] "Die Stunde meines Niederganges, Unterganges." It will be necessary to descend, to work, to bend in order to engrave and carry the new Tables to the valleys, in order to read them and have them read. Writing is the outlet as the descent of meaning outside itself within itself: metaphor-for-others-aimed-at-others-here-and-now, metaphor as the possibility of others here-and-now, metaphor as metaphysics in which Being must hide itself if the other is to appear. Excavation within the other toward the other in which the same seeks its vein and the true gold of its phenomenon. Submission in which the same can always lose (itself). *Niedergang, Untergang.* But the same is nothing, is not (it)self before taking the risk of losing (itself). For the fraternal other is not first in the peace of what is called intersubjectivity, but in the work and the peril of inter-rogation; the other is not certain within the peace of the *response* in which two affirmations *espouse each other,* but is called up in the night by the excavating work of interrogation. Writing is the moment of this original Valley of the other within Being. The moment of depth as decay. Incidence and insistence of inscription.

"Behold, here is a new table; but where are my brethren who will carry it with me to the valley and into hearts of flesh?"[67]

The Instant of Decision is Madness (Kierkegaard)

In any event this book was terribly daring. A transparent sheet separates it from madness. (Joyce, speaking of *Ulysses*)

These reflections have as their point of departure, as the title of this lecture[1] clearly indicates, Michel Foucault's book *Folie et déraison: Histoire de la folie à l'âge classique.*[2]

This book, admirable in so many respects, powerful in its breadth and style, is even more intimidating for me in that, having formerly had the good fortune to study under Michel Foucault, I retain the consciousness of an admiring and grateful disciple. Now, the disciple's consciousness, when he starts, I would not say to dispute, but to engage in dialogue with the master or, better, to articulate the interminable and silent dialogue which made him into a disciple—this disciple's consciousness is an unhappy consciousness. Starting to enter into dialogue in the world, that is, starting to answer back, he always feels "caught in the act," like the "infant" who, by definition and as his name indicates, cannot speak and above all must not answer back. And when, as is the case here, the dialogue is in danger of being taken—incorrectly—as a challenge, the disciple knows that he alone finds himself already challenged by the master's voice within him that precedes his own. He feels himself indefinitely challenged, or rejected or accused; as a disciple, he is challenged by the master who speaks within him and before him, to reproach him for making this challenge and to reject it in advance, having elaborated it before him; and having interiorized the master, he is also challenged by the disciple that he himself is. This interminable unhappiness of the disciple perhaps stems from the fact that he does not yet know—or is still concealing from himself—that the master, like real life, may always be absent. The disciple must break the glass, or better the mirror, the reflection, his infinite speculation on the master. And start to speak.

As the route that these considerations will follow is neither direct nor unilinear—far from it—I will sacrifice any further preamble and go straight to the most general questions that will serve as the focal points of these reflections. General questions that will have to be determined and specified along the way, many of which, most, will remain open.

My point of departure might appear slight and artificial. In this 673-page book, Michel Foucault devotes three pages—and, moreover, in a kind of prologue to his second chapter—to a certain passage from the first of Descartes's *Meditations*. In this passage madness, folly, dementia, insanity seem, I emphasize *seem,* dismissed, excluded, and ostracized from the circle of philosophical dignity, denied entry to the philosopher's city, denied the right to philosophical consideration, ordered away from the bench as soon as summoned to it by Descartes—this last tribunal of a Cogito that, by its essence, *could not possibly* be mad.

In alleging—correctly or incorrectly, as will be determined—that the sense of Foucault's entire project can be pinpointed in these few allusive and somewhat enigmatic pages, and that the reading of Descartes and the Cartesian Cogito proposed to us engages in its problematic the totality of this *History of Madness* as regards both its intention and its feasibility, I shall therefore be asking myself, in two series of questions, the following:

1. First, and in some ways this is a prejudicial question: is the *interpretation* of Descartes's intention that is proposed to us justifiable? What I here call interpretation is a certain passage, a certain semantic relationship proposed by Foucault between, *on the one hand,* what Descartes said—or what he is believed to have said or meant—and *on the other hand,* let us say, with intentional vagueness for the moment, a certain "historical structure," as it is called, a certain meaningful historical totality, a total historical project through which we think what Descartes said—or what he is believed to have said or meant—can *particularly* be demonstrated. In asking if the interpretation is justifiable, I am therefore asking about two things, putting two preliminary questions into one: (a) Have we fully understood the *sign* itself, in itself? In other words, has what Descartes said and meant been clearly perceived? This comprehension of the sign in and of itself, in its immediate materiality as a sign, if I may so call it, is only the first moment but also the indispensable condition of all hermeneutics and of any claim to transition from the sign to the signified. When one attempts, in a general way, to pass from an obvious to a latent language, one must first be rigorously sure of the obvious meaning.[3] The analyst, for example, must first speak the same language as the

patient. (b) Second implication of the first question: once understood as a sign, does Descartes's stated intention have with the total historical structure to which it is to be related the relationship assigned to it? *Does it have the historical meaning assigned to it?* "Does it have the historical meaning assigned to it?" That is, again, two questions in one: Does it have *the* historical meaning assigned to it? does it have *this* meaning, a *given* meaning Foucault assigns to it? Or, second, does it have the *historical* meaning assigned to it? Is this meaning exhausted by its historicity? In other words, is it fully, in each and every one of its aspects, historical, in the classical sense of the word?

2. Second series of questions (and here we shall go somewhat beyond the case of Descartes, beyond the case of the Cartesian Cogito, which will be examined no longer in and of itself but as the index of a more general problematic): in the light of the rereading of the Cartesian Cogito that we shall be led to propose (or rather to recall, for, let it be said at the outset, this will in some ways be the most classical, banal reading, even if not the easiest one), will it not be possible to interrogate *certain* philosophical and methodological presuppositions of this history of madness? *Certain ones* only, for Foucault's enterprise is too rich, branches out in too many directions to be preceded by a method or even by a *philosophy,* in the traditional sense of the word. And if it is true, as Foucault says, as he admits by citing Pascal, that one cannot speak of madness except in relation to that "other form of madness" that allows men "not to be mad," that is, except in relation to reason,[4] it will perhaps be possible not to add anything whatsoever to what Foucault has said, but perhaps only to *repeat* once more, on the site of this *division* between reason and madness of which Foucault speaks so well, the meaning, a meaning of the Cogito or (plural) Cogitos (for the Cogito of the Cartesian variety is neither the first nor the last form of Cogito); and also to determine that what is in question here is an experience which, at its furthest reaches, is perhaps no less adventurous, perilous, nocturnal, and pathetic than the experience of madness, and is, I believe, much less adverse to and accusatory of madness, that is, accusative and objectifying of it, than Foucault seems to think.

As a first stage, we will attempt a commentary, and will accompany or follow as faithfully as possible Foucault's intentions in reinscribing an interpretation of the Cartesian Cogito within the total framework of the *History of Madness.* What should then become apparent in the course of this first stage is the meaning of the Cartesian Cogito as read by Foucault. To this end, it is necessary to recall the general plan of the book and to open several marginal questions, destined to remain open and marginal.

In writing a history of madness, Foucault has attempted—and this is the greatest merit, but also the very infeasibility of his book—to write a history of madness *itself. Itself.* Of madness itself. That is, by letting madness speak for itself. Foucault wanted madness to be the *subject* of his book in every sense of the word: its theme and its first-person narrator, its author, madness speaking about itself. Foucault wanted to write a history of madness *itself,* that is madness speaking on the basis of its own experience and under its own authority, and not a history of madness described from within the language of reason, the language of psychiatry *on* madness—the agonistic and rhetorical dimensions of the preposition *on* overlapping here—on madness already crushed beneath psychiatry, dominated, beaten to the ground, interned, that is to say, madness made into an object and exiled as the other of a language and a historical meaning which have been confused with logos itself. "A history not of psychiatry," Foucault says, "but of madness itself, in its most vibrant state, before being captured by knowledge."

It is a question, therefore, of escaping the trap or objectivist naiveté that would consist in writing a history of untamed madness, of madness as it carries itself and breathes before being caught and paralyzed in the nets of classical reason, from within the very language of classical reason itself, utilizing the concepts that were the historical instruments of the capture of madness—the restrained and restraining language of reason. Foucault's determination to avoid this trap is constant. It is the most audacious and seductive aspect of his venture, producing its admirable tension. But it is also, with all seriousness, the *maddest* aspect of his project. And it is remarkable that this obstinate determination to avoid the trap—that is, the trap set by classical reason to catch madness and which can now catch Foucault as he attempts to write a history of madness itself without repeating the aggression of rationalism—this determination to bypass reason is expressed in two ways difficult to reconcile at first glance. Which is to say that it is expressed uneasily.

Sometimes Foucault globally rejects the language of reason, which itself is the language of order (that is to say, simultaneously the language of the system of objectivity, of the universal rationality of which psychiatry wishes to be the expression, and the language of the body politic—the right to citizenship in the philosopher's city overlapping here with the right to citizenship anywhere, the philosophical realm functioning, within the unity of a certain structure, as the metaphor or the metaphysics of the political realm). At these moments he writes sentences of this type (he has just evoked the broken dialogue between reason and madness at the end of the eighteenth century, a break that was finalized by the annexation of the totality of language—and of the right to language—by psychiatric reason as the delegate of societal and governmental reason; madness has been stifled): "The language of psychiatry, which is a monologue of reason *on* madness, could be established only on the basis of such a silence. I have not tried to write the history of that language but, rather, the archaeology of that silence."[5] And throughout the book runs the theme linking madness to silence, to "words without language" or "without the voice of a subject," "obstinate murmur of a language that speaks by itself, without speaker or interlocutor, piled up upon itself, strangulated, collapsing before reaching the stage of formulation, quietly returning to the silence from which it never departed. The calcinated root of meaning.'' The history of madness itself is therefore the archaeology of a silence.

But, first of all, is there a history of silence? Further, is not an archaeology, even of silence, a logic, that is, an organized language, a project, an order, a sentence, a syntax, a work?[6] Would not the archaeology of silence be the most efficacious and subtle restoration, the *repetition,* in the most irreducibly ambiguous meaning of the word, of the act perpetrated against madness—and be so at the very moment when this act is denounced? Without taking into account that all the signs which allegedly serve as indices of the origin of this silence and of this stifled speech, and as indices of everything that has made madness an interrupted and forbidden, that is, arrested, discourse—all these signs and documents are borrowed, without exception, from the juridical province of interdiction.

Hence, one can inquire—as Foucault does also, at moments other than those when he contrives to speak of silence (although in too lateral and implicit a fashion from my point of view)—about the source and the status of the language of this archaeology, of this language which is to be understood by a reason that is not classical reason. What is the historical responsibility of this logic of archaeology? Where should it be situated? Does it suffice to stack the tools of psychiatry neatly, inside a tightly shut workshop, in order to return to innocence and to end all complicity with the rational or political order which keeps madness captive? The psychiatrist is but the delegate of this order, one delegate among others. Perhaps it does not suffice to imprison or to exile the delegate, or to stifle him; and perhaps it does not suffice to deny oneself the conceptual material of psychiatry in order to exculpate one's own language. All our European languages, the language of everything that has participated, from near or far, in the adventure of Western reason—all this is the immense delegation of the project defined by Foucault under the rubric of the capture or objectification of madness. *Nothing* within this language, and *no one* among those who speak it, can escape the historical guilt—if there is one, and if it is historical in a classical sense— which Foucault apparently wishes to put on trial. But such a trial may be impossible, for by the simple fact of their articulation the proceedings and the verdict unceasingly reiterate the crime. If the *Order* of which we are speaking is so powerful, if its power is unique of its kind, this is so precisely by virtue of the universal, structural, universal, and infinite complicity in which it compromises all those who understand it in its own language, even when this language provides them with the form of their own denunciation. Order is then denounced within order.

Total disengagement from the *totality* of the historical language responsible for the exile of madness, liberation from this language in order to write the archaeology of silence, would be possible in only two ways.

Either do not mention a certain silence (a *certain* silence which, again, can be determined only within a *language* and an *order* that will preserve this silence from contamination by any given muteness), *or* follow the madman down the road of his exile. The misfortune of the mad, the interminable misfortune of their silence, is that their best spokesmen are those who betray them best; which is to say that when one attempts to convey their silence *itself,* one has already passed over to the side of the enemy, the side of order, even if one fights against order from within it, putting its origin into question. There is no Trojan horse unconquerable by Reason (in general). The unsurpassable, unique, and imperial grandeur of the order of reason, that which makes it not just another actual order or structure (a determined historical structure, one structure among other possible ones), is that one cannot speak out against it except by being for it, that one can protest it only from within it; and within its domain, Reason leaves us only the recourse to stratagems and strategies. The revolution against reason, in the historical form of classical reason (but the latter is only a determined example of Reason in general. And because of this oneness of Reason the expression "history of reason" is difficult to conceptualize, as is also, consequently, a "history of madness"), the revolution against reason can be made only within it, in accordance with a Hegelian law to which I myself was very sensitive in Foucault's book, despite the absence of any precise reference to Hegel. Since the revolution against reason, from the moment it is articulated, can operate only *within* reason, it always has the limited scope of what is called, precisely in the language of a department of *internal* affairs, a disturbance. A history, that is, an archaeology against reason doubtless cannot be written, for, despite all appearances to the contrary, the concept of history has always been a rational one. It is the meaning of "history" or *archia* that should have been questioned first, perhaps. A writing that exceeds, by questioning them, the values "origin," "reason," and "history" could not be contained within the metaphysical closure of an archaeology.

As Foucault is the first to be conscious—and acutely so—of this daring, of the necessity of speaking and of drawing his language from the wellspring of a reason more profound than the reason which issued forth during the classical age, and as he experiences a necessity of speaking which must escape the objectivist project of classical reason—a necessity of speaking even at the price of a war declared by the language of reason against itself, a war in which language would recapture itself, destroy itself, or unceasingly revive the act of its own destruction—the allegation of an archaeology of silence, a purist, intransigent, nonviolent, nondialectical allegation, is often counterbalanced, equilibrated, I should even say contradicted by a discourse in Foucault's book that is not only the admission of a difficulty, but the formulation of *another* project, a project that is not an expediency, but a different and more ambitious one, a project more effectively ambitious than the first one.

The admission of the difficulty can be found in sentences such as these, among others, which I simply cite, in order not to deprive you of their dense beauty: "The perception that seeks to grasp them [in question are the miseries and murmurings of madness] in their wild state, necessarily belongs to a world that has already captured them. The liberty of madness can be understood only from high in the fortress that holds madness prisoner. And there madness possesses only the morose sum of its prison experiences, its mute experience of persecution, and we—we possess only its description as a man wanted." And, later, Foucault speaks of a madness "whose wild state can never be restored in and of itself" and of an "inaccessible primitive purity."

Because this difficulty, or this impossibility, must reverberate within the language used to describe this history of madness, Foucault, in effect, acknowledges the necessity of maintaining his discourse within what he calls a "relativity without recourse," that is, without support from an absolute reason or logos. The simultaneous necessity and impossibility of what Foucault elsewhere calls "a language without support," that is to say, a language declining, in principle if not in fact, to articulate itself along the lines of the syntax of reason. In principle if not in fact, but here the fact cannot easily be put between parentheses. The fact of language is probably the only fact ultimately to resist all parenthization. "There, in the simple problem of articulation," Foucault says later, "was hidden and expressed the major difficulty of the enterprise."

One could perhaps say that the resolution of this difficulty is *practiced* rather than *formulated*. By necessity. I mean that the silence of madness is not *said,* cannot be said in the logos of this book, but is indirectly, metaphorically, made present by its *pathos*—taking this word in its best sense. A new and radical praise of folly whose intentions cannot be admitted because the *praise* [*éloge*] of silence always takes place within *logos,* [7] the language of objectification. "To speak well of madness" would be to annex it once more, especially when, as is the case here, "speaking well of" is also the wisdom and happiness of eloquent speech.

Now, to state the difficulty, to state the difficulty of stating, is not yet to surmount it—quite the contrary. First, it is not to say in which language, through the agency of what speech, the difficulty is stated. Who perceives, who enunciates the difficulty? These efforts can be made neither in the wild and inaccessible silence of madness, nor simply in the language of the jailer, that is, in the language of classical reason, but only in the language of someone *for whom* is meaningful and *before whom* appears the dialogue or war or misunderstanding or confrontation or double monologue that opposes reason and madness during the classical age. And thereby we can envision the historic liberation of a logos in which the two monologues, or the broken dialogue, or especially the breaking point of the dialogue between a *determined* reason and a *determined* madness, could be produced and can today be understood and enunciated. (Supposing that they can be; but here we are assuming Foucault's hypothesis.)

Therefore, if Foucault's book, despite all the acknowledged impossibilities and difficulties, was capable of being written, we have the right to ask what, in the last resort, supports this language without recourse or support: who enunciates the possibility of nonrecourse? Who wrote and who is to understand, in what language and from what historical situation of logos, who wrote and who is to understand this history of madness? For it is not by chance that such a project could take shape today. Without forgetting, *quite to the contrary,* the audacity of Foucault's act in the *History of Madness,* we must assume that a certain liberation of madness has gotten underway, that psychiatry has opened itself up, however minimally, and that the concept of madness as unreason, if it ever had a unity, has been dislocated. And that a project such as Foucault's can find its historical origin and passageway in the opening produced by this dislocation.

If Foucault, more than anyone else, is attentive and sensitive to these kinds of questions, it nevertheless appears that he does not acknowledge their quality of being prerequisite methodological or philosophical considerations. And it is true that once the question and the privileged difficulty are understood, to devote a preliminary work to them would have entailed the sterilization or paralysis of all further inquiry. Inquiry can prove through its very act that the movement of a discourse on madness is possible. But is not the foundation of this possibility still too classical?

Foucault's book is not one of those that abandons itself to the prospective lightheartedness of inquiry. That is why, behind the admission of the difficulty concerning the archaeology of silence, a *different* project must be discerned, one which perhaps contradicts the projected archaeology of silence.

Because the silence whose archaeology is to be undertaken is not an original muteness or nondiscourse, but a subsequent silence, a discourse arrested by *command,* the issue is therefore to reach the origin of the protectionism imposed by a reason that insists upon being sheltered, and that also insists upon providing itself with protective barriers against madness, thereby making itself into a barrier against madness; and to reach this origin from within a logos of free trade, that is, from within a logos that preceded the split of reason and madness, a logos which within itself permitted dialogue between what were later called reason and madness (unreason), permitted their free circulation and exchange, just as the medieval city permitted the free circulation of the mad within itself. The issue is therefore to reach the point at which the dialogue was broken off, dividing itself into two soliloquies—what Foucault calls, using a very strong word, the *Decision.* The Decision, through a single act, links and separates reason and madness, and it must be understood at once both as the original act of an order, a fiat, a decree, and as a schism, a caesura, a separation, a dissection. I would prefer *dissension,* to underline that in question is a self-dividing action, a cleavage and torment interior to meaning *in general,* interior to logos in general, a divison

within the very act of *sentire*. As always, the dissension is internal. The exterior
(is) the interior, is the fission that produces and divides it along the lines of the
Hegelian *Entzweiung*.

It thus seems that the project of convoking the first dissension of logos against
itself is quite another project than the archaeology of silence, and raises different
questions. This time it would be necessary to exhume the virgin and unitary
ground upon which the decisive act linking and separating madness and reason
obscurely took root. The reason and madness of the classical age had a common
root. But this common root, which is a logos, this unitary foundation is much
more ancient than the medieval period, brilliantly but briefly evoked by Foucault
in his very fine opening chapter. There must be a founding unity that already
carries within it the "free trade" of the Middle Ages, and this unity is already the
unity of a logos, that is, of a reason; an already historical reason certainly, but a
reason much less determined than it will be in its so-called classical form, having
not yet received the determinations of the "classical age." It is within the
element of this archaic reason that the dissection, the dissension, will present
itself as a modification or, if you will, as an overturning, that is, a revolution but
an internal revolution, a revolution affecting the self, occurring within the self.
For this logos which is in the beginning, is not only the common ground of all
dissension, but also—and no less importantly—the very atmosphere in which
Foucault's language moves, the atmosphere in which a history of madness during
the classical age not only appears *in fact* but is also *by all rights* stipulated and
specified in terms of its limits. In order to account simultaneously for the origin
(or the possibility) of the decision and for the origin (or the possibility) of its
narration, it might have been necessary to start by reflecting this original logos in
which the violence of the classical era played itself out. This history of logos
before the Middle Ages and before the classical age is not, if this need be said at
all, a nocturnal and mute prehistory. Whatever the momentary break, if there is
one, of the Middle Ages with the Greek tradition, this break and this alteration
are late and secondary developments as concerns the fundamental permanence of
the logico-philosophical heritage.

That the embedding of the decision in its true historical grounds has been left
in the shadows by Foucault is bothersome, and for at least two reasons:

1. It is bothersome because at the outset Foucault makes a somewhat enigmatic
allusion to the Greek logos, saying that, unlike classical reason, it "had no
contrary." To cite Foucault: "The Greeks had a relation to something that they
called *hybris*. This relation was not merely one of condemnation; the existence of
Thrasymacus or of Callicles suffices to prove it, even if their language has
reached us already enveloped in the reassuring dialectic of Socrates. But the
Greek Logos had no contrary."[8]

[One would have to assume, then, that the Greek logos had no contrary, which
is to say, briefly, that the Greeks were in the greatest proximity to the elemen-

tary, primordial, and undivided Logos with respect to which contradiction in general, all wars or polemics, could only be ulterior developments. This hypothesis forces us to admit, as Foucault above all does *not,* that the history and lineage of the "reassuring dialectic of Socrates" in their *totality* had already fallen outside and been exiled from this Greek logos that had no contrary. For if the Socratic dialectic is reassuring, in the sense understood by Foucault, it is so only in that it has already expulsed, excluded, objectified or (curiously amounting to the same thing) assimilated and mastered as one of its moments, "enveloped" the contrary of reason; and also only in that it has tranquilized and reassured itself into a pre-Cartesian certainty, a *sophrosyne*, a wisdom, a reasonable good sense and prudence.

Consequently, it must be *either* (a) that the Socratic moment and its entire posterity immediately partake in the Greek logos that has no contrary; and that consequently, the Socratic dialectic could not be reassuring (we may soon have occasion to show that it is no more reassuring than the Cartesian cogito). In this case, in this hypothesis, the fascination with the pre-Socratics to which we have been provoked by Nietzsche, then by Heidegger and several others, would carry with it a share of mystification whose historico-philosophical motivations remain to be examined. *Or* (b) that the Socratic moment and the victory over the Calliclesian hybris already are the marks of a deportation and an exile of logos from itself, the wounds left in it by a decision, a difference; and then the structure of exclusion which Foucault wishes to describe in his book could not have been born with classical reason. It would have to have been consummated and reassured and smoothed over throughout all the centuries of philosophy. It would be essential to the entirety of the history of philosophy and of reason. In this regard, the classical age could have neither specificity nor privilege. And all the signs assembled by Foucault under the chapter heading *Stultifera navis* would play themselves out only on the surface of a chronic dissension. The free circulation of the mad, besides the fact that it is not as simply free as all that, would only be a socioeconomic epiphenomenon on the surface of a reason divided against itself since the dawn of its Greek origin. What seems to me sure in any case, regardless of the hypothesis one chooses concerning what is doubtless only a false problem and a false alternative, is that Foucault cannot *simultaneously* save the affirmation of a reassuring dialectic of Socrates and his postulation of a specificity of the classical age whose reason would reassure itself by excluding its contrary, that is, by *constituting* its contrary as an object in order to be protected from it and be rid of it. In order to lock it up.

The attempt to write the history of the decision, division, difference runs the risk of construing the division as an event or a structure subsequent to the unity of an original presence, thereby confirming metaphysics in its fundamental operation.

Truthfully, for one or the other of these hypotheses to be true and for there to be a real choice between them, it must be assumed in *general* that reason can have a contrary, that there can be an other of reason, that reason itself can construct or discover, and that the opposition of reason to its other is *symmetrical.* This is the heart of the matter. Permit me to hold off on this question.

However one interprets the situation of classical reason, notably as regards the Greek logos (and whether or not this latter experienced dissension) *in all cases* a doctrine of *tradition,* of the tradition of logos (is there any other?) seems to be the prerequisite implied by Foucault's enterprise. No matter what the relationship of the Greeks to *hybris,* a relationship that was certainly not simple ... (Here, I wish to open a parenthesis and a question: in the name of what invariable meaning of "madness" does Foucault associate, whatever the meaning of this association, Madness and *Hybris*? A problem of translation, a philosophical problem of translation is posed—and it is serious—even if *Hybris* is not *Madness* for Foucault. The determination of their difference supposes a hazardous linguistic transition. The frequent imprudence of translators in this respect should make us very wary. I am thinking in particular, and in passing, of what is translated by madness and fury in the *Philebus (45e).*[9] Further, if madness has an invariable meaning, what is the relation of this meaning to the a posteriori *events* which govern Foucault's analysis? For, despite everything, even if his method is not empiricist, Foucault proceeds by inquiry and inquest. What he is writing is a history, and the recourse to events, in the last resort, is indispensable and determining, at least in principle. Now, is not the concept of madness—never submitted to a thematic scrutiny by Foucault—today a false and disintegrated concept, outside current and popular language which always lags longer than it should behind its subversion by science and philosophy? Foucault, in rejecting the psychiatric or philosophical material that has always emprisoned the mad, winds up employing—inevitably—a popular and equivocal notion of madness, taken from an unverifiable source. This would not be serious if Foucault used the word only in quotation marks, as if it were the language of others, of those who, during the period under study, used it as a historical instrument. But everything transpires as if Foucault *knew* what "madness" means. Everything transpires as if, in a continuous and underlying way, an assured and rigorous precomprehension of the concept of madness, or at least of its nominal definition, were possible and acquired. In fact, however, it could be demonstrated that as Foucault intends it, if not as intended by the historical current he is studying, the concept of madness overlaps everything that can be put under the rubric of *negativity.* One can imagine the kind of problems posed by such a usage of the notion of madness. The same kind of questions could be posed concerning the notion of truth that runs throughout the book ... I close this long parenthesis.) Thus, whatever the relation of the Greeks to *hybris,* and of Socrates to the original logos, it is in any event certain that classical reason, and medieval reason before it, bore a relation to Greek reason, and that it is within the milieu of this more or less immediately perceived heritage, which itself is more or less crossed with other traditional lines, that the adventure or misadventure of classical reason developed. If dissension dates from Socrates, then the situation of the madman in the Socratic and post-Socratic worlds—assuming that there is, then, something that can be called mad—perhaps deserves to be examined first. Without this examination, and as Foucault does not proceed in a simply aprioristic fashion, his historical description poses the banal but inevitable problems of periodization and of geographical, political, ethnological limitation, etc. If, on the contrary, the unopposed and unexcluding unity of logos were maintained until the classical "crisis," then this latter is, if I may say so, secondary and derivative. It does not engage the entirety of reason. And in this case, even if stated in passing, Socratic discourse would be nothing less than reassuring. It can be proposed that the classical crisis developed from and within the elementary tradition of a logos that has no opposite but carries within itself and *says* all determined contradictions. This doctrine of the tradition of meaning and of reason would be even further necessitated by the fact that it alone can give meaning and rationality in *general* to Foucault's discourse and to any discourse on the war between reason and unreason. For these discourses intend above all to be understood.]

2. I stated above that leaving the history of the preclassical logos in the shadows is bothersome for *two* reasons. The second reason, which I will adduce briefly before going on to Descartes, has to do with the profound link established by Foucault between the division, the dissension, and the possibility of history itself. *"The necessity of madness,* throughout the history of the West, is linked to the deciding gesture which detaches from the background noise, and from its continuous monotony, a meaningful language that is transmitted and consummated in time; briefly, it is linked to the *possibility of history."*

Consequently, if the decision through which reason constitutes itself by excluding and objectifying the free subjectivity of madness is indeed the origin of history, if it is historicity itself, the condition of meaning and of language, the condition of the tradition of meaning, the condition of the work in general, if the structure of exclusion is the fundamental structure of historicity, then the "classical" moment of this exclusion described by Foucault has neither absolute privilege nor archetypal exemplarity. It is an example as sample and not as model. In any event, in order to evoke the singularity of the classical moment, which is profound, perhaps it would be necessary to underline, not the aspects in which it is a structure of exclusion, but those aspects in which, and especially for what end, its own structure of exclusion is historically distinguished from the others, from all others. And to pose the problem of its exemplarity: are we concerned with an example among others or with a "good example," an example that is revelatory by privilege? Formidable and infinitely difficult problems that haunt Foucault's book, more present in his intentions than his words.

Finally, a *last question:* if this great division is the possibility of history itself, the historicity of history, what does it mean, here, "to write the history of this division"? To write the history of historicity? To write the history of the origin of history? The *hysteron proteron* would not here be a simple "logical fallacy," a fallacy within logic, within an established rationality. And its denunciation is not an act of ratiocination. If there is a historicity proper to reason in general, the history of reason cannot be the history of its origin (which, for a start, demands the historicity of reason in general), but must be that of one of its determined figures.

This second project, which would devote all its efforts to discovering the common root of meaning and nonmeaning and to unearthing the original logos in which *a* language and *a* silence are divided from one another is not at all an expediency as concerns everything that could come under the heading "archaeology of silence," the archaeology which simultaneously claims to say madness itself and renounces this claim. The expression "to say madness itself" is self-contradictory. To say madness without expelling it into objectivity is to let it say itself. But madness is what by essence cannot be said: it is the "absence of the work," as Foucault profoundly says.

Thus, not an expediency, but a different and more ambitious design, one that should lead to a praise of reason (there is no praise [*éloge*], by essence, except of reason),[10] but this time of a reason more profound than that which opposes and determines itself in a historically determined conflict. Hegel again, always ... Not an expediency, but a more ambitious ambition, even if Foucault writes this: "*Lacking* this inaccessible primitive purity [of madness itself], a structural study must go back toward the decision that simultaneously links and separates reason and madness; it must aim to uncover the perpetual exchange, the obscure common root, the original confrontation that gives meaning to the unity, as well as to the opposition, of sense and non-sense" [my italics].

Before describing the moment when the reason of the classical age will reduce madness to silence by what he calls a "strange act of force," Foucault shows how the exclusion and internment of madness found a sort of structural niche prepared for it by the history of another exclusion: the exclusion of leprosy. Unfortunately, we cannot be detained by the brilliant passages of the chapter entitled *Stultifera navis*. They would also pose numerous questions.

We thus come to the "act of force," to the great internment which, with the creation of the houses of internment for the mad and others in the middle of the seventeenth century, marks the advent and first stage of a classical process described by Foucault throughout his book. Without establishing, moreover, whether an event such as the creation of a house of internment is a sign among others, whether it is a fundamental symptom or a cause. This kind of question could appear exterior to a method that presents itself precisely as structuralist, that is, a method for which everything within the structural totality is interdependent and circular in such a way that the classical problems of causality themselves would appear to stem from a misunderstanding. Perhaps. But I wonder whether, when one is concerned with history (and Foucault wants to write a history), a strict structuralism is possible, and, especially, whether, if only for the sake of order and within the order of its own descriptions, such a study can avoid all etiological questions, all questions bearing, shall we say, on the center of gravity of the structure. The legitimate renunciation of a certain style of causality perhaps does not give one the right to renounce all etiological demands.

The passage devoted to Descartes opens the crucial chapter on "the great internment." It thus opens the book itself, and its location at the beginning of the chapter is fairly unexpected. More than anywhere else, the question I have just asked seems to me unavoidable here. We are not told whether or not this passage of the first *Meditation,* interpreted by Foucault as a *philosophical* internment of madness, is destined, as a prelude to the historical and sociopolitical drama, to set the tone for the *entire* drama to be played. Is this "act of force," described in the dimension of theoretical knowledge and metaphysics, a symptom, a cause, a language? What must be assumed or elucidated so that the meaning of this question or dissociation can be neutralized? And if this act of force has a structural affinity with the totality of the drama, what is the status of this affinity? Finally, whatever the place reserved for philosophy in this total historical structure may be, why the sole choice of the Cartesian example? What is the exemplarity of Descartes, while so many other philosophers of the same era were interested or—no less significantly—not interested in madness in various ways?

Foucault does not respond directly to any of these more than methodological questions, summarily, but inevitably, invoked. A single sentence, in his preface, settles the question. To cite Foucault: "To write the history of madness thus will mean the execution of a structural study of an historical ensemble—notions, institutions, juridical and police measures, scientific concepts—which holds captive a madness whose wild state can never in itself be restored." How are these elements organized in the "historical ensemble"? What is a "notion"? Do philosophical notions have a privilege? How are they related to scientific concepts? A quantity of questions that besiege this enterprise.

I do not know to what extent Foucault would agree that the prerequisite for a response to such questions is first of all the internal and autonomous analysis of the philosophical content of philosophical discourse. Only when the totality of this content will have become manifest in its meaning for me (but this is impossible) will I rigorously be able to situate it in its total historical form. It is only then that its reinsertion will not do it violence, that there will be a legitimate reinsertion of *this* philosophical meaning *itself*. As to Descartes in particular, no historical question about him—about the latent historical meaning of his discourse, about its place in a total structure—can be answered before a rigorous and exhaustive internal analysis of his manifest intentions, of the manifest meaning of his philosophical discourse has been made.

We will now turn to this manifest meaning, this properly philosophical intention that is not legible in the immediacy of a first encounter. But first by reading over Foucault's shoulder.

> There had to be folly so that
> wisdom might overcome it.
> (Herder)

Descartes, then, is alleged to have executed the act of force in the first of the *Meditations,* and it would very summarily consist in a summary expulsion of the possibility of madness from thought itself.

I shall first cite the decisive passage from Descartes, the one cited by Foucault. Then we shall follow Foucault's reading of the text. Finally, we shall establish a dialogue between Descartes and Foucault.

Descartes writes the following (at the moment when he undertakes to rid himself of all the opinions in which he had hitherto believed, and to start all over again from the foundations: *a primis fundamentis*. To do so, it will suffice to ruin the ancient foundations without being obliged to submit all his opinions to doubt one by one, for the ruin of the foundations brings down the entire edifice. One of these fragile foundations of knowledge, the most naturally apparent, is sensation. The senses deceive me sometimes; they can thus deceive me all the time, and I will therefore submit to doubt all knowledge whose origin is in sensation): "All that up to the present time I have accepted as most true and certain I have learned either from the senses or through the senses; but it is sometimes proved to me that these senses are deceptive, and it is wiser not to trust entirely to any thing by which we have once been deceived."

Descartes starts a new paragraph.

"But ... " (*sed forte* ... I insist upon the *forte* which the Duc de Luynes left untranslated, an omission that Descartes did not deem necessary to correct when he went over the translation. It is better, as Baillet says, to compare "the French with the Latin" when reading the *Meditations*. It is only in the second French edition by Clerselier that the *sed forte* is given its full weight and is translated by "but yet perhaps ... " The importance of this point will soon be demonstrated.) Pursuing my citation: "But it may be that although the senses sometimes deceive us concerning things which are *hardly perceptible, or very far away,* there are yet many others to be met with as to which we cannot reasonably have any doubt..." [my italics]. There would be, *there would perhaps be* data of sensory origin which cannot reasonably be doubted. "And how could I deny that these hands and this body are mine, were it not perhaps that I compare myself to certain persons, devoid of sense, whose cerebella are so troubled and clouded by the violent vapours of black bile, that they constantly assure us that they think they are kings when they are really quite poor, or that they are clothed in purple when they are really without covering, or who imagine that they have an earthenware head or are nothing but pumpkins or are made of glass . . . ''

And now the most significant sentence in Foucault's eyes: ''But they are mad, *sed amentes sunt isti,* and I should not be any the less insane (*demens*) were I to follow examples so extravagant.''[11]

I interrupt my citation not at the end of this paragraph, but on the first words of the following paragraph, which reinscribe the lines I have just read in a rhetorical and pedagogical movement with highly compressed articulations. These first words are *Praeclare sane* . . . Also translated as *toutefois* [but at the same time—trans.]. And this is the beginning of a paragraph in which Descartes imagines that he can always dream, and that the world might be no more real than his dreams. And he generalizes by hyperbole the hypothesis of sleep and dream (''Now let us assume that we are asleep . . .''); this hypothesis and this hyperbole will serve in the elaboration of doubt founded on natural reasons (for there is also a hyperbolical moment of this doubt), beyond whose reach will be only the truths of nonsensory origin, mathematical truths notably, which are true ''whether I am awake or asleep'' and which will capitulate only to the artificial and metaphysical assault of the evil genius.

How does Foucault read this text?

According to Foucault, Descartes, encountering madness alongside (the expression *alongside* is Foucault's) dreams and all forms of sensory error, refuses to accord them all the same treatment, so to speak. ''In the economy of doubt,'' says Foucault, ''there is a fundamental imbalance between madness, on the one hand, and error, on the other . . .'' (I note in passing that elsewhere Foucault often denounces the classical reduction of madness to error.) He pursues: ''Descartes does not avoid the peril of madness in the same way he circumvents the eventuality of dream and error.''

Foucault establishes a parallelism between the following two procedures:

1. The one by which Descartes wishes to demonstrate that the senses can deceive us only regarding ''things which are hardly perceptible, or very far away.'' These would be the limits of the error of sensory origin. And in the passage I just read, Descartes did say: ''But it may be that although the senses sometimes deceive us concerning things which are hardly perceptible, or very far away, there are yet many others to be met with as to which we cannot reasonably have any doubt . . .'' Unless one is mad, a hypothesis seemingly excluded in principle by Descartes in the same passage.

2. The procedure by which Descartes shows that imagination and dreams cannot themselves create the simple and universal elements which enter into their creations, as, for example, ''corporeal nature in general, and its extension, the figure of extended things, their quantity or magnitude and number,''[12] that is,

everything which precisely is not of sensory origin, thereby constituting the
objects of mathematics and geometry, which themselves are invulnerable to
natural doubt. It is thus tempting to believe, along with Foucault, that Descartes
wishes to find in the analysis (taking this word in its strict sense) of dreams and
sensation a nucleus, an element of proximity and simplicity irreducible to doubt.
It is *in* dreams and *in* sensory perception that I surmount or, as Foucault says, that
I "circumvent" doubt and reconquer a basis of certainty.

Foucault writes thus: "Descartes does not avoid the *peril* of madness in the
same way he circumvents the *eventuality* of dreams or of error.... Neither
image-peopled sleep, nor the clear consciousness that the senses can be decieved
is able to take doubt to the extreme point of its universality; let us admit that our
eyes deceive us, 'let us assume that we are asleep'—truth will not entirely slip
out into the night. For madness, it is otherwise." Later: "In the economy of
doubt, there is an imbalance between madness, on the one hand, and dream and
error, on the other. Their situation in relation to the truth and to him who seeks it
is different; dreams or illusions are surmounted within the structure of truth; but
madness is inadmissible for the doubting subject."

It indeed appears, then, that Descartes does not delve into the experience of
madness as he delves into the experience of dreams, that is, to the point of
reaching an irreducible nucleus which nonetheless would be interior to madness
itself. Descartes is not interested in madness, he does not welcome it as a
hypothesis, he does not consider it. He excludes it by decree. I would be insane if
I thought that I had a body made of glass. But this is excluded, since I am
thinking. Anticipating the moment of the Cogito, which will have to await the
completion of numerous stages, highly rigorous in their succession, Foucault
writes: "impossibility of being mad that is essential not to the object of thought,
but to the thinking subject." Madness is expelled, rejected, denounced in its very
impossibility from the very interiority of thought itself.

Foucault is the first, to my knowledge, to have isolated delirium and madness
from sensation and dreams in this first *Meditation*. The first to have isolated them
in their philosophical sense and their methodological function. Such is the originality of his reading. But if the classical interpreters did not deem this dissociation auspicious, is it because of their inattentiveness? Before answering this
question, or rather before continuing to ask it, let us recall along with Foucault
that this decree of inadmissibility which is a forerunner of the political decree of
the great internment, or corresponds to it, translates it, or accompanies it, or in
any case is in solidarity with it—this decree would have been impossible for a
Montaigne, who was, as we know, haunted by the possibility of being mad, or of
becoming completely mad in the very action of thought itself. The Cartesian
decree therefore marks, says Foucault, "the advent of a *ratio*." But as the advent
of a *ratio* is not "exhausted" by "the progress of rationalism," Foucault leaves
Descartes there, to go on to the historical (politico-social) structure of which the

Cartesian act is only a sign. For "more than one sign," Foucault says, "betrays the classical event."

We have attempted to read Foucault. Let us now naïvely attempt to reread Descartes and, before repeating the question of the relationship between the "sign" and the "structure," let us attempt to see, as I had earlier mentioned, what the *sense of the sign itself* may be. (Since the sign here already has the autonomy of a philosophical discourse, is already a relationship of signifier to signified.)

In rereading Descartes, I notice two things:

1. That in the passage to which we have referred and which corresponds to the phase of *doubt* founded on *natural* reasons, Descartes *does not* circumvent the eventuality of sensory error or of dreams, and does not "surmount" them "within the structure of truth;" and all this for the simple reason that he apparently does not ever, nor in any way, surmount them or circumvent them, and does not ever set aside the possibility of total error for *all* knowledge gained from the senses or from imaginary constructions. It must be understood that the hypothesis of dreams is the radicalization or, if you will, the hyperbolical exaggeration of the hypothesis according to which the senses could *sometimes* deceive me. In dreams, the *totality* of sensory images is illusory. It follows that a certainty invulnerable to dreams would be *a fortiori* invulnerable to *perceptual* illusions of the sensory kind. It therefore suffices to examine the case of dreams in order to deal with, on the level which is ours for the moment, the case of natural doubt, of sensory error in general. Now, which are the certainties and truths that escape perception, and therefore also escape sensory error or imaginative and oneiric composition? They are certainties and truths of a nonsensory and nonimaginative origin. They are *simple* and *intelligible* things.

In effect, if I am asleep, everything I perceive while dreaming may be, as Descartes says, "false and illusory," particularly the existence of my hands and my body and the actions of opening my eyes, moving my head, etc. In other words, what was previously excluded, according to Foucault, as insanity, is admissible within dreams. And we will see why in a moment. But, says Descartes, let us suppose that all my oneirical representations are illusory. Even in this case, there must be some representations of things as naturally certain as the body, hands, etc., however illusory this representation may be, and however false its relation to that which it represents. Now, within these representations, these images, these ideas in the Cartesian sense, everything may be fictitious and false, as in the representations of those painters whose imaginations, as Descartes expressly says, are "extravagant" enough to invent something so new that its like has never been seen before. But in the case of painting, at least, there is a final element which cannot be analyzed as illusion, an element that painters cannot counterfeit: color. This is only an *analogy,* for Descartes does not posit

the necessary existence of color in general: color is an object of the senses among
others. But, *just as* there always remains in a painting, however inventive and
imaginative it may be, an irreducibly simple and real element—color—*similarly,*
there is in dreams an element of noncounterfeit simplicity presupposed by all
fantastical compositions and irreducible to all analysis. But this time—and this is
why the example of the painter and of color was only an analogy—this element is
neither sensory nor imaginative: it is intelligible.

Foucault does not concern himself with this point. Let me cite the passage
from Descartes that concerns us here:

> For, as a matter of fact, painters, even when they study with the greatest
> skill to represent sirens and satyrs by forms the most strange and extraordi-
> nary, cannot give them natures which are entirely new, but merely make a
> certain medley of the members of different animals; or if their imagination is
> extravagant enough to invent something so novel that nothing similar has
> ever before been seen, and that then their work represents a thing purely
> fictitious and absolutely false, it is certain all the same that the colours of
> which this is composed are necessarily real. And for the same reason, al-
> though these general things, to wit, a body, eyes, a head, hands, and such
> like, may be imaginary, we are bound at the same time to confess that there
> are at least some other objects yet more simple and more universal, which
> are real and true; and of these just in the same way as with certain real
> colours, all these images of things which dwell in our thoughts, whether true
> and real or false and fantastic, are formed.
>
> To such a class of things pertains corporeal nature in general, and its
> extension, the figure of extended things, their quantity or magnitude and
> number, as also the place in which they are, the time which measures their
> duration, and so on.
>
> That is possibly why our reasoning is not unjust when we conclude from
> this that Physics, Astronomy, Medicine and all other sciences which have as
> their end the consideration of composite things, are very dubious and uncer-
> tain; but that Arithmetic, Geometry and other sciences of that kind which
> only treat of things that are very simple and very general, without taking
> great trouble to ascertain whether they are actually existent or not, contain
> some measure of certainty and an element of the indubitable. For whether I
> am awake or asleep, two and three together always form five, and the square
> can never have more than four sides, and it does not seem possible that
> truths so clear and apparent can be suspected of any falsity.[13]

And I remark that the following paragraph also starts with a "nevertheless"
(*verumtamen*) which will soon be brought to our attention.

Thus the certainty of this simplicity of *intelligible* generalization—which is
soon after submitted to metaphysical, artificial, and hyperbolical doubt through
the fiction of the evil genius—is in no way obtained by a continuous reduction

which finally lays bare the resistance of a nucleus of sensory or imaginative certainty. There is discontinuity and a transition to another order of reasoning. The nucleus is purely intelligible, and the still natural and provisional certainty which has been attained supposes a radical break with the senses. At this moment of the analysis, no imaginative or sensory signification, as such, has been saved, *no* invulnerability of the senses to doubt has been experienced. *All* significations or "ideas" of sensory origin are *excluded* from the realm of truth, *for the same reason as madness* is excluded from it. And there is nothing astonishing about this: madness is only a particular case, and, moreover, not the most serious one, of the sensory illusion which interests Descartes at this point. It can thus be stated that:

2. The hypothesis of insanity—at this moment of the Cartesian order—seems neither to receive any privileged treatment nor to be submitted to any particular exclusion. Let us reread, in effect, the passage cited by Foucault in which insanity appears. Let us resituate it. Descartes has just remarked that since the senses sometimes deceive us, "it is wiser not to trust entirely to any thing by which we have once been deceived."[14] He then starts a new paragraph with the *sed forte* which I brought to your attention a few moments ago. Now, the entire paragraph which follows does not express Descartes's final, definitive conclusions, but rather the astonishment and objections of the nonphilosopher, of the novice in philosophy who is frightened by this doubt and protests, saying: I am willing to let you doubt certain sensory perceptions concerning "things which are hardly perceptible, or very far away," but the others! that you are in this place, sitting by the fire, speaking thus, this paper in your hands and other seeming certainties! Descartes then assumes the astonishment of this reader or naïve interlocutor, pretends to take him into account when he writes: "And how could I deny that these hands and this body are mine, were it not perhaps that I compare myself to certain persons, devoid of sense, whose . . . and I should not be any the less insane were I to follow examples so extravagant."

The pedagogical and rhetorical sense of the *sed forte* which governs this paragraph is clear. It is the "but perhaps" of the feigned objection. Descartes has just said that all knowledge of sensory origin could deceive him. He pretends to put to himself the astonished objection of an imaginary nonphilosopher who is frightened by such audacity and says: no, not all sensory knowledge, for then you would be mad and it would be unreasonable to follow the example of madmen, to put forth the ideas of madmen. Descartes *echoes* this objection: since I am here, writing, and you understand me, I am not mad, nor are you, and we are all sane. The example of madness is therefore not indicative of the fragility of the sensory idea. So be it. Descartes acquiesces to this natural point of view, or rather he feigns to rest in this natural comfort in order better, more radically and more definitively, to unsettle himself from it and to discomfort his interlocutor. So be it, he says, you think that I would be mad to doubt that I am sitting near the

fire, etc., that I would be insane to follow the example of madmen. I will
therefore propose a hypothesis which will seem much more natural to you, will
not disorient you, because it concerns a more common, and more universal
experience than that of madness: the experience of sleep and dreams. Descartes
then elaborates the hypothesis that will ruin *all* the *sensory* foundations of knowledge and will lay bare only the *intellectual* foundations of certainty. This
hypothesis above all will not run from the possibility of an insanity—an epistemological one—much more serious than madness.

The reference to dreams is therefore not put off to one side—quite the
contrary—in relation to a madness potentially respected or even excluded by
Descartes. It constitutes, in the methodical order which here is ours, the hyperbolical exasperation of the hypothesis of madness. This latter affected only
certain areas of sensory perception, and in a contingent and partial way.
Moreover, Descartes is concerned here not with determining the concept of
madness but with utilizing the popular notion of insanity for juridical and
methodological ends, in order to ask questions of principle regarding only the
truth of ideas.[15] What must be grasped here is that *from this point of view* the
sleeper, or the dreamer, is madder than the madman. Or, at least, the dreamer,
insofar as concerns the problem of knowledge which interests Descartes here, is
further from true perception than the madman. It is in the case of sleep, and not in
that of insanity, that the *absolute totality* of ideas of sensory origin becomes
suspect, is stripped of "objective value" as M. Guéroult puts it. The hypothesis
of insanity is therefore not a good example, a revelatory example, a good instrument of doubt—and for at least two reasons. (a) It does not cover the *totality* of
the field of sensory perception. The madman is not always wrong about everything; he is not wrong often enough, is never mad enough. (b) It is not a useful or
happy example pedagogically, because it meets the resistance of the non-
philosopher who does not have the audacity to follow the philosopher when the
latter agrees that he might indeed be mad at the very moment when he speaks.

Let us turn to Foucault once more. Confronted with the situation of the Cartesian text whose principles I have just indicated, Foucault could—and this time I
am only extending the logic of his book without basing what I say on any
particular text—Foucault could recall *two truths* that on a second reading would
justify his interpretations, which would then only apparently differ from the
interpretation I have just proposed.

1. It appears, on this second reading, that, for Descartes, madness is thought
of only as a single case—and not the most serious one—among all cases of
sensory error. (Foucault would then assume the perspective of the factual determination of the concept of madness by Descartes, and not his juridical usage of
it.) Madness is only a sensory and corporeal fault, a bit more serious than the
fault which threatens all waking but normal men, and much less serious, within
the epistemological order, than the fault to which we succumb in dreams.

Foucault would then doubtless ask whether this reduction of madness to an example, to a case of sensory error, does not constitute an exclusion, an internment of madness, and whether it is not above all a sheltering of the Cogito and everything relative to the intellect and reason from madness. If madness is only a perversion of the senses—or of the imagination—it is corporeal, in alliance with the body. The real distinction of substances expels madness to the outer shadows of the Cogito. Madness, to use an expression proposed elsewhere by Foucault, is confined to the interior of the exterior and to the exterior of the interior. It is the other of the Cogito. I cannot be mad when I think and when I have clear and distinct ideas.

2. Or, while assuming our hypothesis, Foucault could also recall the following: Descartes, by inscribing his reference to madness within the problematic of knowledge, by making madness not only a thing of the body but an *error* of the body, by concerning himself with madness only as the modification of ideas, or the faculties of representation or judgment, intends to neutralize the originality of madness. He would even, in the long run, be condemned to construe it, like all errors, not only as an epistemological deficiency but also as a moral failure linked to a precipitation of the will; for will alone can consecrate the intellectual finitude of perception as error. It is only one step from here to making madness a sin, a step that was soon after cheerfully taken, as Foucault convincingly demonstrates in other chapters.

Foucault would be perfectly correct in recalling these two truths to us if we were to remain at the naïve, natural, and premetaphysical stage of Descartes's itinerary, the stage marked by natural doubt as it intervenes in the passage that Foucault cites. However, it seems that these two truths become vulnerable in turn, as soon as we come to the properly philosophical, metaphysical, and critical phase of doubt.[16]

Let us first notice how, in the rhetoric of the first *Meditation,* the first *toutefois* [at the same time] which announced the "natural" hyperbole of dreams (just after Descartes says, "But they are mad, and I should not be any the less insane," etc.) is succeeded by a second *toutefois* [nevertheless] at the beginning of the next paragraph.[17] To "at the same time," marking the *hyperbolical moment within natural doubt,* will correspond a "nevertheless," marking the *absolutely hyperbolical moment* which gets us out of natural doubt and leads to the hypothesis of the evil genius. Descartes has just admitted that arithmetic, geometry, and simple notions escape the first doubt, and he writes, "Nevertheless I have long had fixed in my mind the belief that an all-powerful God existed by whom I have been created such as I am."[18] This is the onset of the well-known movement leading to the fiction of the evil genius.

Now, the recourse to the fiction of the evil genius will evoke, conjure up, the possibility of a *total madness,* a total derangement over which I could have no control because it is inflicted upon me—hypothetically—leaving me no responsibility for it. Total derangement is the possibility of a madness that is no longer a disorder of the body, of the object, the body-object outside the boundaries of the *res cogitans,* outside the boundaries of the policed city, secure in its existence as thinking subjectivity, but is a madness that will bring subversion to pure thought and to its purely intelligibile objects, to the field of its clear and distinct ideas, to the realm of the mathematical truths which escape natural doubt.

This time madness, insanity, will spare nothing, neither bodily nor purely intellectual perceptions. And Descartes successively judges admissible:

(a) That which he pretended not to admit while conversing with the non-philosopher. To cite Descartes (he has just evoked "some evil genius not less powerful than deceitful"): "I shall consider that the heavens, the earth, colours, figures, sound, and all other external things are nought but the illusions and dreams of which this genius has availed himself in order to lay traps for my credulity; I shall consider myself as having no hands, no eyes, no flesh, no blood, nor any senses, yet falsely believing myself to possess all these things"[19] These ideas will be taken up again in the second *Meditiation.* We are thus quite far from the dismissal of insanity made above.

(b) That which escapes natural doubt: "But how do I know that Hell (i.e., the deceiving God, before the recourse to the evil genius) has not brought it to pass that . . . I am not deceived every time that I add two and three, or count the sides of a square . . . ?"[20]

Thus, ideas of neither sensory nor intellectual origin will be sheltered from this new phase of doubt, and everything that was previously set aside as insanity is now welcomed into the most essential interiority of thought.

In question is a philosophical and juridical operation (but the first phase of doubt was already such) which no longer names madness and reveals all princi-pled possibilities. *In principle* nothing is opposed to the subversion named insan-ity, although *in fact* and from a natural point of view, for Descartes, for his reader, and for us, no natural anxiety is possible regarding this actual subversion. (Truthfully speaking, to go to the heart of the matter, one would have to confront directly, in and of itself, the question of what is *de facto* and what *de jure* in the relations of the Cogito and madness.) Beneath this natural comfort, beneath this apparently prephilosophical confidence is hidden the recognition of an essential and principled truth: to wit, if discourse and philosophical communication (that is, language itself) are to have an intelligible meaning, that is to say, if they are to conform to their essence and vocation as discourse, they must simultaneously in fact and in principle escape madness. They must carry normality within them-selves. And this is not a specifically Cartesian weakness (although Descartes never confronts the question of his own language),[21] is not a defect or mystifica-tion linked to a determined historical structure, but rather is an essential and universal necessity from which no discourse can escape, for it belongs to the meaning of meaning. It is an essential necessity from which no discourse can escape, even the discourse which denounces a mystification or an act of force. And, paradoxically, what I am saying here is strictly Foucauldian. For we can now appreciate the profundity of the following affirmation of Foucault's that curiously also saves Descartes from the accusations made against him: "Madness is the absence of a work." This is a fundamental motif of Foucault's book. Now, the work starts with the most elementary discourse, with the first articulation of a meaning, with the first syntactical usage of an "as such,"[22] for to make a sentence is to *manifest* a possible meaning. By its essence, the sentence is normal. It carries normality within it, that is, *sense,* in every sense of the word—Descartes's in particular. It carries normality and sense within it, and does so whatever the state, whatever the health or madness of him who propounds it, or whom it passes through, on whom, in whom it is articulated. In its most impoverished syntax, logos is reason and, indeed, a historical reason. And if madness in general, beyond any factitious and determined historical structure, is the absence of a work, then madness is indeed, essentially and generally, silence, stifled speech, within a caesura and a wound that *open up* life as *historicity in general.* Not a determined silence, imposed at one given moment rather than at any other, but a silence essentially linked to an act of force and a prohibition which open history and speech. *In general.* Within the dimension of historicity in general, which is to be confused neither with some ahistorical eternity, nor with an empirically determined moment of the history of facts, silence plays the irreducible role of that which bears and haunts language, outside and *against* which alone language can emerge—"against" here simultaneously designating the content from which form takes off by force, and the adversary against whom I assure and reassure myself by force. Although the silence of madness is the absence of a work, this silence is not simply the work's epigraph, nor is it, as concerns language and meaning, outside the work. Like nonmeaning, silence is the work's limit and profound resource. Of course, in essentializing madness this way one runs the risk of disintegrating the factual findings of psychiatric efforts. This is a permanent danger, but it should not discourage the demanding and patient psychiatrist.

So that, to come back to Descartes, any philosopher or speaking subject (and the philosopher is but the speaking subject par excellence) who must evoke madness from the *interior* of thought (and not only from within the body or some other extrinsic agency), can do so only in the realm of the *possible* and in the language of fiction or the fiction of language. Thereby, through his own language, he reassures himself against any actual madness—which may sometimes appear quite talkative, another problem—and can keep his distance, the distance indispensable for continuing to speak and to live. But this is not a weakness or a search for security proper to a given historical language (for example, the search for certainty in the Cartesian style), but is rather inherent in the essence and very project of all language in general; and even in the language

of those who are apparently the maddest; and even and above all in the language
of those who, by their praise of madness, by their complicity with it, measure
their own strength against the greatest possible proximity to madness. Language
being the break with madness, it adheres more thoroughly to its essence and
vocation, makes a cleaner break with madness, if it pits itself against madness
more freely and gets closer and closer to it: to the point of being separated from it
only by the "transparent sheet" of which Joyce speaks, that is, by itself—for this
diaphaneity is nothing other than the language, meaning, possibility, and elementary discretion of a nothing that neutralizes everything. In this sense, I would be
tempted to consider Foucault's book a powerful gesture of protection and internment. A Cartesian gesture for the twentieth century. A reappropriation of
negativity. To all appearances, it is reason that he interns, but, like Descartes, he
chooses the reason of yesterday as his target and not the possibility of meaning in
general.

2. As for the second truth Foucault could have countered with, it too seems
valid only during the natural phase of doubt. Descartes not only ceases to reject
madness during the phase of radical doubt, he not only installs its possible
menace at the very heart of the intelligible, he also in principle refuses to let any
determined knowledge escape from madness. A menace to all knowledge,
insanity—the hypothesis of insanity—is not an internal modification of knowledge. At no point will knowledge alone be able to dominate madness, to
master it in order to objectify it—at least for as long as doubt remains unresolved.
For the end of doubt poses a problem to which we shall return in a moment.

The act of the Cogito and the certainty of existing indeed escape madness the
first time; but aside from the fact that for the first time, it is no longer a
question of objective, representative knowledge, it can no longer literally be
said that the Cogito would escape madness because it keeps itself beyond the
grasp of madness, or because, as Foucault says, "*I* who think, I cannot be
mad"; the Cogito escapes madness only because at its own moment, under
its own authority, it is valid *even if I am mad,* even if my thoughts are completely mad. There is a value and a meaning of the Cogito, as of existence,
which escape the alternative of a determined madness or a determined reason.
Confronted with the critical experience of the Cogito, insanity, as stated in
the *Discourse on Method,* is irremediably on a plane with scepticism. Thought
no longer fears madness: "... remarking that this truth '*I think, therefore I
am*' was so certain and so assured that all the most extravagant suppositions
brought forward by the sceptics were incapable of shaking it."[23] The certainty
thus attained need not be sheltered from an emprisoned madness, for it is
attained and ascertained within madness itself. It is valid *even if I am mad*—a
supreme self-confidence that seems to require neither the exclusion nor the cir-
cumventing of madness. Descartes never interns madness, neither at the stage of
natural doubt nor at the stage of metaphysical doubt. *He only claims to exclude it*

during the first phase of the first stage, during the nonhyperbolical moment of natural doubt.

The hyperbolical audacity of the Cartesian Cogito, its mad audacity, which we perhaps no longer perceive as such because, unlike Descartes's contemporary, we are too well assured of ourselves and too well accustomed to the framework of the Cogito, rather than to the critical experience of it—its mad audacity would consist in the return to an original point which no longer belongs to either a *determined* reason or a *determined* unreason, no longer belongs to them as opposition or alternative. Whether I am mad or not, *Cogito, sum.* Madness is therefore, in every sense of the word, only one *case* of thought (*within* thought). It is therefore a question of drawing back toward a point at which all determined contradictions, in the form of given, factual historical structures, can appear, and appear as relative to this zero point at which determined meaning and nonmeaning come together in their common origin. From the point of view which here is ours, one could perhaps say the following about this zero point, determined by Descartes as Cogito.

Invulnerable to all determined opposition between reason and unreason, it is the point starting from which the history of the determined forms of this opposition, this opened or broken-off dialogue, can appear as such and be stated. It is the impenetrable point of certainty in which the possibility of Foucault's narration, as well as of the narration of the totality, or rather of *all* the determined forms of the exchanges between reason and madness are embedded. It is the point[24] at which the project of thinking this totality by escaping it is embedded. By escaping it: that is to say, by exceeding the totality, which—within existence—is possible only in the direction of infinity or nothingness; for even if the totality of what I think is imbued with falsehood or madness, even if the totality of the world does not exist, even if nonmeaning has invaded the totality of the world, up to and including the very contents of my thought, I still think, I am *while* I think. Even if I do not *in fact* grasp the totality, if I neither understand nor embrace it, I still formulate the project of doing so, and this project is meaningful in such a way that it can be defined only in relation to a precomprehension of the infinite and undetermined totality. This is why, by virtue of this margin of the possible, the principled, and the meaningful, which exceeds all that is real, factual, and existent, this project is mad, and acknowledges madness as its liberty and its very possibility. This is why it is not human, in the sense of anthropological factuality, but is rather metaphysical and demonic: it first awakens to itself in its war with the demon, the evil genius of nonmeaning, by pitting itself against the strength of the evil genius, and by resisting him through reduction of the natural man within itself. In this sense, nothing is less reassuring than the Cogito at its proper and inaugural moment. The project of exceeding the totality of the world, as the totality of what I can think in general, is no more reassuring than the dialectic of Socrates when it, too, overflows the totality of beings, planting us in the light of a hidden sun which is *epekeina tes ousias.* And Glaucon was not mistaken when he cried out: "Lord! what demonic hyperbole? *daimonias hyperboles,"* which is perhaps banally translated as "marvelous transcendence."[25] This demonic hyperbole goes further than the passion of hybris, at least if this latter is seen only as the pathological modification of the being called man. Such a hybris keeps itself within the world. Assuming that it is deranged and excessive, it implies the fundamental derangement and excessiveness of the hyperbole which opens and founds the world as such by exceeding it. Hybris is excessive and exceeds only *within* the space opened by the demonic hyperbole.

The extent to which doubt and the Cartesian Cogito are *punctuated* by this project of a singular and unprecedented excess—an excess in the direction of the nondetermined, Nothingness or Infinity, an excess which overflows the totality of that which can be thought, the totality of beings and determined meanings, the totality of factual history—is also the extent to which any effort to reduce this project, to enclose it within a determined historical structure, however comprehensive, risks missing the essential, risks dulling the *point* itself. Such an effort risks doing violence to this project in turn (for there is also a violence applicable to rationalists and to sense, to *good* sense; and this, perhaps, is what Foucault's book definitely demonstrates, for the victims of whom he speaks are always the bearers of sense, the *true* bearers of the *true* and *good* sense hidden and oppressed by the *determined* "good sense" of the "division"—the "good sense" that never divides itself enough and is always determined too quickly)— risks doing it violence in turn, and a violence of a totalitarian and historicist style which eludes meaning and the origin of meaning.[26] I use "totalitarian" in the structuralist sense of the word, but I am not sure that the two meanings do not beckon each other historically. Structuralist totalitariansim here would be responsible for an internment of the Cogito similar to the violences of the classical age. I am not saying that Foucault's book is totalitarian, for at least at its outset it poses the question of the origin of historicity *in general,* thereby freeing itself of historicism; I am saying, however, that by virtue of the construction of his project he sometimes runs the risk of being totalitarian. Let me clarify: when I refer to the forced entry into the world of that which is not there and is supposed by the world, or when I state that the *compelle intrare* (epigraph of the chapter on "the great internment") becomes *violence itself* when it turns toward the hyperbole in order to make hyperbole reenter the world, or when I say that this reduction to intraworldliness is the origin and very meaning of what is called violence, making possible all straitjackets, I am not invoking an *other world,* an alibi or an evasive transcendence. That would be yet another possibility of violence, a possibility that is, moreover, often the accomplice of the first one.

I think, therefore, that (in Descartes) everything can be reduced to a determined historical totality except the hyperbolical project. Now, this project belongs to the narration narrating itself and not to the narration narrated by Foucault. It cannot be recounted, cannot be objectified as an event in a determined history.

I am sure that within the movement which is called the *Cartesian Cogito* this hyperbolical extremity is not the only element that should be, like pure madness in general, silent. As soon as Descartes has reached this extremity, he seeks to reassure himself, to certify the Cogito through God, to identify the act of the Cogito with a reasonable reason. And he does so as soon as he *proffers* and *reflects* the Cogito. That is to say, he must temporalize the Cogito, which itself is valid only during the instant of intuition, the instant of thought being attentive to itself, at the point, the sharpest point, of the instant. And here one should be attentive to this link between the Cogito and the movement of temporalization. For if the Cogito is valid even for the maddest madman, one must, in fact, not be mad if one is to reflect it and retain it, if one is to communicate it and its meaning. And here, with the reference to God *and* to a certain memory,[27] would begin the hurried repatriation of all mad and hyperbolical wanderings which now take shelter and are given reassurance within the order of reasons, in order once more to take possession of the truths they had left behind. Within Descartes's text, at least, the internment takes place at this point. It is here that hyperbolical and mad wanderings once more become itinerary and method, "assured" and "resolute" progression through our existing world, which is given to us by God as terra firma. For, finally, it is God alone who, by permitting me to extirpate myself from a Cogito that at its proper moment can always remain a silent madness, also insures my representations and my cognitive determinations, that is, my discourse against madness. It is without doubt that, for Descartes, God alone[28] protects me against the madness to which the Cogito, left to its own authority, could only open itself up in the most hospitable way. And Foucault's reading seems to me powerful and illuminating not at the stage of the text which he cites, which is anterior and secondary to the Cogito, but from the moment which immediately succeeds the instantaneous experience of the Cogito at its most intense, when reason and madness have not yet been separated, when to take the part of the Cogito is neither to take the part of reason as reasonable order, nor the part of disorder and madness, but is rather to grasp, once more, the source which permits reason *and* madness to be determined and stated. Foucault's interpretation seems to me illuminating from the moment when the Cogito must reflect and proffer itself in an organized philosophical discourse. That is, *almost always*. For if the Cogito is valid even for the madman, to be mad—if, once more, this expression has a singular philosophical meaning, which I do not believe: it simply says the other of each determined form of the logos—is not to be able to reflect and to say the Cogito, that is, not to be able to make the Cogito appear as such for an other; an other who may be myself. From the moment when Descartes pronounces the Cogito, he inscribes it in a system of deductions and protections that betray its wellspring and constrain the wandering that is proper to it so that error may be circumvented. At bottom, leaving in silence the problem of speech posed by the Cogito, Descartes seems to imply that thinking *and* saying what is clear and distinct are the same thing. One can say *what* one thinks and *that* one thinks without betraying one or the other. Analogously—analogously only—Saint Anselm saw in the *insipiens,* the insane man, someone who could not think because he could not think what he said. Madness was for him, too, a silence, the voluble silence of a thought that did not think its own words. This also is a point which must be developed further. In any event, the Cogito is a work as soon as it is assured of what it says. But before it is a work, it is madness. If the madman could rebuff the evil genius, he could not tell himself so. He therefore cannot say so. And in any event, Foucault is right in the extent to which the project of constraining any wandering already animated a doubt which was always proposed as methodical. This identification of the Cogito with reasonable—normal—reason need not even await—in fact, if not in principle— the proofs of the existence of a veracious God as the supreme protective barrier against madness. This identification intervenes from the moment when Descartes *determines natural light* (which in its undetermined source should be valid even for the mad), from the moment when he pulls himself out of madness by determining natural light through a series of principles and axioms (axiom of causality according to which there must be at least as much reality in the cause as in the effect; then, after this axiom permits the proof of the existence of God, the axioms that "the light of nature teaches us that fraud and deception necessarily proceed from some defect").[29] These dogmatically determined axioms escape doubt, are never even submitted to its scrutiny, are established only reciprocally, on the basis of the existence and truthfulness of God. Due to this fact, they fall within the province of the history of knowledge and the determined structures of philosophy. This is why the act of the Cogito, at the hyperbolical moment when it pits itself against madness, or rather lets itself be pitted against madness, must be repeated and distinguished from the language or the deductive system in which Descartes must inscribe it as soon as he proposes it for apprehension and communication, that is, as soon as he reflects the Cogito for the other, which means for oneself. It is through this relationship to the other as an other self that meaning reassures itself against madness and nonmeaning. And philosophy is perhaps the reassurance given against the anguish of being mad at the point of greatest proximity to madness. This silent and specific moment could be called *pathetic.* As for the functioning of the hyperbole in the structure of Descartes's discourse and in the order of reasons, our reading is therefore, despite all appearances to the contrary, profoundly aligned with Foucault's. It is indeed Descartes—and everything for which this name serves as an index—it is indeed the system of certainty that first of all functions in order to inspect, master, and limit hyperbole, and does so both by deter-

mining it in the ether of a natural light whose axioms are from the outset
exempt from hyperbolical doubt, and by making of hyperbolical doubt a
point of transition firmly maintained within the chain of reasons. But it
is our belief that this movement can be described within its own time and
place only if one has previously disengaged the extremity of hyperbole,
which Foucault seemingly has not done. In the fugitive and, by its essence,
ungraspable moment when it still escapes the linear order of reasons, the
order of reason in general and the determinations of natural light, does
not the Cartesian Cogito lend itself to repetition, up to a certain point,
by the Husserlian Cogito and by the critique of Descartes implied in it?

This would be an example only, for some day the dogmatic and historically
determined grounds—ours—will be discovered, which the critique of Cartesian
deductivism, the impetus and madness of the Husserlian reduction of the totality
of the world, first had to rest on, and then had to fall onto in order to be stated.
One could do for Husserl what Foucault has done for Descartes: demonstrate how
the neturalization of the factual world is a neutralization (in the sense in which to
neutralize is also to master, to reduce, to leave free in a straitjacket) of nonmeaning, the most subtle form of an act of force. And in truth, Husserl increasingly
associated the theme of normality with the theme of the transcendental reduction.
The embedding of transcendental phenomenology in the metaphysics of
presence, the entire Husserlian thematic of the living present is the profound
reassurance of the certainty of *meaning.*

By separating, within the Cogito, *on the one hand,* hyperbole (which I maintain cannot be enclosed in a factual and determined historical structure, for it is
the project of exceeding every finite and determined totality), and, *on the other
hand,* that in Descartes's philosophy (or in the philosophy supporting the
Augustinian Cogito or the Husserlian Cogito as well) which belongs to a factual
historical structure, I am not proposing the separation of the wheat from the tares
in every philosophy in the name of some *philosophia perennis.* Indeed, it is
exactly the contrary that I am proposing. In question is a way of accounting for
the very historicity of philosophy. I believe that historicity in general would be
impossible without a history of philosophy, and I believe that the latter would be
impossible if we possessed only hyperbole, on the one hand, or, on the other,
only determined historical structures, finite *Weltanschauungen.* The historicity
proper to philosophy is located and constituted in the transition, the dialogue
between hyperbole and the finite structure, between that which exceeds the
totality and the closed totality, in the difference between history and historicity;
that is, in the place where, or rather at the moment when, the Cogito and all that
it symbolizes here (madness, derangement, hyperbole, etc.) pronounce and reassure themselves then to fall, necessarily forgetting themselves until their reactivation, their reawakening in another statement of the excess which also later will
become another decline and another crisis. From its very first breath, speech,

confined to this temporal rhythm of crisis and reawakening, is able to open the
space for discourse only by emprisoning madness. This rhythm, moreover, is not
an alternation that additionally would be temporal. It is rather the movement of
temporalization itself as concerns that which unites it to the movement of logos.
But this violent liberation of speech is possible and can be pursued only in the
extent to which it keeps itself resolutely and consciously at the greatest possible
proximity to the abuse that is the usage of speech—just close enough to *say*
violence, to dialogue with itself as irreducible violence, and just far enough to
live and live as speech. Due to this, crisis or oblivion perhaps is not an accident,
but rather the destiny of speaking philosophy—the philosophy which lives only
by emprisoning madness, but which would die as thought, and by a still worse
violence, if a new speech did not at every instant liberate previous madness while
enclosing within itself, in its present existence, the madman of the day. It is only
by virtue of this oppression of madness that finite-thought, that is to say, history,
can reign. Extending this truth to historicity in general, without keeping to a
determined historical moment, one could say that the reign of finite thought can
be established only on the basis of the more or less disguised internment, humili-
ation, fettering and mockery of the madman within us, of the madman who can
only be the fool of a logos which is father, master, and king. But that is another
discourse and another story. I will conclude by citing Foucault once more. Long
after the passage on Descartes, some three hundred pages later, introducing
Rameau's Nephew Foucault writes, with a sigh of remorse: "In doubt's confrontation with its major dangers, Descartes realized that he could not be mad—though
he was to acknowledge for a long time to come that all the powers of unreason
kept vigil around his thought."[30] What we have attempted to do here this
evening is to situate ourselves within the interval of this remorse, Foucault's
remorse, Descartes's remorse according to Foucault; and within the space of
stating that, "though he was to acknowledge for a long time to come," we have
attempted not to extinguish the *other* light, a black and hardly natural light, the
vigil of the "powers of unreason" around the Cogito. We have attempted to
requite ourselves toward the gesture which Descartes uses to requite himself as
concerns the menacing powers of madness which are the adverse origin of
philosophy.

Among all Foucault's claims to my gratitude, there is thus also that of having
made me better anticipate, more so by his monumental book than by the naïve
reading of the *Meditations,* to what degree the philosophical act can no longer no
longer be in memeory of Cartesianism, if to be Cartesian, as Descartes himself
doubtless understood it, is to attempt to be Cartesian. That is to say, as I have at
least tried to demonstrate, to-attempt-to-say-the-demonic-hyperbole from whose
heights thought is announced to itself, *frightens* itself, and *reassures* itself
against being annihilated or wrecked in madness or in death. *At its height* hyperbole, the absolute opening, the uneconomic expenditure, is always reembraced

by an *economy* and is overcome by economy. The relationship between reason, madness, and death is an economy, a structure of deferral whose irreducible originality must be respected. This attempt-to-say-the-demonic-hyperbole is not an attempt among others; it is not an attempt which would occasionally and eventually be completed by the saying of it, or by its object, the direct object of a willful subjectivity. This attempt to say, which is not, moreover, the antagonist of silence, but rather the condition for it, is the original profoundity of will in general. Nothing, further, would be more incapable of regrasping this will than voluntarism, for, as finitude and as history, this attempt is also a first passion. It keeps within itself the trace of a violence. It is more written than said, it is *economized*. The economy of this writing is a regulated relationship between that which exceeds and the exceeded totality: the *différance* of the absolute excess.

To define philosophy as the attempt-to-say-the-hyperbole is to confess—and philosophy is perhaps this gigantic confession—that by virtue of the historical enunciation through which philosophy tranquilizes itself and excludes madness, philosophy also betrays itself (or betrays itself as thought), enters into a crisis and a forgetting of itself that are an essential and necessary period of its movement. I philosophize only in *terror,* but in the *confessed* terror of going mad. The confession is simultaneously, at its *present* moment, oblivion and unveiling, protection and exposure: economy.

But this crisis in which reason is madder than madness—for reason is non-meaning and oblivion—and in which madness is more rational than reason, for it is closer to the wellspring of sense, however silent or murmuring—this crisis has always begun and is interminable. It suffices to say that, if it is classic, it is not so in the sense of the *classical age* but in the sense of eternal and essential classicism, and is also historical in an unexpected sense.

And nowhere else and never before has the concept of *crisis* been able to enrich and reassemble all its potentialities, all the energy of its meaning, as much, perhaps, as in Michel Foucault's book. Here, the crisis is on the one hand, in Husserl's sense, the danger menacing reason and meaning under the rubric of objectivism, of the forgetting of origins, of the blanketing of origins by the rationalist and transcendental unveiling itself. Danger as the movement of reason menaced by its own security, etc.

But the crisis is also decision, the caesura of which Foucault speaks, in the sense of *krinein,* the choice and division between the two ways separated by Parmenides in his poem, the way of logos and the non-way, the labyrinth, the *palintrope* in which logos is lost; the way of meaning and the way of nonmeaning; of Being and of non-Being. A division on whose basis, after which, logos, in the necessary violence of its irruption, is separated from itself as madness, is exiled from itself, forgetting its origin and its own possibility. Is not what is called finitude possibility as crisis? A certain identity between the consciousness of crisis and the forgetting of it? Of the thinking of negativity and the reduction of negativity?

Crisis of reason, finally, access to reason and attack of reason. For what Michel Foucault teaches us to think is that there are crises of reason in strange complicity with what the world calls crises of madness.

Three

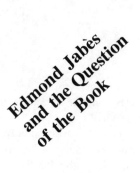

Edmond Jabès
and the Question
of the Book

Our rereadings of *Je bâtis ma demeure*[1] will be better, henceforth. A certain ivy could have hidden or absorbed its meaning, could have turned its meaning in on itself. Humor and games, laughter and dances, songs, circled graciously around a discourse which, as it did not yet love its true root, bent a bit in the wind. Did not yet stand upright in order to enunciate only the rigor and rigidity of poetic obligation.

In *Le livre des questions*[2] the voice has not been altered, nor the intention abandoned, but the accent is more serious. A powerful and ancient root is exhumed, and on it is laid bare an ageless wound (for what Jabès teaches us is that roots speak, that words want to grow, and that poetic discourse *takes root* in a wound): in question is a certain Judaism as the birth and passion of writing. The passion *of* writing, the love and endurance of the letter itself whose subject is not decidably the Jew or the Letter itself. Perhaps the common root of a people and of writing. In any event, the incommensurable destiny which grafts the history of a

> race born of the book (*Livre des questions*, p. 26)

onto the radical origin of meaning as literality, that is, onto historicity itself. For there could be no history without the gravity and labor of literality. The painful folding of itself which permits history to reflect itself as it ciphers itself. This reflection is its beginning.

The only thing that begins by reflecting itself is history. And this fold, this furrow, is the Jew. The Jew who elects writing which elects the Jew, in an exchange responsible for truth's thorough suffusion with historicity and for history's *assignment* of itself to its empiricity.

> *difficulty of being a Jew, which coincides with the difficulty of writing; for Judaism and writing are but the same waiting, the same hope, the same depletion.* (Ibid., p. 132)

The exchange between the Jew and writing as a pure and founding exchange, an exchange without prerogatives in which the original appeal is, in another sense of the word, a *convocation*—this is the most persistent affirmation of the *Livre des questions*:

> *You are he who writes and is written.*
> . . .
> *And Reb Ilde: "What difference is there between choosing and being chosen when we can do nothing but submit to the choice?"* (Ibid., p. 30)

And through a kind of silent displacement toward the essential which makes of this book one long metonymy, the situation of the Jew becomes exemplary of the situation of the poet, the man of speech and of writing. The poet, in the very experience of his freedom, finds himself both bound to language and delivered from it by a speech whose master, nonetheless, he himself is.

> *Words choose the poet . . . .*
> *The art of the writer consists in little by little making words interest themselves in his books. (Je bâtis ma demeure)*

In question is a labor, a deliverance, a slow gestation of the poet by the poem whose father he is.

> *Little by little the book will finish me. (L'espace blanc)*

The poet is thus indeed the *subject* of the book, its substance and its master, its servant and its theme. And the book is indeed the subject of the poet, the speaking and knowing being who *in* the book writes *on* the book. This movement through which the book, *articulated* by the voice of the poet, is folded and bound to itself, the movement through which the book becomes a subject in itself and for itself, is not critical or speculative reflection, but is, first of all, poetry and history. For in its representation of itself the subject is shattered and opened. Writing is itself written, but also ruined, made into an abyss, in its own representation. Thus, within this book, which infinitely reflects itself and which develops as a painful questioning of its own possibility, the form of the book represents itself:

*The novel of Sarah and Yukel, through various dialogues and meditations
attributed to imaginary rabbis, is the story of a love destroyed by men and
by words. It has the dimensions of a book and the bitter obstinacy of a
wandering question. (Livre des questions, p. 26)*

We will see that by another direction of metonymy—but to what extent is it
other?—the *Livre des questions* describes the generation of God himself. The
wisdom of the poet thus culminates its freedom in the passion of translating
obedience to the law of the word into autonomy. Without which, and if passion
becomes subjection, the poet is mad.

The madman is the victim of the rebellion of words. (Je bâtis ma demeure)

Also, through his understanding of this assignment of the root, and through the
inspiration he receives from this injunction of the Law, Jabès perhaps has renounced the *verve,* that is, the *capriciousness* of the early works; but he has in no
way given up his freedom of speech. He has even acknowledged that freedom
must belong to the earth, to the root, or it is merely wind:

*A teaching that Reb Zalé translated with this image: "You think that it is
the bird who is free. You are deceived; it is the flower . . ."
    And Reb Lima: "Freedom is awakened little by little, in the extent to
which we become aware of our ties, like the sleeper of his senses; then
our acts finally have a name." (Ibid., p. 124)*

Freedom allies and exchanges itself with that which restrains it, with everything
it receives from a buried origin, with the gravity which situates its center and its
site. A site whose cult is not necessarily pagan. Provided that this Site is not a
site, an enclosure, a place of exclusion, a province or a ghetto. When a Jew or a
poet proclaims the Site, he is not declaring war. For this site, this land, calling to
us from beyond memory, is always elsewhere. The site is not the empirical and
national Here of a territory. It is immemorial, and thus also a future. Better: it is
tradition as adventure. Freedom is granted to the nonpagan Land only if it is
separated from freedom by the Desert of the Promise. That is, by the Poem.
When it lets itself be articulated by poetic discourse, the Land always keeps itself
beyond any proximity, *illic:*

Yukel, you have always been ill at ease with yourself, you are never HERE, *but*
ELSEWHERE *. . . (Ibid., p. 33)*

*What are you dreaming of?—The Land.—But you are on land.—I am
dreaming of the Land where I will be.—But we are right in front of each
other. And we have our feet on land.—I know only the stones of the way
which leads, as it is said, to the Land.*

The Poet and the Jew are not born *here* but *elsewhere.* They wander, separated
from their true birth. Autochthons only of speech and writing, of Law. *"Race
born of the book"* because sons of the Land to come.

Autochthons of the Book. Autonomous too, as we said. Which assumes that
the poet does not simply receive his speech and his law from God. Judaic
heteronomy has no need of a poet's intercession. Poetry is to prophecy what the
idol is to truth. It it perhaps for this reason that in Jabès the poet and the Jew seem
at once so united and disunited, and that the entire *Livre des questions* is also a
self-justification addressed to the Jewish community which lives under heteronomy and to which the poet does not truly belong. Poetic autonomy, comparable
to none other, presupposes broken Tables.

> *And Reb Lima: Freedom, at first, was engraved ten times in the Tables of
> the Law, but we deserve it so little that the Prophet broke them in his
> anger.''* (Ibid., p. 124)

Between the fragments of the broken Tables the poem grows and the right to
speech takes root. Once more begins the adventure of the text as weed, as outlaw
far from *''the fatherland of the Jews,''* which is a *''sacred text surrounded by
commentaries''* (p. 109). The necessity of commentary, like poetic necessity, is
the very form of exiled speech. In the beginning is hermeneutics. But the *shared*
necessity of exegesis, the interpretive imperative, is interpreted differently by the
rabbi and the poet. The difference between the horizon of the original text and
exegetic writing makes the difference between the rabbi and the poet irreducible.
Forever unable to reunite with each other, yet so close to each other, how could
they ever regain the *realm*? The original opening of interpretation essentially
signifies that there will always be rabbis and poets. And two interpretations of
interpretation.[3] The Law then becomes Question and the right to speech coincides with the duty to interrogate. The book of man is a book of question.

> *''To every question, the Jew answers with a question.''* Reb Lema
> (Ibid., p. 125)

But if this right is absolute, it is because it does not depend upon some accident
within history. The breaking of the Tables articulates, first of all, a rupture within
God as the origin of history.[4]

> *Do not forget that you are the nucleus of a rupture.* (Ibid., p. 137)

God separated himself from himself in order to let us speak, in order to aston-
ish and to interrogate us. He did so not by speaking but by keeping still, by letting silence interrupt his voice and his signs, by letting the Tables be broken. In
Exodus God repented and said so at least twice, before the first and before the
new Tables, between original speech and writing and, within Scripture, between
the origin and repetition (*Exodus* 32:14; 33:17). Writing is, thus, originally
hermetic and secondary. Our writing, certainly, but already His, which starts
with the stifling of his voice and the dissimulation of his Face. This difference,
this negativity in God is our freedom, the transcendence and the verb which can
relocate the purity of their negative origin only in the possibility of the Question.

The question of "the irony of God," of which Schelling spoke, is first, as always, turned in on itself.

> God is in perpetual revolt against God. (*Livre des questions,* p. 177)
>
> God is an interrogation of God. (Ibid., p. 152)

Kafka said: "We are nihilist thoughts in the brain of God." If God opens the question in God, if he is the very opening of the Question, there can be no *simplicity* of God. And, thus, that which was unthinkable for the classical rationalists here becomes the obvious itself. Proceeding within the duplicity of his own questionability, God does not act in the simplest ways; he is not truthful, he is not sincere. Sincerity, which is simplicity, is a lying virtue. It is necessary, on the contrary, to accede to the virtue of the lie.

"*Reb Jacob, who was my first master, believed in the virtue of the lie because, he said, there is no writing without a lie and writing is the way of God*" (p. 92). The clumsy, equivocal way of the detour, *borrowed* by God from God. Irony of God, ruse of God, the oblique way, born of God, the path toward God of which man is not a simple detour. The infinite detour. Way *of* God. "*Yukel, speak to us of the man who is a lie in God*" (p. 94).

This way, preceded by no truth, and thus lacking the prescription of truth's rigor, is the way through the Desert. Writing is the moment of the desert as the moment of Separation. As their name indicates—in Aramaic—the Pharisees, those misunderstood men of literality, were also "separated ones." God no longer speaks to us; he has interrupted himself: we must take words upon ourselves. We must be separated from life and communities, and must entrust ourselves to traces, must become men of vision because we have ceased hearing the voice from within the immediate proximity of the garden. "*Sarah, Sarah with what does the world begin?—With speech?—With vision?*" (p. 173). Writing is displaced on the broken line between lost and promised speech. The *difference* between speech and writing is sin, the anger of God emerging from itself, lost immediacy, work outside the garden. "*The garden is speech, the desert writing. In each grain of sand a sign surprises*" (p. 169). The Judaic experience as reflection, as separation of life and thought, signifies the crossing of the book as an *infinite* anchoritism placed between two immediacies and two self-identifications. "*Yukel, how many pages to live, how many to die, separate you from yourself, separate you from the book to the abandoning of the book?*" (p. 44). The desert-book is made of sand, "*of mad sand,*" of infinite, innumerable and vain sand. "*Pick up a little sand, wrote Reb Ivri . . . then you will know the vanity of the verb*" (p. 122).

The Jewish consciousness is indeed the unhappy consciousness, and *Le livre des questions* is its poem; is the poem inscribed just beyond the phenomenology of the mind, which the Jew can accompany only for a short while, without

eschatological provision, in order not to limit his desert, close his book and
cauterize his cry.[5] *"Mark the first page of a book with a red ribbon, for the
wound is inscribed at its beginning. Reb Alcé"* (p. 122).

If absence is the heart of the question, if separation can emerge only in the
rupture of God—with God—if the infinite distance of the Other is *respected* only
within the sands of a book in which wandering and mirages are always possible,
then *Le livre des questions* is simultaneously the interminable song of absence
and a book on the book. Absence attempts to produce itself in the book and is lost
in being pronounced; it knows itself as disappearing and lost, and to this extent it
remains inaccessible and impenetrable. To gain access to it is to lose it; to show it
is to hide it; to acknowledge it is to lie. *"Nothing is our principle concern, said
Reb Idar"* (p. 188), and Nothing—like Being—can only keep silent and hide
itself.[6]

Absence. *Absence of locality*, first of all. *"Sarah: Speech annihilates distance,
makes the locale despair. Do we formulate speech or does it fashion us?"* The
absence of a place is the title of one of the poems collected in *Je bâtis ma
demeure*. It began thus: *"Vague estate, obsessed page . . ."* And *Le livre des
questions* resolutely keeps itself on the vague estate, in the non-place, between
city and desert, for in either the root is equally rejected or sterilized. Nothing
flourishes in sand or between cobblestones, if not words. City and desert, which
are neither countries, nor countrysides, nor gardens, besiege the poetry of Jabès
and ensure that it will have a necessarily infinite echo. City and desert simultaneously, that is, Cairo, whence Jabès comes to us; he too, as is well known, had his
flight from Egypt. The dwelling built by the poet with his *"swords stolen from
angels"* is a fragile tent of words erected in the desert where the nomadic Jew is
struck with infinity and the letter. Broken by the broken Law. Divided within
himself—(the Greek tongue would doubtless tell us much about the strange
relation between law, wandering, and nonidentification with the self, the common root—*nemein*—of division, naming and nomadism). The poet of writing
can only devote himself to the "unhappiness" that Nietzsche invokes upon, or
promises to invoke upon, him who "hides deserts within him." The poet—or the
Jew—protects the desert which protects both his speech (which can speak only in
the desert), and his writing (which can be traced only in the desert). That is to
say, by inventing, alone, an unfindable and unspecifiable pathway to which no
Cartesian *resolution* can impart rectilinearity and issuance. *"Where is the way?
The way is always to be found. A white sheet of paper is full of ways . . . . We
will go over the same way ten times, a hundred times"* (*Livre des questions*, p.
55). Unwittingly, writing simultaneously designs and discovers an invisible
labyrinth in the desert, a city in the sand. *"We will go over the same way ten
times, a hundred times . . . And all these pathways have their own pathways.—
Other wise they would not be pathways"* (p. 55). The entire first part of the *Livre
de l'absent* can be read as a meditation on the way and the letter. *"At noon, he*

*found himself once more facing infinity, the white page. Every trace of footsteps
had disappeared. Buried"* (p. 56). And again the transition from the desert to the
city, the Limit which is the only habitat of writing: *"When he returned to his
neighborhood and his house—a nomad had taken him on camel's back to the
nearest outpost where he had taken a seat in a military truck headed toward the
city—so many words solicited him. He persisted, however in avoiding them"*
(p. 59).

Absence of the writer too. For to write is to draw back. Not to retire into
one's tent, in order to write, but to draw back from one's writing itself. To be
grounded far from one's language, to emancipate it or lose one's hold on it, to let
it make its way alone and unarmed. To leave speech. To be a poet is to know how
to leave speech. To let it speak alone, which it can do only in its written form.[7]
To leave writing is to be there only in order to provide its passageway, to be the
diaphanous element of its going forth: everything and nothing. For the work, the
writer is at once everything and nothing. Like God:

> *If, wrote Reb Servi, you occasionally think that God does not see you, it is
> because he has made himself so humble that you confuse him with the fly
> buzzing in the pane of your window. But that is the proof of his almighti-
> ness; for he is, simultaneously, Everything and Nothing.* (Ibid., p. 117)

Like God, the writer:

> *As a child, when I wrote my name for the first time I
> felt that I was starting a book. Reb Stein.* (Ibid., p. 23)

> *. . . But I am not this man
> for this man writes
> and the writer is no one.* (Ibid., p. 28)

> *I, Serafi, the absent one, I was born to write books.
> (I am absent because I am the storyteller. Only the
> story is real.)* (Ibid., p. 60)

And yet (this is only one of the contradictory postulations which ceaselessly tear
apart the pages of the *Livre des questions,* and necessarily tear them apart: God
contradicts himself already), only that which is written gives me existence by
naming me. It is thus simultaneously true that things come into existence and lose
existence by being named. Sacrifice of existence to the word, as Hegel said, but
also the consecration of existence by the word. Moreover, it does not suffice to
be written, for one must write in order to have a name. One must be called
something. Which supposes that *"My name is a question . . . Reb Eglal"* (p.
125). *"Without my texts, I am more anonymous than a bedsheet in the wind,
more transparent than a windowpane"* (p. 123).

This necessary *exchange* of one's existence with or for the letter—which is
either to lose or to gain existence—is also imposed upon God:

*I did not seek you Sarah. I sought you. Through you, I ascend to the origin
of the sign, to the unformulated writing sketched by the wind on the sand
and on the sea, the untamed writing of the bird and the mischievous fish.
God, Master of wind, Master of sand, Master of birds and fishes, expected
from man the book that man expected from man; the one in order finally to
be God, the other finally to be man.* (Ibid., p. 189)

All letters form absence.
Thus God is the child of his name.
        Reb Tal. (Ibid., p. 47)

Maister Eckhart said: "God becomes God when creation says God." This assistance given to God by man's writing does not contradict writing's inability to
"help itself" (*Phaedrus*). Is not the divine—the disappearance of man—
announced in this distress of writing?

If absence does not allow itself to be reduced by the letter, this is so because it
is the letter's ether and respiration. The letter is the separation and limit in which
meaning is liberated from its emprisonment in aphoristic solitude. No "logic,"
no proliferation of conjunctive undergrowth can reach the end of its essential
discontinuity and noncontemporaneousness, the ingenuity of its *under-stood*
[*sous-entendu*] silences. The other originally collaborates with meaning. There is
an essential *lapse* between significations which is not the simple and positive
fraudulence of a word, nor even the nocturnal memory of all language. To allege
that one reduces this lapse through narration, philosophical discourse, or the
order of reasons or deduction, is to misconstrue language, to misconstrue that
language is the *rupture* with totality itself. The fragment is neither a determined
style nor a failure, but the form of that which is written. Unless God himself
writes—and he would still have to be the God of the classical philosophers who
neither interrupted nor interrogated himself, did not stifle himself, as did the God
of Jabès. (But the God of the classical philosophers, whose actual infinity did not
tolerate the question, precisely had no vital need for writing.) As opposed to
Being and to the Leibnizian Book,[8] the rationality of the Logos, for which our
writing is responsible, obeys the principle of discontinuity. The caesura does not
simply finish and fix meaning: "The aphorism," says Nietzsche, "the sentence,
in which I, as the first among the Germans, am a master, are the forms of
eternity." But, primarily, the caesura makes meaning emerge. It does not do so
alone, of course; but without interruption—between letters, words, sentences,
books—no signification could be awakened. *Assuming* that Nature refuses the
leap, one can understand why Scripture will never be Nature. It proceeds by
leaps alone. Which makes it perilous. Death strolls between letters. To write,
what is called writing, assumes an access to the mind through having the courage
to lose one's life, to die away from nature.

Jabès is very attentive to this generous distance between signs.

The light is in their absence which you read. (Ibid., p. 25)

All letters form absence. (Ibid., p. 47)

Absence is the permission given to letters to spell themselves out and to
signify, but it is also, in language's twisting of itself, *what* letters say: they say
freedom and a granted emptiness, that which is formed by being enclosed in
letters' net.

Absence, finally as the breath of the letter, for the letter *lives*. "The name must
germinate, otherwise it is false," says André Breton. Signifying absence or
separation, the letter lives as aphorism. It is solitude, articulates solitude, and
lives on solitude. It would no longer be the letter of the law if it were outside
difference, or if it left its solitude, or put an end to interruption, to distance, to
respect, and to its relation to the other, that is, a certain nonrelation. There is,
thus, an animality of the letter which assumes the forms of the letter's desire,
anxiety, and solitude.

> *Your solitude*
> *is an alphabet of squirrels*
> *at the disposition of forests.*
>   ("La clef de voûte," in *Je bâtis ma demeure*)

Like the desert and the city, the forest, in which the fearful signs swarm,
doubtless articulates the non-place and the wandering, the absence of prescribed
routes, the solitary arising of an unseen root, beyond the reach of the sun.
Toward a hidden sky. But the forest, outside the rigidity of its lines, is also trees
clasped by terrified letters, the wood wounded by poetic incision.

> *They engraved the fruit in the pain of the tree of solitude* . . . .
>
> *Like the sailor who grafts a name*
> *On that of the mast*
> *In the sign you are alone.*

The tree of engraving and grafting no longer belongs to the garden; it is the tree
of the forest or of the mast. The tree is to the mast what the desert is to the city.
Like the Jew, like the poet, like man, like God, signs have a choice only between
a natural or an institutionalized solitude. Then they are signs and the other
becomes possible.

The animality of the letter certainly appears, at first, as *one* metaphor among
others. (For example, in *Je bâtis ma demeure* the sex is a vowel, etc., or even
"*Aided by an accomplice, a word sometimes changes its sex and its soul.*" Or,
further: "*Vowels, as they are written, resemble the mouths of fish out of water
pierced by the hook; consonants resemble dispossessed scales. They live uncomfortably in their acts, in their hovels of ink. Infinity haunts them*" [p. 68]). But,
above all, it is metaphor *itself*, the origin of language as metaphor in which Being

and Nothing, the conditions of metaphor, the beyond-metaphor of metaphor, never say themselves. Metaphor, or the animality of the letter, is the primary and infinite equivocality of the signifier as Life. The *psychic* subversion of inert literality, that is to say, of nature, or of speech returned to nature. This overpowerfulness as the life of the signifier is produced within the anxiety and the wandering of the language always richer than knowledge, the language always capable of the movement which takes it further than peaceful and sedentary certitude.

> *How can I say what I know*
> *with words whose signification*
> *is multiple?*
> (*Je bâtis ma demeure*, p. 41)

Betrayed by citation, the organized power of the song keeps itself beyond the reach of commentary, in the *Livre des questions*. Here in particular, is it not born of an extraordinary confluence that weighs upon the canceling lines of words, the punctual singularity of Edmond Jabès's experience, his voice, his style? A confluence in which is recalled, conjoined, and condensed the suffering, the millennial reflection of a people, the *"pain" "whose past and continuity coincide with those of writing,"* the destiny that summons the Jew, placing him between the voice and the cipher; and he weeps for the lost voice with tears as black as the trace of ink. *Je bâtis ma demeure* ("I build my dwelling") is a line borrowed from *La voix de l'encre* (1949) ("The voice of ink"). And *Le livre des questions:*

> *You gather that I attach great value to what is said, more, perhaps,*
> *than to what is written; for in what is written my voice is missing and I*
> *believe in it,—I mean the creative voice, not the auxiliary voice which is a*
> *servant* (*Livre des questions*, p. 88)

(In the work of Emmanuel Levinas can be found the same hesitation, the same anxious movement within the difference between the Socratic and the Hebraic, the poverty and the wealth of the letter, the pneumatic and the grammatical.)[9]

Within original aphasia, when the voice of the god or the poet is missing, one must be satisfied with the vicars of speech that are the cry and writing. This is *Le livre des questions,* the poetic revolution of our century, the extraordinary reflection of man finally attempting today—and always in vain—to retake possession of his language (as if this were meaningful) by any means, through all routes, and to claim responsibility for it against a Father of Logos. One reads, for example, in *Le livre de l'absent:* "A decisive battle in which the vanquished, betrayed by their wounds, describe, as they fall to the ground, a page of writing dedicated by the victors to the chosen one who unwittingly set off the battle. In fact, it is in order to affirm the supremacy of the verb over man, of the verb over the verb, that the battle took place'' (*Livre de l'absent,* p. 69). Is this confluence *Le livre des questions?*

No. The song would no longer be sung if its tension was only confluential. Confluence must repeat the origin. This cry sings because in its enigma, it brings forth water from a cleft rock, the unique source, the unity of a spurting rupture. After which come ''currents,'' ''affluents,'' ''influences.'' A poem always runs the risk of being meaningless, and would be nothing without this risk of being meaningless, and would be nothing without this risk. If Jabès's poem is to risk having a meaning, or if his *question,* at least, is to risk having a meaning, the source must be presumed; and it must be presumed that the unity of the source is not due to a chance encounter, but that beneath this encounter another encounter takes place today. A first encounter, an encounter above all unique because it was a separation, like the separation of Sarah and Yukel. Encounter *is* separation. Such a proposition, which contradicts ''logic,'' breaks the unity of Being—which resides in the fragile link of the ''is''—by welcoming the other and difference into the source of meaning. But, it will be said, Being must always already be conceptualized in order to say these things—the encounter and the separation of what and of whom—and especially in order to say that encounter *is* separation. Certainly, but ''must always already'' precisely signifies the original exile from the kingdom of Being, signifies exile as the conceptualization of Being, and signifies that Being never is, never shows *itself,* is never *present,* is never *now,* outside difference (in all the senses today required by this word).[10] Whether he is Being or the master of beings, God himself is, and appears as what he is, within difference, that is to say, as difference and within dissimulation.

If, in the process of adding pitiful graffiti to an immense poem, as we are doing here, one insisted upon reducing the poem to its ''thematic structure,'' as it is called, one would have to acknowledge that nothing within it is original. The well-worn themes of the question within God, of negativity within God as the liberation of historicity and human speech, of man's writing as the desire and question *of* God (and the double genitive is ontological before being grammatical, or rather is the embedding of the ontological and the grammatical within the *graphein*),[11] of history and discourse as the anger of God emerging himself, etc., etc.—these themes are not first proper to Böhme, to German romanticism, to Hegel, to the final Scheler, etc., etc. Negativity in God, exile as writing, the life of the letter are all already in the Cabala. Which means ''Tradition'' itself. And Jabès is conscious of the Cabalistic resonances of his book. He even plays on them, occasionally (cf., for example, *Le livre de l'absent,* p. 12).

But traditionality is not orthodoxy. Others, perhaps, will articulate the ways in which Jabès *also* severs himself from the Jewish community, assuming that this last notion here has a sense, or has its classical sense. He does not sever himself from it only insofar as concerns dogma, but more profoundly still. For Jabès,

who acknowledges· a very late discovery of a certain way of being part of
Judaism, the Jew is but the suffering allegory: *"You are all Jews, even the
antisemites, for you have all been designated for martyrdom"* (*Livre des questions*, p. 180). He must justify himself to his blood brothers and to rabbis who are
no longer imaginary. They will all reproach him for this universalism, this
essentialism, this skeletal allegorism, this neutralization of the event in the
realms of the symbolic and the imaginary.

> *Addressing themselves to me, my blood brothers said: "You are not Jewish.
> You do not come to the synagogue."* . . . (*Livre des questions*, p. 63)
>
> *The rabbis whose words you cite are charlatans. Have they ever existed?
> And you have nourished yourself on their impious words . . . .*
>
> *You are Jewish for the others and so little Jewish for us.*
>
> *Addressing himself to me, the most contemplative of my blood brothers
> said:*
>   *"To make no difference between a Jew and him who is not Jewish, is this
> not already to cease being a Jew?" And they added: "Brotherhood is to
> give, give, give, and you will never be able to give what you are." Striking
> my chest with my fist I thought: "I am nothing. I have a severed head. But
> is not a man worth a man? And a decapitated one worth a believer?"*
> (Ibid., p. 64)

Jabès is not a defendant in this dialogue, for he carries both it and the charges
within him. In this noncoincidence of the self and the self, he is more and less
Jewish than the Jew. But the Jew's identification with himself does not exist. The
Jew is split, and split first of all between the two dimensions of the letter: allegory
and literality. His history would be but one empirical history among others if he
established or nationalized himself within difference and literality. He would
have no history at all if he let himself be attenuated within the algebra of an
abstract universalism.

Between the too warm flesh of the literal event and the cold skin of the concept
runs meaning. This is how it enters into the book. Everything enters into, transpires in the book. This is why the book is never finite. It always remains suffering
and vigilant.

> —*A lamp is on my table and the house is in the book.*
> —*I will finally live in the house.* (Ibid., p. 15)
>
> *Where is the book found?*
> —*In the book.* (Ibid.)

Every exit from the book is made within the book. Indeed, the end of writing
keeps itself beyond writing: *"Writing that culminates in itself is only a manifestation of spite."* If writing is not a tearing of the self toward the other within a
confession of infinite separation, if it is a delectation of itself, the pleasure of

writing for its own sake, the satisfaction of the artist, then it destroys itself. It syncopates itself in the roundness of the egg and the plenitude of the Identical. It is true that to go toward the other is also to negate oneself, and meaning is alienated from itself in the transition of writing. Intention surpasses itself and disengages from itself in order to be said. *"I hate that which is pronounced in which already I am no longer"* (p. 17). Just as the end of writing passes beyond writing, its origin is not yet in the book. The writer, builder, and guardian of the book posts himself at the entrance to the house. The writer is a ferryman and his destination always has a liminal signification. *"Who are you?—The guardian of the house.— . . . Are you in the book?—My place is on the threshhold"* (p. 15).

But—and this is the heart of the matter—everything that is exterior in relation to the book, everything that is negative as concerns the book, is produced *within the book*. The exit from the book, the other and the threshhold, are all articulated *within the book*. The other and the threshhold can only be written, can only affirm themselves in writing. One emerges from the book only within the book, because, for Jabès, the book is not in the world, but the world is in the book.

"The world exists because the book exists." *"The book is the work of the book"* *"The book multiplies the book"* (p. 33). To be is to-be-in-the-book. even if Being is not the created nature often called the Book of God during the Middle Ages. *"If God is, it is because He is in the book"* (p. 32). Jabès knows that the book is possessed and threatened, that *"its response is still a question, that its dwelling is ceaselessly threatened"* (p. 32). But the book can only be threatened by nothing, non-Being, nonmeaning. If it came *to be,* the threat—as is the case here—would be avowed, pronounced, domesticated. It would be of the house and of the book.

All historic anxiety, all poetic anxiety, all Judaic anxiety thus torments this poem of the interminable question. All affirmations and all negations, all contradictory questions are welcomed into the question within the unity of the book, in a logic like none other, in Logic. Here we would have to say Grammar. But does not this anxiety and this war, this unloosening of all the waters, rest upon the peaceful and silent basis of a nonquestion? Is not the writing of the question, by its decision, by its resolution, the beginning of repose and response? The first violence as regards the question? The first crisis and the first forgetting, the necessary beginning of wandering as history, that is to say, the very dissimulation of wandering?

The nonquestion of which we are speaking is not yet a dogma; and the act of faith in the book can precede, as we know, belief in the Bible. And can also survive it. The nonquestion of which we are speaking is the unpenetrated certainty that Being is a Grammar; and that the world is in all its parts a cryptogram to be constituted or reconstituted through poetic inscription or deciphering; that

the book is original, that everything *belongs to the book* before being and in order
to come into the world; that any thing can be born only by *approaching* the book,
can die only by failing *in sight of* the book; and that always the impassible shore
of the book is *first*.

But what if the Book was only, in all senses of the word, an *epoch* of Being (an
epoch coming to an end which would permit us to see Being in the glow of its
agony or the relaxation of its grasp, and an end which would multiply, like a final
illness, like the garrulous and tenacious hypermnesia of certain moribunds,
books about the dead book)? If the form of the book was no longer to be the
model of meaning? If Being was radically outside the book, outside its letter?
And was such by virtue of a transcendence which could no longer be touched by
inscription and signification, a transcendence which would no longer lie on the
page, and which above all would have arisen before it? If Being lost itself in
books? If books were the dissipation of Being? If the Being of the world, its
presence and the meaning of its Being, revealed itself only in illegibility, in a
radical illegibility which would not be the accomplice of a lost or sought after
legibility, of a page not yet cut from some divine encyclopedia? If the world were
not even, according to Jaspers's expression, "the manuscript of another," but
primarily the other of every possible manuscript? And if it were always too soon
to say *"revolt is a page crumpled in the waste basket"* (p. 177)? And always
too soon to say that evil is only *indecipherable,* due to the effect of some *lapsus
calami* or of God's cacography, and that *"our life, within Evil, has the form of
an inverted letter, a letter excluded because it is illegible in the Book of Books"*
(p. 85)? And if Death did not let *itself* be inscribed in the book in which, as is well
known moreover, the God of the Jews every year inscribes only the names of
those who may live? And if the dead soul were more or less, something other in
any event, than the dead letter of the law which should always be capable of
being reawakened? The dissimulation of an older or younger writing, from an
age other than the age of the book, the age of grammar, the age of everything
announced under the heading of the meaning of Being? The dissimulation of a
still illegible writing?

The radical illegibility of which we are speaking is not irrationality, is not
despair provoking non-sense, is not everything within the domains of the incomprehensible and the illogical that is anguishing. Such an interpretation—or
determination—of the illegible already belongs to the book, is enveloped within
the possibility of the volume. Original illegibility is not simply a moment interior
to the book, to reason or to logos; nor is it any more their opposite, having no
relationship of symmetry to them, being incommensurable with them. Prior to
the book (in the nonchronological sense), original illegibility is therefore the very
possibility of the book and, within it, of the ulterior and eventual opposition of
"rationalism" and "irrationalism." The Being that is announced within the
illegible is beyond these categories, beyond, as it writes itself, its own name.

It would be ludicrous to impugn Jabès for not having pronounced these questions in *Le livre des questions*. They can only sleep within the literary act which needs both their life and their lethargy. Writing would die of the pure vigilance of the question, as it would of the simple erasure of the question. Is not to write, once more, to confuse ontology and grammar? The grammar in which are inscribed all the dislocations of dead syntax, all the aggressions perpetrated by speech against language, every questioning of the letter itself? The written questions addressed to literature, all the tortures inflicted upon it, are always transfigured, drained, forgotten by literature, within literature; having become modifications of itself, by itself, in itself, they are mortifications, that is to say, as always, ruses of life. Life negates itself in literature only so that it may survive better. So that it may *be* better. It does not negate itself any more than it affirms itself: it differs from itself, defers itself, and writes itself as *différance*. Books are always books of *life* (the archetype would be the Book of Life kept by the God of the Jews) or of *afterlife* (the archetype would be the Books of the Dead kept by the Egyptians). When Maurice Blanchot writes: "Is man *capable* of a radical interrogation, that is to say, finally, is man *capable* of literature?" one could just as well say, on the basis of a certain conceptualization of life, "incapable" half the time. Except if one admits that pure literature is nonliterature, or death itself. The question about the origin of the book, the absolute interrogation, the interrogation of all possible interrogations, the "interrogation of God" will never belong to a book. Unless the question forgets itself within the articulations of its memory, the time of its interrogation, the time and tradition of its *sentence,* and unless the memory of itself, the syntax binding the question to itself, does not make a disguised affirmation of this origin. Already a book of the question becoming remote from its origin.

Henceforth, so that God may indeed be, as Jabès says, *an interrogation of God,* would we not have to transform a final affirmation into a question? Literatue would then, perhaps, only be the dreamlike displacement of this question:

> *"There is the book of God in which God questions himself, and there is the book of man which is proportionate to that of God."*
>
> *Reb Rida*

Four

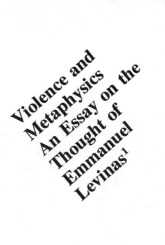

Violence and
Metaphysics
An Essay on the
Thought of
Emmanuel
Levinas[1]

That philosophy died yesterday, since Hegel or Marx,
Nietzsche, or Heidegger—and philosophy should still
wander toward the meaning of its death—or that it has
always lived knowing itself to be dying (as is silently
confessed in the shadow of the very discourse which
declared philosophia perennis); that philosophy died
one day, within history, or that it has always fed on its
own agony, on the violent way it opens history by
opposing itself to nonphilosophy, which is its past and
its concern, its death and wellspring; that beyond the
death, or dying nature, of philosophy, perhaps even
because of it, thought still has a future, or even, as is
said today, is still entirely to come because of what
philosophy has held in store; or, more strangely still,
that the future itself has a future—all these are unan-
swerable questions. By right of birth, and for one time
at least, these are problems put to philosophy as problems philosophy cannot resolve.

It may even be that these questions are not
philosophical, are not *philosophy's* questions. Nevertheless, these should be the only questions today
capable of founding the community, within the world,
of those who are still called philosophers; and called
such in remembrance, at very least, of the fact that
these questions must be examined unrelentingly, despite the diaspora of institutes and languages, despite
the publications and techniques that follow on each
other, procreating and accumulating by themselves,

like capital or poverty. A community of the question, therefore, within that fragile moment when the question is not yet determined enough for the hypocrisy of an answer to have already initiated itself beneath the mask of the question, and not yet determined enough for its voice to have been already and fraudulently articulated within the very syntax of the question. A community of decision, of initiative, of absolute initiality, but also a threatened community, in which the question has not yet found the language it has decided to seek, is not yet sure of its own possibility within the community. A community of the question about the possibility of the question. This is very little—almost nothing—but within it, today, is sheltered and encapsulated an unbreachable dignity and duty of decision. An unbreachable responsibility. Why unbreachable? Because the impossible has *already* occurred. The impossible according to the totality of what is questioned, according to the totality of beings, objects and determinations, the impossible according to the history of facts, has occurred: there is a history of the question, a pure memory of the pure question which in its possibility perhaps authorizes all inheritance and all pure memory in general and as such. The question has already begun—we know it has—and this strange certainty about an *other* absolute origin, an other absolute decision that has secured the past of the question, liberates an incomparable instruction: the discipline of the question. Through (through, that is to say that we must *already* know how to read) this discipline, which is not yet even the inconceivable tradition of the negative (of negative determination), and which is completely previous to irony, to maieutics, to *epoché,* and to doubt, an injunction is announced: the question must be maintained. As a question. The liberty *of the question* (double genitive)[2] must be stated and protected. A founded dwelling, a realized tradition of the question remaining a question. If this commandment has an ethical meaning, it is not in that it belongs to the *domain* of the ethical, but in that it ultimately authorizes every ethical law in general. There is no stated law, no commandment, that is not addressed to a freedom of speech. There is therefore neither law nor commandment which does not confirm and *enclose*—that is, does not dissimulate by presupposing it—the possibility of the question. Thus, the question is always enclosed; it never appears immediately as such, but only through the hermetism of a proposition in which the answer has already begun to determine the question. The purity of the question can only be indicated or recalled through the difference of a hermeneutical effort.

Thus, those who look into the possibility of philosophy, philosophy's life and death, are already engaged in, already overtaken by the dialogue of the question about itself and with itself; they always act in remembrance of philosophy, as part of the correspondence of the question with itself. Essential to the destiny of this correspondence, then, is that it comes to speculate, to reflect, and to question about itself within itself. This is where the objectification, secondary interpretation, and determination of the question's own history in the world all

begin; and this is where the combat embedded in the difference between the
question in general and "philosophy" as a determined—finite and mortal—
moment or mode of the question itself also begins. The difference between
philosophy as a power and adventure *of* the question itself and philosophy as a
determined event or turning point *within* this adventure.

This difference is better conceived today. That this difference has come to light,
has been conceptualized *as such,* is doubtless an unnoticed and inessential sign
for the historian of facts, techniques, and ideas. But, understood in all its implications, it is perhaps the most deeply inscribed characteristic of our age. And
would not better thinking this difference be knowing that if something is still to
transpire within the tradition by which philosophers always know themselves to
be overtaken, then the tradition's origin will have to be summoned forth and
adhered to as rigorously as possible? Which is not to stammer and huddle lazily
in the depths of childhood, but precisely the opposite.

Close to us and since Hegel, in his mighty shadow, the two great voices which
have ordered us to this total repetition—which itself has recalled us to ourselves
and has been acknowledged as of utmost philosophical urgency—are those of
Husserl and Heidegger. Despite the most profound dissimilarities, the appeal to
tradition—which is in no way traditional—is shaped by an intention common to
Husserlian phenomenology and to what we will call provisionally, by approxima-
tion and for reasons of economy, Heideggerean "ontology."[3]

Thus, very briefly:

1. The entirety of philosophy is conceived on the basis of its Greek source. As
is well known, this amounts neither to an occidentalism, nor to a historicism.[4] It
is simply that the founding concepts of philosophy are primarily Greek, and it
would not be possible to philosophize, or to speak philosophically, outside this
medium. That Plato, for Husserl, was the founder of a reason and a philosophical
task whose telos was still sleeping in the shadows; or that for Heidegger, on the
contrary, Plato marks the moment at which the thought of Being forgets itself and
is determined as philosophy—this difference is decisive only at the culmination
of a common root which is Greek. The difference is fraternal in its posterity,
entirely submitted to the same domination. Domination of the same too, which
will disappear neither in phenomenology nor in "ontology."

2. The archaeology to which Husserl and Heidegger lead us by different paths
entails, for both, a subordination or transgression, in any event a *reduction of
metaphysics.* Even though, for each, this gesture has an entirely different meaning, or at least does so apparently.

3. Finally, the category of the *ethical* is not only dissociated from metaphysics
but coordinated with something other than itself, a previous and more radical
function. When ethics is not treated this way, when law, the power of resolution,
and the relationship to the other are once more part of the *archia,* they lose their
ethical specificity.[5]

These three motifs arrayed at the unique source of the unique philosophy would indicate the only possible direction to be taken by any philosophical resource in general. Any possible dialogue between Husserlian phenomenology and Heideggerean "ontology," at every point where they are more or less directly implicated, can be understood only from within the Greek tradition. At the moment when the fundamental conceptual system produced by the Greco-European adventure is in the process of taking over all of humanity, these three motifs would predetermine the totality of the logos and of the worldwide historico-philosophical situation. No philosophy could possibly dislodge them without first succumbing to them, or without finally destroying itself as a philosophical language. At a historical depth which the science and philosophies of history can only presuppose, we know that we are consigned to the security of the Greek element; and we know it with a knowledge and a confidence which are neither habitual nor comfortable but, on the contrary, permit us to experience torment or distress in general. For example, the consciousness of crisis is for Husserl but the provisional, almost necessary covering up of a transcendental motif which in Descartes and in Kant was already beginning to accomplish the Greek aim: philosophy as science. When Heidegger says that "for a long time, too long, thought has been desiccated," like a fish out of water, the element to which he wishes to return thought is still—already—the Greek element, the Greek thought of Being, the thought of Being whose irruption or call produced Greece. The knowledge and security of which we are speaking are therefore not in the world: rather, they are the possibility of our language and the nexus of our world.

It is at this level that the thought of Emmanuel Levinas can make us tremble.

At the heart of the desert, in the growing wasteland, this thought, which fundamentally no longer seeks to be a thought of Being and phenomenality, makes us dream of an inconceivable process of dismantling and dispossession.

1. In Greek, in our language, in a language rich with all the alluvia of its history—and our question takes shape already—in a language that admits to its powers of seduction while playing on them unceasingly, this thought summons us to a dislocation of the Greek logos, to a dislocation of our identity, and perhaps of identity in general; it summons us to depart from the Greek site and perhaps from every site in general, and to move toward what is no longer a source or a site (too welcoming to the gods), but toward an *exhalation,* toward a prophetic speech already emitted not only nearer to the source than Plato or the pre-Socratics, but inside the Greek origin, close to the other of the Greek (but will the other of the Greek be the non-Greek? Above all, can it be *named* the non-Greek? And our question comes closer.) A thought for which the entirety of the Greek logos has already erupted, and is now a quiet topsoil deposited not over bedrock, but around a more ancient volcano. A thought which, without philology and solely by remaining faithful to the immediate, but buried nudity of experi-

ence itself, seeks to liberate itself from the Greek domination of the Same and the One (other names for the light of Being and of the phenomenon) as if from oppression itself—an oppression certainly comparable to none other in the world, an ontological or transcendental oppression, but also the origin or alibi of all oppression in the world. A thought, finally, which seeks to liberate itself from a philosophy fascinated by the "visage of being that shows itself in war" which "is fixed in the concept of totality which dominates Western philosophy" (*Totality and Infinity* [hereafter *TI*], p. 21).

2. This thought nevertheless seeks to define itself, in its primary possibility, as metaphysical (a Greek notion however, if we follow the vein of our question). A metaphysics that Levinas seeks to raise up from its subordinate position and whose concept he seeks to restore in opposition to the entire tradition derived from Aristotle.

3. This thought calls upon the ethical relationship—a nonviolent relationship to the infinite as infinitely other, to the Other[6]—as the only one capable of opening the space of transcendence and of liberating metaphysics. And does so without supporting ethics and metaphysics by anything other than themselves, and without making them flow into other streams at their source.

In question, therefore, is a powerful will to explication of the history of Greek speech. Powerful because, if this attempt is not the first of its kind, it reaches a height and a level of penetration in its dialogue at which the Greeks—and foremost among them the two Greeks named Husserl and Heidegger—are called upon to respond. If the messianic eschatology from which Levinas draws inspiration seeks neither to assimilate itself into what is called a philosophical truism, nor even to "complete" (*TI*, p. 22) philosophical truisms, nevertheless it is developed in its discourse neither as a theology, nor as a Jewish mysticism (it can even be understood as the trial of theology and mysticism); neither as a dogmatics, nor as *a* religion, nor as *a* morality. In the last analysis it never bases its authority on Hebraic theses or texts. It seeks to be understood from within a *recourse to experience itself*. Experience itself and that which is most irreducible within experience: the passage and departure toward the other; the other itself as what is most irreducibly other within it: Others. A recourse not to be confused with what has always been called a philosophical enterprise, but which reaches a point at which an exceeded philosophy cannot not be brought into question. Truthfully, messianic eschatology is never mentioned literally: it is but a question of designating a space or a hollow within naked experience where this eschatology can be understood and where it must resonate. This hollow space is not an opening among others. It is opening itself, the opening of opening, that which can be enclosed within no category or totality, that is, everything within experience which can no longer be described by traditional concepts, and which resists every philosopheme.

What do this explication and this reciprocal surpassing of two origins and two historical speeches signify? Do a new élan and some strange community begin to take shape, without being the spiraling return of Alexandrian promiscuity? If we recall that Heidegger, too, seeks to open the passageway to a former speech which, supporting itself from within philosophy, carries us to the outer or inner reaches of philosophy, what do this other speech and this other passageway signify here? It is this space of interrogation that we have chosen for a very partial[7] reading of Levinas's work. Of course it is not our intention to explore this space, even in the name of a timid beginning. Faintly and from afar, we will only attempt to point it out. First of all, in the style of commentary, we will try to remain faithful to the themes and audacities of a thought—and this despite several parentheses and notes which will enclose our perplexity. Faithful also to its history, whose patience and anxiety capitulate and carry within themselves the reciprocal interrogation of which we wish to speak.[8] Then we will attempt to ask several questions. If they succeed in approaching the heart of this explication, they will be nothing less than objections, but rather the questions put to *us* by Levinas.

We have just spoken of "themes" and of the "history of a thought." The difficulty is classical and concerns not only method. The brevity of these pages will only intensify it. We will not choose. We will refuse to sacrifice the history of Levinas's thought and works to the order or aggregate of themes—which must not be called a system—assembled and enriched in the great book *Totality and Infinity*. And if we must, for once, have faith in him who stands most accused in the trial conducted by this book, the result is nothing without its becoming.[9] But neither will we sacrifice the self-coherent unity of intention to the becoming, which then would be no more than pure disorder. We will not choose between the opening and the totality. Therefore we will be incoherent, but without systematically resigning ourselves to incoherence. The possibility of the impossible system will be on the horizon to protect us from empiricism. Without reflecting here upon the philosophy of this hesitation, let us note between parentheses that by simply articulating it we have already come close to Levinas's own problematic.

I
The Violence of Light

The departure from Greece was discreetly premeditated in *Théorie de l'intuition dans la phénoménologie de Husserl*. In France, in 1930, this was the first major work devoted to the entirety of Husserl's thought. Through a remarkable exposition of the developments of phenomenology, such as were then available from the published works and teachings of the master, and through precautions which already acknowledged the "surprises" that Husserl's meditations and unpublished works might "hold in store," a reticence was announced. The imperialism of *theoria* already bothered Levinas. More than any other philosophy, *phenomenology,* in the wake of Plato, was to be struck with light. Unable to reduce the last naïveté, the naïveté of the glance, it predetermined Being as object.[10]

At this point, the accusation remains timid and is not of a piece.

(a) First, it is difficult to maintain a philosophical discourse against light. And thirty years later, when the charges against theoretism and (Husserlian) phenomenology became the essential motifs in the break with tradition, the nudity of the face of the other—this epiphany of a certain non-light before which all violence is to be quieted and disarmed—will still have to be exposed to a certain enlightenment. Especially as concerns the violence implicit in phenomenology.

(b) Next, it is difficult to overlook the fact that Husserl so little predetermined Being as object that in *Ideas I* absolute existence is accorded only to pure consciousness. True, it has often been argued that the difference hardly counts, and that a philosophy of consciousness is always a philosophy of the object. Levinas's reading of Husserl on this point has always been nuanced, supple, contrasted. As early as in the *Theory of Intuition,* theory is correctly distinguished from objectivity in general. As we shall see later, practical, axiological, etc., consciousness is for Husserl too a consciousness of the object. Levinas openly acknowledges this. Therefore, the accusation is really directed against the irreducible primacy of the subject-object correlation. But, later, Levinas will insist more and more on those aspects of Husserlian phenomenology which take us to the inner or outer reaches of the "subject-object correlation." For example, this would be "intentionality as a relationship with otherness," as an "exteriority which is not objective," sensibility, passive genesis, the movement of temporalization, etc.[11]

(c) Further, for Levinas the sun of the *epekeina tes ousias* will always illuminate the pure awakening and inexhaustible source of thought (*TI,* p. 127) . It is not only the Greek ancestor of the Infinite which transcends totality (the totality of being or of *noema,* the totality of the same or the ego),[12] but is also the instrument of destruction for the phenomenology and ontology subjected to the neutral totality of the Same as Being or as Ego. All the essays in 1947 grouped under the title *De l'existence à l'existant* will be placed under the sign of "the Platonic formulation placing the Good beyond Being." (In *Totality and Infinity* the "Phenomenology of Eros" describes the movement of the *epekeina tes ousias* in the very experience of the caress.) In 1947 Levinas calls this movement, which is not theological, not a transcendence toward "a superior existence," "ex-cendence." With a foothold in being, excendence is a "departure from being and from the categories which describe it." This ethical excendence designates the site—rather the non-site—of metaphysics as metatheology, metaontology, metaphenomenology. We will have to return to this reading of the *epekeina tes ousias* and its relationship to ontology. Since we are speaking of light, let us note for the moment that the Platonic movement is interpreted such that it leads no longer to the sun but even beyond light and Being, beyond the light *of* Being. "We thus encounter *in our own way* the Platonic idea of the Good beyond Being," we read at the end of *Totality and Infinity* (p. 293—my italics), concerning creation and fecundity. *In our own way,* which is to say that ethical excendence is not projected toward the neutrality of the good, but toward the Other, and that which (is) *epekeina tes ousias* is not essentially light but fecundity or generosity. Creation is but creation *of* the other; it can be only as paternity, and the relations of the father to son escape all the logical, ontological, and phenomenological categories in which the absoluteness of the other is necessarily the same. (But did not the Platonic sun already enlighten the visible sun, and did not excendence play upon the meta-phor of these two suns? Was not the Good the necessarily nocturnal source of all light? The light of light beyond light. The heart of light is black, as has often been noticed.[13] Further, Plato's sun does not only enlighten: it engenders. The good is the father of the visible sun which provides living beings with "creation, growth and nourishment" *Republic,* 508a–509b.)

(d) Finally, Levinas is certainly quite attentive to everything in Husserl's analyses which tempers or complicates the primordiality of theoretical consciousness. In a paragraph devoted to *nontheoretical consciousness,* it is acknowledged that the primacy of objectivity in general is not necessarily confused, in *Ideas I,* with the primacy of the theoretical attitude. There are nontheoretical acts and objects "of a new and irreducible ontological structure." "For example, says Husserl, the act of valorization constitutes an *axiological* object (*Gegenständlichkeit*), specific in relation to the world of things; constitutes a being from a new region." Levinas also admits on several occasions that the importance accorded to theoretical objectivity has to do with the transcendental guide most often chosen in *Ideas I:* the perception of extended things. (However, we already know that this guide could be only a provisional example.)

Despite all these precautions, despite a constant oscillation between the letter and the spirit of Husserlianism (the former most often contested in the name of the latter),[14] and despite Levinas's insistence upon what is called a "fluctuation in Husserl's thought," a break not to be reconsidered is signified. The phenomenological reduction, whose "historical role ... is not even a problem" for Husserl, remains a prisoner of the natural attitude which is possible "in the extent to which the latter is theoretical."[15] "Husserl gives himself the liberty of theory as he gives himself theory itself." Chapter 4 of *La conscience théorique* designates, within a compressed and nuanced analysis, the point of departure: one cannot simultaneously maintain the primacy of the objectifying act and the irreducible originality of nontheoretical consciousness. And if "the conception of consciousness in the 5th *Untersuchung* seems to us not only to affirm a primacy of theoretical consciousness, but sees it as the only access to what creates the *being* of the object," if "the existing world, which is revealed to us, has the mode of existence of the object given over to the theoretical glance," if "the real world is the world of knowledge," if "in his [Husserl's] philosophy ... knowledge and representation[16] is not a mode of life to the same degree as the others, nor a secondary mode," then "we will have to take our leave."

One already foresees the unease to which a thought rejecting the excellence of theoretical rationality will have to resign itself later, especially in that it never ceases to appeal to the most uprooted rationalism and universalism against the violences of mysticism and history, against the ravishing of enthusiasm and ecstasy. One foresees too, the difficulties of a progression which leads to a metaphysics of separation through a reduction of theoretism. For separation, distance or impassiveness heretofore have been the targets of the classical objections against theoretism and objectivism. On the contrary, there will be more force—and danger—in denouncing the blindness of theoretism, its inability to depart from itself towards absolute exteriority, towards the totally-other, the infinitely-other "more objective than objectivity" (*TI*). The complicity of theoretical objectivity and mystical communion will be Levinas's true target. The premetaphysical unity of one and the same violence. An alternation which always modifies the same confinement of the other.

In 1930 Levinas turns toward Heidegger against Husserl. *Sein und Zeit* is published, and Heidegger's teaching begins to spread. Everything which overflows the commentary and "letter" of Husserl's texts moves toward "ontology," "in the very special sense Heidegger gives to the term" (*Théorie de l'intuition* [hereafter *THI*]). In his critique of Husserl, Levinas retains two Heideggerean themes: (1) despite "the idea, so profound, that in the ontological order the world of science is posterior to the concrete and vague world of perception, and depends upon it," Husserl "perhaps was wrong to see in this concrete world, a world of perceived objects above all" (*THI*). Heidegger goes further, since for him this world is not primarily given over to the glance, but is rather—and we wonder whether Heidegger would have accepted this formulation—"in its very Being like a center of action, a field of activity or of *solicitude*" (ibid.). (2) if Husserl was right in his opposition to historicism and naturalistic history, he neglected "the historical situation of man ... understood in another sense."[17] There exist a historicity and a temporality of man that are not only predicates but "the very substantiality of his substance." It is "this structure ... which occupies such an important place in Heidegger's thought" (ibid.).

One already foresees the unease to which a thought rejecting the excellence of a "philosophy" which "appears ... as independent of man's historical situation as a theory seeking to consider everything *sub specie aeternitatis*" (*THI*) will have to resign itself later, especially in that it never ceases to call upon the "eschatology" which like experience "as the 'beyond' of history withdraws beings from history's jurisdiction." There is no contradiction here but rather a displacement of concepts—in this case the concept of history—which we must follow. Perhaps then the appearance of contradiction will vanish as the fantasy of a philosophy enveloped in its own fundamental conceptions. A contradiction according to what Levinas often will call "formal logic."

Let us follow this displacement. The respectful, moderate reproach directed against Husserl in a Heideggerean style will soon become the main charge of an indictment this time directed against Heidegger, and made with a violence that will not cease to grow. Certainly it is not a question of denouncing as militant theoretism a thought which, in its initial act, refused to treat the self-evidence of the object as its ultimate recourse; a thought for which the historicity of meaning, according to Levinas's own terms, "destroys clarity and constitution as authentic modes of the existence of the mind" (*En découvrant l'existence* [hereafter *EDE*]); and for which, finally, "the self-evident is no longer the fundamental mode of intellection," for which "existence is irreducible to the light of the self-evident" and "the drama of existence" is played out "before light" (ibid.). Nevertheless, at a singular depth—but the fact and the accusation are made only more significant by it—Heidegger still would have questioned and reduced theoretism from within, and in the name of, a Greco-Platonic tradition under the surveillance of the agency of the glance and the metaphor of light. That is, by the spatial pair inside-outside (but is this, in all its aspects, a *spatial* pair?) which gives life to the opposition of subject and object. By allegedly reducing this last schema, Heidegger would have retained what made it possible and necessary: light, unveiling, comprehension or precomprehension. This what the texts written after *En découvrant l'existence* tell us. "Heideggerean care, illuminated as it is by comprehension (even if comprehension offers itself as care), is already determined by the structure 'inside-outside' that characterizes light." In making the strucutre "inside-outside" tremble at the point where it would have resisted Heidegger, Levinas in no way pretends to erase it, or to deny its meaning and existence. Nor does he do so, moreover, when the opposition subject-object or cogito-cogitatum is in question. In the style by which strong and faithful thought is recognized (this is Heidegger's style too), Levinas respects the zone or layer of traditional truth; and the philosophies whose presuppositions he describes are in general neither refuted nor criticized. Here, for example, it is a question simply of revealing beneath this truth, as that which founds it and is dissimulated within it, "a situation which precedes the division of Being into an inside and an outside." However it is also a question of inaugurating, in a way that is to be new, quite new, a metaphysics of radical separation and exteriority. One anticipates that this metaphysics will have some difficulty finding its language in the medium of a traditional logos entirely governed by the structure "inside-outside," "interior-exterior."

Thus, "without being knowledge, Heidegger's temporality is ecstasy, 'being

outside itself.' Not a transcendence of theory, but already deportation from an
interior toward an exterior.'' The structure of *Mitsein*[18] itself will be interpreted
as a Platonic inheritance, belonging to the world of light. In effect, through the
experience of eros and paternity, through the waiting for death, there should arise
a relationship to the other which can no longer be understood as a modification of
''the Eleatic notion of Being'' (*Le temps et l'autre* [hereafter *TA*]). The latter
would demand that multiplicity be included in, subjected to, the domination of
unity. And it would still govern Plato's philosophy, according to Levinas, even
unto its concept of femininity (conceived as matter in the categories of activity
and passivity) and its concept of the city-state which ''must imitate the world
of ideas.''

''It is . . . toward a pluralism which does not fuse into unity that we wish to
make our way; and, if it can be dared, to break with Parmenides'' (*TA*). Thus,
Levinas exhorts us to a second parricide. The Greek father who still holds us
under his sway must be killed; and this is what a Greek—Plato—could never
resolve to do, deferring the act into a hallucinatory murder. A hallucination
within the hallucination that is already speech. But will a non-Greek ever succeed
in doing what a Greek in this case could not do, except by disguising himself as a
Greek, by *speaking* Greek, by feigning to speak Greek in order to get near the
king? And since it is a question of killing a speech, will we ever know who is the
last victim of this stratagem? Can one feign speaking a language? The Eleatic
stranger and disciple of Parmenides had to give language its due for having
vanquished him: shaping non-Being according to Being, he had to ''say farewell
to an unnamable opposite of Being'' and had to confine non-Being to its relativity
to Being, that is to the movement of alterity.

Why was the repetition of the murder necessary according to Levinas? Because the Platonic gesture will be ineffectual for as long as multiplicity and
alterity are not understood as the absolute *solitude* of the *existent* in its *existence*.
These are the translations of *Seiendes* and *Sein* chosen by Levinas at this point
''for reasons of euphony'' (*TA*).[19] This choice will always retain a certain ambiguity: by *existent,* in effect, Levinas almost if not always understands the being
which is man, being in the form of *Dasein*. Now, thus understood, the existent is
not being (*Seiendes*) in general, but refers to what Heidegger calls *Existenz*—
mainly because it has the same root—that is ''the mode of Being, and precisely,
the Being of the being which keeps itself open for the aperture of Being, and
within it.'' ''Was bedeutet 'Existenz' in Sein und Zeit? Das wort nennt eine
Weise des Seins, und zwar das Sein desjenigen Seienden, das offen steht für die
Offenheit des Seins, in der es steht, indem es sie aussteht'' (Introduction to *Was
ist Metaphysik*).

Now this solitude of the ''existent'' in its ''existence'' would be primordial
and could not be conceived on the basis of the neutral unity of *existence* which
Levinas often and profoundly describes under the heading of the ''*there is*.'' But

is not the "there is" the totality of indeterminate, neutral, anonymous beings rather than Being itself? The theme of the "there is" calls for systematic confrontation with Heidegger's allusions to the *"es gibt"* (*Being and Time, Letter on Humanism*), and for a confrontation too, of terror, which Levinas opposes to Heideggerean anguish, with the experience of fright, which Heidegger says, in the *Nachwort* to *Was ist Metaphysik,* "always resides near essential anxiety."

The relationship to the other arises from the depths of this solitude. Without it, without this primordial secret, parricide is philosophy's theatrical fiction. To understand the secret on the basis of the unity of existence, on the pretext that it *exists* or that it *is* the secret of the existent, "is to confine oneself to unity, and to let Parmenides escape every parricide" (*TA*). Therefore, Levinas henceforth will move toward a thought of original difference. Is this thought in contradiction with Heidegger's intentions? Is there a difference between this difference and the difference of which Heidegger speaks? Is their juxtaposition anything but verbal? And which difference is more original? We will consider these questions later.

A world of light and of unity, a "philosophy of a world of light, a world without time." In this heliopolitics "the social ideal will be sought in an ideal of fusion . . . the subject . . . losing himself in a collective representation, in a common ideal . . . . It is the collectivity which says 'us,' and which, turned toward the intelligible sun, toward the truth, experience, the other at his side and not face to face with him . . . . *Miteinandersein* also remains the collectivity of the with, and its authentic form is revealed around the truth." Now, "we hope to show, for our part, that it is not the preposition *mit* which must describe the original relation with the other." Beneath solidarity, beneath companionship, before *Mitsein,* which would be only a derivative and modified form of the originary relation with the other, Levinas already aims for the face-to-face, the encounter with the face. "Face to face without intermediary" and without "communion." Without intermediary and without communion, neither mediate nor immediate, such is the truth of our relation to the other, the truth to which the traditional logos is forever inhospitable. This unthinkable truth of living experience, to which Levinas returns ceaselessly, cannot possibly be encompassed by philosophical speech without immediately revealing, by philosophy's own light, that philosophy's surface is severely cracked, and that what was taken for its solidity is its rigidity. It could doubtless be shown that it is in the nature of Levinas's writing, at its decisive moments, to move along these cracks, masterfully progressing by negations, and by negation against negation. Its proper route is not that of an "either this . . . or that," but of a "neither this . . . nor that." The poetic force of metaphor is often the trace of this rejected alternative, this wounding of language. Through it, in its opening, experience itself is silently revealed.

Without intermediary and without communion, absolute proximity and absolute distance: "eros in which, within the proximity to the other, distance is

integrally maintained; eros whose pathos is made simultaneously of this proximity and this duality.'' A community of nonpresence, and therefore of non-
phenomenality. Not a community without light, not a blindfolded synagogue, but
a community anterior to Platonic light. A light before neutral light, before the
truth which arrives as a third party, the truth "which we look toward together,"
the judgmental arbitrator's truth. Only the other, the totally other, can be man-
ifested as what it is before the shared truth, within a certain nonmanifestation and
a certain absence. It can be said only of the other that its phenomenon is a certain
nonphenomenon, its presence (*is*) a certain absence. Not pure and simple absence, for there logic could make its claim, but a *certain* absence. Such a
formulation shows clearly that within this experience of the other the logic of
noncontradiction, that is, everything which Levinas designates as "formal
logic," is contested in its root. This root would be not only the root of our
language, but the root of all of western philosophy,[20] particularly phenomenology and ontology. This naïveté would prevent them from thinking the other (that
is from thinking; and this would indeed be the reason why, although Levinas,
"the enemy of thought," does not say so), and from aligning their discourse with
the other. The consequence would be double. (a) Because they do not think the
other, they do not have time. Without time, they do not have history. The
absolute alterity of each instant, without which there would be no time, cannot be
produced—constituted—within the identity of the subject or the existent. It
comes into time through the Other. Bergson and Heidegger would have overlooked this (*De l'existence à l'existent* [hereafter *EE*]), and Husserl even more so.
(b) More seriously, to renounce the other (not by being weaned from it, but by
detaching oneself from it, which is actually to be in relation to it, to respect it
while nevertheless overlooking it, that is, while knowing it, identifying it, as-
similating it), to renounce the other is to enclose oneself within solitude (the bad
solitude of solidity and self-identity) and to repress ethical transcendence. In
effect, if the Parmenidean tradition—we know now what this means for Levinas—
disregards the irreducible solitude of the "existent," by the same token it disregards the relationship to the other. It does not think solitude, it does not appear
to itself to be solitude, because it is the solitude of totality and opacity. "Solipsism is neither observation nor sophism; it is the very structure of reason."
Therefore, there is a soliloquy of reason and a solitude of light. Incapable of
respecting the Being and meaning of the other, phenomenology and ontology
would be philosophies of violence. Through them, the entire philosophical tradition, in its meaning and at bottom, would make common cause with oppression
and with the totalitarianism of the same. The ancient clandestine friendship
between light and power, the ancient complicity between theoretical objectivity
and technico-political possession.[21] "If the other could be possessed, seized, and
known, it would not be the other. To possess, to know, to grasp are all synonyms
of power" (*TA*). To see and to know, to have and to will, unfold only within the

oppressive and luminous identity of the same; and they remain, for Levinas, fundamental categories of phenomenology and ontology. Everything given to me within light appears as given to myself by myself. Henceforward, the heliological *metaphor* only turns away our glance, providing an alibi for the historical violence of light: a displacement of technico-political oppression in the direction of philosophical discourse. For it has always been believed that metaphors exculpate, lift the weight of things and of acts. If there is no history, except through language, and if language (except when it names Being *itself* or nothing: almost never) is elementally metaphorical, Borges is correct: "Perhaps universal history is but the history of several metaphors." Light is only one example of these "several" fundamental "metaphors," but what an example! Who will ever dominate it, who will ever pronounce its meaning without first being pronounced by it? What language will ever escape it? How, for example, will the metaphysics of the face as the *epiphany* of the other free itself of light? Light perhaps has no opposite; if it does, it is certainly not night. If all languages combat within it, *modifying only* the same metaphor and choosing the *best* light, Borges, several pages later, is correct again: "Perhaps universal history is but the history of the diverse *intonations* of several metaphors" (*La sphère de Pascal;* my italics).

II
Phenomenology,
Ontology, Metaphysics

These measures were critical, but they obeyed the voice of full certainty. They appeared, through the essays, the concrete and subtle analyses concerning exoticism, the caress, insomnia, fecundity, work, the instant, fatigue, only at the point, at the edge of the indescribable indestructible which opens up classical conceptuality, seeking its own conceptuality between rejections. *Totality and Infinity,* the great work, not only enriches these concrete analyses but organizes them within a powerful architecture. Levinas calls the positive movement which takes itself beyond the disdain or disregard of the other, that is, beyond the appreciation or possession, understanding and knowledge of the other, *metaphysics* or *ethics.* Metaphysical transcendence is *desire.*

This concept of desire is as anti-Hegelian as it can possibly be. It does not designate a movement of negation and assimilation, the negation of alterity first necessary in order to become "self-consciousness" "certain of itself" (*Phenomenology of the Mind* and *Encyclopedia*). For Levinas, on the contrary, desire is the respect and knowledge of the other as other, the ethico-metaphysical moment whose transgression consciousness *must* forbid itself. According to Hegel, on the contrary, this gesture of transgression and assimilation is necessary and essential. Levinas sees in it a premetaphysical, natural necessity, and in several splendid analyses separates desire from enjoyment—which Hegel does not appear to do. Enjoyment is only deferred in work:[22] thus, Hegelian desire

would be only need, in Levinas's sense. But one rightly suspects that things
would appear more complicated, if one followed closely the movement of certitude and the truth of desire in the *Phenomenology of the Mind*. Despite his
anti-Kierkegaardian protests, Levinas here returns to the themes of *Fear and
Trembling:* the movement of desire can be what it is only paradoxically, as the
renunciation of desire.

Neither theoretical intentionality nor the affectivity of need exhaust the movement of desire: they have as their meaning and end their own accomplishment,
their own fulfillment and satisfaction within the totality and identity of the same.
Desire, on the contrary, permits itself to be appealed to by the absolutely irreducible exteriority of the other to which it must remain infinitely inadequate. Desire
is equal only to excess. No totality will ever encompass it. Thus, the metaphysics
of desire is a metaphysics of infinite separation. Not a consciousness of separation as a Judaic consciousness, as an unhappy consciousness:[23] in the Hegelian
Odyssey Abraham's unhappiness is an expediency, the provisional necessity of a
figure and a transition within the horizons of a reconciliatory return to self and
absolute knowledge. Here there is no return. For desire is not unhappy. It is
opening and freedom. Further, a desired infinite may govern desire itself, but it
can never appease desire by its presence. "And if desire were to cease with God /
Ah, I would envy you hell." (May we cite Claudel to comment upon Levinas,
when the latter also polemizes against "this spirit admired since [our] earliest youth"?)

The infinitely other is the invisible, since vision opens up only the illusory and
relative exteriority of theory and of need. A provisional exteriority, given only
within *sight of* its own consummation, its own consumption. Inaccessible, the
invisible is the most high. This expression—perhaps inhabited by the Platonic
resonances Levinas evokes, but more so by others more readily recognizable—
tears apart, by the superlative excess, the spatial literality of the metaphor. No
matter how high it is, height is always accessible; the most high, however, is
higher than height. No addition of more height will ever measure it. It does not
belong to space, is not of this world. But what necessity compels this inscription
of language in space at the very moment when it exceeds space? And if the pole
of metaphysical transcendence is a spatial non-height, what, in the last analysis,
legitimates the expression of trans-ascendance, borrowed from Jean Wahl? The
theme of the face perhaps will help us understand it.

The ego is the same. The alterity or negativity interior to the ego, the interior
difference, is but an appearance: an *illusion,* a "play of the Same," the "mode
of identification" of an ego whose essential moments are called body, possession, home, economy, etc. Levinas devotes some splendid descriptions to them.
But this play of the same is not monotonous, is not repeated as monologue and
formal tautology. As the work of identification and the concrete production of
egoity, it entails a *certain* negativity. A finite negativity, an internal and relative

modification through which the ego affects itself by itself, within its own movement of identification. Thus it alters itself toward itself within itself. The resistance to work, by provoking it, remains a moment of the same, a finite moment
that forms a system and a totality with the agent. It necessarily follows, then, that
Levinas will describe *history* as a blinding to the other, and as the laborious
procession of the same. One may wonder whether history can be history, *if there
is history,* when negativity is enclosed within the circle of the same, and when
work does not truly meet alterity, providing itself with its own resistance. One
wonders whether history itself does not begin with this relationship to the other
which Levinas places beyond history. The framework of this question should
govern the entire reading of *Totality and Infinity.* In any event, one observes
the displacement of the concept of historicity of which we spoke above. It
must be acknowledged that without this displacement no anti-Hegelianism could
be logically consequent. The *necessary* condition for this anti-Hegelianism is
therefore fulfilled.

A precaution must be made: the theme of the concrete (nonformal) tautology
or of false (finite) heterology—this very difficult theme is proposed rather discreetly at the beginning of *Totality and Infinity,* but it conditions every affirmation made in the book. If negativity (work, history, etc.) never has a relation to
the other, if the other is not the simple negation of the same, then neither
separation nor metaphysical transcendence can be conceived under the category
of negativity. Just as—as we saw above—simple internal consciousness could
not provide itself with time and with the absolute alterity of every instant without
the irruption of the totally-other, so the ego cannot engender alterity within itself
without encountering the Other.

If one is not convinced by these initial propositions authorizing the equation of
the ego and the same, one never will be. If one does not follow Levinas when he
affirms that the things offered to work or to desire—in the Hegelian sense: for
example, natural objectivity—belong to the ego, to the ego's economy (to the
same), and do not offer the absolute resistance reserved for the other (Others); if
one is tempted to think that this last resistance supposes, in its innermost meaning, the possibility of the resistance of things—the existence of the world which
is not myself and in which I am, in as original a way as one may wish, for
example as origin of the world within the world, although it is not to be confused
with this possibility; if one does not follow Levinas when he affirms that the true
resistance to the same is not that of things, is not *real* but rather is *intelligible,* [24]
and if one rebels against the notion of a purely intelligible resistance, then in all
these cases one will follow Levinas no further. Nor will one be able to follow,
without an indefinable malaise, the conceptual operations liberated by the
classical dissymetry of the same and other, as they are overturned; or (as a
classical mind would say), while they *feign* permitting themselves to be overturned, all the while remaining the *same,* impassive beneath an algebraic substitution.

What, then, is this encounter with the absolutely-other? Neither representation, nor limitation, nor conceptual relation to the same. The ego and the other do not permit themselves to be dominated or made into totalities by a concept of relationship. And first of all because the concept (material of language), which is always *given to the other,* cannot encompass the other, cannot include the other. The dative or vocative dimension which opens the original direction of language, cannot lend itself to inclusion in and modification by the accusative or attributive dimension of the object without violence. Language, therefore, cannot make its own possibility a totality and *include* within itself its own origin or its own end.

Truthfully, one does not have to wonder *what* this encounter is. It is *the* encounter, the only way out, the only adventuring outside oneself toward the unforeseeably-other. *Without hope of return.* In every sense of this expression, which is why this eschatology which awaits *nothing* sometimes appears infinitely hopeless. Truthfully, in *La trace de l'autre* eschatology does not only "appear" hopeless. It is given as such, and renunciation belongs to its essential meaning. In describing liturgy, desire, and the work of art as ruptures of the Economy and the Odyssey, as the impossibility of return to the same, Levinas speaks of an "eschatology without hope for the self or without liberation in my time."

Therefore, there is no way to conceptualize the encounter: it is made possible by the other, the unforeseeable "resistant to all categories." Concepts suppose an anticipation, a horizon within which alterity is amortized as soon as it is announced precisely because it has let itself be foreseen. The infinitely-other cannot be bound by a concept, cannot be thought on the basis of a horizon; for a horizon is always a horizon of the same, the elementary unity within which eruptions and surprises are always welcomed by understanding and recognized. Thus we are obliged to think in opposition to the truisms which we believed— which we still cannot not believe—to be the very ether of our thought and language. To attempt to think the opposite is stifling. And it is a question not only of thinking the opposite which is still in complicity with the classical alternatives, but of liberating thought and its language for the encounter occurring beyond these alternatives. Doubtless this encounter, which for the first time does not take the form of an intuitive contact (in ethics, in the sense given to it by Levinas, the principal, central prohibition is that of contact) but the form of a separation (encounter as separation, another rupture of "formal logic").[25] Doubtless this encounter of the unforeseeable *itself* is the only possible opening of time, the only pure future, the only pure expenditure *beyond* history as economy. But this future, this beyond, is not another time, a day after history. It is *present* at the heart of experience. Present not as a total presence but as a *trace.* Therefore, before all dogmas, all conversions, all articles of faith or philosophy, experience itself is eschatological at its origin and in each of its aspects.

Face to face with the other within a glance *and* a speech which both maintain distance and interrupt all totalities, this being-together as separation precedes or exceeds society, collectivity, community. Levinas calls it *religion.* It opens ethics. The ethical relation is a religious relation (*Difficile liberté* [hereafter *DL*]). Not *a* religion, but *the* religion, the religiosity of the religious. This transcendence beyond negativity is not accomplished by an intuition of a positive presence; it "only institutes language at the point where neither no nor yes is the first word" (*TI*) but an interrogation. Not a theoretical interrogation, however, but a total question, a distress and denuding, a supplication, a demanding prayer addressed to a freedom, that is, to a commandment: the only possible ethical imperative, the only incarnated nonviolence in that it is respect for the other. An immediate respect for the other himself—one might say, although without following any literal indication by Levinas—because it does not pass through the neutral element of the universal, and through respect—in the Kantian sense[26]— for the law.

This restitution of metaphysics then permits the radicalization and systematization of the previous reductions of phenomenology and ontology. The act of *seeing* is at the outset a respectful knowledge, and light passes for the medium which—as faithfully and neutrally as possible, as a third party—permits the known to be. It is not by chance that the theoretical relation has been the preferred framework of the metaphysical relation (cf. *TI*). When the third term, in its most neutral indetermination, is the light of Being—which is neither a being nor a non-being, while the same and the other *are*—the theoretical relation is ontology. According to Levinas, the latter always brings the other back into the midst of the same and does so for the benefit of the unity of Being. And the theoretical freedom which accedes to the thought of Being is but the identification of the same, the light in which I provide myself with what I claim to encounter, that is, an *economic* freedom, in the particular sense Levinas gives to this word. A freedom in immanence, a premetaphysical, one could almost say a physical, freedom, an empirical freedom, even if it is called reason within history. Reason would be nature. Metaphysics begins when theory criticizes itself as ontology, as the dogmatism and spontaneity of the same, and when metaphysics, in departing from itself, lets itself be put into question by the other in the movement of ethics. Although in fact it is secondary, metaphysics as the critique of ontology is rightfully and philosophically primary. If it is true that "Western philosophy most often has been an ontology" dominated since Socrates by a Reason which receives only what it gives itself,[27] a Reason which does nothing but recall itself to itself, and if ontology is tautotology and egology, then it has always *neutralized* the other, in every sense of the word. Phenomenological neutralization, one might be tempted to say, gives the most subtle and modern form to this historical, political and authoritarian neutralization. Only metaphysics can free the other from the light of Being or from the phenomenon which "takes away from Being its resistance."

Heideggerean "ontology," despite its seductive appearance, would not escape this framework. It would still remain "egology" and even "egoism": "*Sein und*

Zeit has argued perhaps but one sole thesis: Being is inseparable from the comprehension of Being (which unfolds as time); Being is already an appeal to
subjectivity. The primacy of ontology for Heidegger does not rest on the truism:
'to know the *existent* it is necessary to have comprehended the Being of the
existent.' To affirm the priority of *Being* over the *existent* is, indeed, to decide
the essence of philosophy; it is to subordinate the relation with *someone,* who is
an existent (the ethical relation), to a relation with the *Being of the existent,*
which, impersonal, permits the apprehension, the domination of the existent (a
relationship of knowing), subordinates justice to freedom . . . the mode of remaining the same in the midst of the other'' (*TI,* p. 45). Despite all the misunderstandings which may be embedded in this treatment of Heideggerean
thought—we will study them for themselves later—Levinas's intention, in any
event, seems clear. The neutral thought of Being neutralizes the Other as a being:
''Ontology as first philosophy is a philosophy of power'' (*TI,* p. 46), a philosophy of the neutral, the tyranny of the state as an anonymous and inhuman
universality. Here we find the premises for a critique of the state's alienation
whose anti-Hegelianism would be neither subjectivist, nor Marxist; nor anar-
chist, for it is a philosophy of the ''principle, which can be only as a commandment.'' The Heideggerean ''possibilities'' remain powers. Although they are
pretechnical and preobjective, they are nonetheless oppressive and possessive.
By another paradox, the philosophy of the neutral communicates with a philosophy of the site, of rootedness, of pagan violence, of ravishment, of enthusiasm,
a philosophy offered up to the sacred, that is, to the anonymous divinity, the
divinity without the Deity (*DL*). It is a ''shameful materialism'' in that it is
complete, for at heart materialism is not primarily sensualism, but a recognized
primacy of the neutral (*TI*). The notion of *primacy,* employed so frequently by
Levinas, well translates the gesture of his entire critique. According to the
indication present in the notion of *archia,* the philosophical beginning is immediately transposed into an ethical or philosophical command. From the very
first, *primacy* indicates principle *and* chief. All the classical concepts interrogated by Levinas are thus dragged toward the *agora,* summoned to justify themselves in an ethico-political language that they have not always sought—or
believed that they sought—to speak, summoned to transpose themselves into this
language by confessing their violent aims. Yet they already spoke this language
in the city, and spoke it well, by means of the detours of philosophy and despite
philosophy's apparent disinterest, notwithstanding its eventual return to power.
Here we find the premises for a non-Marxist reading of philosophy as ideology.
The ways chosen by Levinas are decidedly difficult: rejecting idealism and the
philosophies of subjectivity, he must also denounce the neutrality of a ''Logos
which is the verb of no one'' (*TI*). (It could no doubt be demonstrated that
Levinas, uncomfortably situated in the difference between Husserl and
Heidegger—and, indeed, by virtue of the history of his thought—always

criticizes the one in a style and according to a scheme borrowed from the other, and finishes by sending them off into the wings together as partners in the "play of the same" and as accomplices in the same historico-philosophical coup.) The verb must not only be the verb of someone—it must overflow, in its movement toward the other, what is called the speaking subject. Neither the philosophies of the neutral nor the philosophies of subjectivity can acknowledge this trajectory of speech that no speech can make into a totality. By definition, if the other is the other, and if all speech is for the other, no logos as absolute knowledge can *comprehend* dialogue and the trajectory toward the other. This incomprehensibility, this rupture of logos is not the beginning of irrationalism but the wound or inspiration which opens speech and then makes possible every logos or every rationalism. A total logos still, in order to be logos, would have to let itself be proffered toward the other beyond its own totality. If, for example, there is an ontology or a logos of the comprehension of the Being (of beings), it is in that "already the comprehension of Being is said to the existent, who again arises behind the theme in which he is presented. This 'saying to the other'—this relationship to the other as interlocutor, this relation with an *existent*—precedes all ontology; it is the ultimate relation in Being. Ontology presupposes metaphysics" (*TI,* pp. 47–48). "Prior to the unveiling of Being in general, as the basis of knowledge and meaning of Being, there is a relationship with the existent which is expressed; before the ontological level, the ethical level." Ethics is therefore metaphysics. "Morality is not a branch of philosophy, but first philosophy."

The absolute overflowing of ontology—as the totality and unity of the same: Being—by the other occurs as infinity because no totality can constrain it. The infinity irreducible to the *representation* of infinity, the infinity exceeding the ideation in which it is thought, thought of as more than I can think, as that which cannot be an object or a simple "objective reality" of the idea—such is the pole of metaphysical transcendence. After the *epekeina tes ousias,* the Cartesian idea of infinity made metaphysics emerge for a second time in Western ontology. But what neither Plato nor Descartes recognized (along with several others, if we may be permitted not to believe to the same extent as Levinas in their solitude among the philosophical crowd which understands neither true transcendence nor the strange idea of Infinity) is that the expression of this infinity is the *face.*

The face is not only a visage which may be the surface of things or animal facies, aspect, or species. It is not only, following the origin of the word, what is *seen,* seen because it is naked. It is also that which sees. Not so much that which sees things—a theoretical relation—but that which exchanges its glance. The visage is a face only in the face-to-face. As Scheler said (but our citation must not make us forget that Levinas is nothing less than Schelerian): "I see not only the eyes of an other, I see also that he looks at me."

Did not Hegel say this too? "If we ask ourselves now in which particular organ the soul appears as such in its entirety we shall at once point to the eye. For in the eye the soul concentrates itself; it not merely uses the eye as its instrument, but is itself therein manifest. We have, however, already stated, when referring to the external covering of the human body, that in contrast with the bodies of animals, the heart of life pulses through and throughout it. And in much the same sense it can be asserted of art that it has to invent every point of the external appearance into the direct testimony of the human eye, which is the source of soul-life, and reveals spirit.''[28] This is perhaps the occasion to emphasize, concerning a precise point, a theme that we will enlarge upon later: Levinas is very close to Hegel, much closer than he admits, and at the very moment when he is apparently opposed to Hegel in the most radical fashion. This is a situation he must share with all anti-Hegelian thinkers, and whose final significance calls for much thought. Here, in particular, on the relations between desire and the eye, between sound and theory, the convergence is as profound as the difference, being neither simply added to nor juxtaposed with it. In effect, like Levinas Hegel thought that the eye, not aiming at "consumption," suspends desire. It is the very limit of desire (and perhaps, thereby, its resource) and is the first theoretical sense. We must not conceive light and the eye's opening on the basis of any physiology, but on the basis of the relation between death and desire. After having spoken of taste, touch, and smell, Hegel again writes, in the *Aesthetics:* "*Sight,* on the other hand, possesses a purely ideal relation to objects by means of light, a material which is at the same time immaterial, and which suffers on its part the objects to continue in their free self-subsistence, making them appear and re-appear, but which does not, as the atmosphere or fire does, consume them actively either by imperceptible degrees or patently. Everything, then is an object of the appetiteless vision, [la vue exempte de désirs] which, however, in so far as it remains unimpaired in its integrity, merely is disclosed in its form and colour.''[29]

This neutralization of desire is what makes sight excellent for Hegel. But for Levinas, this neutralization is also, and for the same reasons, the first violence, even though the face is not what it is when the glance is absent. Violence, then, would be the solitude of a mute glance, of a face without speech, *the abstraction* of seeing. According to Levinas the glance *by itself,* contrary to what one may be led to believe, does not *respect* the other. Respect, beyond grasp and contact, beyond touch, smell and taste, can be only as desire, and metaphysical desire does not seek to consume, as do Hegelian desire or need. This is why Levinas places sound above light. ("Thought is language and is thought in an element analogous to sound and not to light." What does this *analogy* mean here, a difference and a resemblance, a relation between the sensible sound and the sound of thought as intelligible speech, between sensibility and signification, the senses and sense? This is a question also posed by Hegel, admiring the word *Sinn.*)

In *Totality and Infinity* the movement of metaphysics is thus also the transcendence of hearing in relation to seeing. But in Hegel's *Aesthetics* too: "The remaining ideal sense is hearing. This is in signal contrast to the one just described. Hearing is concerned with the tone, rather than the form and colour of an object, with the vibration of what is corporeal; it requires no process of dissolution, as the sense of smell requires, but merely a trembling of the object, by which the same is in no wise impoverished. This ideal motion, in which through its sound what is as it were the simple individuality [*subjectivité*] the soul of the material thing expresses itself, the ear receives also in an ideal way, just as the eye shape and colour, and suffers thereby what is ideal or not external in the object to appeal to what is spiritual or non-corporeal."[30] But:

> Hearing, which, as also the sight, does not belong to the senses of action [*sens pratiques*] but those of contemplation [*sens théoriques*]; and is, in fact, still more ideal than sight. For the unruffled, aesthetic observation of works of art no doubt permits the objects to stand out quietly in their freedom just as they are without any desire to impair that effect in any way; but that which it apprehends is not that which is itself essentially ideally composed, but rather on the contrary, that which receives its consistency in its sensuous existence. The ear, on the contrary, receives the result of that ideal vibration of material substance, without placing itself in a practical relation towards the objects, a result by means of which it is no longer the material object in its repose, but the first example of the more ideal activity of the soul itself which is apprehended.[31]

The question of the analogy would thus lead us back to the notion of *trembling*, which seems to us decisive in Hegel's *Aesthetics* in that it opens the passage to ideality. Further, in order to confront systematically Hegel's and Levinas's thoughts on the theme of the face, one would have to consult not only the pages of the *Phenomenology of the Mind* devoted to physiognomy, but also paragraph 411 of the *Encyclopedia* on mind, face, and language.

For reasons now familiar to us, the face-to-face eludes every category. For within it the face is given simultaneously as expression and as speech. Not only as glance, but as the original unity of glance and speech, eyes and mouth, that speaks, but also pronounces its hunger. Thus it is also that which *hears* the invisible, for "thought is language," and "is thought in an element analogous to sound and not to light." This unity of the face precedes, in its signification, the dispersion of senses and organs of sensibility. Its signification is therefore irreducible. Moreover, the face does not *signify*. It does not incarnate, envelop, or signal anything other than self, soul, subjectivity, etc. Thought is speech, and is therefore immediately face. In this, the thematic of the face belongs to the most modern philosophy of language and of the body itself. The other is not signaled by his face, he is this face: "Absolutely present, in his face, the Other—without any metaphor—faces me."[32] The other, therefore, is given "in person" and

without allegory only in the face. Let us recall what Feuerbach, who also made
the themes of height, substance, and face communicate with each other, said on
this subject: "That which is situated highest in space is also in its quality the
highest part of man, that which is closest to him, that which one can no longer
separate from him—and this is his *head*. If I see a man's head, it is the man
himself who I see; but if I only see his torso, I see no more than his torso."[33]
That which can no longer be separated from . . . is substance in its essential
predicates and "in itself." Levinas also often says *kath' auto* and "substance" in
speaking of the other as face. The face is presence, *ousia.*

The face is not a metaphor, not a figure. The discourse on the face is neither
allegory nor, as one might be tempted to believe, prosopopoeia. Consequently
the height of the face (in relation to the rest of the body) perhaps determines *in
part* (in part only, as we will see later) the expression *most-high* which we
examined above. If the height of the most-high, as we might be tempted to say,
does not belong to space (and this is why the superlative must destroy space as it
constructs the metaphor), it is not because it is foreign to space, but because
(within) space it is the origin of space, orienting space through speech and
glance, through the face, the chief who commands body and space from above.
(Aristotle, indeed, compares the transcendental principle of the good to the chief
of the armies; however, he overlooks both the face, and the fact that the god of
the armies is the Face.) The face does not signify, does not present itself as a
sign, but *expresses itself,* offering itself *in person,* in itself, *kath' auto:* "the thing
in itself expresses itself." To express oneself is to be *behind* the sign. To be
behind the sign: is this not, *first of all,* to be capable of attending (to) one's
speech, to assist it, according to the expression used in the *Phaedrus* as argument
against Theuth (or Hermes)—an expression Levinas makes his own on several
occasions. Only living speech, in its mastery and magisteriality, is able to assist
itself; and only living speech is expression and not a servile sign—on the condition
that it is truly speech, "the creative voice, and not the accomplice voice which is
a servant" (E. Jabès). And we know that all the gods of writing (Greece, Egypt,
Assyria, Babylonia) have the status of auxiliary gods, servile secretaries of the
great god, lunar and clever couriers who occasionally dethrone the king of the
gods by dishonorable means. The written and the work are not expressions but
signs for Levinas.

Along with the reference to the *epekeina tes ousias,* this is at very least the
second Platonic theme of *Totality and Infinity.* It is also to be found in Nicholas
of Cusa. "While the worker abandons his work, which then pursues its independent destiny, the verb of the professor is inseparable from the very person who
proffers it."[34] The critique of the work thus implied separates Hegel from
Nicholas of Cusa for one time at least.

This problematic requires separate consideration in and of itself. Is "oral
discourse" "the plenitude of discourse?" Or, is it, in another sense, the "speech

activity'' in which I "am absent, missing from my products" which then betray me more than they express me? Is the "frankness" of expression essentially an aspect of living speech for him who is not God? This question is meaningless for Levinas, who conceives the face in terms of the "resemblance" of man and God. Are not weight and magisterial instruction an aspect of writing? Is it not possible to invert all of Levinas's statements on this point? By showing, for example, that writing can assist itself, for it *has time* and freedom, escaping better than speech from empirical urgencies. That, by neutralizing the demands of empirical "economy," writing's essence is more "metaphysical" (in Levinas's sense) than speech? That the writer absents himself better, that is, expresses himself better as other, addresses himself to the other more effectively than the man of speech? And that, in depriving himself of the *enjoyments* and effects of his signs, the writer more effectively renounces violence? It is true that he perhaps intends only to multiply his signs to infinity, thus forgetting—at very least—the other, the infinitely other as death, and thus practicing writing as *deferral* and as an *economy of death*. The limit between violence and nonviolence is perhaps not between speech and writing but within each of them. The thematic of the *trace* (which Levinas distinguishes from the effect, the path, or the sign which is not related to the other as the invisible absolute) should lead to a certain rehabilitation of writing. Is not the "He" whom transcendence and generous absence uniquely announce in the trace more readily the author of writing than of speech? The work, trans-economy, the pure expenditure as determined by Levinas, is neither play nor death. It is not simply to be confused with either the letter or with speech. It is not a sign, and therefore its concept cannot include the concept of the work found in *Totality and Infinity*. Levinas is thus at once quite close to and quite far from Nietzsche and Bataille.

Maurice Blanchot speaks of his disagreement with this preeminence of oral discourse, which resembles "the tranquil humanist and socratic speech which brings us close to the speaker."[35] Moreover, how could Hebraism belittle the letter, in praise of which Levinas writes so well? For example:_"To admit the action of literature on men—this is perhaps the ultimate wisdom of the West, in which the people of the Bible will be recognized" (*DL*); and "The spirit is free in the letter, and subjugated in the root"; and then, "To love the Torah more than God" is "protection against the madness of a direct contact with the Sacred" (*DL*). The aspect of living and original speech *itself* which Levinas seeks to save is clear. Without its possibility, outside its horizon, writing is nothing. In this sense, writing will always be secondary. To liberate it from this possibility and this horizon, from this essential secondariness, is to deny it as writing, and to leave room for a grammar or a lexicon without language, for cybernetics or electronics. But it is only in God that speech, as presence, as the origin and horizon of writing, is realized without defect. One would have to be able to show that only this reference to the speech of God distinguishes Levinas's intentions

from those of Socrates in the *Phaedrus;* and that for a thought of original finitude
this distinction is no longer possible. And that if writing is secondary at this
point, nothing, however, has occurred before it.

As for Levinas's ties to Blanchot, it seems to us that despite the frequent
rapprochements he proposes, the profound and incontestable affinities between
them all belong to the critical and negative moment, within the hollow space of
finitude in which messianic eschatology comes to resonate, within the expectation of expectation in which Levinas has begun to hear a response. This response
is still called expectation, of course, but Levinas no longer has to await it. The
affinity ceases, it seems to us, at the moment when eschatalogical positivity
retrospectively comes to illuminate the common route, to lift the finitude and
pure negativity of the question, when the neutral is determined. Blanchot could
probably extend over all of Levinas's propositions what he says about the dissymmetry within the space of communication: "Here, I believe, is what is decisive
in the affirmation which we must hear, and which must be maintained indepen-
dently of the theological context in which it occurs." But is this possible?
Independent of its "theological context" (an expression that Levinas would most
likely reject) does not this entire discourse collapse?

To be behind the sign which is in the world is *afterward* to remain invisible to
the world within epiphany. In the face, the other is given over in person *as other,*
that is, as that which does not reveal itself, as that which cannot be made
thematic. I could not possibly speak of the Other, make of the Other a theme,
pronounce the Other as object, in the accusative. I can only, I *must* only speak to
the other; that is, I must call him in the vocative, which is not a category, a *case*
of speech, but, rather the bursting forth, the very raising up of speech. Categories
must be missing for the Other not to be overlooked; but for the Other not to be
overlooked, He must present himself as absence, and must appear as nonphenomenal. Always behind its signs and its works, always within its secret interior,
and forever discreet, interrupting all historical totalities through its freedom of
speech, the face is not "of this world." It is the origin of the world. I can speak
of it only by speaking *to it;* and I *may* reach it only as I *must* reach it. But I must
only *reach* it as the inaccessible, the invisible, the intangible. Secret, separate,
invisible like Gyjès ("the very condition of man")—this is the very state, the
very status of what is called the *psyche*. This absolute separation, this natural
atheism, this lying freedom in which truth and discourse take root—all this is a
"great glory for the creator." An affirmation which, for once at least, is hardly
disorienting.

For the face to present the other without metaphor, speech must not only
translate thought. Thought, of course, already must be speech, but above all the
body must also remain a language. Rational knowledge must not be the first word
of words. If one is to believe Levinas, Husserl and Heidegger, at bottom,
accepted the classical subordination of language to thought, and body to lan-

guage. On the contrary, Merleau-Ponty, "better than others," would have shown "that disincarnated thought, thinking of speech before speaking it, thought as constitutive of the world of speech, was a myth." But by the force of a movement proper to Levinas, he accepts this extreme "modern" audacity only to redirect it toward an infinitism that this audacity itself must suppose, according to himself; and the form of this infinitism is often quite classical, pre-Kantian rather than Hegelian. Thus, the themes of one's own body as language and as intentionality cannot get around the classical dangers, and thought cannot *first* be language unless it is acknowledged that thought is *first* and irreducibly a relation to the other (which it seems to us did not escape Merleau-Ponty);[36] but a relation to an irreducible other who summons me without possibility of return from without, for in this order is presented the infinity which no thought can enclose and which forbids all monologue "even if it had 'the corporal intentionality' of Merleau-Ponty." Despite all appearances and all habitual thinking, it must be acknowledged here that the dissociation of thought and language, and the subordination of the latter to the former, are proper to a philosophy of finitude. And this demonstration would refer us once more to the Cartesian Cogito of the third *Meditation*, beyond Merleau-Ponty, Heidegger, and Husserl. And does so according to a schema that seems to us to support the entirety of Levinas's thought: the other is the other only if his alterity is absolutely irreducible, that is, infinitely irreducible; and the infinitely Other can only be Infinity.

As speech and glance the face is not in the world, since it opens and exceeds the totality. This is why it marks the limit of all power, of all violence, and the origin of the ethical. In a sense, murder is always directed against the face, but thereby always misses it. "Murder exerts a power over that which escapes power. Still, a power, for the face expresses itself in the sensible; but already impotence, because the face rips apart the sensible." "The Other is the only being who I may wish to kill," but the only one, also, who orders that "thou shalt commit no murders," and thus absolutely limits my power. Not by opposing me with another force in the world, but by speaking to me, and by looking at me from an *other* origin of the world, from that which no finite power can restrict: the strange, unthinkable notion of unreal resistance. Since his 1953 article (already cited), Levinas no longer, to our knowledge, speaks of "intelligible resistance"—an expression whose sense still belongs at least literally, to the realm of the same, and which was utilized, apparently, only to signify an unreal resistance. In *Totality and Infinity* Levinas speaks of "ethical resistance."

That which escapes the concept as power, therefore, is not existence in general, but the existence of the Other. And first of all because, despite all appearances, there is no concept of the Other. We would have to reflect upon this word "Other" [*Autrui*] in an artisan-like way, in the realm where philosophy and philology constrain each other, uniting their concerns and their rigor—this word "Other" circumscribed in silence by the capital letter which ever increases the neutrality of the *other,* and which we use so familiarly, even though it is the very disorder of our conceptuality. Is it only a common noun without concept? But, first of all, is it a noun? It is not an adjective, or a pronoun; therefore it is a substantive—and such it is classed by the dictionaries—but a substantive which is not, as usual, a species of noun: neither common noun, for it cannot take, as in the category of the other in general, the *heteron,* the definite article. Nor the plural. "In the chancellery location *l'autrui* [the Other], *le* must not be understood as the article of *autrui:* implied is *property, rights: the property, the rights of Others,"* notes Littré, who began thus: *"Autrui,* from *alter-huic,* this other, in regimen: this is why *autrui* is always in regimen, and why *autrui* is less general than *les autres* [the others]." Thus, without making language the accident of thought, we would have to account for this: that, within language, that which is always "in regimen" and in the least generality is, in its meaning, undeclinable and beyond genre. What is the origin of this *case* of meaning in language, of this *regimen* in which language places meaning? Nor is *autrui* a proper noun, even though its anonymity signifies but the unnamable source of every proper noun. We would have to examine patiently what emerges in language when the Greek conception of *heteron* seems to run out of breath when faced by the *alter-huic;* what happens when the *heteron* seems to become incapable of mastering what it alone, however, is able to precomprehend by concealing it as alterity (other in general), and which, in return, will reveal to *heteron* its irreducible center of meaning (the other *as* Other [*autrui*]). We would have to examine the complicity of the concealment and the precomprehension which does not occur within a conceptual movement, for the French word *autrui* does not designate a category of the genre *autre.* We would have to examine this thought of the other *in general* (which is not a genre), the Greek thought within which this nonspecific *difference* realizes (itself in) our history. Or, rather: what does *autre* mean before its Greek determination as *heteron,* and its Judeo-Christian determination as *autrui?* This is the kind of question which Levinas seems to contest profoundly: according to him, only the irruption of the Other permits access to the absolute and to the irreducible alterity of the other. We would have to examine, therefore, this *Huic* of *autrui* whose transcendence is not yet that of a thou. Here, Levinas's opposition to Buber or to Gabriel Marcel becomes meaningful. After opposing the magisterial height of the *You* to the intimate reciprocity of the Me-Thou (*TI*), Levinas seems to move toward a philosophy of the *Ille,* of the *He* (*Il*) in his meditation of the *Trace* (that is, of the neighbor as a distant stranger, according to the original ambiguity of the word translated as the "neighbor" to be loved). A philosophy of the *He* who would not be an impersonal object opposed to the *thou,* but the invisible transcendence of the Other.[37] If the face's expression is not revelation, then the unrevealable is expressed beyond all thematization, beyond all constitutive analysis, all phenomenology. At its various stages, the transcendental constitution of the *alter ego*—of which Husserl attempts to reassemble the description in the fifth of the *Cartesian Meditations*—would presuppose that whose genesis it allegedly traces (according to Levinas). The Other could not be constituted as an alter ego, as a phenomenon of the ego, by and for a nomadic subject proceeding by appresentative analogy. All the difficulties encountered by Husserl could be "surmounted" if the ethical relationship were recognized as the original face-to-face, as the emergence of absolute alterity, the emergence of an exteriority which can be neither derived, nor engendered, nor constituted on the basis of anything other than itself. An absolute outside, an exteriority infinitely overflowing the monad of the *ego cogito*. Here again, Descartes against Husserl, the Descartes of the *Third Meditation* allegedly misconstrued by Husserl. While Descartes, in his reflections on the *cogito,* becomes aware that infinity not only cannot be constituted as a (dubitable) object, but has already made infinity possible as a *cogito* overflowing the object, (a nonspatial overflowing, against which metaphor shatters), Husserl, on the other hand, "sees in the cogito a subjectivity with no support from without, constituting the idea of infinity itself, and providing himself with it as object" *(TI)*. Now, the infinite(-ly other) cannot be an object because it is speech, the origin of meaning and the world. Therefore, no phenomenology can account for ethics, speech, and justice.

But if all justice begins with speech, all speech is not just. Rhetoric may amount to the violence of theory, which *reduces* the other when it *leads* the other, whether through psychology, demagogy, or even pedagogy which is not instruction. The latter descends from the heights of the master, whose absolute exteriority does not impair the disciple's freedom. Beyond rhetoric, speech uncovers the nudity of the face, without which no nudity would have any meaning. All nudity, "even the nudity of the body experienced in shame," is a "figure of speech" in relation to the nonmetaphorical nudity of the face. This is already quite explicit in *Is Ontology Fundamental?* "The nudity of the face is not a stylistic figure." And it is shown, still in the form of negative theology, that this nudity is not even an opening, for an opening is relative to a "surrounding plenitude." The word "nudity" thus destroys itself after serving to indicate something beyond itself. An entire reading and interrogation of *Totality and Infinity* could be developed around this affirmation. For this affirmation seems to us quite implicitly—perhaps even too implicitly—to support the decisive division between what Levinas calls the face and that which is *Beyond the Face,* the section which considers, aside from the *Phenomenology of Eros,* Love, Fecundity, and Time. This nudity of the face, speech, and glance, being neither theory nor theorem, is offered and exposed as denuding, as demanding supplication, as the unthinkable únity of a speech able to assist itself and a glance which calls for assistance.

Asymmetry, non-light, and commandment then would be violence and injustice themselves—and, indeed, so they are commonly understood—if they estab-

lished relations between finite beings, or if the other was but a negative determination of the (finite or infinite) same. But we have seen that this is not the case.
Infinity (as infinitely other) cannot be violent as is totality (which is thus always
defined by Levinas, always determined by an option, that is, an initial decision of
his discourse, as *finite totality:* totality, for Levinas, means a finite totality. This
functions as a silent axiom.) This is why God alone keeps Levinas's world from
being a world of the pure and worst violence, a world of immorality itself. The
structures of living and naked experience described by Levinas are the very
structures of a world in which war would rage—strange conditional—if the
infinitely other were not infinity, if there were, by chance, one naked man, finite
and alone. But in this case, Levinas would no doubt say, there no longer would
be any war, for there would be neither face nor true asymmetry. Therefore the
naked and living experience in which God has *already* begun to speak could no
longer be our concern. In other words, in a world where the face would be fully
respected (as that which is not of this world), there no longer would be war. In a
world where the face no longer would be absolutely respected, where there no
longer would be a face, there would be no more cause for war. God, therefore, is
implicated in war. His name too, like the name of peace, is a function within the
system of war, the only system whose basis permits us to speak, the only system
whose language may ever be spoken. With or without God, there would be no
war. War supposes and excludes God. We can have a relation to God only within
such a system. Therefore war—*for war there is*—is the difference between the
face and the finite world without a face. But is not this difference that which has
always been called the world, in which the absence-presence of God *plays*? Only
the play of the world permits us *to think the essence* of God. In a sense that our
language—and Levinas's also—accommodates poorly the play of the world
precedes God.

The face-to-face, then, is not originally determined by Levinas as the vis-à-vis
of two equal and upright men. The latter supposes the face-to-face of the man
with bent neck and eyes raised toward the God on high. Language is indeed the
possibility of the face-to-face and of being-upright, but it does not exclude
inferiority, the humility of the glance at the father as the glance of the child made
in memory of having been expulsed before knowing how to walk, and of having
been delivered, prone and *infans,* into the hands of the adult masters. Man, one
might say, is a God arrived too early, that is, a God who knows himself forever
late in relation to the already-there of Being. But it is certain that these last
remarks—and this is the least one might say—do not belong to the genre of
commentary. And we are not referring, here, to the themes known under the
name of psychoanalysis, nor to the embryological or anthropological hypothesis
on the structurally premature birth of man's offspring. Let it suffice us to know
that man is born.[38]

God's name is often mentioned, but this return to experience, and to "things themselves,'' as a relation to the infinite(ly) other is not theological, even if it alone is capable, afterward, of founding theological discourse, which up to now has ''imprudently considered the idea of the relationship between God and creation in ontological terms'' *(TI)*. The foundation of metaphysics—in Levinas's sense—is to be encountered in the return to things themselves, where we find the common root of humanism and theology: the resemblance between man and God, man's visage and the Face of God. ''The Other resembles God'' *(ibid.)*. Via the passageway of this resemblance, man's speech can be lifted up toward God, an almost unheard of *analogy* which is the very movement of Levinas's discourse on discourse. Analogy as dialogue with God: ''Discourse is discourse with God . . . . Metaphysics is the essence of this language with God.'' Discourse with God, and not in God as *participation*. Discourse with God, and not discourse on God and his attributes as *theology*. And the dissymmetry of my relation to the other, this ''curvature of inter-subjective space signifies the divine intention of all truth.'' It ''is, perhaps, the very presence of God.'' Presence as separation, presence-absence—again the break with Parmenides, Spinoza and Hegel, which only ''the idea of creation *ex nihilo*'' can consummate. Presence as separation, presence-absence as resemblance, but a resemblance which is not the ''ontological mark'' of the worker imprinted on his product, or on ''beings created in his image and resemblance'' (Malebranche);[39] a resemblance which can be understood neither in terms of communion or knowledge, nor in terms of participation and incarnation. A resemblance which is neither a sign nor an effect of God. Neither the sign nor the effect exceeds the same. We are ''in the Trace of God.'' A proposition which risks incompatability with every allusion to the ''very presence of God.'' A proposition readily converted into atheism: and if God was an *effect of the trace?* If the idea of divine presence (life, existence, parousia, etc.), if the name of God was but the movement of erasure of the trace in presence? Here it is a question of knowing whether the trace permits us to think presence in its system, or whether the reverse order is the true one. It is doubtless the *true order*. But it is indeed the *order of truth* which is in question. Levinas's thought is maintained between these two postulations.

The face of God disappears forever in showing itself. Thus are reassembled in the unity of their metaphysical signification, at the very heart of the experience denuded by Levinas, the diverse evocations of the Face of Yahweh, who of course is never named in *Totality and Infinity*. The face of Yahweh is the *total* person and the *total* presence of ''the Eternal speaking face to face with Moses,'' but saying to him also: ''Thou canst not see my face: for there shall be no man see me and live . . . . thou shalt stand upon a rock: and it shall come to pass, while my glory passeth by, that I will put thee in a clift of the rock, and will cover thee with my hand while I pass by: And I will take away mine hand, and thou shalt see my back parts: but my face shall not be seen'' (Exodus 33:20–23). The face of God which commands while hiding itself is at once more and less a face than all faces. Whence, perhaps, despite all Levinas's precautions, the equivocal complicity of theology and metaphysics in *Totality and Infinity*. Would Levinas subscribe to this infinitely ambiguous sentence from the *Book of Questions* by Edmond Jabès: "All faces are His; this is why HE has no face"?

The face is neither the face of God nor the figure of man: it is their resemblance. A resemblance which, however, we must think before, or without, the assistance of the Same. [40]

III
Difference and
Eschatology

The questions whose principles we now will attempt to indicate are all, in several senses, questions of language: questions of language and the question of language. But if our commentary has not been too unfaithful, it is already clear that there is no element of Levinas's thought which is not, in and of itself, engaged by such questions.

Of the Original Polemic

First, let it be said, for our own reassurance: the route followed by Levinas's thought is such that all our questions already belong to his own interior dialogue, are displaced into his discourse and only listen to it, from many vantage points and in many ways.

A. Thus, for example, *De l'existence à l'existant* and *Le temps et l'autre* seemed to proscribe the "logic of genre," as well as the categories of the Same and Other. These lacked the originality of the experience to which Levinas wished to lead us back: "To the cosmos which is Plato's world is opposed the world of the mind, in which the implications of eros are not reduced to the logic of genre, in which the ego is substituted for the *same,* and Others for *the other.*" Now, in *Totality and Infinity,* where the categories of Same and Other return in force, the *vis demonstrandi* and very energy of the break with tradition is precisely the adequation of Ego to the Same, and of Others to the Other. Without using these terms themselves, Levinas often warned us against confusing *identity* and *ipseity,* Same and Ego: *idem* and *ipse.* This confusion, which, in a certain way, is immediately practiced by the Greek concept of *autos* and the German concept of *selbst,* does not occur as spontaneously in French; nevertheless, it returns as a kind of silent axiom in *Totality and Infinity.* [41] We have seen this: according to Levinas there would be no interior difference, no fundamental and autochthonous alterity within the ego. If, formerly, interiority, the secret and original separation, had permitted the break with the classical use of the Greek concepts of Same and Other, the amalgamation of Same and Ego (Same and Ego homogenized, and homogenized with the concept, as well as with the finite totality) now permits Levinas to include within the same condemnation both the Greek and the most modern philosophies of subjectivity, the philosophies most careful to distinguish, as did Levinas previously, the Ego from the Same and Others from the other. Without close attention to this double movement, to this progress which seems to contest its own condition and its own initial stage, we would miss the originality of this protest against the concept, the state and totality: it is not made, as is generally the case, in the name of subjective existence, but against it. Simultaneously against Hegel and against Kierkegaard.

Levinas often warns us against confusing—as one is so tempted to do—his anti-Hegelianism with a subjectivism, or with a Kierkegaardian type of existentialism, both of which would remain, according to Levinas, violent and premetaphysical egoisms. "It is not I who do not accept the system, as Kierkegaard thought, it is the other." Can one not wager that Kierkegaard would have been deaf to this distinction? And that he, in turn, would have protested against this conceptuality? It as subjective existence, he would have remarked perhaps, that the other does not accept the system. The other is not myself—and who has ever maintainèd that it is?—but it is *an* Ego, as Levinas must suppose in order to maintain his own discourse. The passage from Ego to other as *an Ego* is the passage to the essential, non-empirical *egoity* of subjective existence *in general*. The philosopher Kierkegaard does not *only* plead for Sören Kierkegaard, ("the egoistic cry of a subjectivity still concerned with Kierkegaard's happiness or salvation"), but for subjective existence in general (a noncontradictory expression); this is why his discourse is philosophical, and not in the realm of empirical egoism. The name of a philosophical subject, when he says *I,* is always, in a certain way, a pseudonym. This is a truth that Kierkegaard adopted systematically, even while protesting against the "possibilization" of individual existence which resists the concept. And is not this essence of subjective existence presupposed by the respect for the other, which can be what it is—the other—only as subjective existence? In order to reject the Kierkegaardian notion of subjective existence Levinas should eliminate even the notions of an *essence* and a *truth* of subjective existence (of the Ego, and primarily of the Ego of the Other). Moreover, this gesture would comply with the logic of the break with phenomenology and ontology. The least one might say is that Levinas does not do so, and cannot do so, without renouncing philosophical discourse. And, if you will, the attempt to achieve an opening toward the beyond of philosophical discourse, by means of philosophical discourse, which can never be shaken off completely, cannot possibly succeed *within language*—and Levinas recognizes that there is no thought before language and outside of it—except by *formally* and *thematically* posing *the question of the relations between belonging and the opening, the question of closure.* Formally—that is by posing it in the most effective and most formal, the most formalized, way possible: not in a *logic,* in other words in a philosophy, but in an inscribed description, in an inscription of the relations between the philosophical and the nonphilosophical, in a kind of unheard of *graphics,* within which philosophical conceptuality would be no more than a *function.*

Let us add, in order to do him *justice,* that Kierkegaard had a sense of the relationship to the irreducibility of the totally-other, not in the egoistic and esthetic here and now, but in the religious beyond of the concept, in the direction of a certain Abraham. And did he not, in turn—for we must let the other speak—see in Ethics, as a moment of Category and Law, the forgetting, in anonymity, of the subjectivity of religion? From his point of view, the ethical moment is Hegelianism itself, and he says so explicitly. Which does not prevent him from reaffirming ethics in repetition, and from reproaching Hegel for not having constituted a morality. It is true that Ethics, in Levinas's sense, is an Ethics without law and without concept, which maintains its non-violent purity only before being determined as concepts and laws. This is not an objection: let us not forget that Levinas does not seek to propose laws or moral rules, does not seek to determine *a* morality, but rather the essence of the ethical relation in general. But as this determination does not offer itself as a *theory* of Ethics, in question then, is an Ethics of Ethics. In this case, it is perhaps serious that this Ethics of Ethics can occasion neither a determined ethics nor determined laws without negating and forgetting itself. Moreover, is this Ethics of Ethics beyond all laws? Is it not the Law of laws? A coherence which breaks down the coherence of the discourse against coherence—the infinite concept, hidden within the protest against the concept.

If juxtaposition with Kierkegaard has often imposed itself upon us, despite the author's own admonitions, we are certain that as concerns the essential in its initial inspiration Levinas's protest against Hegelianism is foreign to Kierkegaard's protest. Inversely, a confrontation of Levinas's thought with Feuerbach's anti-Hegelianism would necessarily uncover, it seems to us, more profound convergences and affinities that the meditation of the Trace would confirm further still. We are speaking here of convergences, and not of influences; primarily because the latter is a notion whose philosophical meaning is not clear to us; and next because, to our knowledge, Levinas nowhere alludes to Feuerbach or to Jaspers.

But why does Levinas return to categories he seemed to have rejected previously in attempting this very difficult passage beyond the debate—which is also a complicity—between Hegelianism and classical anti-Hegelianism?

We are not denouncing, here, an incoherence of language or a contradiction in the system. We are wondering about the meaning of a necessity: the necessity of lodging oneself within traditional conceptuality in order to destroy it. Why did this necessity finally impose itself upon Levinas? Is it an extrinsic necessity? Does it not touch upon only an instrument, only an "expression," which can be put between quotation marks? Or does it hide, rather, some indestructible and unforeseeable resource of the Greek logos? Some unlimited power of envelopment, by which he who attempts to repel it would always already be *overtaken?*

B. During the same period, Levinas had expelled the concept of *exteriority*. The latter referred to an enlightened unity of space which neutralized radical alterity: the relation to the other, the relation of Instants to each other, the relation to Death, etc.—all of which are not relations of an Inside to an Outside. "The relation with the other is a relation with a Mystery. It is the other's exteriority, or rather his alterity, for exteriority is a property of space, and brings the subject back to himself through the light which constitutes his entire being" *(TA)*. Now *Totality and Infinity,* subtitled *Essay on Exteriority,* does not only abundantly employ the notion of exteriority. Levinas also intends to show that *true* exteriority is not spatial, for space is the Site of the Same. Which means that the Site is always a site of the Same. Why is it necessary still to use the word "exteriority" (which, if it has a meaning, if it is not an algebraic X, obstinately beckons toward space and light) in order to signify a nonspatial relationship? And if every "relationship" is spatial, why is it necessary still to designate as a (nonspatial) "relationship" the respect which absolves the other? Why is it necessary to *obliterate* this notion of exteriority without erasing it, without making it illegible, by stating that its truth is its untruth, that *true* exteriority is not spatial, that is, is not exteriority? That it is necessary to state infinity's *excess* over totality *in* the language of totality; that it is necessary to state the other in the language of the Same; that it is necessary to think *true* exteriority as non-*exteriority,* that is, still by means of the Inside-Outside structure and by spatial metaphor; and that it is necessary still to inhabit the metaphor in ruins, to dress oneself in tradition's shreds and the devil's patches—all this means, perhaps, that there is no philosophical logos which must not *first* let itself be expatriated into the structure Inside-Outside. This deportation from its own site toward the Site, toward spatial locality is the *metaphor* congenital to the philosophical logos. Before being a rhetorical procedure within language, metaphor would be the emergence of language itself. And philosophy is only this language; in the best of cases, and in an unaccustomed sense of the expression, philosophy can only *speak it,* state the metaphor *itself,* which amounts to *thinking* the metaphor within the silent horizon of the nonmetaphor: Being. Space being the wound and finitude of birth (of *the* birth) without which one could not even open language, one would not even have a true or false exteriority to speak of. Therefore, one can, by using them, *use up* tradition's words, rub them like a rusty and devalued old coin; one can say that true exteriority is nonexteriority without being interiority, and one can write by crossing out, by crossing out what already has been crossed out: for crossing out writes, still draws in space. The syntax of the Site whose archaic description is not legible *on* the metal of language cannot be erased: it is this metal itself, its too somber solidity and its too shining brilliance. Language, son of earth and sun:

writing. One would attempt in vain, in order to wean language from exteriority
and interiority, in order to wean language from weaning, to forget the words
"inside," "outside," "exterior," "interior," etc., and to banish them by decree; for one would never come across a language without the rupture of space,
an aerial or aquatic language in which, moreover, alterity would be lost more
surely than ever. For the meanings which radiate from Inside-Outside, from
Light-Night, etc., do not only inhabit the proscribed words; they are embedded,
in person or vicariously, at the very heart of conceptuality itself. This is because
they do not signify an immersion *in* space. The structure Inside-Outside or
Day-Night has no meaning *in* a pure space given over to itself and disoriented. It
emerges on the basis of an *included* origin, an *inscribed* eastern horizon which is
neither within nor without space. This text of the glance is *also* the text of
speech. Therefore it can be called Face. But one must not expect, henceforth, to
separate language and space, to empty language of space, to snatch speech away
from light, to speak while a Hand hides Glory. In vain would one exile any given
word ("inside," "outside," "exterior," "interior," etc.), and in vain would
one burn or emprison the letters of light, for language in its entirety already has
awakened as a fall into light. That is, if you will, language arises with the sun.
Even if "the sun is never named . . . its power is in our midst" (Saint-John
Perse). To say that the infinite exteriority of the other *is not* spatial, is *non*-
exteriority and *non*-interiority, to be unable to designate it otherwise than
negatively—is this not to acknowledge that the infinite (also designated negatively in its current positivity: in-finite) cannot be stated? Does this not amount
to acknowledging that the structure "inside-outside," which is language itself,
marks the original finitude of speech and of whatever befalls it? No philosophical
language will ever be able to reduce the naturality of a spatial praxis in language;
and one would have to meditate the unity of Leibniz's distinction between "civil
language" and "scholarly" or philosophical language. And here one would have
to meditate even more patiently the irreducible complicity, despite all of the
philosopher's rhetorical efforts, between everyday language and philosophical
language; or, better, the complicity between certain historical languages and
philosophical language. A certain ineradicable naturality, a certain original
naïveté of philosophical language could be verified for each speculative concept
(except, of course, for the nonconcepts which are the name of *God* and the verb
to be). Philosophical language belongs to a system of language(s). Thereby, its
nonspeculative ancestry always brings a certain equivocality into speculation.
Since this equivocality is original and irreducible, perhaps philosophy must adopt
it, think it and be thought in it, must accommodate duplicity and difference
within speculation, within the very purity of philosophical meaning. No one, it
seems to us, has attempted this more profoundly than Hegel. Without naïvely
using the category of chance, of happy predestination or of the chance encounter,
one would have to do for each concept what Hegel does for the German notion of

Aufhebung, whose equivocality and presence in the German language he calls *delightful:* "*Aufheben* has in the German language a double sense: that of preserving, *maintaining,* and that of leaving off, *bringing to an end.* To preserve, moreover, has a negative sense . . . . Lexicologically, these two determinations of the *Aufheben* may be considered as two *meanings* of the word. It is remarkable that a language comes to use one and the same word to express two opposed meanings. Speculative thought is *delighted* [*my italics*] to find in language words which by themselves have a speculative sense; the German language possesses several of these" (*Wissenschaft der Logik* I, pp. 124–25). In the *Vorlesungen über die Philosophie der Geschichte* (*Lectures on the Philosophy of History*) Hegel also notes that the union of two meanings (*historia rerum gestarum* and *res gestas*) of the word *Geschichte* "in our language" is not a "simple exterior contingency."

Henceforth, if I cannot designate the (infinite) irreducible alterity of the Other execpt through the negation of (finite) spatial exteriority, perhaps the meaning of this alterity is finite, is not positively infinite. The infinitely other, the infinity of the other, is not the other *as* a positive infinity, as God, or as resemblance with God. The infinitely Other would not be what it is, other, if it was a positive infinity, and if it did not maintain within itself the negativity of the indefinite, of the *apeiron.* Does not "infinitely other" primarily signify that which does not come to an end, despite my interminable labor and experience? Can one respect the Other as Other, and expel negativity—labor—from transcendence, as Levinas seeks to do? The positive Infinity (God)—if these words are meaningful—cannot be infinitely Other. If one thinks, as Levinas does, that positive Infinity tolerates, or even requires, infinite alterity, then one must renounce all language, and first of all the words *infinite* and *other.* Infinity cannot be understood as Other except in the form of the in-finite. As soon as one attempts to think Infinity as a positive plenitude (one pole of Levinas's nonnegative transcendence), the other becomes unthinkable, impossible, unutterable. Perhaps Levinas calls us toward this unthinkable-impossible-unutterable beyond (tradition's) Being and Logos. But it must not be possible either to think or state this call. In any event, that the positive plenitude of classical infinity is translated into language only by betraying itself in a negative word (in-finite), perhaps situates, in the most profound way, the point where thought breaks with language. A break which afterward will but resonate throughout all language. This is why the modern philosophies which no longer seek to distinguish between thought and language, nor to place them in a hierarchy, are essentially philosophies of original finitude. But then they should be able to abandon the word "finitude," forever prisoner of the classical framework. Is this possible? And what does it mean *to abandon* a classical notion?

The other cannot be what it is, infinitely other, except in finitude and mortality (mine *and* its). It is such as soon as it comes into language, of course, and only then, and only if the word *other* has a meaning—but has not Levinas taught us that there is no thought before language? This is why our questions certainly would be less bothersome for a classical infinitism of the Cartesian type, for example, which would dissociate thought and language, the latter never going as fast or as far as the former. Not only would these questions be less bothersome for a classical infinitism, but they could be its own questions. In another way: to neutralize space within the description of the other, in order thereby to liberate positive infinity—is this not to neutralize the essential finitude of a face (glance-speech) which *is a body*, and not, as Levinas continually insists, the corporeal metaphor of etherealized thought? Body: that is, *also* exteriority, locality in the fully spatial, literally spatial, meaning of the word; a zero point, the origin of space, certainly, but an origin which has no meaning before the *of*, an origin inseparable from genitivity and from the space that it engenders and orients: an *inscribed* origin. The *inscription* is the written origin: traced and henceforth *inscribed in* a system, in a figure which it no longer governs. Without which there no longer would be a body proper to oneself. If the face of the other was not *also, irreducibly*, spatial exteriority, we would still have to distinguish between soul and body, thought and speech; or better, between a true, nonspatial face, and its mask or metaphor, its spatial figure. The entire Metaphysics of the Face would collapse. Again, this question could be derived as much from a classical infinitism (duality of thought and language, but also of thought and body) as from the most modern philosophy of finitude. This strange alliance in the question perhaps signifies that within philosophy and within language, within *philosophical discourse* (supposing there are any others), one cannot simultaneously save the themes of positive infinity and of the face (the nonmetaphorical unity of body, glance, speech, and thought). This last unity, it seems to us, can be thought only within the horizon of infinite (indefinite) alterity as the irreducibly *common* horizon of Death and the Other. The horizon of finitude or the finitude of the horizon.

But, let us repeat, all this *within philosophical discourse*, where the thought of Death *itself* (without metaphor) and the thought of a positive Infinity have never been able to understand each other. If the face *is body*, it is mortal. Infinite alterity as death cannot be reconciled with infinite alterity as positivity and presence (God). Metaphysical transcendence cannot be at once transcendence toward the other as Death and transcendence towards the other as God. Unless God means Death, which after all has never been *excluded* by the entirety of the classical philosophy within which we understand God both as Life and as the Truth of Infinity, of positive Presence. But what does this *exclusion* mean if not the exclusion of every particular *determination?* And that God is *nothing* (determined), is not life, because he is *everything?* and therefore is at once All and

Nothing, Life and Death. Which means that God is or appears, *is named,* within
the difference between All and Nothing, Life and Death. Within difference, and
at bottom as Difference itself. This difference is what is called *History.* God is
inscribed in it.

It will be said that Levinas stands opposed to precisely this kind of philosophical discourse. But in this combat, he already has given up the best weapon:
disdain of discourse. In effect, when confronted by the classical difficulties of
language we are referring to, Levinas cannot provide himself with the classical
resources against them. At arms with the problems which were equally the
problems of negative theology and of Bergsonism, he does not give himself the
right to speak, as they did, in a language resigned to its own failure. Negative
theology was spoken in a speech that knew itself failed and finite, inferior to
logos as God's understanding. Above all, negative theology never undertook a
Discourse with God in the face to face, and breath to breath, of two free
speeches; and this despite the humility and the haughtiness of breaking off, or
undertaking, the exchange. Analogously, Bergson had the right to announce the
intuition of duration, and to denounce intellectual spatialization, within a language given over to space. It was not a question of saving, but of destroying
discourse within "metaphysics," the science which allegedly does without symbols" (Bergson). Antagonistic metaphors were multiplied systematically in this
autodestruction of language which adovcated silent metaphysical intuition. Language being defined as a historical residue, there was no contradiction in utilizing
it, for better or for worse, in order to denounce its own betrayal, and then to
abandon it to its own insufficiency as rhetorical refuse, *speech lost to
metaphysics.* Like negative theology, a philosophy of intuitive communion gave
itself the right (correctly or incorrectly, another problem) to travel through
philosophical discourse as through a foreign medium. But what happens when
this right is no longer given, when the possibility of metaphysics is the possibility
of speech? When metaphysical responsibility is responsibility for language, because "thought consists of speaking" (*TI*), and metaphysics is a language with
God? How to think the other, if the other can be spoken only as exteriority and
through exteriority, that is, nonalterity? And if the speech which must inaugurate
and maintain absolute separation is by its essence rooted in space, which cannot
conceive separation and absolute alterity? If, as Levinas says, only discourse
(and not intuitive contact) is righteous, and if, moreover, all discourse essentially
retains within it space and the Same—does this not mean that discourse is
originally violent? And that the philosophical logos, the only one in which peace
may be declared, is inhabited by war? The distinction between discourse and
violence[42] always will be an inaccessible horizon. Nonviolence would be the
telos, and not the essence of discourse. Perhaps it will be said that something like
discourse has its essence in its telos, and the presence of its present in its future.

This certainly is so, but on the condition that its future and its telos be nondiscourse: peace as a *certain* silence, a certain beyond of speech, a certain possibility, a certain silent horizon of speech. And telos has always had the form of presence, be it a future presence. There is war only after the opening of discourse, and war dies out only at the end of discourse. Peace, like silence, is the strange vocation of a language called outside itself by itself. But since *finite* silence is also the medium of violence, language can only indefinitely tend toward justice by acknowledging and practicing the violence within it. Violence against violence. *Economy* of violence. An economy irreducible to what Levinas envisions in the word. If light is the element of violence, one must combat light with a certain other light, in order to avoid the worst violence, the violence of the night which precedes or represses discourse. This *vigilance* is a violence chosen as the least violence by a philosophy which takes history, that is, finitude, seriously; a philosophy aware of itself as *historical* in each of its aspects (in a sense which tolerates neither finite totality, nor positive infinity), and aware of itself, as Levinas says in another sense, as *economy*. But again, an economy which in being history, can be *at home* neither in the finite totality which Levinas calls the Same nor in the positive presence of the Infinite. Speech is doubtless the first defeat of violence, but paradoxically, violence did not exist before the possibility of speech. The philosopher (man) *must* speak and write within this war of light, a war in which he always already knows himself to be engaged; a war which he knows is inescapable, except by denying discourse, that is, by risking the worst violence. This is why this avowal of the war within discourse, an avowal which is not yet peace, signifies the opposite of bellicosity; the bellicosity—and who has shown this better than Hegel?—whose best accomplice *within history* is irenics. *Within history* which the philosopher cannot escape, because it is not history in the sense given to it by Levinas (totality), but is the history of the departures from totality, history as the very movement of transcendence, of the excess over the totality without which no totality would appear as such. History is not the totality transcended by eschatology, metaphysics, or speech. It is transcendence itself. If speech is a movement of metaphysical transcendence, it is history, and not beyond history. It is difficult to think the origin of history in a perfectly finite totality (the Same), as well as, moreover, in a perfectly positive infinity. If, in this sense, the movement of metaphysical transcendence is history, it is still violent, for—and this is the legitimate truism from which Levinas always draws inspiration—history is violence. Metaphysics is *economy:* violence against violence, light against light: philosophy (in general). About which it can be said, by transposing Claudel's intention, that everything in it "is painted on light as if with condensed light, like the air which *becomes* frost." This becoming is war. This polemic is language itself. Its inscription.

Of Transcendental
Violence

In addition, metaphysics, unable to escape its ancestry in light, always supposes a phenomenology in its very critique of phenomenology, and especially if, like Levinas's metaphysics, it seeks to be discourse and instruction.

A. Does metaphysics suppose this phenomenology only as a method, as a technique, in the strict sense of these words? Although he rejects the majority of the literal results of Husserl's researches, Levinas keeps to the methodological inheritance: "The presentation and development of the notions employed owes everything to the phenomenological method" *(TI; DL)*. But are not the presentation and development of ideas but the vestments of thought? And can a method be borrowed, like a tool? Thirty years earlier, in the wake of Heidegger, did not Levinas maintain that method cannot be isolated? For method always shelters, especially in Husserl's case, "an anticipated view of the 'sense' of the being which one encounters" *(THI)*. Levinas wrote at this time: "Consequently, in our exposition we cannot separate the theory of intuition, as a philosophical method, from what might be called Husserl's *ontology*" *(THI)*.

Now, what the phenomenological method refers to, explicitly and in the last analysis (and this would be too easy to show), is Western philosophy's very decision, since Plato, to consider itself as science, as theory: that is, precisely as that which Levinas wishes to put into question by the ways and means of phenomenology.

B. Beyond its method, the aspect of "Husserl's essential teaching" *(TI)* which Levinas intends to retain is not only its supple and necessary descriptions, the fidelity to the meaning of experience, but also the concept of intentionality. An intentionality enlarged beyond its representative and theoretical dimension, beyond the noetico-noematical structure which Husserl incorrectly would have seen as the primordial structure. Repression of the infinite would have kept Husserl from access to the true depths of intentionality as desire and as metaphysical transcendence toward the other beyond phenomenality or Being. This repression would occur in two ways.

On the one hand, in the value of *adequation.* As vision and theoretical intuition, Husserlian intentionality would be adequation. This latter would exhaust and interiorize all distance and all true alterity. "Vision, in effect, is essentially an adequation of exteriority to interiority: exteriority is reabsorbed in the contemplating soul, and, as an *adequate idea,* is revealed a priori, resulting in a *Sinngebung*" *(TI)*. Now, "intentionality, in which thought remains *adequation* to its object, does not define . . . consciousness at its fundamental level." Certainly Husserl is not named here, at the very moment when Levinas speaks of intention-

ality as adequation; one may always suppose that by the expression "intentionality, in which thought remains *adequation,*" Levinas means "an intentionality
such that, etc., an intentionality in which at least, etc." But the context, numerous other passages and the allusion to the *Sinngebung,* all clearly indicate that
Husserl, in the letter of his texts, was unable to recognize that "as intentionality
all knowledge already supposes the idea of infinity, which is adequation par
excellence" *(TI)*. Thus, supposing that Husserl had foreseen the infinite horizons which overflow objectivity and adequate intuition, he would have interpreted them, *literally,* as "thoughts aiming at objects": "What does it matter if
in Husserlian phenomenology, understood literally, these unsuspected horizons
are interpreted, in turn, as thoughts aiming at objects!" (cited above).

On the other hand, supposing that the Husserlian Cogito opened onto the
infinite, according to Levinas, it would open onto an object-infinity, an infinity
without alterity, a false infinity: "If Husserl sees in the cogito a subjectivity with
no support outside itself, he is constituting the idea of infinity itself, giving it to
himself as an object." The "false-infinity," a Hegelian expression which
Levinas never uses, nevertheless seems to us, perhaps because it is Hegelian, to
haunt numerous gestures of denunciation in *Totality and Infinity.* As it was for
Hegel, the "false-infinity" for Levinas would be the indefinite, *negative* form of
infinity. But, since Levinas conceives *true* alterity as nonnegativity (nonnegative
transcendence), he can make the other the true infinity, and make the same (in
strange complicity with negativity) the false-infinity. Which would have seemed
absolutely mad to Hegel (and to all the metaphysics expanded and rethought in
him): how can alterity be separated from negativity, how can alterity be separated
from the "false infinity"? Or inversely, how could absolute sameness not be
infinity? If, as Levinas says, the same is a violent totality, this would mean that it
is a finite totality, and therefore is abstract, more other than the other (than an
other totality), etc. The same as finite totality would not be the same, but still the
other. Levinas would be speaking of the other under the rubric of the same, and
of the same under the rubric of the other, etc. If the finite totality was the same, it
could not be thought, or posed as such, without becoming other than itself (and
this is war). If it did not do so, it could not enter into war with others (finite
totalities), nor could it be violent. Henceforth, not being violent, it would not be
the same in Levinas's sense (finite totality). Entering into war—and war there
is—it is conceived, certainly, as the other's other, that is, it gains access to the
other as an other (self). But again, it is no longer a totality in Levinas's sense. In
this language, which is the only language of western philosophy, can one not
repeat Hegelianism, which is only this language coming into absolute possession
of itself?

Under these conditions, the only effective position to take in order not to be
enveloped by Hegel would seem to be, for an instant, the following: to consider
the false-infinity (that is, in a profound way, original finitude) irreducible.

Perhaps this is what Husserl does, at bottom, by demonstrating the irreducibility of intentional incompleteness, and therefore of alterity; and by showing that since consciousness is irreducible, it can never possibly, by its own essence, become self-consciousness, nor be reassembled absolutely close to itself in the parousia of an absolute knowledge. But can this *be said,* can one think the "false infinity" as such (time, in a word), can one pause alongside it as alongside the truth of experience, without *already* (an already which permits us to think time!) having let the *true* infinity, which then must be recognized as such, be indicated, presented, thought and stated? What we call philosophy, which perhaps is not the entirety of thought, cannot think the false, nor even choose the false, without paying homage to the anteriority and the superiority of the true (same relationship between the other and the same). This last question, which indeed could be Levinas's question to Husserl, would demonstrate that as soon as *he speaks* against Hegel, Levinas can only confirm Hegel, has confirmed him already.

But is there a more rigorously and, especially, a more literally Husserlian theme than the theme of inadequation? Of the infinite overflowing of horizons? Who was more obstinately determined than Husserl to show that vision was originally and essentially the inadequation of interiority and exteriority? And that the perception of the transcendent and extended thing was essentially and forever incomplete? That immanent perception occurred within the infinite horizon of the flux of experience? (cf., for example, *Ideas I,* paragraph 83, passim). And above all, who better than Levinas first gave us to understand these Husserlian themes? Therefore, it is not a question of recalling their existence, but of asking whether Husserl finally *summarized* inadequation, and reduced the infinite horizons of experience to the condition of available objects. And whether he did so by the secondary interpretation of which Levinas accuses him.

We can hardly believe so. In the two intentional directions of which we have just spoken, the *Idea in the Kantian sense* designates the infinite overflowing of a horizon which, by reason of an absolute and essential necessity which itself is absolutely principled and irreducible, *never* can become an object itself, or be completed, *equaled,* by the intuition of an object. Even by God's intuition. The horizon itself cannot become an object because it is the unobjectifiable wellspring of every object in general. This impossibility of adequation is so radical that neither the *originality* nor the *apodicticity* of evident truths are necessarily adequations. (Cf., for example, *Ideas I,* sec. 3; *Cartesian Meditations,* sec. 9, passim.) (Of course, this does not imply that certain possibilities of adequate evident truths—particular and founded ones—are overlooked by Husserl.) The importance of the concept of horizon lies precisely in its inability to *make* any constitutive act *into* an object, and in that it opens the work of objectification to infinity. In phenomenology there is never a constitution of horizons, but horizons of constitution. That the infinity of the Husserlian horizon has the form of an indefinite opening, and that it offers itself without any possible end to the negativity of constitution (of the work of objectification)—does this not certainly keep it from all totalization, from the illusion of the immediate presence of a plenitudinous infinity in which the other suddenly becomes unfindable? If a consciousness of infinite inadequation to the infinite (and even to the finite) distinguishes a body of thought careful to respect exteriority, it is difficult to see how Levinas can depart from Husserl, on this point at least. Is not intentionality respect itself? The eternal irreducibility of the other to the same, but of the other *appearing as* other for the same? For without the phenomenon of other as other no respect would be possible. The phenomenon of respect supposes the respect of phenomenality. And ethics, phenomenology.

In this sense, phenomenology is respect itself, the development and becoming-language of respect itself. This was Husserl's aim in stating that reason does not tolerate being distinguished into theoretical, practical, etc. (cf. above). This does not mean that respect as ethics is *derived* from phenomenology, that it supposes phenomenology as its premise, or as a previous or superior value. The presupposition of phenomenology is of a unique kind. It "commands" nothing, in the worldly (real, political, etc.) sense of commandment. It is the very neutralization of this kind of commandment. But it does not neutralize the worldly type of commandment in order to substitute another type of commandment for it. It is profoundly foreign to all hierarchies. Which is to say that ethics not only is neither dissipated in phenomenology nor submitted to it, but that ethics finds within phenomenology its own meaning, its freedom and radicality. Moreover, it seems incontestable to us that the themes of nonpresence (temporalization and alterity) contradict that which makes phenomenology a metaphysics of presence, *working* it ceaselessly, and we emphasize this elsewhere.

C. Can Levinas separate himself from Husserl more legitimately as concerns theoretism and the primacy of the consciousness of the object? Let us not forget that the "primacy" necessarily in question here is that of the object or of objectivity *in general*. Now phenomenology has surely contributed nothing if not an infinite renewal, enlargement, and suppling of the notion of object in general. The ultimate jurisdiction of evident truths is infinitely open, is open for every type of possible object, that is, for every conceivable sense present for consciousness in general. No discourse (for example, the discourse in *Totality and Infinity* which seeks to reawaken ethical truths to their absolute independence, etc.) could be meaningful, could be thought or understood, if it did not draw upon this layer of phenomenological evidence in general. It suffices that ethical meaning be *thought* in order for Husserl to be right. Not only nominal definitions but, before them, possibilities of essence which guide all concepts, are presupposed when one speaks of ethics, of transcendence, of infinity, etc. These expressions must have a meaning for concrete consciousness in general, or no discourse and no thought would be possible. This domain of absolutely "prior" truths is the domain of the transcendental phenomenology in which a phenomenology of ethics must take root. This rooting is not *real,* does not signify a real dependence; it would be vain to reproach transcendental phenomenology for being *in fact* incapable of engendering ethical values or behaviors (or, amounting to the same thing for being able to repress them, more or less directly). Since every determined meaning, every thought meaning, every noema (for example, the meaning of ethics) supposes the possibility of *noema in general,* it is fitting to begin *rightfully* with transcendental phenomenology. To begin *rightfully* with the general possibility of a noema which—let us recall this decisive point—is not a *real (reell)* moment for Husserl, and therefore is without any real (hierarchical or other) relationship to *anything else:* anything else being capable of conception only in noematicity. In particular, this means that from Husserl's point of view ethics *in fact,* in existence and in history, could not be *subordinated* to transcendental neutralization, nor be submitted to it in any way. Neither ethics, nor anything else in the world, moreover. Transcendental neutralization is in principle, by its meaning, foreign to all factuality, all existence in general. In fact it is neither before nor after ethics. Neither before nor after anything that is.

Thus, one may speak of ethical objectivity, or of ethical values or imperatives as objects (noemas) with all their originality, without reducing this objectivity to any of those which incorrectly (but the fault is not Husserl's) function as the model for what commonly is understood as objectivity (theoretical objectivity, political, technical, natural, etc. objectivity). Truthfully, there are two meanings of the theoretical: the current meaning, the one Levinas's protest particularly aims at; and the more hidden sense in which *appearance* in general is maintained, including the appearance of the nontheoretical (in the first sense) in particular. In this second sense, phenomenology is indeed a theoretism, but it is so in the extent to which all thought and all language are tied to theoretism, de facto and de jure. Phenomenology measures this extent. I know the meaning of the nontheoretical as such (for example, ethics or the metaphysical in Levinas's sense), with a theoretical knowledge (in general), and I respect it as such, as what it is, in its meaning. I have regard[43] for recognizing that which cannot be regarded as a thing, as a façade, as a theorem. I have regard for the face itself.

D. But, as we know, the fundamental disagreement between Levinas and Husserl is not here. Nor does it bear upon the ahistoricity of meaning with which Levinas formerly reproached Husserl, and concerning which the latter had "held in store surprises" (as Levinas's eschatology was to surprise us thirty years later in speaking *"from beyond the totality* or history" *TI).* Which supposes, once more, that the totality is finite (a supposition in no way inscribed in its concept), that history as such can be a finite totality, and that there is no history beyond the finite totality. Perhaps one would have to show, as was suggested above, that history is impossible, meaningless, in the finite totality, and that it is impossible, meaningless, in the positive and actual infinity; that history keeps to the difference between totality and infinity, and that history precisely is that which Levinas calls transcendence and eschatology. A *system* is neither finite nor infinite. A structural totality escapes this alternative in its functioning. It escapes the archaeological and the eschatological, and inscribes them in itself.

The disagreement appears definite as concerns the Other. As we have seen: according to Levinas, by making the other, notably in the *Cartesian Meditations,* the ego's phenomenon, constituted by analogical appresentation on the basis of belonging to the ego's own sphere, Husserl allegedly missed the infinite alterity of the other, reducing it to the same. To make the other an alter ego, Levinas says frequently, is to neutralize its absolute alterity.

(a) Now, it would be easy to show the degree to which Husserl takes pains to respect, in its meaning, the alterity of the Other, particularly in the *Cartesian Meditations.* He is concerned with describing how the other *as other,* in its irreducible alterity, is presented to me. Is presented to me, as we will see later, as originary nonpresence. It is the other as other which is the ego's phenomenon: the phenomenon of a certain non-phenomenality which is irreducible for the ego as ego in general (the eidos ego). For it is impossible to encounter the alter ego (in the very form of the encounter[44] described by Levinas), impossible to respect it in experience and in language, if this other, in its alterity, does not *appear* for an ego (in general). One could neither speak, nor have any sense of the totally other, if there was not a phenomenon of the totally other, or evidence of the totally other as such. No one more than Husserl has been sensitive to the singular and irreducible style of this evidence, and to the original non-phenomenalization indicated within it. Even if one neither seeks nor is able to thematize the other *of which* one does not speak, but *to whom* one speaks, this impossibility and this imperative themselves can be thematized (as Levinas does) only on the basis of a certain appearance of the other as other for an ego. Husserl speaks of this *system,* of this appearance, and of the impossibility of thematizing the other in person. This is *his* problem: "They, (the other *egos*) however, are not simple representations or objects represented within me, synthetic unities of a process of verification taking place 'within me,' but precisely 'others' ... 'subjects for this same world ... subjects who perceive the world ... and who thereby experience me, just as I experience the world and in it, 'others' " (*Cartesian Meditations*). It is this appearance of the other as that which I can never be, this originary non-phenomenality, which is examined as the ego's *intentional phenomenon.*

(b) For—and here we are keeping to the most manifest and most massively incontestable meaning of the fifth of the *Cartesian Meditations* whose course is so mazelike—Husserl's most central affirmation concerns the *irreducibly mediate* nature of the intentionality aiming at the other as other. It is evident, by an essential, absolute and definitive self-evidence that the other as transcendental other (other absolute origin and other zero point in the orientation of the world), can never be given to me in an original way and in person, but only through analogical appresentation. The necessary reference to analogical appresentation, far from signifying an analogical and assimilatory reduction of the other to the same, confirms and respects separation, the unsurpassable necessity of (nonobjective) mediation. If I did not approach the other by way of analogical appresentation, if I attained to the other immediately and originally, silently, in communion with the other's own experience, the other would cease to be the other. Contrary to appearances, the theme of appresentative transposition translates the recognition of the radical separation of the absolute origins, the relationship of absolved absolutes and nonviolent respect for the secret: the opposite of victorious assimilation.

Bodies, transcendent and natural things, are others in general for my consciousness. They are outside, and their transcendence is the sign of an already irreducible alterity. Levinas does not think so; Husserl does, and thinks that "other" already means something when things are in question. Which is to take seriously the reality of the external world. Another sign of this alterity in general, which things share here with others, is that something within them too is always hidden, and is indicated only by anticipation, analogy and appresentation. Husserl states this in the fifth of the *Cartesian Meditations:* analogical appresentation belongs, to a certain extent, to *every perception.* But in the case of the other as transcendent thing, the principled possibility of an originary and original presentation of the hidden visage is always open, in principle and a priori. This possibility is absolutely rejected in the case of Others. The alterity of the transcendent thing, although already irreducible, is such only by means of the indefinite incompleteness of my original perceptions. Thus it is incomparable to the alterity of Others, which is also irreducible, and adds to the dimension of incompleteness (the body of the Other in space, the history of our relations, etc.) a more profound dimension of nonoriginality—the radical impossibility of going around to see things from the other side. But without the first alterity, the alterity of bodies (and the Other is also a body, from the beginning), the second alterity could never emerge. The system of these two alterities, the one inscribed in the other, must be thought together: the alterity of Others, therefore, by a double power of indefiniteness. The stranger is infinitely other because by his essence no enrichment of his profile can give me the subjective face of his experience *from his perspective,* such as he has lived it. Never will this experience be given to me originally, like everything which is *mir eigenes,* which is *proper* to me. This transcendence of the nonproper no longer is that of the entirety, always inaccessible on the basis of always partial attempts: transcendence of *Infinity,* not of *Totality.*

Levinas and Husserl are quite close here. But by acknowledging in this infinitely other *as such* (appearing as such) the status of an intentional modification of the ego in general, Husserl gives himself the *right to speak* of the infinitely other as such, accounting for the origin and the legitimacy of his language. He describes the phenomenal system of nonphenomenality. Levinas *in fact* speaks of the infinitely other, but by refusing to acknowledge an intentional modification of the ego—which would be a violent and totalitarian act for him—he deprives himself of the very foundation and possibility of his own language. What authorizes him to say "infinitely other" if the infinitely other does not appear as such in the zone he calls the same, and which is the neutral level of transcendental description? To return, as to the only possible point of departure, to the intentional phenomenon in which the other appears as other, and lends itself to language, *to every possible language,* is perhaps to give oneself over to violence, or to make oneself its accomplice at least, and to *acquiesce*—in the critical sense—to the violence of the fact; but in question, then, is an irreducible zone of factuality, an original, transcendental violence, previous to every ethical choice, even supposed by ethical nonviolence. Is it meaningful to speak of a preethical violence? If the transcendental "violence" to which we allude is tied to phenomenality itself, and to the possibility of language, it then would be embedded in the root of meaning and logos, before the latter had to be determined as rhetoric, psychagogy, demagogy, etc.

(c) Levinas writes: "The other, as other, is not only an alter ego. It is what I myself am not" (*EE* and *TA*). "Decency" and "everyday life" incorrectly lead us to believe that "the other is known through sympathy, as an other like myself, as alter ego" (*TA*). This is exactly what Husserl does not do. He seeks to recognize the other as Other only in its form as ego, in its form of alterity, which cannot be that of things in the world. If the other were not recognized as a transcendental alter *ego,* it would be entirely in the world and not, as ego, the origin of the world. To refuse to see in it an ego in this sense is, within the ethical order, the very gesture of all violence. If the other was not recognized as ego, its entire alterity would collapse. Therefore, it seems that one may not suppose that Husserl makes of the other an other like myself (in the factual sense of the word), or a *real* modification of *my life,* without misconstruing his most permanent and openly stated intentions. If the Other was a real moment of my egological life, if "inclusion of an other monad within my own" (*Cartesian Meditations*) was real, I would perceive it *originaliter*. Husserl does not cease to emphasize that this is an absolute impossibility. The other as alter ego signifies the other as other, irreducible to *my* ego, precisely because it is an ego, because it has the form of the ego. The egoity of the other permits him to say "ego" as I do; and this is why he is Other, and not a stone, or a being without speech *in my real economy*. This is why, if you will, he is face, can speak to me, understand me, and eventually command me. Dissymmetry itself would be impossible without this symmetry, which is not of the world, and which, having no real aspect, imposes no limit upon alterity and dissymmetry—makes them possible, on the contrary. This dissymmetry is an *economy* in a new sense; a sense which would probably be intolerable to Levinas.

Despite the logical absurdity of this formulation, this economy is the transcendental symmetry of two empirical asymmetries. The other, for me, is an ego which I know to be in relation to me as to an other. Where have these movements been better described than in *The Phenomenology of the Mind*? The movement of transcendence toward the other, as invoked by Levinas, would have no meaning if it did not bear within it, as one of its essential meanings, that in my ipseity I know myself to be other for the other. Without this, ''I'' (in general: egoity), unable to be the other's other, would never be the victim of violence. The violence of which Levinas speaks would be a violence without victim. But since, in the dissymmetry which he describes, the author of violence could never be the other himself, but always the same (ego), and since all egos are others for others, the violence without victim would be also a violence without author. And all these propositions can be reversed without difficulty. It will be easily understood that if the Parmenides of the *Poem* gives us to believe, through interposed historical phantasms, that he lent himself to parricide several times, the great and fearful white shadow which spoke to the young Socrates continues to smile when we undertake grand discourses on separate beings, unity, difference, the same and the other. To what exercises would Parmenides give himself over, at the frontiers of *Totality and Infinity,* if we attempted to make him understand that *ego* equals *same,* and that the other is what it is only as the absolute infinitely other absolved of its relationship to the Same. For example: (1) The infinitely other, he would say perhaps, can be what it is only if it is other, that is, other *than. Other than* must be *other than* myself. Henceforth, it is no longer absolved of a relation to an ego. Therefore, it is no longer infinitely, absolutely other. It is no longer what it is. If it was absolved, it would not be the other either, but the Same. (2) The infinitely other cannot be what it is—infinitely other—except by being absolutely not the same. That is, in particular, by being other than itself (non ego). Being other than itself, it is not what it is. Therefore, it is not infinitely other, etc.

At bottom, we belive, this exercise is not just verbiage, or dialectical virtuosity in the ''play of the Same.'' It would mean that the expression ''infinitely other'' or ''absolutely other'' cannot be stated and thought simultaneously; that the other cannot be absolutely exterior[45] to the same without ceasing to be other; and that, consequently, the same is not a totality closed in upon itself, an identity playing with itself, having only the appearance of alterity, in what Levinas calls economy, work, and history. How could there by a ''play of the Same'' if alterity itself was not already *in* the Same, with a meaning of inclusion doubtless betrayed by the word *in?* Without alterity *in* the same, how could the "play of the Same" occur, in the sense of playful activity, or of dislocation, in a machine or organic totality which *plays* or *works?* And it could be shown that for Levinas work, always enclosed inside totality and history, fundamentally remains a game. A proposition that we can accept, with several precautions, more easily than he.

Finally, let us confess our total deafness to propositions of this type: "Being occurs as multiple, and as divided into Same and Other. This is its ultimate structure" (*TI*). What is the division *of being between* the same and the other? Is it a division *between* the same and the other, which does not suppose, at very least, that the same *is* the other's other, and the other the same as oneself? We are not only thinking of Parmenides' exercise, playing with the young Socrates. The Stranger in the *Sophist* who, like Levinas, seems to break with Eleatism in the name of alterity, knows that alterity can be thought only as negativity, and above all, can be *said* only as negativity, which Levinas begins by refusing; he knows too, that differing from Being, the other is always relative, is stated *pros eteron,* which does not prevent it from being an *eidos* (or a *genre,* in a nonconceptual sense), that is, from being the same as itself ("same as itself" already supposing, as Heidegger notes in *Identity and Difference,* precisely as concerns the *Sophist,* mediation, relation, and difference: *eksastan auto tauton*). Levinas, from his perspective, would refuse to assimilate the Other to the *eteron* in question here. But how can the "Other" be thought or said without reference—we do not say reduction—to the alterity of the *eteron* in general? This last notion, henceforth, no longer has the restricted meaning which permits its simple opposition to the notion of *Other,* as if it was confined to the region of real or logical objectivity. The *eteron,* here, belongs to a more profound and original zone than that in which this philosophy of subjectivity (that is, of objectivity), still implicated in the notion of the Other, is expanded.

The other, then, would not be what he is (my fellow man as foreigner) if he were not alter ego. This is a self-evidence greatly prior to "decency" and to the dissimulations of "daily life." Does not Levinas treat the expression *alter ego* as if *alter* were the epithet of a real subject (on a pre-eidetic level)? As an ephithetical, accidental modification of my real (empirical) identity? Now, the transcendental syntax of the expression *alter ego* tolerates no relationship of substantive to adjective, of absolute to epithet, in one sense or the other. This is its strangeness. A necessity due to the finitude of meaning: the other is absolutely other only if he is an ego, that is, in a certain way, if he is the same as I. Inversely, the other as *res* is simultaneously less other (not absolutely other) and less "the same" than I. Simultaneously more and less other, which means, once more, that the absolute of alterity is the same. And this contradiction (in

terms of a formal logic which Levinas follows for once, since he refuses to call
the other *alter ego*), this impossibility of translating my relation to the Other into
the rational coherence of language—this contradiction and this impossibility are
not the signs of "irrationality": they are the sign, rather, that one may no longer
draw inspiration from *within* the coherence of the *Logos,* but that thought is
stifled in the region of the origin of language as dialogue and difference. This
origin, as the concrete condition of rationality, is nothing less than "irrational,"
but it could not be "included" in language. This origin is an inscribed inscription.

Further, every reduction of the other to a *real* moment of *my* life, its reduction
to the state of empirical alter-ego, is an empirical possibility, or rather eventuality, which is called violence; and violence presupposes the necessary eidetic
relationships envisaged in Husserl's descriptions. For, on the contrary, to gain
access to the egoity of the alter ego as if to its alterity itself is the most peaceful
gesture possible. *We do not say absolutely peaceful.* We say *economical.* There
is a transcendental and preethical violence, a (general) dissymmetry whose archia
is the same, and which eventually permits the inverse dissymmetry, that is, the
ethical nonviolence of which Levinas speaks. In effect, *either* there is only the
same, which can no longer even appear and be said, nor even exercise violence
(pure infinity or finitude); *or* indeed there is the same *and* the other, and then the
other cannot be the other—of the same—except by being the same (as itself:
ego), and the same cannot be the same (as itself: ego) except by being the other's
other: alter ego. That I am also essentially the other's other, and that I know I am,
is the evidence of a strange symmetry whose trace appears nowhere in Levinas's
descriptions. Without this evidence, I could not desire (or) respect the other in
ethical dissymmetry. This transcendental violence, which does not spring from
an ethical resolution or freedom, or from a *certain way* of encountering or
exceeding the other, originally institutes the relationship between two finite
ipseities. In effect, the necessity of gaining access to the meaning of the other (in
its irreducible alterity) on the basis of its "face," that is, its nonphenomenal
phenomenon, its nonthematic theme, in other words, on the basis of an intentional modification of my ego (in general), (an intentional modification upon
which Levinas indeed must base the meaning of his discourse); and the necessity
of speaking of the other as other, or to the other as other, on the basis of its
appearing-for-me-as-what-it-is: the other (an appearing which dissimulates its
essential dissimulation, takes it out of the light, stripping it, and hiding that
which is hidden in the other), as the necessity from which no discourse can
escape, from its earliest origin—these necessities are violence itself, or rather the
transcendental origin of an irreducible violence, supposing, as we said above,
that it is somehow meaningful to speak of preethical violence. For this transcendental origin, as the irreducible violence of the relation to the other, is at the

same time nonviolence, since it opens the relation to the other. It is an *economy*.
And it is this economy which, by this opening, will permit access to the other to
be determined, in ethical freedom, as moral violence or nonviolence. It is difficult
to see how the notion of violence (for example, as the dissimulation or oppression of the other by the same, a notion which Levinas employs as self-evident,
and which, however, already signifies alteration of the same, of the other as what
it is) could be determined rigorously on a purely ethical level, without prior
eidetic-transcendental analysis of the relations between ego and alter-ego in
general, between several origins of the world in general. That the other appears
as such only in its relationship to the same, is a self-evidence that the Greeks had
no need to acknowledge in the transcendental egology which would confirm it
later; and, it is violence as the origin of meaning and of discourse in the reign of
finitude.[46] The difference between the same and the other, which is not a difference or a relation among others, has no meaning in the infinite, except to
speak, as Hegel does and against Levinas, of the anxiety of the infinite which
determines and negates itself. Violence, certainly, appears within the horizon of
an idea of the infinite. But this horizon is not the horizon of the infinitely other,
but of a reign in which the difference between the same and the other, *différance*,
would no longer be valid, that is, of a reign in which peace itself would no longer
have meaning. And first of all because there would be no more phenomenality or
meaning in general. The infinitely other and the infinitely same, if these words
have meaning for a finite being, is the same. Hegel himself recognized negativity, anxiety or war in the infinite absolute only as the movement of the absolute's
own history, whose horizon is a final pacification in which alterity would be
absolutely *encapsulated,* if not lifted up, in parousia.[47] How are we to interpret
the *necessity* of *thinking* the *fact* of what is first of all *on the horizon* in what is
generally called the end of history? Which amounts to asking what the *thought* of
the other *as* other means, and whether or not the light of the "as such" is
dissimulation in this unique case. Unique case? No, we must reverse the terms:
"other" is the name, "other" is the meaning of this unthinkable unity of light
and night. What "other" means is phenomenality as disappearance. Is it a
question, here, of a "third route excluded by these contradictory ones" (revelation and dissimulation, *The Trace of the Other*)? But this route cannot appear,
cannot be stated as tertiary. If it is called "trace," the word can emerge only as a
metaphor whose philosophical elucidation will ceaselessly call upon "contradictions." Without which its originality—that which distinguishes it from the *Sign*
(the word conventionally chosen by Levinas)—would not appear. For it *must* be
made to appear. And the phenomenon supposes original contamination by the
sign.

War, therefore, is congenital to phenomenality, is the very emergence of
speech and of appearing. Hegel does not abstain by chance from pronouncing the

word "man" in the *Phenomenology of the Mind;* and he describes war (for example, the dialectic of the Master and the Slave) without anthropological reference, within the realm of a science of *consciousness,* that is, of phenomenality itself, in the necessary structure of its movement: a science of experience and of consciousness.

Discourse, therefore, if it is originally violent, can only *do itself violence,* can only negate itself in order to affirm itself, make war upon the war which institutes it without ever *being able* to reappropriate this negativity, to the extent that it is discourse. *Necessarily* without reappropriating it, for if it did so, the horizon of peace would disappear into the night (worst violence as previolence). This secondary war, as the avowal of violence, is the least possible violence, the only way to repress the worst violence, the violence of primitive and prelogical silence, of an unimaginable night which would not even be the opposite of day, an absolute violence which would not even be the opposite of nonviolence: nothingness or pure non-sense. Thus discourse chooses itself violently in opposition to nothingness or pure non-sense, and, in philosophy, against nihilism. For this not to be so, the eschatology which animates Levinas's discourse would have to have had kept its promise already, even to the extent of no longer being able to occur within discourse as eschato*logy,* and as the idea of a peace "beyond history." The "messianic triumph" "armed against evil's revenge" would have to have been ushered in. This messianic triumph, which is the horizon of Levinas's book, but which "overflows its framework" *(TI),* could abolish violence only by suspending the difference (conjunction or opposition) between the same and the other, that is, by suspending the *idea* of peace. But here and now (in a present in general), this horizon cannot be stated, an end cannot be stated, eschato*logy* is not possible, except *through violence.* This infinite passage through violence is what is called history. To overlook the irreducibility of this last violence, is to revert—within the order of philosophical discourse which one cannot *seek to reject,* except by risking the *worst violence*—to an infinitist dogmatism in pre-Kantian style, one which does not pose the question of responsibility for its own finite philosophical discourse. It is true that the delegation of this responsibility to God is not an abdication, God not being a finite third party: thus conceived, divine responsibility neither excludes nor diminishes the integrity of my own responsibility, the responsibility of the finite philosopher. On the contrary, divine responsibility requires and calls for this latter responsibility, as its telos or its origin. But the *fact* of the inadequation of these two responsibilities, or of this unique responsibility for itself—this history or anxiety of the infinite—is not yet a *theme* for the pre-Kantian, or rather even pre-Hegelian, rationalists.

Nor will it be so for as long as the absolutely principial self-evidence, in Levinas's own terms, of "the impossibility for the ego not to be itself" is not dissolved. The ego cannot not be itself even when it ventures out toward the other, nor could it venture forth with this impossibility, which thus "marks the innate tragedy of the ego, the fact that it is riveted to its own being" (*EE*), according to Levinas's strong statement. And above all, marks the fact that the ego knows this. This knowledge is the first discourse and first word of escha-to*logy;* it is that which permits separation and speaking to the other. It is not a knowledge among others, but is knowledge itself. "It is this 'always-being-one-and-yet-always-other' which is the fundamental characteristic of knowledge, etc." (Schelling). No philosophy responsible for its language can renounce ipseity in general, and the philosophy or eschatology of separation may do so less than any other. Between original tragedy and messianic triumph there is *philosophy,* in which violence is returned against violence within knowledge, in which original finitude appears, and in which the other is respected within, and by, the same. This finitude makes its appearance in an irreducibly open question which is the *philosophical question in general: why* is the essential, irreducible, absolutely general and unconditioned form of experience as a venturing forth toward the other still egoity? *Why* is an experience which would not be lived as *my own* (for an ego in general, in the eidetic-transcendental sense of these words) impossible and unthinkable? This unthinkable and impossible are the limits of reason in general. In other words: *why finitude,* if, as Schelling had said, "egoity is the general principle of finitude"? And *why Reason,* if it is true that "Reason and Egoity, in their true Absoluteness, are one and the same" (Schelling), and true that "reason . . . is a kind of universal and essential structure of transcendental subjectivity in general" (Husserl)? The philosophy which is the discourse of this reason as phenomenology cannot answer such a question by essence, for every answer can be made only in language, and language is opened by the question. Philosophy (in general) can only open itself to the question, within it and by it. It can only *let itself be questioned.*

Husserl knew this. And he called the irreducibly egoic essence of experience "archi-factuality" (*Urtatsache*), nonempirical factuality, transcendental factuality (a notion to which attention has never been paid, perhaps). "This *I am* is for me, for the I who says it and understands it accordingly, the *primordial intentional foundation of my world* (*der intentionale Urgrund für meine Welt*)."[48] *My world* is the opening in which all experience occurs, including, as the experience par excellence, that which is transcendence toward the Other as such. Nothing can appear outside the appurtenance to "my world" for an "I am." "Whether it is suitable or not, whether it appears to me monstrous (due to whatever prejudices) or not, *I must stand firm before the primordial fact* (*die Urtatsache, der ich standhalten muss*),from which I cannot turn my glance for an instant, as a philosopher. For philosophical children this indeed may be the dark corner to which the ghosts of solipsism, or of psychologism or relativism, return. The true philosopher will prefer, instead of fleeing from these ghosts, to illuminate the dark corner.''[49] Understood in this sense, the intentional relationship of "ego to my world" cannot be opened on the basis of an infinite-other radically foreign to "my world," nor can it be imposed upon me by a God who determines this relationship: "The subjective a priori is that which precedes the Being of God and of everything, without exception, which exists for me, a thinking being. God too, is for me what he is by my own conscious production; I cannot look away from this in the anguished fear of what may be considered blasphemy, but on the contrary must see in it the problem. Here too, just as concerning the *alter ego,* 'conscious production' does not mean that I invent and fashion this supreme transcendence.''[50] God no more really depends upon me than does the *alter-ego.* But he has *meaning* only for an ego in general. Which means that before all atheism or all faith, before all theology, before all language about God or with God, God's divinity (the infinite alterity of the infinite other, for example) must have a meaning for an ego in general. Let us note in passing that the "subjective a priori" recognized by transcendental phenomenology is the only possible way to check the totalitarianism of the neutral, the impersonal "absolute Logic," that is, eschatology without dialogue and everything classed under the conventional—quite conventional—rubric of Hegelianism.

The question about egoity as transcendental archi-factuality can be repeated more profoundly in the direction of the archi-factuality of the "living present." For egological life has as its irreducible and absolutely universal form the living present. There is no experience which can be lived other than in the present. The absolute impossibility of living other than in the present, this eternal impossibility, defines the unthinkable as the limit of reason. The notion of a past whose meaning could not be thought in the form of a (past) present marks the *impossible-unthinkable-unstatable* not only for philosophy in general but even for a thought of being which would seek to take a step outside philosophy. This notion, however, does become a theme in the meditation of the trace announced in Levinas's most recent writings. In the living present, the notion of which is at once the most simple and most difficult of notions, all temporal alterity can be constituted and appear as such: as other past present, other future present, other absolute origins relived in intentional modification, in the unity and actuality of my living present. Only the actual unity of my living present permits other presents (other absolute origins) from appearing as such, in what is called memory or anticipation (for example, but in truth in the constant movement of temporalization). But only the alterity of past and future presents permits the absolute identity of the living present as the self-identity of non-self identity. One would have to show, [51] on the basis of the *Cartesian Meditations,* and given the reduction of every problem of factual genesis, how the question of *anteriority* in the relation between the constitution of other as *other present* and the constitution of the other as *Others* is a false question, which must refer to a common structural root. Although in the *Cartesian Meditations* Husserl evokes only the *analogy* of the two movements (Sec. 52), in many of the unpublished works he seems to hold them to be inseparable.

In the last analysis, if one wishes to determine violence as the necessity that the other not appear as what it is, that it not be respected except in, for, and by the same, that it be dissimulated by the same in the very freeing of its phenomenon, then time is violence. This movement of freeing absolute alterity in the absolute same is the movement of temporalization in its most absolutely unconditioned universal form: the living present. If the living present, the absolute form of the opening of time to the other in itself, is the absolute form of egological life, and if egoity is the absolute form of experience, then the present, the presence of the present, and the present of presence, are all originally and forever violent. The living present is originally marked by death. Presence as violence is the meaning of finitude, the meaning of meaning as history.

But why? Why finitude? Why history?[52] And why may we, on what basis may we, examine this violence as finitude and as history? Why the why? And from whence does it permit itself to be understood in its philosophical determination?

Levinas's metaphysics in a sense presupposes—at least we have attempted to show this—the transcendental phenomenology that it seeks to put into question. And yet the legitimacy of this putting into question does not seem to us any less radical. What is the origin of the question about transcendental archi-factuality as violence? Upon what basis does one ask questions about finitude as violence? Upon what basis does the original violence of discourse permit itself to be commanded to be returned against itself, to be always, as language, the return against itself which recognizes the other as other? Of course, one cannot *answer* these questions (for example, by saying that the question about the violence of finitude can be posed only on the basis of finitude's other and the idea of infinity), except by undertaking a new discourse which once more will seek to justify transcendental phenomenology. But the naked opening of the question, its silent opening, escapes phenomenology, as the origin and end of phenomenology's logos. The silent opening of the question about history as finitude and violence permits the appearance of history *as such;* it is the call (to) (of) an eschatology which dissimulates its own opening, covers this opening with its own noise as soon as the opening stands forth and is determined. This is the opening of a question, in the inversion of transcendental dissymmetry, put to philosophy as logos, finitude, history, violence: an interpellation of the Greek by the non-Greek at the heart of a silence, an ultralogical affect of speech, a question which can be stated only by being forgotten in the language of the Greeks; and a question which can be stated, as forgotten, only in the language of the Greeks. The strange dialogue of speech and silence. The strange community of the silent question of which we spoke above. It seems to us that this is the point at which, beyond any misunderstandings about Husserl's literal ambitions, phenomenology and eschatology can *open* a dialogue interminably, *be opened* in it, calling each other to silence.

Of Ontological Violence

Silence is a word which is not a
word, and breath an object which
is not an object. (G. Bataille)

Does not the movement of this dialogue also govern the explication with Heidegger? It would not be surprising. To be persuaded of this, it would suffice to notice, in the most schematic way possible, the following: in order to speak, as we have just spoken, of the present as the absolute form of experience, one *already* must understand *what time is,* must understand the *ens of the praes-ens,* and the proximity of the *Being of this ens.* The present of presence and the presence of the present suppose the horizon, the precomprehending anticipation of Being as time. If the meaning of Being always has been determined by philosophy as presence, then the *question of* Being, posed on the basis of the transcendental horizon of time (first stage, in *Being and Time*) is the first tremor of philosophical security, as it is of self-confident presence.

Now, Husserl never unfolded this question of Being. If phenomenology carries this question within itself each time that it considers the themes of temporalization, and of the relationship to the alter ego, it nonetheless remains dominated by a metaphysics of presence. The question of Being does not govern its discourse.

Phenomenology in general, as the passageway to essentiality, presupposes an anticipation of the *esse* of essence, the unity of the *esse* prior to its distribution into essence and existence. Via another route, one could probably show that Husserl silently presupposes a metaphysical anticipation or decision when, for example, he affirms Being (*Sein*) as the nonreality (*Realität*) of the ideal (*Ideal*). Ideality is unreal, but it *is*—as object or as thought-being. Without a presupposed access to a meaning of Being not exhausted by reality, the entire Husserlian theory of ideality would collapse, and with it all of transcendental phenomenology. For example, Husserl could no longer write: "Offenbar muss überhaupt jeder Versuch, das Sein des Idealen in ein mögliches Sein von Realem umzudeuten, daran scheitern, dass Möglichkeiten selbst wieder ideale Gegenstände sind. So wenig in der realen Welt Zahlen im allgemeinen, Dreiecke im allgemeinen zu finden sind so wenig Möglichkeiten" ("Manifestly every attempt to reinterpret the Being of the ideal as a possible Being of the real must fail, on the whole, for the possibilities themselves are in turn ideal. In the real world, one finds as few possibilities as one does numbers in general, or triangles in general).''[53] The meaning of Being—before each of its regional determinations—must be thought *first,* if one is to distinguish the ideal which *is* not only from the real which it is *not,* but also from the fictional which belongs to the domain of the possible real. ("Naturally, it is not our intention to place the *Being of the ideal* on the same level as the *Being-thought of the fictional or the absurd.*''[54] Hundreds of analogous texts could be cited.) But if Husserl can write this, and if, therefore, he presupposes access to a meaning of Being in general, how can he distinguish his idealism as a theory of knowledge from metaphysical idealism? The latter too, posited the unreal Being of the ideal. Husserl doubtless would respond, thinking of Plato, that the ideal was *realized* within metaphysical idealism, that is, that it was substantified, hypostasized, as soon as it was not understood essentially, in each of its aspects, as noema, and as soon as one imagined that it could be without in some way being thought or envisaged. This situation would not have been totally modified later when the *eidos* became originally and essentially noema only in the Understanding or Logos of an infinite subject: God. But to what extent does transcendental idealism, whose way is opened thereby, escape the horizon—at the very least—of this infinite subjectivity? This cannot be debated here.

However, if he had previously opposed Heidegger to Husserl, Levinas now contests what he calls "Heideggerean ontology": "The primacy of ontology for Heidegger does not rest on the truism, 'To know the *existent* it is necessary to have comprehended the Being of the existent.' To affirm the priority of *Being* over the *existent* is to decide the essence of philosophy; it is to subordinate the relation with *someone,* who is an existent, (the ethical relation) to a relation with the *Being of the existent,* which, impersonal, permits the apprehension, the domination of the existent (a relationship of knowing), subordinates justice to freedom" (*TI,* p. 45). This ontology would be valid for every existent, "except for the Other."[55]

Levinas's phrase overwhelms "ontology": not only would the thought of the Being of the existent have the impoverished logic of the truism, but it escapes this poverty only in order to seize and to murder the Other. It is a laughably self-evident but criminal truism, which places ethics under the heel of ontology.

Therefore, what of "ontology" and the "truism" ("in order to know the *existent* it is necessary to have comprehended the Being of the existent")? Levinas says that "the primacy of ontology does not rest" on a "truism." Is this certain? If the *truism* (*true, truth*) is fidelity to truth (that is, to the Being of what is as what it is, and such as it is), it is not certain that thought (Heidegger, for example) has ever sought to avoid it. "What is strange about this thought of Being is its simplicity," says Heidegger, at the very moment, moreover, when he demonstrates that this thought entertains no theoretical or practical aims. "The accomplishment of this thought is neither theoretical nor practical; no more does it consist in the union of these two modes of behavior."[56] Is not this gesture of return to what is within the dissociation of theory and practice also Levinas's gesture?[57] Does he not have to define metaphysical transcendence, therefore, as a not (yet) practical ethics? We are concerned here with some rather strange truisms. It is "by the simplicity of its essence" that "the thought of Being makes itself unknowable for us."[58]

If, on the contrary, by "truism" one understands, in the realm of *judgment*, analytic affirmation and the poverty of tautology, then the incriminated proposition is perhaps the least analytic of all; for if there were to be only one thought in the world which escapes the form of the truism, it would be this one. First, what Levinas envisages in the word "truism" is not a judicative proposition but a truth previous to judgment, which in turn founds all possible judgment. A banal truism is the repetition of the subject in the predicate. Now, Being is not simply a predicate of the existent, no more than it is the existent's subject. If it is taken as essence or as existence (as Being-such or Being-there), if it is taken as copula or as position of existence, or, more profoundly and more originally, if it is taken as the unitary focal point of all these possibilities, then the Being of the existent does not belong to the realm of predication, because it is already implied in all predication in general, and makes predication possible. And it makes every synthetic or analytic judgment possible. It is beyond genre and categories, transcendental in the scholastic sense, before scholasticism had made of the transcendental a supreme and infinite existent, God himself. It must be a singular truism that, through which is sought, in the most profound way, as the most concrete thought of all thoughts, the common root of essence and existence, without which no judgment, no language would be possible, and which every concept can only presuppose, by dissimulating it.[59] But if "ontology" is not a truism, or at least a truism among others, and if the strange difference between Being and the existent has a meaning, or is meaning, can one speak of the "priority" of Being in relation to the existent? An important question, here, for it is this alleged "priority" which, for Levinas, would enslave ethics to "ontology."

There can be an order of priority only between two determined things, two existents. Being, since *it is nothing* outside the existent, a theme which Levinas had commented upon so well previously, could in no way *precede* the existent, whether in time, or in dignity, etc. Nothing is more clear, as concerns this, in Heidegger's thought. Henceforth, one cannot legitimately speak of the "subordination" of the existent to Being, or, for example, of the ethical relation to the ontological relation. To precomprehend or explicate the implicit relation of Being to the existent[60] is not to submit the existent (for example, someone) to Being in a violent fashion. Being is but the *Being-of* this existent, and does not exist outside it as a foreign power, or as a hostile or neutral impersonal element. The neutrality so often denounced by Levinas can only be the characteristic of an undetermined existent, of an anonymous ontic power, of a conceptual generality, or of a principle. Now, Being is not a principle, is not a principial existent, an *archia* which would permit Levinas to insert the face of a faceless tyrant under the name of Being. The thought of Being (of the existent) is radically foreign to the search for a principle, or even for a root (although certain images lead us to believe this, occasionally), or for a "tree of knowledge": it is, as we have seen,

beyond theory, and is not the first word of theory. It is even beyond all hierarchies. If every "philosophy," every "metaphysics," has always sought to
determine the first existent, the excellent and truly existent existent, then the
thought of the Being of the existent is not this metaphysics or first philosophy. It
is not even ontology (cf. above), if ontology is another name for first philosophy.
Since it is not first philosophy concerned with the archi-existent, that is, the first
thing or first cause which governs, then the thought of Being is neither concerned
with, nor exercises, any power. For power is a relationship between existents.
"Such thinking has no result. It produces no effect" (*Humanismus*). Levinas
writes: "Ontology, as first philosophy, is a philosophy of power" (*TI*). This is
perhaps true. But we have just seen that the thought of Being is neither ontology,
nor first philosophy, nor a philosophy of power. Foreign to every first philosophy, it is not opposed to any kind of first philosophy. Not even to morals, if, as
Levinas says, "morals is not a branch of philosophy but first philosophy" (*TI*).
Foreign to the search for an ontic *archia* in general, for an ethical or political
archia in particular, it is not *foreign*, in the sense understood by Levinas who
accuses it precisely of this foreignness, in the way violence is foreign to nonviolence, or evil to good. One may say of it what Alain said of philosophy: it "is no
more politics" (or ethics) . . . "than it is agriculture." Which does not mean that
it is an industry. Radically foreign to ethics, it is not a counterethics, nor a
subordination of ethics to a function in the realm of ethics that is already secretly
violent: the neutral. Levinas always reconstructs, and not only in the case of
Heidegger, the *polis* or kind of social organization whose delicate outline he
believes can be traced through a discourse offered neither as sociological, nor as
political, nor as ethical. Thus it is paradoxical to see the Heideggerean city
governed by a neutral power, by an anonymous discourse, that is, by the "one"
(*man*) whose inauthenticity Heidegger was the first to describe. And if it is true,
in a difficult sense, that the Logos, according to Heidegger, "is the Logos of no
one," this certainly does not mean that it is the anonymity of oppression, the
impersonality of the State, or the neutrality of the "one says." It is anonymous
only as the *possibility* of the name and of responsibility. "But if man must one
day arrive in the neighborhood of Being, he must first learn to exist in that which
has no name" (*Humanism*). Did not the Kabbala also speak of the unnameable
possibility of the Name?

The thought of Being, therefore, can have no *human* design, secret or not.
Taken by itself, it is doubtless the only thought which no anthropology, no
ethics, and above all, no ethico-anthropological psychoanalysis will ever
enclose.[61]

Quite the contrary. Not only is the thought of Being not ethical violence, but it
seems that no ethics—in Levinas's sense—can be opened without it. Thought—
or at least the precomprehension of Being—*conditions* (in its own fashion, which
excludes every ontic conditionality: principles, causes, premises, etc.) the

recognition of the essence of the existent (for example someone, existent *as other, as* other self, etc.). It conditions the *respect* for the other *as what it is: other.* Without this acknowledgment, which is not a knowledge, or let us say without this "letting-be" of an existent (Other) as something existing outside me in the essence of what it is (first in its alterity), no ethics would be possible. "To let be" is an expression of Heidegger's which does not mean, as Levinas seems to think,[62] to let be as an "object of comprehension first," and, in the case of the Other, as "interlocutor afterward." The "letting-be" concerns all possible forms of the existent, and even those which, *by essence,* cannot be transformed into "objects of comprehension."[63] If it belongs to the essence of the Other first and foremost to be an "interlocutor" and to be "interpellated," then the "letting-be" will let the Other be what it is, will respect it as interpellated-interlocutor. The "letting-be" does not only, or by privilege, concern impersonal things. To let the other be in its existence and essence as other means that what gains access to thought, or *(and)* what thought gains access to, is that which is essence and that which is existence; and that which is the Being which they both presuppose. Without this, no letting-be would be possible, and first of all, the letting be of respect and of the ethical commandment addressing itself to freedom. Violence would reign to such a degree that it would no longer even be able to appear and be named.

Therefore, the "relation to the Being of the existent" cannot possibly dominate the "relation to the existent." Heidegger not only would criticize the notion of a *relation* to Being, just as Levinas criticizes that of a *relation to the other,* but also the notion of *domination:* Being is not elevated, is not the land of the existent, for elevation belongs to the existent. There are few themes which have demanded Heidegger's insistence to this extent: Being is not an excellent existent.

That Being is not *above* the existent does not imply that it is *beside* it. For then it would be another existent. Therefore, it is difficult to speak of "the ontological significance of the *existent* in the general economy of Being—which Heidegger simply places *beside* Being through a distinction . . ." (EE) It is true that Levinas acknowledges elsewhere that "if there is distinction, there is not separation" (TA); and this is already to acknowledge the impossibility of every relationship of ontic domination between Being and existent. In reality, there is not even a *distinction* in the usual sense of the word, between Being and existent. For reasons of essence, and first because Being is nothing outside the existent, and because the opening amounts to the ontico-ontological difference, it is impossible to avoid the ontic metaphor in order to articulate Being in language, in order to let Being circulate in language. This is why Heidegger says of language that it is *"lichtend-verbergende Ankunft des seins selbst"* (*Humanismus*). At one and the same time language illuminates and hides Being itself. Nevertheless, Being itself is *alone* in its absolute resistance to *every metaphor.* Every philology which allegedly reduces the *meaning* of Being to the metaphorical origin of the *word* "Being," whatever the historical (scientific) value of its hypotheses, misses the history of the meaning of Being. This history is to such an extent the history of a liberation of Being as concerns the determined existent, that one existent among others has come to be thought of as the eponymous existent of Being, for example, *respiration.* Renan and Nietzsche, for example, refer to respiration as the etymological origin of the word *Being* when they wish to reduce the meaning of what they take to be a concept—the indeterminate generality of Being—to its modest metaphorical origin. (Renan: *On the Origin of Language.* Nietzsche: *The Birth of Philosophy*).[64] Thus is explained all of empirical history, except precisely for the essential, that is, the thought that respiration and *non-respiration are,* for example. And are in a determined way, among other ontic determinations. Etymological empiricism, the hidden root of all empiricism, explains everything except that at a given moment the metaphor, has been thought *as* metaphor, that is, has been ripped apart as the veil of Being. This moment is the emergence of the thought of Being itself, the very movement of metaphoricity. For this emergence still, and always, occurs beneath an *other* metaphor. As Hegel says somewhere, empiricism always forgets, at very least, that it employs the words to be. Empiricism is thinking *by* metaphor without thinking the metaphor *as such.*

Concerning "Being" and "respiration," let us permit ourselves a juxtaposition which does not only have the value of a historical curiosity. In a letter to X . . ., dated March 1638, Descartes explains that the proposition "'I breathe, therefore I am' concludes nothing, if it has not been proven previously that one exists, or if one does not imply: *I think that* I breathe (even if I am mistaken in this), therefore I am; and it is nothing other to state in this sense *I breathe, therefore I am* than *I think, therefore I am.*" Which means, in terms of what concerns us here, that the *meaning* of respiration is always but a dependent and particular determination of my thought and my existence, and a fortiori of thought and of Being in general. Supposing that the word "Being" is derived from a word meaning "respiration" (or any other determined thing), no etymology or philology—as such, and as determined sciences—will be able to account for the thought for which "respiration" (or any other determined thing) becomes a determination of Being among others. Here, for example, no philology will be able to account for the gesture of Descartes's thought. One must travel other roads—or an other reading of Nietzsche—in order to trace the genealogy of the unheard-of meaning of Being.

This is a first reason why the "relation with an existent," with someone (the ethical relation), cannot be "dominated" by "a relation with the Being of the existent (a relation of knowledge)."

Second reason: the "relation with the Being of the existent," which is in no way a relation, above all is not a "relation of knowledge."[65] It is not a theory, as we have seen, and teaches us nothing about what is. It is because it is not science that Heidegger sometimes refuses it even the name of ontology, after having distinguished it from metaphysics, and even from fundamental ontology. Since it is not knowledge, the thought of Being is not to be confused with the concept of pure Being as undetermined generality. Formerly, Levinas had given us to understand this: "Precisely because Being is not an existent, it must not be apprehended *per genus et differentiam specificam*" *(EDE)*. Now, according to Levinas, all violence is a violence of the concept; and both *Is Ontology Fundamental?* and *Totality and Infinity* interpret the thought of Being as a concept of Being. Opposing himself to Heidegger, Levinas writes, among many other similar passages: "In our relation with the Other, the latter does not affect us on the basis of a concept" *(Is Ontology Fundamental?)*. According to Levinas, it is finally the absolutely undetermined concept of Being which offers the Other to our understanding, that is, to our power and our violence. Now Heidegger is emphatic on this point: the Being *which is in question* is not the concept to which the existent (for example, someone) is to be submitted (subsumed). Being is not the concept of a rather indeterminate and abstract predicate, seeking to cover the totality of existents in its extreme universality: (1) because it is not a predicate, and authorizes all predication; (2) because it is "older" than the concrete *presence* of the *ens;* (3) because belonging to Being does not cancel any predicative difference, but, on the contrary, permits the emergence of every possible difference.[66] Being is therefore transcategorical, and Heidegger would say of it what Levinas says of the other: it is "refractory to the category" *(TI)*. "The question of Being as a question of the possibility of the concept of Being arises from the preconceptual comprehension of Being,"[67] writes Heidegger, opening a dialogue and a repetition, (as concerns the Hegelian concept of pure Being as nothingness), which will not cease to deepen and, in the style which is almost always that of Heidegger's dialogue with the thinkers of tradition, will not cease to permit Hegel's discourse to grow and to speak—Hegel's discourse as that of all of metaphysics (Hegel included, or rather, being entirely included in Hegel).

Thus, the thought or pre-comprehension of Being signifies nothing less than a conceptual or totalitarian com-prehension. What we have just said of Being could also be said of the same.[68] To treat Being (and the same) as categories, or to treat the "relationship to Being" as a relation to a category which itself could be (by "reversal of terms," *TI*) posed afterward, or subordinated to a determined relation (an ethical relation, for example)—is this not to forbid oneself every determination (the ethical one, for example) from the outset? Every determination, in effect, presupposes the thought of Being. Without it, how can one give meaning to Being as other, as other self, to the irreducibility of the existence and the essence of the other, and to the consequent responsibility? etc. "This prerogative . . . *of being answerable to oneself as essent,* in short, this prerogative of existing, involves in itself the necessity of a comprehension of Being."[69] If to understand Being is to be able to let be (that is, to respect Being in essence and existence, and to be responsible for one's respect), then the understanding of Being always concerns alterity, and par excellence the alterity of the Other in all its originality: one can have to let be only that which one is not. If Being is always to be let be, and if to think is to let Being be, then Being is indeed the other of thought. But since it is what it is only by the letting-be of thought, and since the latter is thought only by virtue of the presence of the Being which it lets be, then thought and Being, thought and the other, are the same; which, let us recall, does not mean identical, or one, or equal.

This amounts to stating that the thinking of Being does not make of the other a species of the genre Being. Not only because the other is "refractory to the category," but because Being is not a category. Like the Other, Being is not at all the accomplice of the totality, whether of the finite totality, (the violent totality of which Levinas speaks) or of an infinite totality. The notion of totality is always related to the existent. It is always a "metaphysical" or "theological" notion, and the notions of finite and infinite take on meaning in relation to it.[70] Foreign to the finite totality, or to the infinity of existents, *foreign* in the sense specified above, foreign without being another existent or another totality of existents, Being could not oppress or enclose the existent and its differences. If the glance of the other is to command me, as Levinas says, and is to command me to command, then I must be able to let be the other in his freedom as Other, and vice versa. But Being itself commands nothing or no one. As Being is not the lord of the existent, its priority (ontic metaphor) is not an *archia*. The best liberation from violence is a certain putting into question, which makes the search for an *archia* tremble. Only the thought of Being can do so, and not traditional "philosophy" or "metaphysics." The latter are therefore "politics" which can escape ethical violence only by economy: by battling violently against the violences of the *an-archy* whose possibility, in history, is still the accomplice of archism.

Just as he implicitly had to appeal to phenomenological self-evidences against phenomenology, Levinas must ceaselessly suppose and practice the thought of precomprehension of Being in his discourse, even when he directs it against "ontology." Otherwise, what would "exteriority as the essence of Being" mean (*TI*)? And that "eschatology places one in relation to Being, *beyond the totality* or history, and not with Being beyond past and present" (*TI*)? And "to support pluralism as the structure of Being" (*DL*)? And that "the encounter with the face is, absolutely, a relation to what is. Perhaps man alone is substance, and this is why he is face"?[71] Ethico-metaphysical transcendence therefore presupposes ontological transcendence. The *epekeina tes ousias* (in Levinas's interpretation) would not lead beyond Being itself, but beyond the totality of the existent or the existent-hood of the existent (the Being existent of the existent), or beyond ontic

history. Heidegger also refers to the *epekeina tes ousias* in order to announce
ontological transcendence,[72] but he also shows that the undetermined *agathon*
toward which transcendence breaks through has been determined too quickly.

Thus, the thought of Being could not possibly occur as ethical violence. On the
contrary, without it one would be forbidden to let be the existent, and one would
enclose transcendence within identification and empirical economy. By refusing,
in *Totality and Infinity,* to accord any dignity to the ontico-ontological difference,
by seeing in it only a ruse of war, and by calling the intra-ontic movement of
ethical transcendence (the movement respectful of one existent toward another)
metaphysics, Levinas confirms Heidegger in his discourse: for does not the latter
see in metaphysics (in metaphysical ontology) the forgetting of Being and the
dissimulation of the ontico-ontological difference? "Metaphysics does not pose
the question of the truth of Being itself."[73] It thinks Being in an implicit fashion,
as is inevitable in every language. This is why the thinking of Being must take its
driving force from metaphysics, and must first occur as the metaphysics of
metaphysics in the question "What is Metaphysics?" But the difference between
the implicit and the explicit is the entirety of thought; and if correctly determined,
it imprints its form on all ruptures and on the most radical questions. "It is true,"
says Heidegger once more, "that Metaphysics represents the existent in its
Being, and thus thinks the Being of the existent. But it does not think the
difference of Being and the existent."[74]

For Heidegger, it is therefore metaphysics (or metaphysical ontology) which
remains a closure of the totality, and transcends the existent only toward the
(superior) existent, or toward the (finite or infinite) totality of the existent. This
metaphysics essentially would be tied to a humanism which never asks itself "in
what manner the essence of man belongs to the truth of Being."[75] "What is
proper to all metaphysics is revealed in its 'humanism.'"[76] Now, Levinas simultaneously proposes to us a humanism and a metaphysics. It is a question of
attaining, via the royal road of ethics, the supreme existent, the truly existent
("substance" and "in itself" are Levinas's expressions) as other. And this
existent is man, determined as face in his essence as man on the basis of his
resemblance to God. Is this not what Heidegger has in mind when he speaks of
the unity of metaphysics, humanism and onto-theology? "The encounter with the
face is not only an anthropological fact. It is, absolutely speaking, a relation with
what is. Perhaps man alone is substance, and this is why he is face." Certainly.
But it is the analogy between the face and God's visage that, in the most classical
fashion, distinguishes man from animal, and determines man's substantiality:
"The Other resembles God." Man's substantiality, which permits him to be
face, is thus founded in his resemblance to God, who is therefore both The Face
and absolute substantiality. The theme of the Face thus calls for a second reference to Descartes. Levinas never formulates it: it is, as recognized by the
Schoolmen, the ambiguity of the notion of substance as concerns God and his

creatures (cf. for example, *Principes,* I, sec. 51). By means of more than one
mediation we thus are referred to the Scholastic problem of the analogy. We do
not intend to enter into it here.[77] Let us simply notice that conceived on the basis
of a doctrine of analogy, of "resemblance," the expression "human face" is no
longer, at bottom, as foreign to metaphor as Levinas seems to wish. " . . . The
Other resembles God . . . ." Is this not the original metaphor? The question of
Being is nothing less than a disputation of the *metaphysical* truth of this schema;
which, let us note in passing, "atheistic humanism" employs precisely in order
to denounce the very process of alienation. The question of Being draws back
into this schema, this opposition of humanisms, in the direction of the thought of
Being presupposed by the determination of the existent-man, the existent-God,
and the analogical relationship between them; for the possibility of this relationship can be opened solely by the pre-conceptual and pre-analogical unity of
Being. It is a question neither of substituting Being for God, nor of founding God
on Being. The Being of the existent (for example, God)[78] is not the absolute
existent, nor the infinite existent, nor even the foundation of the existent in
general. This is why the question of Being cannot budge the metaphysical edifice
of *Totality and Infinity* (for example). It is simply forever out of reach for the
"inversion of the terms" *ontology* and *metaphysics* that Levinas proposes. The
theme of this inversion, therefore, does not play an indispensable role, have
meaning and necessity, except in the economy and coherence of Levinas's book
in its entirety.

What would it mean, for metaphysics and for humanism, to ask "in what
manner the essence of man belongs to the truth of Being" (*Humanismus*)?
Perhaps this: would the experience of the face be possible, could it be stated, if
the thought of Being were not already implied in it? In effect, the face is the
inaugural unity of a naked glance and of a right to speech. But eyes and mouth
make a face only if, beyond need, they can "let be," if they see and they say
what is such as it is, if they reach the Being of what is. But since Being is, it
cannot simply be produced, but precisely must be respected by a glance and a
speech; Being must provoke them, interpellate them. There is no speech without
the thought and statement *of* Being. But as Being is nothing outside the determined existent, it would not appear as such without the possibility of speech.
Being *itself* can only be thought and stated. It is the contemporary of the Logos,
which itself can only be as the Logos *of* Being, *saying* Being. Without this
double genitivity, speech, cut off from Being and enclosed in the determined
existent, would be only (according to Levinas's terminology) the cry of need
before desire, the gesture of the self in the realm of the homogenous. It is only
then, in the reduction or subordination of thought to Being, that "philosophical
discourse itself" would not be "only a failed act, the pretext for an uninterrupted
psychoanalysis or philology or sociology in which the appearance of discourse
vanishes into the All" (*TI*). It is only then that the relation to exteriority would

no longer catch its breath. The metaphysics of the face therefore *encloses* the thought of Being, presupposing the difference between Being and the existent at the same time as it stifles it.

If this difference is original, if to think Being outside the existent is to think *nothing,* or if it is to *think* nothing no more than it is to approach the existent other than in its Being, doubtless one has some right to say with Levinas (excepting the ambiguous expression "Being in general") that "the relation to the expressed existent *preexists* . . . the unveiling of Being in general . . . ; at the ontological plane, the ethical one" *(TI;* my italics). If preexistence has the ontic sense which it must have, then this is incontestable. In fact, in existence the relationship with the *expressed* existent precedes the unveiling, the explicit thinking, of Being itself. With the limitation that there is no *expression,* in the sense of speech and not of need, except if there is already, implicitly, thought of Being. Likewise, *in fact,* the natural attitude precedes the transcendental reduction. But we know that ontological or transcendental "priority" is not of this order, and no one has ever alleged that it was. This "priority" no more contradicts than it confirms ontic or factual precedence. It follows that Being, since it is always, in fact, determined as an existent and is nothing outside the existent, is always dissimulated. Levinas's phrase—the preexistence of the relation to the existent—is the very formula of this initial concealment. Being not existing before the Existent—and this is why it *is History*—it begins by hiding itself beneath its determination. This determination as the revelation of the existent (Metaphysics) is the very veiling of Being. There is nothing accidental or regrettable about this. "The unconcealing of the existent, the clarity accorded to it, darkens the light of Being. Being draws back in that it is disclosed in the existent" *(Holzwege* p. 310). Is it not risky, then, to speak of the thinking of Being as of a thought dominated by the theme of unveiling *(TI)?* Without this dissimulation of Being by the existent there would be nothing, and there would be no history. That Being occurs in all respects as history and as world means that it can only retire beneath ontic determinations in the history of metaphysics. For historical "epochs" are metaphysical (ontotheological) determinations of the Being which thus brackets itself, reserves itself beneath metaphysical concepts. In the strange light of this being-history Heidegger permits the reemergence of the notion of "eschatology," as it appears, for example, in *Holzwege:* "Being itself . . . is in itself eschatological" (p. 302). The relationship between this eschatology and messianic eschatology requires closer examination. The first supposes that war is not an accident which overcomes Being, but rather Being itself. "Das Sein selber das Strittige ist" *(Brief über den Humanismus,* p. 189). A proposition which must not be understood in consonance with Hegelianism: here, negativity has its origin neither in negation, nor in the anxiety of an infinite and primary existent. War, perhaps, is no longer even conceivable as negativity.

Heidegger, as is well known, calls the original dissimulation of Being beneath the existent, which is prior to the error in judgment, and which nothing precedes in the ontic order, erring [*Irren:* erring, going astray]: "Every epoch of world history is an epoch of erring" (*Holzwege* p. 311). If Being is time and history, then erring and the epochal essence of Being are irreducible. Henceforth, how can one accuse this thought of interminable wandering of being a new paganism of the Site, a complacent cult of the Sendentary? (*TI, DL*).[79] Here, the solicitation of the Site and the Land is in no way, it must be emphasized, a passionate attachment to territory or locality, is in no way a provincialism or particularism. It is, at very least, as little linked to empirical "nationalism" as is, or should be, the Hebraic nostalgia for the Land, a nostalgia *provoked* not by an empirical passion, but by the irruption of a speech or a promise.[80] Is not to interpret the Heideggerean theme of the Land or the Dwelling as a nationalism or a Barrèsism first of all to express an *allergy*—the word, the accusation, which Levinas plays upon so often—to the "climate" of Heidegger's philosophy? Levinas acknowledges, moreover, that his "reflections," after having submitted to inspiration by "the philosophy of Martin Heidegger," "are governed by a profound need to depart from the climate of this philosophy" (*EE*). In question here is a need whose natural legitimacy we would be the last to question; what is more, we believe that its climate is never totally exterior to thought itself. But does not the naked truth of the other appear beyond "need," "climate," and a certain "history"? And who has taught us this better than Levinas?

The Site, therefore, is not an empirical Here but always an *Illic:* for Heidegger, as for the Jew and the Poet. The proximity of the Site is always held in reserve, says Hölderlin as commented on by Heidegger.[81] The thinking of Being thus is not a pagan cult of the *Site,* because the Site is never a given proximity but a promised one. And then also because it is not a *pagan cult.* The Sacred of which it speaks *belongs* neither to religion in general, nor to a particular theology, and thus cannot be determined by any history of religion. It is first the essential experience of divinity or of deity. As the latter is neither a concept nor a reality, it must provide access to itself in a proximity foreign to mystical theory or affectivity, foreign to theology and to enthusiasm. Again, in a sense which is neither chronological nor logical, nor ontical in general, it *precedes* every relationship to God or to the Gods. This last relationship, of whatever type, in order to be lived and stated supposes some precomprehension of the Deity, of God's Being-god, of the "dimension of the divine" of which Levinas also speaks by saying that it "is opened on the basis of the human face" (*TI*). This is all, and as usual it is simple and difficult. The sacred is the "only essential space of divinity which in turn opens only a dimension for the gods and the god . . . " (*Humanismus*). This space (in which Heidegger also names Elevation)[82] is within faith and atheism. Both presuppose it. "It is only on the basis of the truth of Being that the essence of the Sacred can be thought. It is only on the basis of the essence of the Sacred that the essence of Divinity must be thought. It is only in the light of the

essence of Divinity that one can think and say what the word 'God' must designate'' (*Humanismus*). This precomprehension of the Divine cannot not be
presupposed by Levinas's discourse at the very moment when he seeks to oppose
God to the Sacred divine. That the gods or God cannot be indicated except in the
Space of the Sacred and in the light of the deity, is at once the *limit* and the
wellspring of finite-Being as history. Limit, because divinity is *not* God. In a
sense it is nothing. ''The sacred, it is true, appears. But the god remains distant.''[83] Wellspring, because this anticipation as a thought of Being (of the
existent God) always *sees* God *coming,* opens the possibility (the eventuality) of
an encounter with God and of a dialogue with God.[84]

That the Deity of God, which permits the thinking and naming of God, is
nothing, and above all is not God himself, is what Meister Eckhart, in particular,
said this way: ''God and the deity are as different from one another as heaven and
earth. . . . God operates, deity does not operate, has nothing to operate, has no
operation in it, has never any operation in view'' (Sermon *Nolite timere cos*). But
this deity is still determined as the essence-of-the-threefold-God. And when
Meister Eckhart seeks to go beyond these determinations, the movement which
he sketches seems to remain enclosed in ontic transcendence. ''When I said that
God was not a Being and was above Being, I did not thereby contest his Being,
but on the contrary attributed to him a *more elevated Being*'' (*Quasi stella
matutina* . . .). This negative theology is still a theology and, *in its literality at
least,* it is concerned with liberating and acknowledging the ineffable transcendence of an infinite existent, ''Being above Being and superessential negation.'' *In its literality at least,* but the difference between metaphysical ontotheology, on the one hand, and the thought of Being (of difference), on the
other, signifies the essential importance of the *letter.* Since everything occurs in
movements of increasing explicitness, the literal difference is almost the entire
difference of thought. This is why, here, when the thought of Being goes beyond
ontic determinations it is not a negative theology, nor even a negative ontology.

''Ontological'' anticipation, transcendence toward Being, permits, then, an
understanding of the word God, for example, even if this understanding is but the
ether in which dissonance can resonate. This transcendence inhabits and founds
language, and along with it the possibility of all Being-together; the possibility of
a *Mitsein* much more original than any of the eventual forms with which it has
often been confused: solidarity, the team, companionship.[85] Implied by the
discourse of *Totality and Infinity,* alone permitting to *let* be others in their truth,
freeing dialogue and the face to face, the thought of Being is thus as close as
possible to nonviolence.

We do not say pure nonviolence. Like pure violence, pure nonviolence is a
contradictory concept. Contradictory beyond what Levinas calls ''formal logic.''
Pure violence, a relationship between beings without face, is not yet violence, is
pure nonviolence. And inversely: pure nonviolence, the nonrelation of the same

to the other (in the sense understood by Levinas) is pure violence. Only a face can arrest violence, but can do so, in the first place, only because a face can provoke it. Levinas says it well: "Violence can only aim at the face" ("La violence ne peut viser qu'un visage" *TI*). Further, without the thought of Being which opens the face, there would be only pure violence or pure nonviolence. Therefore, the thought of Being, in its unveiling, is never foreign to a certain violence.[86] That this thought always appears in difference, and that the same— thought (and) (of) Being—is never the identical, means first that Being is history, that Being dissimulates itself in its occurrence, and originally does violence to itself in order to be stated and in order to appear. A Being without violence would be a Being which would occur outside the existent: nothing; nonhistory; nonoc- currence; nonphenomenality. A speech produced without the least violence would determine nothing, would say nothing, would offer nothing to the other; it would not be *history,* and it would *show* nothing: in every sense of the word, and first of all the Greek sense, it would be speech without *phrase.*

In the last analysis, according to Levinas, nonviolent language would be a language which would do without the verb *to be,* that is, without predication. Predication is the first violence. Since the verb *to be* and the predicative act are implied in every other verb, and in every common noun, nonviolent language, in the last analysis, would be a language of pure invocation, pure adoration, proffer- ing only proper nouns in order to call to the other from afar. In effect, such a language would be purified of all *rhetoric,* which is what Levinas explicitly desires; and purified of the first sense of rhetoric, which we can invoke without artifice, that is, purified of every *verb.* Would such a language still deserve its name? Is a language free from all rhetoric possible? The Greeks, who taught us what *Logos* meant, would never have accepted this. Plato tells us in the *Cratylus* (425a), the *Sophist* (262 ad) and in Letter VII (342b), that there is no *Logos* which does not suppose the interlacing of nouns and verbs.

Finally, if one remains within Levinas's intentions, what would a language without phrase, a language which would say nothing, offer to the other? Lan- guage must give the world to the other, *Totality and Infinity* tells us. A master who forbids himself the *phrase* would give nothing. He would have no disciples but only slaves. The work—or liturgy—that is the expenditure which breaks with economy, and which must not be thought, according to Levinas, as a Game, would be forbidden to him.

Thus, in its most elevated nonviolent urgency, denouncing the passage through Being and the moment of the concept, Levinas's thought would not only propose an ethics without law, as we said above, but also a language without phrase. Which would be entirely coherent if the face was only glance, but it is also speech; and in speech it is the phrase which makes the cry of need become the expression of desire. Now, there is no phrase which is indeterminate, that is, which does not pass through the violence of the concept. Violence appears with

articulation. And the latter is opened only by (the at first preconceptual) circulation of Being. The very elocution of nonviolent metaphysics is its first disavowal.
Levinas doubtless would not deny that every historical language carries within it
an irreducible conceptual moment, and therefore a certain violence. From his
point of view, the origin and possibility of the concept are simply not the thought
of Being, but the gift of the world to the other as totally-other (cf., for example,
TI, p. 175). In its original possibility as *offer*, in its still silent intention, language
is nonviolent (but can it be language, in this pure intention?). It becomes violent
only in its history, in what we have called the phrase, which obliges it to
articulate itself in a conceptual syntax opening the circulation of the same,
permitting itself to be governed both by "ontology" and by what remains, for
Levinas, the concept of concepts: Being. Now, for Levinas, the concept of Being
would be only an abstract means produced for the gift of the world to the other
who is *above Being*. Hence, only in its silent origin, before Being, would
language be nonviolent. But why history? Why does the phrase impose itself?
Because if one does not uproot the silent origin from itself violently, if one
decides not to speak, then the worst violence will silently cohabit the *idea* of
peace? Peace is made only in a *certain silence*, which is determined and protected by the violence of speech. Since speech says nothing other than the
horizon of this silent peace by which it has itself summoned and that it is its
mission to protect and to prepare, speech *indefinitely* remains silent. One never
escapes the *economy of war*.

It is evident that to separate the original possibility of speech—as non-violence
and gift—from the violence necessary in historical actuality is to prop up thought
by means of transhistoricity. Which Levinas does explicitly, despite his initial
critique of Husserlian "anhistoricism." For Levinas, the origin of meaning is
nonhistory, is "beyond history." One would then have to ask whether it is any
longer possible to identify thought and language as Levinas seeks to do; and one
would have to ask whether this transhistoricity of meaning is authentically Hebraic in its inspiration; and finally, whether this nonhistory uproots itself from
history in general, or only from a certain empirical or ontic dimension of history.
And whether the eschatology invoked can be separated from every reference to
history. *For our own reference to history, here, is only contextual. The economy
of which we are speaking does not any longer accommodate the concept of
history such as it has always functioned, and which it is difficult, if not impossible, to lift from its teleological or eschatological horizon.*

The anhistoricity of meaning at its origin is what profoundly separates Levinas
from Heidegger, therefore. Since Being is history for the latter, it *is not* outside
difference, and thus, it originally occurs as (nonethical) violence, as dissimulation of itself in its own unveiling. That language, thereby, always hides its own
origin is not a contradiction, but history itself. In the ontological-historical[87]
violence which permits the thinking of ethical violence, in economy as the

thought of Being, Being is necessarily dissimulated. The first violence is this dissimulation, but it is also the first defeat of nihilistic violence, and the first epiphany of Being. Being, thus, is less the *primum cognitum,* as was said, than the *first dissimulated,* and these two propositions are not contradictory. For Levinas, on the contrary, Being (understood as concept) is the *first dissimulating,* and the ontico-ontological difference thereby would neutralize difference, the infinite alterity of the totally-other. The ontico-ontological difference, moreover, would be conceivable only on the basis of the idea of the Infinite, of the unanticipatable irruption of the totally-other existent. For Levinas, as for Heidegger, language would be at once a coming forth and a holding back [*réserve*], enlightenment and obscurity; and for both, dissimulation would be a conceptual gesture. But for Levinas, the concept is on the plane of Being; for Heidegger it is on the plane of ontic determination.

This schema accentuates their opposition but, as is often the case, also permits one to conjecture about their proximity: the proximity of two "eschatologies" which by opposed routes repeat and put into question the entire "philosophical" adventure issued from Platonism. Interrogate it simultaneously from within and without, in the form of a question to Hegel, in whom this adventure is thought and recapitulated. This proximity would be indicated in questions of this type: *on the one hand,* is God (the infinite-other-existent) still an existent which can be precomprehended on the basis of a thought of Being (singularly, of divinity)? In other words, can infinity be called an ontic determination? Has not God always been thought of as the name of that which is not a supreme existent precomprehended on the basis of a thought of Being? Is not God the name of that which cannot be anticipated on the basis of the dimension of the divine? Is not God the other name of Being (name because nonconcept), the thinking of which would open difference and the ontological horizon, instead of being indicated in them only? Opening of the horizon, and not *in* the horizon. Through the thought of infinity, the ontic enclosure would have already been broken—but in a sense of the unthought that would have to be examined more closely—by means of what Heidegger calls metaphysics and onto-theology. *On the other hand:* is not the thought of Being the thought *of* the other before being the homogeneous identity of the concept, and the asphixiation of the same? Is not the beyond-history of eschatology the other name of the transition to a more profound history, to History itself? But to a history which, unable any longer to be *itself* in any original or final *presence,* would have to change its name?

In other words, perhaps one might say that ontology precedes theology *only* by putting between brackets the content of the ontic determination which, in post-Hellenic philosophical thought, is called God: to wit, the positive infinity. The positive infinity would only have the (nominal) appearance of what is called an ontic determination. In truth, it would be that which refuses to be an ontic determination which is included as such in the thought of Being, that is, on the basis and in the light of a thought of Being. On the contrary, it is infinity—as nondetermination and concrete operation—which would permit the thinking of the difference between Being and ontic determination. The ontic content of infinity would destroy ontic closure. Implicitly or not, the thought of infinity would open the question, and the ontico-ontological difference. Paradoxically, it would be this thought of infinity (what is called the thought of God) which would permit one to affirm the priority of ontology over theology, and to affirm that the thought of Being is presupposed by the thought of God. Doubtless, it is for this reason that Duns Scotus or Malebranche, respectful of the presence in all thought of *uniform* Being, or Being in general, did not believe it necessary to distinguish between the levels of ontology (or metaphysics) and theology. Heidegger often reminds us of the "strange simplicity" of the thought of Being: this is both its difficulty and that which properly touches upon the "unknowable." For Heidegger, infinity would be only one eventual determination of this simplicity. For Malebranche, infinity is its very form: "The idea of the extended infinite thus encloses more reality than that of the heavens; and the idea of the infinite in all genres of Being, that which corresponds to this word, *Being,* the infinitely perfect being, contains infinitely more [reality], although the perception with which this idea affects us is the slightest of all; and is slighter to the extent that it is more vast, and consequently infinitely slight because infinite" (*Entretien d'un philosophe chrétien avec un philosophe chinois.*) Since Being is nothing (determined), it is necessarily produced in difference (*as* difference). Is, on the one hand, to say that Being is infinite, or to say, on the other, that it is revealed as produced only "in simultaneity with" (*in eins mit*) Nothingness (*What Is Metaphysics?*)—which means that it is "finite in its essence" (ibid.)—fundamentally to say anything else? But one would have to show that Heidegger never meant "anything else" than classical metaphysics, and that the transgression of metaphysics is not a new metaphysical or onto-theological thesis. Thus, the question about the Being of the existent would not only introduce—among others—the question about the existent-God; it already *would suppose* God as the very possibility of its question, and as the answer within its question. God always would be implied in every question about God, and would precede every "method." The very content of the thought of God is that of a being *about* which no question could be asked (except by being asked by it), and which cannot be determined as an existent. *The Idiot (Idiota),* an admirable meditation by Nicholas of Cusa, develops this implication of God in every question, and first in the question of God. For example:

> *The Idiot:* See how easie the difficultie is in divine things, that it always offers it self to the seeker, in the same manner that it is sought for. *The Orator:* Without doubt, there is nothing more wonderfull. *Id:* Every question concerning God presupposeth the thing questioned; and that must be answered, which in every question concerning God, the question presupposeth:

for God, although he be unsignifiable, is signified in every signification of terms. *Or:* Declare thy self more at large . . . . *Id:* Doth not the question, whether a thing be or no, presuppose the Entitie? *Or:* Yes. *Id:* Therefore when it is demanded of thee, whether God be, (or whether there be a God?) answer that which is presupposed, namely that he is; because that is the Entitie presupposed in the question. So, if any man shall ask thee, what is God? considering that this question presupposeth a quidditie to be; thou shalt answer, that God is absolute quiddity itself. And so for all things. Nor need there be any hesitation or doubt in this; for God is the absolute presupposition itself, of all things, which (after what manner soever) are presupposed as in every effect the cause is presupposed. See therefore, Oratour, how easie Theologicall difficulty is . . . . If that which in every question is presupposed, be in divine matters an answer unto the question, then of God there can be no proper question, because the answer coincides with it.[88]

By making the origin of language, meaning, and difference the relation to the infinitely other, Levinas is resigned to betraying his own intentions in his philosophical discourse. The latter is understood, and instructs, only by first permitting the same and Being to circulate within it. A classical schema here complicated by a metaphysics of dialogue and instruction, of a demonstration which contradicts what is demonstrated by the very rigor and truth of its development. The thousand-times-denounced circle of historicism, psychologism, relativism, etc. But the true name of this inclination of thought to the Other, of this resigned acceptance of incoherent incoherence inspired by a truth more profound than the "logic" of philosophical discourse, the true name of this renunciation of the concept, of the a prioris and transcendental horizons of language, is *empiricism*. For the latter, at bottom, has ever committed but one fault: the fault of presenting itself as a philosophy. And the profundity of the empiricist intention must be recognized beneath the naïveté of certain of its historical expressions. It is the *dream* of a purely *heterological* thought at its source. A *pure* thought of *pure* difference. Empiricism is its philosophical name, its metaphysical pretention or modesty. We say the *dream* because it must vanish *at daybreak,* as soon as language awakens. But perhaps one will object that it is language which is sleeping. Doubtless, but then one must, in a certain way, become classical once more, and again find other grounds for the divorce between speech and thought. This route is quite, perhaps too, abandoned today. Among others, by Levinas.

By radicalizing the theme of the infinite exteriority of the other, Levinas thereby assumes the aim which has more or less secretly animated all the philosophical gestures which have been called *empiricisms* in the history of philosophy. He does so with an audacity, a profundity, and a resoluteness never before attained. By taking this project to its end, he totally renews empiricism, and inverses it by revealing it to itself as metaphysics. Despite the Husserlian and Heideggerean stages of his thought, Levinas does not even seek to draw back from the word *empiricism*. On two occasions, at least, he speaks for "the radical empiricism confident in the instruction of exteriority" (*TI*). The experience of the other (of the infinite) is irreducible, and is therefore "the experience par excellence" (*TI*). And, concerning death which is indeed its irreducible resource, Levinas speaks of an "empiricism which is in no way a positivism."[89] But can one speak of an *experience* of the other or of difference? Has not the concept of experience always been determined by the metaphysics of presence? Is not experience always an encountering of an irreducible presence, the perception of a phenomenality?

This complicity between empiricism and metaphysics is in no way surprising. By criticizing them, or rather by limiting them with one and the same gesture, Kant and Husserl indeed had recognized their solidarity. It calls for closer meditation. Schelling went quite far in this direction.[90]

But empiricism always has been determined by philosophy, from Plato to Husserl, as *nonphilosophy:* as the philosophical pretention to nonphilosophy, the inability to justify oneself, to come to one's own aid as speech. But this incapacitation, when resolutely assumed, contests the resolution and coherence of the logos (philosophy) at its root, instead of letting itself be questioned by the logos. Therefore, nothing can so profoundly *solicit* the Greek logos—philosophy—than this irruption of the totally-other; and nothing can to such an extent reawaken the logos to its origin as to its mortality, its other.

But if one calls this experience of the infinitely other Judaism (which is only a hypothesis for us), one must reflect upon the necessity in which this experience finds itself, the injunction by which it is ordered to occur as logos, and to reawaken the Greek in the autistic syntax of his own dream. The necessity to avoid the worst violence, which threatens when one silently delivers oneself into the hands of the other in the night. The necessity to borrow the ways of the unique philosophical logos, which can only invert the "curvature of space" for the benefit of the same. A same which is not the identical, and which does not enclose the other. It was a Greek who said, "If one has to philosophize, one has to philosophize; if one does not have to philosophize, one still has to philosophize (to say it and think it). One always has to philosophize." Levinas knows this better than others: "One could not possibly reject the Scriptures without knowing how to read them, nor say philology without philosophy, nor, if need be, arrest philosophical discourse without philosophizing" (*DL*). "One must refer—I am convinced—to the medium of all comprehension and of all understanding in which all truth is reflected—precisely to Greek civilization, and to what it produced: to the logos, to the coherent discourse of reason, to life in a reasonable State. This is the true grounds of all understanding" (*DL*). Such a site of encounter cannot only offer *occasional* hospitality to a thought which would remain foreign to it. And still less may the Greek absent himself, having loaned his house and his language, while the Jew and the Christian meet in his home (for this is the encounter in question in the text just cited). Greece is not a neutral, provisional territory, beyond borders. The history in which the Greek logos is produced cannot be a happy accident providing grounds for understanding to those who understand eschatological prophecy, and to those who do not understand it at all. It cannot be *outside* and *accidental* for any thought. The Greek miracle is not this or that, such and such astonishing success; it is the impossibility for any thought ever to treat its sages as "sages of the outside," according to the expression of Saint John Chrysostom. In having proferred the *epekeina tes ousias,* in having recognized from its second word (for example, in the *Sophist*) that alterity had to circulate at the origin of meaning, in welcoming alterity in general into the heart of the logos, the Greek thought of Being forever has protected itself against every absolutely *surprising* convocation.

Are we Jews? Are we Greeks? We live in the difference between the Jew and the Greek, which is perhaps the unity of what is called history. We live in and of difference, that is, in *hypocrisy,* about which Levinas so profoundly says that it is "not only a base contingent defect of man, but the underlying rending of a world attached to both the philosophers and the prophets" (*TI,* p. 24).

Are we Greeks? Are we Jews? But who, *we*? Are we (not a chronological, but a pre-logical question) *first* Jews or *first* Greeks? And does the strange dialogue between the Jew and the Greek, peace itself, have the form of the absolute, speculative logic of Hegel, the living logic which *reconciles* formal tautology and empirical heterology[91] after having *thought* prophetic discourse in the preface to the *Phenomenology of the Mind?* Or, on the contrary, does this peace have the form of infinite separation and of the unthinkable, unsayable transcendence of the other? To what horizon of peace does the language which asks this question belong? From whence does it draw the energy of its question? Can it account for the historical *coupling* of Judaism and Hellenism? And what is the legitimacy, what is the meaning of the *copula* in this proposition from perhaps the most Hegelian of modern novelists: "Jewgreek is greekjew. Extremes meet"?[92]

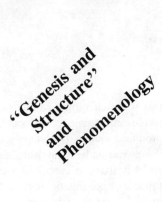

Five

"Genesis and Structure" and Phenomenology

I must begin with a *precaution* and a *confession*. When, in order to approach a philosophy, one is armed not only with a pair of concepts—here, "structure and genesis"—that has been determined or overburdened with reminiscences by a long problematical tradition, but also with a speculative grid in which the classical figure of an antagonism is apparent from the start, then the operative debate which one prepares to undertake from within this philosophy, or on the basis of it, is in danger of appearing to be not so much an attentive scrutiny as a putting into question, that is, an abusive investigation which introduces beforehand what it seeks to find, and does violence to the physiology proper to a body of thought. No doubt, to treat a philosophy by introducing the foreign substance of a debate may be efficacious, may surrender or set free the meaning of a latent process, but it begins with an aggression and an infidelity. We must not forget this.

In the case at hand, this is truer than ever. Husserl has always indicated his aversion for debate, dilemma, and aporia, that is, for reflection in the alternative mode whereby the philosopher, at the end of his deliberations, seeks to reach a conclusion, that is, to close the question, to enclose his expectations or his concern in an option, a decision, a solution; and this would be the result of a speculative or "dialectical" attitude, in the sense that Husserl, at least, always sought to ascribe to this word. Not only are the metaphysicians guilty of this attitude, but often, unbeknownst to themselves, so are the adherents of the empirical sciences: both groups would be congenitally guilty of a certain sin of explicationism. The phenomenologist, on the contrary, is the "true positivist" who returns to the things themselves, and who is self-effacing before the originality and primordiality of meanings. The process of a faithful comprehension or description, and the continuity of explication must dispel the shadow of a choice. Thus one might say, and in an entirely prejudicial fashion, that Husserl, by his rejection of system and speculative closure, and by virtue of the style of his thought, is attuned to the historicity of meaning and to the possibility of its becoming, and is also already respectful of that which remains open within structure. And even when one comes to think that the opening of the structure is "structural," that is, essential, one already has progressed to an order heterogeneous to the first one: the *difference* between the (necessarily closed) minor structure and the structurality of an opening—such, perhaps, is the unlocatable site in which philosophy takes root. Particularly when it speaks of and describes structures. Thus, the presumption of a conflict between the genetic approach and the structural approach from the outset appears to be superimposed upon the specificity of what is given to a virgin glance. And if the question "structure *or* genesis" had been exposed to Husserl *ex abrupto,* I wager that he would have been quite astonished to see himself called into such a debate; he would have answered that it depends upon what one intends to speak about. There are some givens which must be described in terms of structure, and others which must be described in terms of genesis. There are layers of meaning which appear as systems, or complexes, or static configurations, within which, moreover, are possible a movement and a genesis which must obey both the legality proper to and the functional significance of the structure under consideration. Other layers, sometimes more profound, sometimes more superficial, are given in the essential mode of creation and movement, that is, in the modes of primordial origin, of becoming, or of tradition; and these require that in speaking of them one use the language of genesis, supposing that there is one, or that there is only one.

The image of this fidelity to the theme of the description can be found in Husserl's (at least apparent) fidelity to himself all along his itinerary. To show this, I will take two examples.

1. The transition from the genetic researches in the only book whose method, or some of whose psychologistic presuppositions, Husserl renounced (I am thinking of *Philosophie der Arithmetik*), to the *Logische Untersuchungen* in particular (where above all it was a question of describing the objectivity of ideal objectivities in a certain atemporal fixedness, and in their autonomy as concerns a certain subjective becoming). This transition has an explicative continuity, and Husserl is so sure of this that more than forty years later he writes: "This fixing of

attention on the formal, and a first understanding of its meaning, I acquired through my *Philosophie der Arithmetik* (1891), which, despite its immaturity as a first text, nonetheless represented a first attempt to attain clarity as to the true meaning, the authentic and original meaning, of the concepts of set theory and number theory, and did so by returning to the spontaneous activities of colligation and numeration in which collections ('totalities', 'sets') and numbers are given in an originally productive way. Therefore it was, to use my later way of expressing myself, a research deriving from constitutive phenomenology . . ." etc.[1]

It will be objected that fidelity is easily explained here, since it is a question of grasping, in the dimension of the "transcendental genesis," an intention that was first attached perhaps more "naïvely" but with sure uncertainty to a psychological genesis.

2. But one cannot say the same about the transition—within phenomenology this time—from the structural analyses of static constitution practiced in *Ideen I* (1913) to the analyses of genetic constitution which follow, and which are sometimes quite new in their content. And yet this transition is still a simple progress which implies no "surpassing" (as it is called) and still less an option, and especially not a repentance. It is the deepening of a work which leaves intact what has been uncovered, a work of excavation in which the baring of both the genetic foundations and the original productivity not only neither shakes nor ruins the superficial structures already unearthed, but also brings eidetic forms once again to light, that is the "structural a prioris"—this is Husserl's expression—of genesis itself.

Thus, in Husserl's mind at least, there was never a "structure-genesis" problem but only a privilege of one or the other of these two operative concepts, according to the space of description, the *quid* or the *quomodo* of the givens. In this phenomenology, where, at first glance, and if one takes inspiration from traditional schemas, motifs of conflict or of tension appear numerous (it is a philosophy of essences always considered in their objectivity, their intangibility, their apriority; but, by the same token, it is a philosophy of experience, of becoming, of the temporal flux of what is lived, which is the ultimate reference; it is also a philosophy in which the notion of "transcendental experience" designates the very field of reflection, in a project which, in Kant's eyes for example, would have derived from teratology), one finds no clashes; and the mastery of the phenomenologist at work would have assured Husserl of a perfect serenity in the usage of these two always complementary operative concepts. Phenomenology, in the clarity of its intention, would be offended, then, by our preliminary question.

Having taken these precautions as concerns Husserl's aims, I must now confess my own. In effect, I would like to attempt to show:

First, that beneath the serene use of these concepts is to be found a debate that regulates and gives its rhythm to the progression of the description, that gives to the description its "animation," and whose incompleteness, which leaves every major stage of phenomonology unbalanced, makes new reductions and explications indefinitely necessary;

Second, that this debate, at every instant endangering the very principles of the method, appears—I say "appears," for this is a hypothesis which even if it is not confirmed might permit us, at least, to accentuate the original characteristics of the Husserlian attempt—appears thus to force Husserl to transgress the purely descriptive space and transcendental pretention of his research, and to move toward a metaphysics of history in which the solid structure of a *Telos* would permit him to reappropriate, by making it essential and by in some way prescribing its horizon, an untamed genesis which grew to greater and greater expanse, and seemed to accommodate itself less and less to phenomenological apriorism and to transcendental idealism.

I will follow alternately the thread of a debate interior to Husserl's thought, and the thread of a combat on the flank of Husserl's field of research into which he had to enter on two occasions; I refer to the two polemics which placed him in opposition to those philosophies of structure called *Diltheyism* and *Gestaltism*.

Husserl, thus, ceaselessly attempts to reconcile the *structuralist* demand (which leads to the comprehensive description of a totality, of a form or a function organized according to an internal legality in which elements have meaning only in the solidarity of their correlation or their opposition), with the *genetic* demand (that is the search for the origin and foundation of the structure). One could show, perhaps, that the phenomenological project itself is born of an initial failure of this attempt.

In *Philosophie der Arithmetik,* the objectivity of a structure, that of numbers and arithmetical series—and, correlatively, that of the arithmetical attitude—is tied to the concrete genesis which must make it possible. From the start, Husserl refuses, and will always refuse, to accept the intelligibility and normativity of this universal structure as manna fallen from a "heavenly place" (*topos ouranios*),[2] or as an eternal truth created by an infinite reason. To seek out the subjective origin of arithmetical objects and values, here, is to turn back toward perception, toward perceptual ensembles, and toward the pluralities and totalities found in perception in a premathematical organization. By virtue of its style this return to perception and to acts of colligation or numeration yields to the then frequent temptation vaguely named "psychologism."[3] But Husserl indicates his reservations on more than one score and he never reaches the point of construing an *actual* genetic constitution as an epistemological validation, as Lipps, Wundt, and several others had the tendency to do (although it is true that read attentively, and for themselves, they would appear more prudent and less simplistic than one would be tempted to believe on the basis of Husserl's criticisms of them).

Husserl's originality is to be recognized in that: (*a*) he distinguishes number from concept, that is, from a *constructum,* a psychological artifact; (*b*) he underlines that mathematical or logical synthesis is irreducible to the *order*—in both senses of the word—of psychological temporality; (*c*) he bases his entire psychological analysis on the *already given* possibility of an objective *etwas überhaupt,* which Frege will criticize under the denomination *bloodless specter (blutloses Gespenst)* but which designates the intentional[4] dimension of objectivity, the transcendental relation to the object that no psychological genesis can institute but can only presuppose in its own possibility. Consequently, the respect for arithmetical *meaning,* for its *ideality* and its *normativity,* forbids Husserl any psychological deduction of the number at the very moment when both his stated method and the tendencies of the period should have pushed him toward one. It remains that the intentionality presupposed by the movement of genesis is still conceived by Husserl as a *trait,* as a *psychological structure of consciousness,* like character and the state of something factual. Now, the meaning of the number can do very well without the intentionality of a factual consciousness. This meaning, that is, this ideal objectivity and normativity is precisely independence from any factual consciousness; and Husserl quickly will be obliged to acknowledge the legitimacy of Frege's criticisms: the essence of the number derives from psychology to the same extent as does the existence of the North Sea. Moreover, neither unity nor zero can be engendered on the basis of a multiplicity of positive acts, facts, or psychic events. What is true for arithmetical unity is also true for the unity of every object in general.

If Husserl gives up the psychological route[5] when confronted by all the difficulties of accounting for a structure of ideal meaning on the basis of a factual genesis, he no less rejects the logicizing conclusion with which his critics wished to corner him. Whether in the then current Platonic or Kantian style, this logicism was preoccupied above all with the autonomy of logical ideality as concerns all consciousness in general, or all concrete and non-formal consciousness. Husserl, for his part, seeks to *maintain* simultaneously the normative autonomy of logical or mathematical ideality as concerns all factual consciousness, and its original dependence in relation to a subjectivity *in general; in general,* but *concretely.* Thus he had to navigate between the Scylla and Charybdis of logicizing structuralism and psychologistic genetism (even in the subtle and pernicious form of the "transcendental psychologism" attributed to Kant). He had to open up a new direction of philosophical attention and permit the discovery of a concrete, but nonempirical, intentionality, a "transcendental experience" which would be "constitutive," that is, like all intentionality, simultaneously productive and revelatory, active and passive. The original unity, the common root of activity and passivity is from quite early on the very possibility of meaning for Husserl. And this common root will ceaselessly be experienced as the common root of structure *and* genesis which is dogmatically presupposed by all the *ulterior* problematics and dissociations concerning them. Husserl will attempt to prepare an access to this common radicality through the diverse "reductions," which are presented initially as neutralizations of psychological genesis and even of every factual genesis in general. The first phase of phenomenology, in its style and its objects, is structuralist, because first and foremost it seeks to stay clear of psychologism and historicism. But it is not genetic description *in general* which is disqualified, but only the genetic description which borrows its schemas from naturalism and causalism, and depends upon a science of "facts" and therefore on an empiricism; and therefore, concludes Husserl, depends upon a relativism incapable of insuring its own truth; therefore, on a skepticism. The transition to the phenomenological attitude is made necessary, thus, by the impotence or philosophical fragility of genetism when the latter, by means of a positivism which does not understand itself, believes itself capable of enclosure by a "science-of-facts" *(Tatsachenwissenschaft),* whether this be a natural science or a science of the mind. The expression "worldly genesis" covers the domain of these sciences.

For as long as the phenomenological space has not been uncovered, and for as long as the transcendental description has not been undertaken, the problem of "structure and genesis" seems to have no meaning. Neither the idea of structure, which isolates the different spheres of objective signification with respect for their static originality, nor the idea of genesis, which effects abusive transitions from one region to another, appears adequate to clarify the problem which is already Husserl's, that is, the problem of the *foundation of objectivity.*

This might appear to be inconsequential: can one not imagine, in effect, a methodological fecundity of these two notions in the various domains of the natural and social sciences to the extent that the latter, in their own movement and moment, in their actual labor, do not have to answer for the meaning and value of their objectivity? Not at all. Even the most naïve utilization of the notion of genesis, and especially of the notion of structure, supposes at very least that the natural regions and the domains of objectivity have been rigorously circumscribed. Now, this prior circumscription, this elucidation of the meaning of each regional structure can derive only from a phenomenological critique. The latter is always *rightfully* primary, because it alone can answer, before every empirical inquiry and in order for such an inquiry to be possible, questions of this kind: what is the physical thing, what is the psychological thing, what is the historical thing, etc. etc.?—questions whose answer was more or less dogmatically implied by the structural or genetic techniques.

Let us not forget that if *Philosophie der Arithmetik* is the contemporary of the most ambitious, systematic, and optimistic of psychogenetic attempts, Husserl's first phenomenological works were developed approximately at the same time as the first structuralist projects, or at least those which stated structure as a theme, for it would not be difficult to show that a certain structuralism has always been philosophy's most spontaneous gesture. Now, Husserl states his objections to

Diltheyism and Gestaltism, those first philosophies of structure, in a way that is identical in principle to his objections to genetism.

In Husserl's eyes the structuralism of the *Weltanschauungsphilosophie* is a historicism. And despite Dilthey's vehement protests, Husserl will persist in thinking that, like all historicism, and despite its originality, the *Welt-anschauungsphilosophie* avoids neither relativism nor skepticism.[6] For it reduces the norm to a historical factuality, and it ends by confusing, to speak the language of Leibniz and of the *Logische Untersuchungen* (vol. I, p. 188), the *truths of fact* and the *truths of reason*. Pure truth or the pretension to pure truth is missed in its *meaning* as soon as one attempts, as Dilthey does, to account for it from within a determined historical totality, that is, from within a factual totality, a finite totality all of whose manifestations and cultural productions are structurally solidary and coherent, and are all regulated by the same function, by the same finite unity of a total subjectivity. This meaning of truth, or of the pretension to truth, is the requirement of an absolute, infinite omni-temporality and universality, without limits of any kind. The Idea of truth, that is the Idea of philosophy or of science, is an infinite Idea, an Idea in the Kantian sense. Every totality, every finite structure is inadequate to it. Now the Idea or the project which animates and unifies every *determined* historical structure, every *Welt-anschauung*, is *finite:*[7] on the basis of the structural description of a *vision of the world* one can account for everything except the infinite opening to truth, that is, philosophy. Moreover, it is always something like an *opening* which will frustrate the structuralist project. What I can never understand, in a structure, is that by means of which it is not closed.

If Husserl attacked Diltheyism[8] with such violence, it is that he found in Diltheyism a *seductive* attempt, a tempting aberration. Dilthey, in effect, has the merit of protesting against the positivist naturalization of the life of the mind. The act of "understanding" that he opposes to explication and objectification must be the first and major route to be followed by the sciences of the mind. Husserl thus pays homage to Dilthey, and shows himself quite hospitable: *first,* to the idea of a principle of "understanding" or of re-understanding, of "re-living" (*Nachleben*)—notions simultaneously to be juxtaposed with the notion of *Ein-fühlung,* borrowed from Lipps and transformed by Husserl, and with the notion of *Reaktivierung,* which is the active reliving of the past intention of an *other* mind and the reawakening of a production of meaning—in question here is the very possibility of a science of the mind; *second,* to the idea that there exist totalitarian structures endowed with a unity of internal meaning, spiritual organisms in a sense, cultural worlds all of whose functions and manifestations are solidary and to which *Weltanschauungen* correspond correlatively; *third,* to the distinction between physical structures, in which the principle of relationship is external causality, and mental structures, in which the principle of relationship is what Husserl will call "motivation."

But this renewal is not fundamental, and it only intensifies the historicist

menace. History does not cease to be an empirical science of "facts" because it
has reformed its methods and techniques, or because it has substituted a comprehensive structuralism for causalism, atomism, and naturalism, or because it
has become more attentive to cultural totalities. Its pretension to founding normativity on a better understood factuality does not become more legitimate, but
only increases its powers of philosophical seduction. A confusion of value and
existence, and more generally, of all types of realities and all types of idealities is
sheltered beneath the equivocal category of the historical.[9] Thus, the theory of
the *Weltanschauung* must revert back or be reduced to the strict limits of its own
domain; its contours are sketched by a certain *difference* between wisdom and
knowledge; and by an ethical indictment and impatience. This irreducible difference is due to an interminable *delaying* [*différance*] of the theoretical foundation. The exigencies of life demand that a practical response be organized on the
field of historical existence, and that this response precede an absolute science
whose conclusions it cannot await. The system of this anticipation, the structure
of this interrupted response is what Husserl calls *Weltanschauung*. One might
say, with some precautions, that he sees in it the situation and meaning of a
"provisional morality,"[10] whether it be personal or communal.

Up to now, we have been interested in the "structure-genesis" problem which
first presented itself to Husserl outside the borders of phenomenology. It is the
radicalization of the presuppositions of psychology and history that made the
transition to the phenomenological attitude necessary. Let us now attempt to
catch up with the same problem in the field of phenomenology, keeping in mind
Husserl's methodological premises, notably the "reduction" in its eidetic and
transcendental forms. Truthfully, we will see that it cannot be a question of the
same problem, but only of an analogous or "parallel" problem, as Husserl
would say; and the meaning of this notion of "parallelism," which we will touch
upon shortly, presents problems that are not among the least difficult.

If the first phase of the phenomenological description and the "constitutive
analyses" (a phase of which *Ideas* is the most elaborated trace) is resolutely static
and structural in its design, it seems to be so for at least two reasons. (A)
Reacting against the historicist or psychologistic genetism with which he continues to be at loggerheads, Husserl systematically excludes every genetic preoccupation.[11] The protests made against this attitude perhaps have contaminated
and indirectly have determined Husserl's own attitude: everything occurs as if at
this point he considered *every* genesis as associative, causal, factual and worldly.
(B) Concerned above all else with formal ontology and with objectivity in
general, Husserl applies himself especially to the articulation between the object
in general (whatever its regional appurtenance) and consciousness in general
(*Ur-Region*). He defines the forms of self-evidence in general, and thereby seeks
to attain the ultimate critical and phenomenological jurisdiction, under which the
most ambitious genetic description later will be subsumed.

Thus, if Husserl distinguishes between empirical and eidetic structure on the one hand, and between empirical and eidetic-transcendental structure on the other, at this time he has not yet taken the same step as concerns genesis.

Within the pure transcendentality of consciousness, at this phase of the description, our problem would take on at least—since we must choose—two forms. And in both cases, it is a question of *closure* or of *opening*.

1. Differing from mathematical essences, the essences of pure consciousness are not, and in principle cannot be, *exact*. The difference between *exactitude* and *rigor* recognized by Husserl is well known. An eidetic descriptive science, such as phenomenology, may be rigorous, but it is necessarily inexact—I would rather say "anexact"—due to no failure on its part. Exactitude is always a product derived from an operation of "idealization" and of "transition to the limit" which can only concern an abstract moment, an *abstract* eidetic element (spatiality, for example) of a thing materially determined as an objective body, setting aside, precisely, the other eidetic elements of a body in general. This is why geometry is a "material" and "abstract" science.[12] It follows that a "geometry of experience," a "mathematics of phenomena" is impossible: this is an "attempt doomed to miscarry."[13] This means in particular, for what concerns us here, that the essences of consciousness, and therefore the essences of "phenomena" in general, cannot belong to a structure or "multiplicity" of the mathematical type. Now what is it that characterizes such a multiplicity for Husserl, and at this time? In a word, the possibility of *closure*.[14] Here, we cannot enter into the intramathematical difficulties always raised by this Husserlian conception of mathematical "definitude," especially when confronted by certain later developments of axiomatics and by Gödel's discoveries. What Husserl seeks to underline by means of this comparison between an exact and a morphological science, and what we must retain here, is the principled, essential, and structural impossibility of closing a structural phenomenology. It is the infinite opening of what is experienced, which is designated at several moments of Husserlian analysis by reference to an *Idea in the Kantian sense,* that is, the irruption of the infinite into consciousness, which permits the unification of the temporal flux of consciousness just as it unifies the object and the world by anticipation, and despite an irreducible incompleteness. It is the strange *presence* of this Idea which also permits every transition to the limit and the production of all exactitude.

2. Transcendental intentionality is described in *Ideas I* as an original structure, an archi-structure *(Ur-Struktur)* with four poles and two correlations: the noetico-noematic correlation or structure and the *morphe-hyle* correlation or structure. That this complex structure is the structure both of intentionality, that is, the structure of the origin of meanings and of the opening to the light of phenomenality, and that the occlusion of this structure is non-sense itself, is indicated by at least two signs: (A) Noesis and noema, the intentional moments of the structure, can be distinguished in that the noema does not belong to

consciousness in a *real* way. *Within* consciousness, in general there is an agency which *does not really* belong to it. This is the difficult but decisive theme of the non-real (*reell*) inclusion of the noema.[15] Noema, which is the objectivity of the object, the meaning and the "as such" of the thing for consciousness, is neither the determined thing itself in its untamed existence (whose appearing the noema precisely is), nor is it a properly subjective moment, a "really" subjective moment, since it is indubitably given as an object for consciousness. It is neither of the world nor of consciousness, but it is the world or something of the world *for* consciousness. Doubtless it can rightfully be laid bare only on the basis of intentional consciousness, but it does not borrow from intentional consciousness what metaphorically we might call, by avoiding the realization of consciousness, its "material." This real nonappurtenance to any region at all, even to the archi-region, this *anarchy* of the noema is the root and very possibility of objectivity and of meaning. This irregionality of the noema, the opening to the "as such" of Being and to the determination of the totality of regions in general, cannot be described, *stricto sensu and simply,* on the basis of a determined regional structure. This is why the transcendental reduction (to the extent that it must remain an eidetic reduction if one is to know what one will continue to speak about, and if one is to avoid empirical or absolute idealism) may appear deceitful, since it does provide access to a determined region, whatever its founding privilege. One might think that once the nonreality of the noema was acknowledged, a conversion of the entire phenomenological method would have followed, as well as an abandonment of transcendental idealism along with the Reduction. But would this not have been, then, to condemn oneself to silence—which is always possible, moreover—and in any event to renounce a rigor that only the eidetic-transcendental *limitation* and a certain regionalism can ensure? In any event, the transcendentality of the opening is simultaneously the origin and the undoing, the condition of possibility and a certain impossibility of every structure and of every systematic structuralism. (B) While the noema is an intentional and non-real element, the *hylē* is a real but not intentional element of the experienced. It is the sensate (experienced and not real) material of affect before any animation by intentional form. It is the pole of pure passivity, of the nonintentionality without which consciousness could not receive anything *other* than itself, nor exercise its intentional activity. This receptiveness is also an essential opening. If, on the level at which *Ideas* remains, Husserl recounces the description and interrogation of the *hylē* for itself and in its pure ingenuity, if he renounces the examination of the possibilities entitled *formless materials and immaterial forms,*[16] if he keeps to the constituted *hylē-morphic* correlation, it is that his analyses are still developed (and will they not always be so, in a certain way?) from within a constituted temporality.[17] Now, at its greatest depth and in its pure specificity the *hylē* is primarily temporal matter. It is the possibility of genesis itself. Thus at these two poles of opening and from within the very transcendental structure of all consciousness there would arise the necessity for the transition to a genetic constitution and for the new "transcendental aesthetic" which will be announced unceasingly but will be deferred always, and within which the themes of the Other and of Time were to have permitted their irreducible complicity to appear. It is that the constitution of the other and of time refers phenomenology to a zone in which its "principle of principles" (as we see it, its *metaphysical* principle: the *original self-evidence* and *presence* of the thing itself in person) is radically put into question. In any event, as can be seen, the necessity of this transition from the structural to the genetic is nothing less than the necessity of a break or a conversion.

Before following this movement interior to phenemonology and the transition to the genetic analyses, let us pause for a moment at a second border problem.

All the problematical schemas which we have just indicated belong to the transcendental sphere. But might not a psychology renewed by the double influence of phenomenology and *Gestalt psychology,* [18] one which maintains its distance from associationism, atomism, causalism, etc., alone pretend to assume such a description and such problematical schemas? In a word, can a structuralist psychology, one allegedly independent from transcendental phenomenology if not from phenomenological psychology, make itself invulnerable to the reproach of psychologism formerly directed against classical psychology? It was all the more tempting to think so in that Husserl himself prescribed the establishment of a phenomenological psychology, an "apriorical" psychology, to be sure, but also a worldly one (in that it cannot exclude the position of the worldly thing that the *psyche* is), and strictly *parallel* to transcendental phenomenology. Now the overcoming of the invisible difference which separates parallel things is not innocent: it is the most subtle and ambitious gesture of psychologistic abuse. And this is the principle of the critiques which Husserl addresses to the psychologies of structure or of totality in his *Nachwort* to *Ideen I. Gestaltpsychologie* is mentioned explicitly. [19] To avoid "naturalism" it does not suffice to escape atomism. And in order to clarify the *distance* which must separate a phenomenological psychology from a transcendental phenomenology, one would have to examine the *nothing* which prevents them from coming together, the parallelism which liberates the space of a transcendental question. This *nothing* is what permits the transcendental reduction. The transcendental reduction is what directs our attention toward this *nothing* in which the totality of meaning and the meaning of totality permit their origin to appear. That is, according to Fink's expression, the *origin of the world.*

If we had the time and the means, we would now have to approach the enormous problems of genetic phenomenology, as the latter is developed after *Ideas.* I will simply note the following points.

The profound unity of this genetic description is diffracted, without being dispersed, along *three lines.* (A) The *logical* route. The task of *Erfahrung und Urteil, Formaler und Transzendentaler Logik,* and numerous analogous texts is to undo, to "reduce" not only the superstructures of scientific idealizations and the values of objective exactitude, but also all predicative sedimentation belonging to the cultural layer of subjective-relative truths in the *Lebenswelt*. This in order to regrasp and "reactivate" the emergence of theoretical or practical predication in general, and on the basis of the most untamed precultural life. (B) The *egological* route. In a sense this route is already latent beneath the preceding one. First, because in the most general fashion, phenomenology cannot and may not ever describe anything but the intentional modifications of the *eidos ego* in general.[20] Next, because the genealogy of logic kept to the realm of *cogitata* and the acts of the *ego* as if to its proper existence and *life;* and these were read only on the basis of noematic signs and results. Now however, as stated in the *Cartesian Meditations,* it is a question of returning once more to the couple *cogito-cogitatum,* if you will, in order to reapprehend the genesis of the *ego itself,* the ego existing for itself and "continuously constituting [itself] as existing."[21] Aside from the delicate problems of *passivity and activity,* this genetic description of the *ego* will encounter limits which we would be tempted to call definitive, but which Husserl, of course, considers provisional. They derive from the fact, he says, that phenomenology is only at its beginnings.[22] In effect the genetic description of the ego at every instant prescribes the formidable task of a *universal* genetic phenomenology. This is announced in the third route. (C) The *historico-teleological* route: " . . . a teleological reason [runs] throughout all historicity"[23] and particularly "the unity of the history of the *ego*."[24] This third route, which is to provide access to the *eidos* of historicity in general (that is, to its *telos,* for the eidos of a historicity, and thus of the movement of meaning— which is a necessarily rational movement—can be only a norm, a value more than an essence) cannot be a route among others. The eidetics of history cannot be an eidetics among others: it embraces the totality of beings. In effect the irruption of the *logos,* the accession to human consciousness of the idea of an infinite task of reason, does not occur only through a series of revolutions which at the same time would be self-conversions, seeming to tear open a previous finitude in order to lay bare the power of a hidden infinity and to give voice to the *dynamis* of a silence. These ruptures, which at the same time are unveilings, (and also coverings up, for the origin dissimulates itself immediately beneath the new domain of uncovered or produced objectivity) *are always already indicated,* Husserl recognizes, "in confusion and in the dark," that is, not only in the most elementary forms of life and human history, but closer and closer in animality and nature in general. How can such an affirmation, made necessary *by* and *in* phenomenology itself, be totally certain within phenomenology? For it does not only concern phenomena that are experienced and self-evident. Does its inability to *be indicated* rigorously anywhere else than in a phenomenology prevent it from already—or still—being a metaphysical assertion, the affirmation of a metaphysics which articulates itself in a phenomenological discourse? I am satisfied only to raise these questions here.

Reason, thus, unveils itself. Reason, Husserl says, is the *logos* which is produced in history. It traverses Being with itself in sight, in sight of appearing to itself, that is, to state itself and hear itself as *logos*. It is speech as auto-affection: hearing oneself speak.[25] It emerges from itself in order to take hold of itself within itself, in the "living present" of its self-presence. In emerging from itself, hearing oneself speak constitutes itself as the history of reason through the detour of *writing. Thus it differs from itself in order to reappropriate itself. The Origin of Geometry* describes the necessity of this exposition of reason in a worldly inscription. An exposition indispensable to the constitution of truth and the ideality of objects, but which is also the danger to meaning from what is outside the sign. In the moment of writing, the sign can always "empty" itself, take flight from awakening, from "reactivation," and may remain forever closed and mute. As for Cournot, writing here is the "critical epoch."

Here, one must become quite attentive to the fact that this language is not *immediately* speculative and metaphysical, as certain consonant phrases of Hegel's seemed to be for Husserl, correctly or incorrectly. For this *logos* which calls to itself and summons itself by itself as *telos,* and whose *dynamis* tends toward its *energeia* or *entelechia*—this *logos* does not occur *in* history and does not traverse Being as a foreign empiricity into which both its metaphysical transcendence and the actuality of its infinite essence would descend and condescend. *Logos is nothing* outside history and Being, since it is discourse, infinite discursiveness and not an actual infinity, and since it is meaning. Now, the irreality of meaning was discovered by phenomenology as one of its very own premises. Inversely, no history as self-tradition and no Being could have meaning without the *logos* which is *the* meaning which projects and proffers itself. Despite all these classical notions, phenomenology does not *abdicate* itself for the benefit of a classical metaphysical speculation which on the contrary, according to Husserl, would have to recognize in phenomenology the clarified energy of its own intentions. Which amounts to saying that in criticizing classical metaphysics, phenomenology accomplishes the most profound project of metaphysics. Husserl acknowledges or rather claims this himself, particularly in the *Cartesian Meditations.* The results of phenomenology are "metaphysical, if it be true that ultimate cognitions of being should be called metaphysical. On the other hand, what we have here is *anything but metaphysics, in the customary* sense with which metaphysics, as 'first philosophy,' was instituted originally."[26] "Phenomenology indeed *excludes every naïve metaphysics* ... but *does not exclude metaphysics as such.*"[27] For within the most universal *eidos* of mental historicity, the conversion of philosophy into phenomenology would be the final degree of differentiation (stage, that is, *Stufe,* structural level or genetic stage).[28] The two previous degrees would be, first, that of a pretheoretical culture, and next, that of the theoretical or philosophical project (the Greco-European moment).[29]

The presence of *Telos* or *Vorhaben*—the infinite theoretical anticipation which simultaneously is given as an infinite practical task—for phenomenological consciousness is indicated every time that Husserl speaks of the *Idea in the Kantian sense*. The latter is offered within phenomenological self-evidence as evidence of an essential overflowing of actual and adequate self-evidence. One would have to examine quite closely the intervention of the Idea in the Kantian sense at various points along Husserl's itinerary. Perhaps it would appear then that this Idea is the Idea or very project of phenomenology, that which makes it possible by overflowing its system of self-evidences or factual determinations, or by overflowing this system as phenomenology's source or end.

Since *Telos* is totally open, is opening itself, to say that it is the most powerful structural a priori of historicity is not to designate it as a static and determined value which would inform and enclose the genesis of Being and meaning. It is the concrete possibility, the very birth of history and the meaning of becoming in general. Therefore it is structurally genesis itself, as origin and as becoming.

All these formulations have been possible thanks to the initial distinction between different irreducible types of genesis and structure: worldly genesis and transcendental genesis, empirical structure, eidetic structure, and transcendental structure. To ask oneself the following historico-semantic question: "What does the notion of genesis *in general,* on whose basis the Husserlian diffraction could come forth and be understood, mean, and what has it always meant? What does the notion of structure *in general,* on whose basis Husserl *operates* and operates distinctions between empirical, eidetic, and transcendental dimensions mean, and what has it always meant throughout its displacements? And what is the historico-semantic relationship between genesis and structure *in general?*" is not only simply to ask a prior linguistic question. It is to ask the question about the unity of the historical ground on whose basis a transcendental reduction is possible and is motivated by itself. It is to ask the question about the unity of the world from which transcendental freedom releases itself, in order to make the origin of this unity appear. If Husserl has not asked these questions in terms of historical philology, if he did not first ask himself about the meaning of his operative instruments *in general,* it is not due to naïveté, dogmatic precipitation, or a neglect of the historical weight of language. It is rather because to ask oneself about the meaning of the notions of structure or genesis *in general,* before the dissociations introduced by reduction, is to interrogate that which precedes the transcendental reduction. Now the latter is but the free act of the question, which frees itself from the totality of what precedes it in order to be able to gain access to this totality, particularly to its historicity and its past. The question of the possibility of the transcendental reduction cannot expect an answer. It is the question of the possibility of the question, opening itself, the gap on whose basis the *transcendental I,* which Husserl was tempted to call "eternal" (which in his thought, in any event, means neither infinite nor ahistorical, quite the contrary) is called upon to ask itself about everything, and particularly about the possibility of the unformed and naked factuality of the nonmeaning, in the case at hand, for example, of its own death.

Six

La parole
soufflée

When I write there is nothing other than what I write. Whatever else I felt I have not been able to say, and whatever else has escaped me are ideas or a stolen verb which I will destroy, to replace them wtih something else. (Artaud, Rodez, April 1946)

. . . whatever way you turn you have not even *started* thinking. (Artaud, *Collected Works* I, p. 89)

Naïveté of the discourse we begin here, speaking toward Antonin Artaud. To diminish this naïveté we would have had to wait a long time: in truth, a dialogue would have to have been opened between— let us say as quickly as possible—*critical* discourse and *clinical* discourse. And the dialogue would have to have borne upon that which is beyond their two trajectories, pointing toward the common elements of their origin and their horizon. Happily for us, this horizon and this origin are more clearly perceptible today. Close to us, Maurice Blanchot, Michel Foucault, and Jean Laplanche have questioned the problematic unity of these two discourses, have attempted to acknowledge the passing of a discourse which, without doubling itself, without even distributing itself (along the division between the critical and the clinical), but with a single and simple characteristic speaks of madness *and* the work,[1] driving, primarily, at their enigmatic conjunction.

For a thousand not simply material reasons, we cannot evince, here, the questions that these essays seem to leave unresolved, even though we acknowledge the priority due these questions. We feel that even if, in the best of cases, the common ground of the two discourses—the medical commentary and the other one—has been designated from afar, *in fact* the two have never been confused in any text. (And is this so because we are concerned, first of all, with

commentary? Let us throw out these questions in order to see, further on, where
Artaud necessarily makes them land.)

We have said *in fact*. Describing the "extraordinarily rapid oscillations"
which in [Laplanche's] *Hölderlin et la question du père* produce the illusion of
unity, "permitting, in both senses, the imperceptible transfer of analogical
figures," and the crossing of the "domain included betweeen poetic forms and
psychological structures," Michel Foucault concludes that a *principled* and essential conjunction of the two is impossible. Far from brushing aside this impossibility, he posits that it proceeds from a kind of infinite closeness: "Despite the
fact that these two discourses have a demonstrably identical content which can
always be transferred from one to the other, they are profoundly incompatible. A
conjoined deciphering of poetic and psychological structures will never reduce
the distance between them. And yet, they are always infinitely close to one
another, just as is close to something possible the possibility that founds it; the
continuity of meaning between the work and madness is possible only on the
basis of the *enigma of the same* which permits the *absoluteness of the rupture*
between them to appear." But Foucault adds a little further on: "And this is not
an abstract figuration but a historical relationship in which our culture must
question itself."[2] Could not the fully *historical* field of this interrogation, in
which the overlapping of the two discourses is as much to be constituted as it is to
be restored, show us how something that is impossible de facto could present
itself as impossible de jure? It would still be necessary to conceive historicity,
and the difference between the two impossibilities, in an unexpected way, and
this initial task is not the easiest. This historicity, long since eliminated from
thought, cannot be more thoroughly erased than at the moment when commentary, that is, precisely, the "deciphering of structures," has commenced its reign
and determined the position of the question. This moment is even more absent
from our memory in that it is not *within* history.

We feel, indeed, that if clinical commentary and critical commentary
everywhere demand their own autonomy and wish to be acknowledged and
respected by one another, they are no less complicit—by virtue of a unity which
refers, through as yet unconceived mediations, to the mediation we sought an
instant ago—in the same abstraction, the same misinterpretation and the same
violence. At the moment when criticism (be it aesthetic, literary, philosophical,
etc.) allegedly protects the meaning of a thought or the value of a work against
psychomedical reductions, it comes to the same result [that a reduction would
come to] through the opposite path: *it creates an example*. That is to say, *a case*.
A work or an adventure of thought is made to bear witness, as example or martyr,
to a structure whose essential permanence becomes the prime preoccupation of
the commentary. For criticism to *make a case* of meaning or of value, to take
them seriously, is to read an essence into the example which is falling between
the phenomenological brackets. And this happens according to the most irrepres-

sible movement of even the commentary which most respects the untamed singularity of its theme. Although they are radically opposed for good reasons that are well known, the *psychological reduction* and the *eidetic reduction* function in the same way when confronted with the problem of the work or of madness, and unwittingly pursue the same end. Assuming that psychopathology, whatever its style, could attain in its reading the sure profundity of a Blanchot, whatever mastery it could gain of the case of Artaud would result in the same *neutralization* of "poor M. Antonin Artaud." Whose entire adventure, in *Le livre à venir,* becomes *exemplary*. In question is a reading—an admirable one, moreover—of the "unpower" (Artaud speaking of himself) "essential to thought" (Blanchot). "It is as if, despite himself and through a pathetic error from whence come his cries, he touched upon the point at which to think is always already to be able to think no more: *'unpower,'* as he calls it, which is as if essential to thought."[3] The *pathetic error* is that part of the example which belongs to Artaud himself: it will not be retained in the decoding of the essential truth. The error is Artaud's history, his erased trace on the way to truth. A pre-Hegelian concept of the relations between truth, error, and history.[4] "That poetry is linked to this impossibility of thought which is thought itself, is the truth that cannot be revealed, for it always turns away, thereby obliging him to experience it below the point at which he would truly experience it."[5] Artaud's pathetic error: the weight of example and existence which keeps him remote from the truth he hopelessly indicates: the nothingness at the heart of the word, the "lack of being," the "scandal of thought separated from life," etc. That which belongs to Artaud without recourse—his experience itself—can without harm be abandoned by the critic and left to the psychologists or doctors. But "for our sake, we must not make the mistake of reading the precise, sure, and scrupulous descriptions he gives us of this state as psychological analyses." That which no longer belongs to Artaud, as soon as we can read it through him, and thereby articulate, repeat, and take charge of it, that to which Artaud is only a witness, is a universal essence of thought. Artaud's entire adventure is purportedly only the index of a transcendental structure: "For never will Artaud accept the scandal of thought separated from life, even when he is given over to the most direct and untamed experience ever undergone of the essence of thought understood as separation, the experience of thought's inability to affirm anything opposed to itself as the limit of its infinite power."[6] Thought separated from life—this is, as is well known, one of the great figurations of the mind of which Hegel gave several examples.[7] Artaud, thus, would be another.

And Blanchot's meditation stops there: without questioning for themselves either that which irreducibly amounts to Artaud, or the idiosyncratic affirmation[8] which supports the nonacceptance of this scandal, or what is "untamed" in this experience. His meditation stops there or almost: it gives itself just the time to invoke a temptation which *would have to be* avoided but which, in fact, never has been: "It would be tempting to juxtapose what Artaud tells us with what Hölderlin and Mallarmé tell us: that inspiration is primarily the pure point at which it is missing. But we must resist the temptation to make overgeneralized affirmations. Each poet says the same, which, however, is not the same, is the unique, we feel. What is Artaud's is his alone. What he says has an intensity that we should not bear." And in the concluding lines that follow nothing is said of the unique. We return to essentiality: "When we read these pages, we learn what we cannot ever come to learn: that the fact of thinking can only be overwhelming; that what is to be thought is that which turns away from thought within thought, inexhaustibly exhausting itself within thought; that to suffer and to think are linked in a secret way."[9] Why this return to essentiality? Because, by definition, there is nothing to say about the unique? We will not rush toward this too solid commonplace here.

Blanchot must have been even more tempted to assimilate Artaud and Hölderlin in that his text devoted to the latter, *La folie par excellence,*[10] is advanced within the same framework. While asserting the necessity of escaping the alternative of the two discourses ("for the mystery stems also from this simultaneously double reading of an event which, however, is no more situated in one than in the other of the two versions," and primarily because this event is a demonic one which "keeps itself outside the opposition sickness-health"), Blanchot narrows the field of medical knowledge which misses the singularity of the event and masters every surprise in advance. "For medical knowledge, this event is in 'the rules,' or at least is not surprising; it corresponds to what is known about patients inspired to write by nightmare" (p. 15). This reduction of the clinical reduction is an essentialist reduction. While protesting, here too, against "overgeneralized . . . formulations," Blanchot writes: "One cannot be content with viewing Hölderlin's fate as that of an admirable or sublime individuality which, having too strongly desired something great, had to go to the breaking point. His fate belongs only to him, but he himself belongs to what he has expressed and discovered, which exists not as his alone, but as the truth and affirmation of the essence of poetry. . . . He does not decide upon his fate but upon the fate of poetry, the meaning of the truth that he has set out to achieve, . . . and this movement is not his alone but the very achievement of truth, which, despite him, at a certain point demands that his personal reason become the pure impersonal transcendence from which there is no return" (p. 26). Thus the unique is hailed in vain; it is indeed the very element which disappears from this commentary. And not by chance. The disappearance of unicity is even presented as the meaning of the truth of Hölderlin: "Authentic speech, the speech that mediates because the mediator disappears within it, puts an end to its particularities and returns to the element from whence it came" (p. 30). And thus, what authorizes one to say "the poet" instead of Hölderlin, what authorizes this dissolution of the unique is a conception of the unity or unicity of the unique—here the unity of madness and the work—as conjunction, composition or "combination": "A like combination is not encountered twice" (p. 20).

Jean Laplanche reproaches Blanchot for his "idealist interpretation," "resolutely anti-'scientific' and anti-'psychological' " and proposes to substitute another type of unitary theory for the theory of Hellingrath, which Blanchot, despite his own differences, also leans toward.[11] Not wanting to renounce unitarism, Laplanche wants "to include within a single movement his [Hölderlin's] work, and his evolution toward and within madness, even if this movement has the scansion of a dialectic and the multilinearity of counterpoint" (p. 13). In fact, one very quickly realizes that this "dialectic" scansion and this multilinearity do nothing but, as Foucault correctly says, increase the rapidity of oscillations, until the rapidity is difficult to perceive. At the end of the book, we are still out of breath searching for the unique, which itself, as such, eludes discourse and always will elude it: "The assimilation of the evolution of schizophrenia to the evolution of the work that we are proposing leads to results which absolutely cannot be generalized: in question is the relationship of poetry to mental illness within a particular, perhaps unique, case" (p. 132). Again, a conjoined and chance unicity. For, once one has from afar even mentioned it as such, one returns to the expressly criticized exemplarism[12] of Blanchot. The psychological style and, opposed to it, the structuralist or essentialist style have almost totally disappeared, certainly, and the philosophical gesture is seductive: it is no longer a question of understanding the poet Hölderlin on the basis of a schizophrenic or a transcendental structure whose meaning would be known to us, and which would hold in store no surprises. On the contrary, in Hölderlin we must read, and see designated, an access, the best one perhaps, an exemplary access to the essence of schizophrenia in general. And this essence of schizophrenia is not a psychological or anthropological fact available to the determined sciences called psychology or anthropology: "It is he [Hölderlin] who reopens the question of schizophrenia as a universal problem" (p. 133). A universal and not only human problem, not a primarily human problem because a true anthropology could be constituted upon the possibility of schizophrenia—which does not mean that the possibility of schizophrenia can *in fact* be encountered in beings other than man. Schizophrenia simply is not one among other attributes of an essence of man that would have to be constituted and acknowledged as the prerequisite basis of the study of man. Just as "in certain societies, the accession to Law, to the Symbolic has fallen to institutions other than that of the father" (p. 133)—whose precomprehension the institution of paternity thus permits—similarly, analogically, schizophrenia is not one among other dimensions or possibilities of the existent called man, but indeed the structure that opens the truth of man. This opening is produced in an exemplary way in the case of Hölderlin. It could be thought that, by definition, the unique cannot be an example or case of a universal figure. But it can. Exemplarity only apparently contradicts unicity. The equivocality lodged in the notion of example is well known: it is the resource of the complicity between clinical discourse and critical discourse, the complicity between the discourse which reduces meaning or value and the one that attempts to restore them. This is what permits Foucault to conclude for his purposes: "Hölderlin occupies a unique and exemplary place" (p. 209).

Such is the case that has been made of Hölderlin and Artaud. Our intention is above all not to refute or to criticize the principle of these readings. They are legitimate, fruitful, true; here, moreover, they are admirably executed, and informed by a critical vigilance which makes us make immense progress. If, on the other hand, we seem unsure of the treatment reserved for the unique, it is not because we think, and this credit will have to be granted us, that subjective existence, the originality of the work or the singularity of the beautiful, must be protected against the violence of the concept by means of moral or aesthetic precautions. No, inversely, when we appear to regret a silence or defeat before the unique, it is because we believe in the necessity of reducing the unique, of analyzing it and decomposing it by shattering it even further. Better: we believe that no commentary can escape these defeats, unless it destroys itself as commentary by exhuming the unity in which is embedded the differences (of madness and the work, of the psyche and the text, of example and essence, etc.) which implicitly support both criticism and the clinic. This ground, which we are approaching only by the negative route here, is *historical* in a sense which, it seems to us, has never been given thematic value in the commentaries of which we have just spoken, and which truthfully can hardly be tolerated by the metaphysical concept of history. The tumultuous presence of this archaic ground will thus magnetize the discourse which will be attracted into the resonance of the cries of Antonin Artaud. Will be attracted from afar, again, for our initial stipulation of naïveté was not a stipulation of style.

And if we say, to begin, that Artaud teaches us this unity prior to dissociation, we do not say so in order to construe Artaud as an example of what he teaches. If we understand him, we expect no instruction from him. Also, the preceding considerations are in no way methodological prologomena or generalizations announcing a new treatment of the case of Artaud. Rather, they indicate the very question that Artaud wants to destroy from its root, the question whose derivativeness, if not impossibility, he indefatigably denounced, upon which his cries furiously and unceasingly hurled themselves. For what his howls promise us, articulating themselves under the headings of *existence, flesh, life, theater, cruelty* is the meaning of an art prior to madness *and* the work, an art which no longer yields works, an artist's existence which is no longer a route or an experience that gives access to something other than itself; Artaud promises the existence of a speech that is a body, of a body that is a theater, of a theater that is a text because it is no longer enslaved to a writing more ancient than itself, an ur-text or an ur-speech. If Artaud absolutely resists—and, we believe, as was never done before—clinical or critical exegeses, he does so by virtue of that part of his adventure (and with this word we are designating a totality anterior to the separation of the life and the work) which is the very protest *itself* against exemplification *itself*. The critic and the doctor are without resource when confronted by an existence that refuses to signify, or by an art without works, a language without a trace. That is to say, without difference. In pursuit of a manifestation which would not be an expression but a pure creation of life, which would not fall far from the body then to decline into a sign or a work, an object, Artaud attempted to destroy a history, the history of the dualist metaphysics which more or less subterraneously inspired the essays invoked above: the duality of the body and the soul which supports, secretly of course, the duality of speech and existence, of the text and the body, etc. The metaphysics of the commentary which authorized "commentaries" because it *already* governed the works commented upon. Nontheatrical works, in the sense understood by Artaud, works that are already deported commentaries. Beating his flesh in order to reawaken it at the eve prior to the deportation, Artaud attempted to forbid that his speech be spirited away [*soufflé*][13] from his body.

Spirited [*soufflé*]: let us understand *stolen* by a possible commentator who would acknowledge speech in order to place it in an order, an order of essential truth or of a real structure, psychological or other. The first commentator, here, is the reader or the listener, the receiver which the "public" must no longer be in the theater of cruelty.[14] Artaud knew that all speech fallen from the body, offering itself to understanding or reception, offering itself as a spectacle, immediately becomes stolen speech. Becomes a signification which I do not possess because it is a signification. Theft is always the theft of speech or text, of a trace. The theft of a possession does not become a theft unless the thing stolen is a possession, unless it has acquired meaning and value through, at least, the consecration of a vow made in discourse. And this proposition could only foolishly be interpreted as the dismissal of every other theory of theft advanced within the order of morals, economics, or politics. For this proposition is anterior to such discourses, because it explicitly, and within a single question, establishes communication between the essence of theft and the origin of discourse in general. Now every discourse on theft, each time that it is determined by a given set of circumstances, has already obscurely resolved or repressed this question, has already reassured itself into the familiarity of an initial knowledge: everyone knows what theft means. But the theft of speech is not a theft among others; it is confused with the very possibility of theft, defining the fundamental structure of theft. And if Artaud makes us think this, it is no longer as the example of a structure, because in question is the very thing—theft—which constitutes the structure of the example as such.

Spirited [*soufflé*]: at the same time let us understand *inspired* by an *other* voice that itself reads a text older than the text of my body or than the theater of my gestures. Inspiration is the drama, with several characters, of theft, the structure of the classical theater in which the invisibility of the prompter [*souffleur*] ensures the indispensable *différance* and intermittence between a text already written by another hand and an interpreter already dispossessed of that which he receives. Artaud desired the conflagration of the stage upon which the prompter [*souffleur*] was possible and where the body was under the rule of a foreign text. Artaud wanted the machinery of the prompter [*souffleur*] spirited away [*soufflé*], wanted to plunder the structure of theft. To do so, he had to destroy, with one and the same blow, both poetic inspiration and the economy of classical art, singularly the economy of the theater. And through the same blow he had to destroy the metaphysics, religion, aesthetics, etc., that supported them. He would thus open up to Danger a world no longer sheltered by the structure of theft. To restore Danger by reawakening the stage of cruelty—this was Antonin Artaud's *stated* intention, at very least. It is this intention that we will follow here, with the exception of a calculated slip.

Unpower, which appears thematically in the letters to Jacques Rivière,[15] is not, as is known, simple impotence, the sterility of having "nothing to say," or the lack of inspiration. On the contrary, it is inspiration itself: the force of a void, the cyclonic breath [*souffle*] of a prompter [*souffleur*] who draws his breath in, and thereby robs me of that which he first allowed to approach me and which I believed I could say *in my own name.* The generosity of inspiration, the positive irruption of a speech which comes from I know not where, or about which I know (if I am Antonin Artaud) that I do not know where it comes from or who speaks it, the fecundity of the *other* breath [*souffle*] is unpower: not the absence but the radical irresponsibility of speech, irresponsibility as the power and the origin of speech. I am in relation to myself within the ether of a speech which is always spirited away [*soufflé*] from me, and which steals from me the very thing that it puts me in relation to. Consciousness of speech, that is to say, consciousness in general is not knowing who speaks at the moment when, and in the place where, I proffer my speech. This consciousness is thus also an unconsciousness ("In my unconsciousness it is others whom I hear," 1946), in opposition to which another consciousness will necessarily have to be reconstituted; and this time, consciousness will be cruelly present to itself and will hear itself speak. It is within the province of neither morals, nor logic, nor aesthetics to define this irresponsibility: it is a total and original loss of existence itself. According to Artaud it also, and primarily, occurs in my Body, in my Life—expressions whose sense must be understood beyond any metaphysical determinations and beyond the "limitations of being" which separated body from soul, speech from gesture, etc. Loss, precisely, is the metaphysical determination into which I will have to slip my works if they are to be understood within a world and a literature unwittingly governed by the metaphysics for which Jacques Rivière served as delegate. "Here, too, I fear a misunderstanding. I would like you to realize that it is not a matter of the higher or lower existence involved in what is known as inspiration, but of a total absence, of a veritable dwindling away" (*Artaud Anthology*, [San Francisco, 1965; hereafter *AA*], p. 8). Artaud ceaselessly repeated this: the origin and urgency of speech, that which impelled him into expression, was confused with his own lack of speech, with "having nothing to say" in his own name. "The dispersiveness of my poems, their formal defects, the constant sagging of my thinking, are to be attributed not to lack of practice, of mastery of the instrument I wield, of *intellectual development,* but to a central collapse of the mind, to a kind of erosion, both essential and fleeting, of my thinking, to the passing nonpossession of the material gains of my development, to the abnormal separation of the elements of thought . . . . There is thus something that is destroying my thinking, a something which does not prevent me from being what I might be, but which leaves me, if I may say so, in abeyance. A something furtive which takes away from me the words *which I have found*" (*AA*, pp. 10–11; Artaud's italics).

It would be tempting, easy, and, to a certain extent, legitimate to underline the exemplarity of this description. The "essential" and "fleeting" erosion, "both essential and fleeting," is produced by the "something furtive which takes away from me the words which *I have found.*" The furtive is fleeting, but it is more than fleeting. Furtiveness—in Latin—is the manner of the thief, who must act very quickly in order to steal from me the words which I have found. Very quickly, because he must invisibly slip into the nothing that separates me from my words, and must purloin them before I have even found them, so that having found them, I am certain that I have always already been divested of them. Furtiveness is thus the quality of dispossession which always empties out speech as it eludes itself. Spoken language has erased the reference to theft from the word "furtive," the subtle subterfuge which makes signification slip—and this is the theft of theft, the furtiveness that eludes itself through a necessary gesture— toward an invisible and silent contact with the fugitive, the fleeting and the fleeing. Artaud neither ignores nor emphasizes the proper sense of the word, but stays within the movement of erasure: in *Nerve-Scales,* à propos of "wasting," "loss," "traps in our thought" he speaks, without being simply redundant, of "stealthy abductions" (*rapts furtifs*) (*Collected Works* [London, 1971; hereafter *CW*], 1:70–71).

As soon as I speak, the words I have found (as soon as they are words) no longer belong to me, are originally *repeated* (Artaud desires a theater in which repetition[16] is impossible. Cf. *The Theater and its Double* [New York, 1958; hereafter *TD*], p. 82). I must first hear myself. In soliloquy as in dialogue, to speak is to hear oneself. As soon as I am heard, as soon as I hear myself, the I who hears *itself,* who hears *me,* becomes the I who speaks and takes speech from the I who thinks that he speaks and is heard in his own name; and becomes the I who takes speech *without ever cutting off* the I who thinks that he speaks. Insinuating itself into the name of the person who speaks, this difference is nothing, is furtiveness itself: it is the structure of instantaneous and original elusion without which no speech could ever catch its breath [*souffle*]. Elusion is produced as the original *enigma*, that is to say, as the speech or history (*ainos*) which hides its origin and meaning; it never says where it is going, nor where it is coming from, primarily because it does not know where it is coming from or going to, and because this not knowing, to wit, the absence of its own subject, is not subsequent to this enigma but, rather, constitutes it. Elusion is the initial unity of that which afterward is diffracted into theft and dissimulation. To understand elusion as rapt or as rape exclusively or fundamentally is within the province of a psychology, an anthropology, or a metaphysics of subjectivity (consciousness, unconsciousness, or the individual body). No doubt that this metaphysics is powerfully at work in Artaud's thought.

Henceforth, what is called the speaking subject is no longer the person himself, or the person alone, who speaks. The speaking subject discovers his irreducible secondarity, his origin that is always already eluded; for the origin is always already eluded on the basis of an organized field of speech in which the speaking subject vainly seeks a place that is always missing. This organized field is not uniquely a field that could be described by certain theories of the psyche or of linguistic fact. It is first—but without meaning anything else—the cultural field from which I must draw my words and my syntax, the historical field which I must read by writing on it. The structure of theft already lodges (itself in) the relation of speech to language. Speech is stolen: since it is stolen from language it is, thus, stolen from itself, that is, from the thief who has always already lost speech as property and initiative. Because its forethought cannot be predicted, the act of reading perforates the act of speaking or writing. And through this perforation, this hole, I escape myself. The form of the hole—which mobilizes the discourse of a certain existentialism and a certain psychoanalysis for which "poor M. Antonin Artaud" provides examples—communicates with a scato-theological thematic in Artaud's works which we will examine later. That speech and writing are always unavowably taken from a reading is the form of the original theft, the most archaic elusion, which simultaneously hides me and *purloins* my powers of inauguration. The mind *purloins*. The *letter*,[17] inscribed or propounded speech, is always stolen. Always stolen because it is always *open*. It never belongs to its author or to its addressee, and by nature, it never follows the trajectory that leads from subject to subject. Which amounts to acknowledging the autonomy of the signifier as the letter's historicity; before me, the signifier on its own says more than I believe that I mean to say, and in relation to it, my meaning-to-say is submissive rather than active. My meaning-to-say finds itself lacking something in relation to the signifier, and is inscribed passively, we might say, even if the reflection of this lack determines the urgency of expression as excess: the autonomy of the signifier as the stratification and historical potentialization of meaning, as a historical system, that is, a system that is open at some point.[18] The oversignification which overburdens the word "spirit" [*souffle*], for example, has not finished illustrating this.

Let us not overextend the banal description of this structure. Artaud does not exemplify it. He wants to explode it. He opposes to this inspiration of loss and dispossession a good inspiration, the very inspiration that is missing from inspiration as loss. Good inspiration is the spirit-breath [*souffle*] of life, which will not take dictation because it does not read and because it precedes all texts. It is the spirit [*souffle*] that would take possession of itself in a place where property would not yet be theft. This inspiration would return me to true communication with myself and would give me back speech: "The difficult part is to find out exactly where one is, to re-establish communication with one's self. The whole thing lies in a certain flocculation of objects, the gathering of these mental gems about one as yet undiscovered (*à trouver*) nucleus. / Here, then, is what I think of thought: / INSPIRATION CERTAINLY EXISTS" (*CW* 1:72) The expression "as yet undiscovered" [*à trouver*] will later punctuate another page. It will then be time to wonder whether Artaud does not thereby designate, each time, the undiscoverable itself.

If we wish to gain access to this metaphysics of life, then life, as the source of good inspiration, must be understood as prior to the life of which the biological sciences speak: "Furthermore, when we speak the word 'life,' it must be understood we are not referring to life as we know it from its surface of fact, but that fragile, fluctuating center which forms never reach. And if there is still one hellish, truly accursed thing in our time, it is our artistic dallying with forms, instead of being like victims burnt at the stake, signaling through the flames" (*TD*, p. 13). Life referred to "from its surface of fact" is thus the life of forms. In *Situation of the Flesh* Artaud will oppose to it "the life-force"[19] (*CW* 1:165) The theater of cruelty will have to reduce this difference between force and form.

What we have just called elusion is not an abstraction for Artaud. The category of furtiveness is not valid solely for the disincarnated voice or for writing. If difference, within its phenomenon, is the sign of theft or of the purloined breath [*souffle*], it is primarily, if not in itself, the total dispossession which constitutes me as the deprivation of myself, the elusion of my existence; and this makes difference the simultaneous theft of both my body and my mind: my flesh. If my speech is not my breath [*souffle*], if my letter is not my speech, this is so because my spirit was already no longer my body, my body no longer my gestures, my gestures no longer my life. The integrity of the flesh torn by all these differences must be restored in the theater. Thus the metaphysics of flesh which determines Being as life, and the mind as the body itself, as unseparated thought, "obscure" thinking (for "Clear mind is a property of matter," *CW* 1:165)—this is the continuous and always unperceived trait which links *The Theater and Its Double* to the early works and to the theme of unpower. This metaphysics of the flesh is also governed by the anguish of dispossession, the experience of having lost life, of separation from thought, of the body exiled far from the mind. Such is the initial cry. "I am reflecting on life. All the systems I could devise would never equal these cries by a man occupied in rebuilding his life.... My reason will certainly one day have to receive these unformulated forces exteriorly shaped like a cry which are besieging me, and they may then supplant higher thought. These are intellectual cries, cries which stem from the marrow's *delicacy*. This is what I personally call the Flesh. I do not separate my thought from my life.... But what am I in the midst of this theory about the Flesh or more correctly, Existence? I am a man who has lost his life and who is seeking every way of re-integrating it in its proper place.... But I must look into this aspect of the flesh which is supposed to give me a metaphysics of Being and a positive understanding of life" (*CW* 1:164–65).

Let us not be detained here by a possible resemblance to the essence of the mythic itself: the dream of a life without difference. Let us ask, rather, what difference within the flesh might mean for Artaud. My body has been stolen from me by effraction. The Other, the Thief, the great Furtive One, has a proper name: God. His history has taken place. It has its own place. The place of effraction can be only the opening of an orifice. The orifice of birth, the orifice of defecation to which all other gaps refer, as if to their origin. "It is filled, / it is not filled, / there is a void, / a lack / a missing something / which is always taken by a parasite on flight" (August 1947). *Flight:* the pun is certain.

Ever since I have had a relation to my body, therefore, ever since my birth, I no longer am my body. Ever since I have had a body I am not this body, hence I do not possess it. This deprivation institutes and informs my relation to my life. My body has thus always been stolen from me. Who could have stolen it from me, if not an Other, and how could he have gotten hold of it from the beginning unless he had slipped into my place inside my mother's belly, unless I had been *stolen from my birth,* unless my birth had been purloined from me, "as if being born has for a long time smelled of dying"? (*84,* p. 11) Death yields to conceptualization within the category of theft; it is not what we believe we can anticipate as the termination of the process or adventure that we (assuredly) call life. Death is an articulated form of our relationship to the Other. I die only *of* the other: through him, for him, in him. My death is *represented,* let one modify this word as one will. And if I die by representation, then at the "extreme moment of death" this representative theft has not any less shaped the entirety of my existence, from its origin. This is why, in the last extremity " ... one does not commit suicide alone. / No one was ever born alone. / Nor has anyone died alone ... / ... And I believe that there is always someone else, at the extreme moment of death, to strip us of our own life" (*AA,* pp. 161–62) The theme of death as theft is at the center of "La mort et l'homme" (Sur un dessin de Rodez, in *84,* no. 13).

And who could the thief be if not the great invisible Other, the furtive perse-cutor who *doubles* me everywhere, that is, redoubles and surpasses me, always arrives before me where I have chosen to go, like "the body which pursued me" (persecuted me) "and did not follow" (preceded me)—who could he be if not God? "AND WHAT HAVE YOU DONE WITH MY BODY, GOD?"(*84,* p. 108). And here is the answer: ever since the black hole of my birth, god has "*flayed me alive* / during my entire existence / and has done so / uniquely because of the fact that / it is I / who was god, / truly god, / I a man / and not the so-called ghost / who was only the projection into the clouds / of the body of a man other than myself, / who called himself the / Demiurge / Now, the hideous history of the Demiurge / is well known / It is the history of the body / which *pursued* (and did not follow) mine / and which, in order to go first and be born, / projected itself across my body / and / was born / through the disemboweling of my body / of which he kept a piece / in order to / pass himself off / as me. / Now, there was no one but he and I, / he / an abject body / unwanted by space, / I / a body being mad / consequently not yet having reached completion / but evolving / toward integral purity / like the body of the so-called Demiurge, / who, knowing that he has no chance of being received / and yet wanting to live at any price, / found nothing better / in order *to be* / than to be born at the price of my assassination. / Despite everything, my body reshaped itself / against and through a thousand attacks of evil / and of hatred / which each time deteriorated him / and left me dead. / And it is thus that through dying / I have come to achieve real immortality. / And / this is the true story of things / as they really happened / and not / as seen in the legendary atmosphere of myths / which obscure reality" (*84,* pp. 108–10).

God is thus the proper name of that which deprives us of our own nature, of our own birth; consequently he will always have spoken before us, on the sly. He is the difference which insinuates itself between myself and myself as my death. This is why—such is the concept of true suicide according to Artaud—I must die away from my death in order to be reborn "immortal" at the eve of my birth. God does not take hold of any one of our innate attributes, but of our innateness itself, of the innateness proper to our being itself: "There are some fools who think of themselves as beings, as innately being. / I am he who, in order to be, must whip his innateness. / One who must be a being innately, that is, always whipping this sort of nonexistent kennel, O! bitches of impossibility"(*CW,* I:19).

Why is this original alienation conceived as pollution, obscenity, "filthiness," etc.? Why does Artaud, bemoaning the loss of his body, lament a loss of purity as much as he laments dispossession, lament the loss of propriety as much as the loss of property? "I have been tortured too much ... / ... / I have worked too hard at being pure and strong / ... / I have sought to have a proper body too much" (*84,* p. 135).

By definition, I have been robbed of my possessions, my worth, my value. My truth, what I am worth, has been purloined from me by some One who in my stead became God at the exit from the Orifice, at birth. God is false value as the initial worth of that which is born. And this false value becomes Value, because it has always already *doubled* true value which has never existed, or, amounting to the same thing, existed only prior to its own birth. Henceforth, original value, the ur-value that I should have retained within myself, or rather should have retained as myself, as my value and my very being, that which was stolen from me as soon as I fell far from the Orifice, and which is stolen from me again each time that a part of me falls far from myself—this is the work, excrement, dross, the value that is annulled because it has not been retained, and which can become, as is well known, a persecuting arm, an arm eventually directed against myself. Defecation, the "daily separation with the feces, precious parts of the body" (Freud), is, as birth, as my birth, the initial theft which simultaneously depreciates[20] me and soils me. This is why the history of God as a genealogy of stolen value is recounted as the history of defecation. "Do you know anything more outrageously fecal / than the history of God...." ("Le théâtre de la cruauté," in *84*, p. 121).

It is perhaps due to God's complicity with the origin of the work that Artaud also calls him the Demiurge. In question is a metonym of the name of God, the proper name of the thief and the metaphorical name of myself: the metaphor of myself is my dispossession within language. In any event, God-the-Demiurge does not *create,* is not life, but is the subject of *œuvres* and maneuvers, is the thief, the trickster, the counterfeiter, the pseudonymous, the usurper, the opposite of the creative artist, the artisanal being, the being of the artisan: Satan. I am God and God is Satan; and as Satan is part of God's creation (. . . "the history of God / of his being: SATAN . . ." in *84*, p. 121), God is of my own creation, my double who slipped into the difference that separates me from my origin, that is, into the nothing that opens my history. What is called the presence of God is but the forgetting of this nothing, the eluding of elusion, which is not an accident but the very movement of elusion: " . . .Satan, / who with his overflowing nipples / hid from us / only Nothingness?" (ibid.).

This history of God is thus the history of the work as excrement. Scato-logy itself. The work, as excrement, supposes separation and is produced within separation. The work thus proceeds from the separation of the mind from a pure body. It belongs to the mind, and to relocate an unpolluted body is to reconstitute oneself as a body without a work. "For one must have a mind in order / to shit, / a *pure* body cannot / shit. / What it shits / is the glue of minds / furiously determined to steal something from him / for without a body one cannot exist" (*84*, p. 113). One can read in *Nerve-Scales:* "Dear Friends, What you took to be my works were only my waste matter" (*CW* 1:72).

My work, my trace, the excrement that robs *me of* my possessions after I have been *stolen from* my birth, must thus be rejected. But to reject it is not, here, to refuse it but to retain it. To keep myself, to keep my body and my speech, I must retain the work within me,[21] conjoin myself with it so that there will be no opportunity for the Thief to come between it and me: it must be kept from falling far from my body as writing. For "writing is all trash" (*CW* 1:75). Thus, that which dispossesses me and makes me remote from myself, interrupting my proximity to myself, also soils me: I relinquish all that is proper to me. Proper is the name of the subject close to himself—who is what he is—and abject the name of the object, the work that has deviated from me. I have a proper name when I am proper. The child does not appropriate his true name in Western society—initially in school—is not well named until he is proper, clean, toilet-trained. The unity of these significations, hidden beneath their apparent dispersion, the unity of the proper as the nonpollution of the subject absolutely close to himself, does not occur before the Latin era of philosophy (*proprius* is attached to proper); and, for the same reason, the metaphysical determination of madness as the disease of alienation could not have begun its development before this era. (It goes without saying that we are not construing the linguistic phenomenon as a cause or a symptom: the concept of madness, quite simply, is solidified only during the era of the metaphysics of a proper subjectivity.) Artaud *solicits* this metaphysics, *shakes* it when it lies to itself and establishes the proper departure from that which is proper to oneself (the alienation of alienation) as the condition for the phenomenon of the proper; and Artaud still *summons* this metaphysics, draws upon its fund of values, and attempts to be more faithful to it than it is to itself by means of an absolute restoration of the proper to the eve prior to all dissociation.

Like excrement, like the turd, which is, as is also well known, a metaphor of the penis,[22] the work *should* stand upright. But the work, as excrement, is but matter without life, without force or form. It always falls and collapses as soon as it is outside me. This is why the work—be it poetic or other—will never help me stand upright. I will never be erect in it. Thus salvation, status, uprightness will be possible only in an art without works. The work always being the work of death, the art without works—dance or the theater of cruelty—will be the art of life itself. "I have therefore said 'cruelty' as I might have said 'life'" (*TD*, p. 114).

Rigid with rage against God, convulsed with anger against the work, Artaud does not renounce salvation. On the contrary, soteriology will be the eschatology of one's proper body. "It is the *state* of my / body which will make / the Last Judgment" (*84,* p. 131). One's-proper-body-upright-without-detritus. Evil, pollution, resides in the *critical* or the *clinical:* it is to have one's speech and body become works, objects which can be offered up to the furtive haste of the commentator because they are supine. For, by definition, the only thing that is not subject to commentary is the life of the body, the living flesh whose integrity, opposed to evil and death, is maintained by the theater. Disease is the impossibility of standing upright in dance and in the theater. "There is plague, / cholera / smallpox / only because dance / and consequently theater / have not yet begun to exist" (*84, p. 127*).

The tradition of mad poets? Hölderlin: "Yet, fellow poets, us it behoves to stand / Bare headed beneath God's thunderstorms, / To grasp the Father's rays, no less, with our own two hands / And, wrapping in song the heavenly gift, / To offer it to the people."[23] Nietzsche: ". . . need I add that one must also be able to dance with the pen . . .?"[24] Or further: "Only those thoughts that come by walking have any value."[25] On this point, as on many others, one could be tempted to envelop these three mad poets, in the company of several others, within the thrust of a single commentary and the continuity of a single genealogy.[26] A thousand other texts on standing upright and on the dance could effectively encourage such a project. But would it not then miss Artaud's essential decision? From Hölderlin to Nietzsche, standing upright and the dance remain metaphorical, perhaps. In any event, erection is not obliged to exile itself into the work or to delegate itself to the poem, to expatriate itself into the sovereignty of speech or writing, into the literal uprightness of the letter or the tip of the pen. The uprightness of the work, to be more precise, is the reign of literality over breath [*souffle*]. Nietzsche had certainly denounced the grammatical structure embedded within a metaphysics to be demolished; but, did he ever question, as to its origin, the relationship between grammatical security, which he acknowledged, and the uprightness of the letter? Heidegger foretells this relationship in a brief suggestion in the *Introduction to Metaphysics:* "In a certain broad sense the Greeks looked on language from a visual point of view, that is, starting from the written language. It is in writing that the spoken language comes to stand. Language is, i.e. it stands, in the written image of the word, in the written signs, the letters, *grammata*. Consequently, grammar represents language in being. But through the flow of speech language seeps away into the impermanent. Thus, down to our time, language has been interpreted grammatically."[27] This does not contradict, but confirms, paradoxically, the disdain of writing which, in the *Phaedrus* for example, saves metaphorical writing as the initial inscription of truth upon the soul—saves it and initially refers to it as to the most assured knowledge and the proper meaning of writing (276a).

It is metaphor that Artaud wants to destroy. He wishes to have done with standing upright as metaphorical erection within the written work.[28] This alienation of the written work into metaphor is a phenomenon that belongs to superstition. And "We must get rid of our superstitious valuation of texts and written poetry" (*TD*, p. 78). Superstition is thus the essence of our relation to God, of our persecution by the great furtive one. The death of God[29] will ensure our salvation because the death of God alone can reawaken the Divine. Man's name—man as the scato-theological being, the being capable of being soiled by the work and of being constituted by his relation to the thieving God—designates the historical corruption of the unnamable Divine. "And this faculty is an exclusively human one. I would even say that it is this infection of the human which contaminates ideas that should have remained divine; for far from believing that man invented the supernatural and the divine, I think it is man's age-old intervention which has ultimately corrupted the divine within him" (*TD,* p. 8). God is thus a sin against the divine. The essence of guilt is scato-theological. The body of thought in which the scato-theological essence of man appears as such cannot simply be a metaphysical anthropology or humanism. Rather it points to the way beyond man, beyond the metaphysics of Western theater whose "preoccupations ... stink unbelievably of man, provisional, material man, I shall even say *carrion man*" (*TD,* p. 42. Cf. also, in *CW* 3, the letter of insults to the Comédie-Française which, in explicit terms, denounces the scatological vocation of that institution's concept and operations).

By virtue of this rejection of the metaphorical stance within the work, and despite several striking resemblances (here, the passage beyond man and God), Artaud is not the son of Nietzsche. And even less so of Hölderlin. The theater of cruelty, by killing metaphor (upright-being-outside-itself-within-the-stolen-work), pushes us into "a new idea of *Danger*" (letter to Marcel Dalio in *Œuvres complètes,* [Paris, 1970], 5:95). The adventure of the Poem is the last anguish to be suppressed before the adventure of the Theater.[30] Before Being in its proper station.

How will the theater of cruelty save me, give me back the institution of my flesh itself? How will it prevent my life from falling outside me? How will it help me avoid "having lived / like the 'Demiurge' / with / a body stolen by effraction" (*84,* p. 113)?

First, by summarily reducing the organ. The first gesture of the destruction of classical theater—and the metaphysics it puts on stage—is the reduction of the organ. The classical Western stage defines a theater of the organ, a theater of words, thus a theater of interpretation, enregistration, and translation, a theater of deviation from the groundwork of a preestablished text, a table written by a God-Author who is the sole wielder of the primal word. A theater in which a master disposes of the stolen speech which only his slaves—his directors and actors—may make use of. "If, then, the author is the man who arranges the language of speech and the director is his slave, there is merely a question of words. There is here a confusion over terms, stemming from the fact that, for us, and according to the sense generally attributed to the word *director,* this man is merely an artisan, an adapter, a kind of translator eternally devoted to making a dramatic work pass from one language into another; this confusion will be possible, and the director will be forced to play second fiddle to the author, only so long as there is a tacit agreement that the language of words is superior to others and that the theater admits none other than this one language" (*TD,* p. 119).[31] The differences upon which the metaphysics of Occidental theater lives (author-text / director-actors), its differentiation and its divisions, transform the "slaves" into commentators, that is, into organs. Here, they are recording organs. Now, "We must believe in a sense of life renewed by the theater, a sense of life in which man fearlessly makes himself *master of what does not yet exist* (my italics), and brings it into being. And everything that has not been born can still be brought to life if we are not satisfied to remain mere recording organisms" (*TD*, p. 13).

But what we will call organic differentiation had already raged within the body, before it had corrupted the metaphysics of the theater. *Organization* is articulation, the interlocking of functions or of members (*artho, artus*), the labor and play of their differentiation. This constitutes both the "membering" and dismembering of my proper body. For one and the same reason, through a single gesture, Artaud is as fearful of the articulated body as he is of articulated language, as fearful of the member as of the word. For articulation is the structure of my body, and structure is always a structure of expropriation. The division of the body into organs, the difference interior to the flesh, opens the lack through which the body becomes absent from itself, passing itself off as, and taking itself for, the mind. Now, "there is no mind, nothing but the differentiation of bodies" (March, 1947). The body, which "always seeks to reassemble itself,"[32] escapes itself by virtue of that which permits it to function and to express itself; as is said of those who are ill, the body listens to itself and, thus, disconcerts itself. "The body is the body, / it is alone / and has no need of organs, / the body is never an organism, / organisms are the enemies of bodies, / everything one does transpires by itself without the aid of any organ, / every organ is a parasite, / it overlaps with a parasitic function / destined to bring into existence a being which should not be there" (*84*, p. 101). The organ thus welcomes the difference of the stranger into my body: it is always the organ of my ruin, and this truth is so original that neither the heart, the central organ of life, nor the sex, the first organ of life, can escape it: "It is thus that there is in fact nothing more ignominiously useless and superfluous than the organ called the heart / which is the dirtiest means that any being could have invented for pumping life inside me. / The movements of the heart are nothing other than a maneuver to which being ceaselessly abandons itself above me, in order to take from me that which I ceaselessly deny it" (*84*, p. 103). Further on: "A true man has no sex" (p. 112). [33] A true man has no sex for he must be his sex. As soon as the sex becomes an organ, it becomes foreign to me, abandons me, acquiring thereby the arrogant autonomy of a swollen object full of itself. This swelling of the sex become a separate object is a kind of castration. "He said he saw a great preoccupation with sex in me. But with taut sexual organs, swollen like an object" (Art and Death, in *CW* 1:108).

The organ: place of loss because its center always has the form of an orifice. The organ always functions as an embouchure. The reconstitution and reinstitution of my flesh will thus always follow along the lines of my body's closing in on itself and the reduction of the organic structure: "I was alive / and I have been *here* since *always*. / Did I eat? / No, / but when I was hungry I retreated with my body and did not eat myself / but all that has been decomposed, / a strange operation has taken place . . . / Did I sleep? / No, I did not sleep, / one must be chaste to know not to eat. / To open one's mouth is to give oneself over to miasms. / No mouth, then! / No mouth, / no tongue, / no teeth, / no larynx, / no esophagus, / no stomach, / no belly, / no anus. / I will reconstruct the man that I am" (November 1947, in *84,* p. 102) Further on: "(It is not especially a question of the sex or the anus / which, moreover, are to be hewn off and liquidated)" (*84,* p. 125). The reconstitution of the body must be autarchic; it cannot be given any assistance and the body must be remade of a single piece: "It is / I / who / will   be / remade / by   me / myself / entirely / . . . by   myself / who am a body / and have no regions within me" (March 1947.)

The dance of cruelty punctuates this reconstruction, and once more in question is a *place to be found:* "Reality has not yet been constructed because the true organs of the human body have not yet been assembled and put in place. / The theater of cruelty has been created to complete this putting into place and to undertake, through a new dance of the body of man, the disruption of this world of microbes which is but coagulated nothingness. / The theater of cruelty wants to make eyelids dance cheek to cheek with elbows, patellas, femurs and toes, and to have this dance be seen" (*84,* p. 101).

Thus, theater could not have been a genre among others for Artaud, who was a man of the theater before being a writer, poet, or even a man of the theater: an actor as much as an author, and not only because he acted a great deal, having written but a single play, and having demonstrated for an "aborted theater," but because theater summons the totality of existence and no longer tolerates either the incidence of interpretation or the distinction between actor and author. The initial urgent requirement of an in-organic theater is emancipation from the text. Although the rigorous system of this emancipation is found only in *The Theater and Its Double,* protest against the letter had always been Artaud's primary concern. Protest against the dead letter which absents itself far from breath [*souffle*] and flesh. Artaud initially dreamed of a graphism which would not begin as deviation, of a nonseparated inscription: an incarnation of the letter and a bloody tatoo: "In deference to this letter (from Jean Paulhan, 1923) I continued for a further month to work at writing a verbally, not a grammatically, successful poem. / Then I gave up. As far as I was concerned, the problem was not to find out what might manage to worm its way into the structures of written language, / but into the web of my living soul. / By which words entered like knives in lasting carnation, / a fitting, dying in-carnation under a span, the burning island of a gallows lantern" (*CW,* 1:18).[34]

But the tattoo paralyzes gesture and silences the voice which also belongs to the flesh. It represses the shout and the chance for a still unorganized voice. And later, proposing the withdrawal of the theater from text, prompter [*souffleur*], and the omnipotence of a primary logos, Artaud will not simply wish to give it over to mutism. He will only attempt the resituation and subordination of speech—the until now enormous, pervasive, ubiquitous, bloated speech [*parole soufflée*]—which had exorbitantly weighed upon theatrical space. Without disappearing, speech will now have to keep to its place; and to do so it will have to modify its very function, will have no longer to be a language of words, of terms "in a single defined sense" (*TD*, p. 118), of concepts which put an end to thought and life. It is within the silence of definition-words that "we could listen more closely to life" (ibid.). Thus, onomatopoeia, the gesture dormant in all classical speech, will be reawakened, and along with it sonority, intonation, intensity. And the syntax governing the succession of word gestures will no longer be a grammar of predication, a logic of "clear thinking" or of a knowing consciousness. "When I say I will perform no written play, I mean that I will perform no play based on writing and speech . . . and that even the spoken and written portions will be spoken and written in a new sense" (*TD*, p. 111). "It is not a question of suppressing the spoken language, but of giving words approximately the importance they have in dreams" (*TD*, p. 94).[35]

Foreign to dance, as immobile and monumental as a definition, materialized, that is to say, part of "clear thinking," the tattoo is thus still all too silent. It maintains the silence of a liberated letter that speaks on its own and assigns itself more importance than speech has in dreams. The tatoo is a depository, a work, and it is precisely the work that must be destroyed, as we now know. A fortiori the masterpiece: "no more masterpieces" (the title of one of the most important texts of *The Theater and Its Double*). Here again, to overthrow the power of the literal work is not to erase the letter, but only to subordinate it to the incidence of illegibility or at least of illiteracy. "I am writing for illiterates."[36] As can be seen in certain non-Western civilizations, precisely the ones that fascinated Artaud, illiteracy can quite well accommodate the most profound and living culture. The traces inscribed on the body will no longer be graphic incisions but wounds received in the destruction of the West, its metaphysics and its theater, the stigmata of this pitiless war. For the theater of cruelty is not a new theater destined to escort some new novel that would modify from within an unshaken tradition. Artaud undertakes neither a renewal, nor a critique, nor a new interrogation of classical theater; he intends the effective, active, and nontheoretical destruction of Western civilization and its religions, the entirety of the philosophy which provides traditional theater with its groundwork and decor beneath even its more apparently innovative forms.

The stigmata and not the tattoo: thus, in the résumé of what should have been the first production of the theater of cruelty (*The Conquest of Mexico*), incarnating the "question of colonization," and which "revives in a brutal and implacable way the ever active fatuousness of Europe" (*TD*, p. 126), the stigmata are substituted for the text. "Out of this clash of moral disorder and Catholic monarchy with pagan order, the subject can set off unheard-of explosions of forces and images, sown here and there with brutal dialogues. Men battling hand to hand, bearing within themselves, like stigmata, the most opposed ideas" (*TD*, p. 127).

The subversive efforts to which Artaud thus had always submitted the imperialism of the letter had the negative meaning of a *revolt* for as long as they took place within the milieu of literature as such. Thus, the initial works surrounding the letters to Jacques Rivière. The *revolutionary*[37] affirmation which was to receive a remarkable theoretical treatment in *The Theater and Its Double* nevertheless had surfaced in *The Alfred Jarry Theater* (1926–30). There we already find prescribed a descent toward the depth at which the distinction of theatrical organs (author-text / director-actor-public), in the manifestation of forces, no longer would be possible. Now this system of organic divisions, this *difference,* has never been possible, except when distributed around an object, book, or libretto. The depth sought after must thus be the depth of illegibility: "Whatever is part of . . . illegibility" "we want to see sparkle and triumph on stage" (*CW* 2:23). In theatrical illegibility, in the night that precedes the book, the sign has not yet been separated from force.[38] It is not quite yet a sign, in the sense in which we understand sign, but is no longer a *thing,* which we conceive only as opposed to the sign. It has, then, no chance to become, in this state, a written text or an articulated speech; no chance to rise and to inflate itself above *energeia* in order to be invested, according to Humboldt's distinction, with the somber and objective impassivity of the *ergon.* Now Europe lives upon the ideal of this separation between force and meaning as text, at the very moment when, as we suggested above, in purportedly elevating the mind above the letter, it states a preference for metaphorical writing. This derivation of force within the sign divides the theatrical act, exiles the actor far from any responsibility for meaning, makes of him an interpreter who lets his life be breathed into [*insoufflé*] him, and lets his words be whispered [*soufflé*] to him, receiving his delivery as if he were taking orders, submitting like a beast to the pleasure of docility. Like the seated public, he is but a consumer, an aesthete, a "pleasure-taker." The stage is no longer cruel, is no longer the stage, but a decoration, the luxurious illustration of a book. In the best of cases, another literary genre. "Dialogue—a thing written and spoken—does not belong specifically to the stage, it belongs to books, as is proved by the fact that in all hand-books of literary history a place is reserved for the theater as a subordinate branch of the history of the spoken language" (*TD,* p. 37).

To let one's speech be spirited away [*soufflé*] is, like writing itself, the ur-phenomenon of the *reserve:* the abandoning of the self to the furtive, to discretion and separation, is, at the same time, accumulation, capitalization, the security of the delegated or deferred decision. To leave one's speech to the furtive is to tranquilize oneself into deferral, that is to say, into economy. The theater of the prompter [*souffleur*] thus constructs the system of fear, and manages to keep fear at a distance with the learned machinations of its materialized meditations. And, as we know, Artaud, like Nietzsche, but through the theater, wants to return us to Danger as Becoming. "The comtemporary theater is decadent because . . . it has broken away from . . . Danger" (*TD,* p. 42), broken away from Becoming: "It seems, in brief, that the highest possible idea of the theater is one that reconciles us philosophically with Becoming" (*TD,* p. 109).

To reject the work, to let one's speech, body, and birth be spirited away [*soufflé*] by the furtive god is thus to defend oneself against the theater of fear which multiplies the differences between myself and myself. Restored to its absolute and terrifying proximity, the stage of cruelty will thus return me to the autarchic immediacy of my birth, my body and my speech. Where has Artaud better defined the stage of cruelty than in *Here Lies,* outside any apparent reference to the theater: "I, Antonin Artaud, am my son / my father, my mother / and myself" (*AA,* p. 238)?

But does not the theater which is no longer a colony succumb to its own cruelty? Will it resist its own danger? Liberated from diction, withdrawn from the dictatorship of the text, will not theatrical atheism be given over to improvisational anarchy and to the actors' capricious inspirations? Is not another form of subjugation in preparation? Another flight of language into arbitrariness and irresponsibility? To thwart this danger, which inwardly threatens danger itself, Artaud, through a strange movement, disposes the language of cruelty within a new form of writing: the most rigorous, authoritarian, regulated, and mathematical—the fost formal form of writing. This apparent incoherence suggests a hasty objection. In truth, the will to maintain speech by defending oneself against it governs, with its omnipotent and infallible logic, a reversal that we will have to follow here.

To Jean Paulhan: "I do not believe that if you had once read my Manifesto you could persevere in your objections, so either you have not read it or you have read it badly. My plans have nothing to do with Copeau's improvisations. However thoroughly they are immersed in the concrete and external, however rooted in free nature and not in the narrow chambers of the brain, they are not, for all that, left to the caprice of the wild and thoughtless inspiration of the actor, especially the actor who, once cut off from the text, plunges in without any idea of what he is doing. I would not care to leave the fate of my plays and of the theater to that kind of chance. No" (*TD,* pp. 109–10). "I give myself up to feverish dreams, but I do so in order to deduce new laws. In delirium, I seek multiplicity, subtlety and the eye of reason, not rash prophecies" (*CW* 1:167).

If it is necessary, thus, to renounce "the theatrical superstition of the text and the dictatorship of the writer" (*TD*, p. 124), it is because they could not have imposed themselves without the aid of a certain model of speech and writing: the speech that represents clear and willing thought, the (alphabetic, or in any event phonetic) writing that represents representative speech. Classical theater, the theater of diversions, was the representation of all these representations. And this deferral, these delays, these stages of representation extend and liberate the play of the signifier, thus multiplying the places and moments of elusion. For the theater to be neither subjected to this structure of language, nor abandoned to the spontaneity of furtive inspiration, it will have to be governed according to the requirements of another language and another form of writing. The themes, but also occasionally the models, of writing doubtless will be sought outside Europe, in Balinese theater, in the ancient Mexican, Hindu, Iranian, Egyptian, etc., cosmogonies. This time, writing not only will no longer be the transcription of speech, not only will be the writing *of* the body itself, but it will be produced, within the movements of the theater, according to the rules of hieroglyphics, a system of signs no longer controlled by the institution of the voice. "The overlapping of images and movements will culminate, through the collusion of objects, silences, shouts, and rhythms, or in a genuine physical language with signs, not words, as its root" (*TD*, p. 287). Words themselves will once more become physical signs that do not trespass toward concepts, but "will be construed in an incantational, truly magical sense—for their shape and their sensuous emanations" (*TD*, p. 125). Words will cease to flatten theatrical space and to lay it out horizontally as did logical speech; they will reinstate the "volume" of theatrical space and will utilize this volume "in its undersides (*dans ses dessous*)" (*TD*, p. 124). It is not by chance, henceforth, that Artaud speaks of "hieroglyphics" rather than ideograms: "And it can be said that the spirit of the most ancient hieroglyphs will preside at the creation of this pure theatrical language" (ibid.). (In saying hieroglyphics, Artaud is thinking only of the *principle* of the writing called hieroglyphic, which, as we know, did not *in fact* set aside all phoneticism.)

Not only will the voice no longer give orders, but it will have to let itself be punctuated by the law of this theatrical writing. The only way to be done with the freedom of inspiration and with the spiriting away of speech [*la parole soufflée*] is to create an absolute mastery over breath [*le souffle*] within a system of nonphonetic writing. Whence *An Affective Athleticism,* the strange text in which Artaud seeks the laws of breath in the Cabbala and in Yin and Yang, and wants "through the hieroglyph of a breath . . . to recover an idea of the sacred theater" (*TD*, p. 141). Having always preferred the shout to the text, Artaud now attempts to elaborate a rigorous textuality of shouts, a codified system of onomatopoeias, expressions, and gestures—a veritable theatrical pasigraphy reaching beyond empirical languages,[39] a universal grammar of cruelty. "Similarly the ten thousand and one expressions of the face caught in the form of masks can be labeled and catalogued, so they may eventually participate directly and symbolically in this concrete language of the stage'' (*TD*, p. 94). Artaud even attempts to recognize, beneath their apparent contingency, the necessity of unconscious formations; he therefore, after a fashion, traces the form of theatrical writing from the model of unconscious writing. This is perhaps the unconscious writing of which Freud speaks in the ''Note on the Mystic Writing Pad,'' as a writing which erases and retains itself; although Freud speaks of this writing after having warned, in *The Interpretation of Dreams,* against metaphorizing the unconscious as an original text subsisting alongside the *Umschrift* (transcription), and after having compared dreams, in a short text from 1913, to ''a system of writing'' and even of ''hieroglyphic'' writing, rather than to ''a language.''

Despite all appearance, that is, despite the entirety of Western metaphysics, this mathematizing formalization would liberate both the festival and repressed ingenuity. ''This may perhaps shock our European sense of stage freedom and spontaneaous inspiration, but let no one say that this mathematics creates sterility or uniformity. The marvel is that a sensation of richness, of fantasy and prodigality emanates from this spectacle ruled with a maddening scrupulosity and consciousness'' (*TD*, p. 55). ''The actors with their costumes constitute veritable living, moving hieroglyphs. And these three-dimensional hieroglyphs are in turn brocaded with a certain number of gestures—mysterious signs which correspond to some unknown, fabulous, and obscure reality which we here in the Occident have completely repressed'' (*TD*, p. 61).

How are this liberation and this raising of the repressed possible? And not despite, but with the aid of a totalitarian codification and rhetoric of forces? With the aid of *cruelty,* which initially signifies ''rigor'' and ''submission to necessity'' (*TD*, p. 102)? It is that by prohibiting chance and by repressing the play of the machine, this new theatrical arrangement sutures all the gaps, all the openings, all the differences. Their origin and active movement—differing, deferral—are *enclosed.* At this point, eluded speech is definitively returned to us. And at this point, perhaps, cruelty pacifies itself within its regained absolute proximity, within another summary reduction of becoming, within the perfection and *economy* of its return to the stage. ''I, Antonin Artaud, am my son, / my father, my mother, / and myself.'' Such is, according to Artaud's stated desire, the *law of the house,* the initial organization of a dwelling space, the ur-stage. The ur-stage is then *present,* reassembled into its presence, *seen,* mastered, terrifying, and pacifying.

Furtive *différance* could not have insinuated itself with the aid of writing but, rather, slipped in between two forms of writing, thereby placing my life outside the work and making its origin—my flesh—into the epigraph and breathless [*essoufflé*] sarcophagous of my discourse. Only through writing made flesh, only through the theatrical hieroglyphic, could the necessary destruction of the double take place, and with it the erasure of *apo-cryphal* writing which eludes my being as life, keeping me at a remove from hidden force. Discourse can now be reunited with its birth in a perfect and permanent self-presence. "It happens that this mannerism, this excessively hieratic style, with its rolling alphabet, its shrieks of splitting stones, noises of branches, noises of the cutting and rolling of wood, compose a sort of animated material murmur in the air, in space, a visual as well as audible whispering. And after an instant the magic identification is made: WE KNOW IT IS WE WHO WERE SPEAKING" (*TD*, p. 67). The present knowledge of the *proper-past* of our speech.

A magic identification, of course. The temporal differences would sufficiently bear witness to this. And to say that it is magic is to say very little. It could even be demonstrated that it is the very essence of magic. A magic and, what is more, an unfindable identification. Unfindable is "the grammar of this new language," which Artaud concedes "is still to be found" (*TD*, p. 110). *In fact*, against all his intentions, Artaud had to reintroduce the prerequisite of the written text into "productions" ... "rigorously composed and *fixed* once and for all before being played" (*Œuvres complètes* [hereafter *OC*], 5:41). "All these groupings, researches, and shocks will culminate nevertheless in a work *written down*, fixed in its least details, and recorded by new means of notation. The composition, the creation, instead of being made in the brain of an author, will be made in nature itself, in real space, and the final result will be as strict and as calculated as that of any written work whatsoever, with an immense objective richness as well" (*TD*, pp. 11–112). Even if Artaud had not, as *in fact he did*,[40] had to respect the rights of the work and of the written work, does not his very project (the reduction of the work and of difference, therefore of historicity) indicate the very essence of madness? But this madness, as the metaphysics of inalienable life and historic indifference—the "I speak / from above time" (*AA*, p. 248)—no less legitimately has denounced, with a gesture that does not give shelter to another metaphysics, the *other* madness, as the metaphysics which lives *within* difference, within metaphor and the work, and thus within alienation; and lives within them without conceiving them *as such,* beyond metaphysics. Madness is as much alienation as inalienation. It is the work or the absence of the work.[41] These two determinations indefinitely confront one another within the closed field of metaphysics, just as those whom Artaud calls evident or authentic madmen confront the other madmen within history. They necessarily confront one another and exchange themselves for each other; they articulate themselves within the categories—acknowledged or not, but always recognizable—of a single historico-metaphysical discourse. The concepts of madness, alienation, or inalienation irreducibly belong to the history of metaphysics. Or, more narrowly: they belong to the epoch of metaphysics that determines Being as the life of a proper subjectivity. Now difference—or deferral, with all the modifications laid bare by Artaud—can only be conceived as such beyond metaphysics, towards the Difference—or Duplicity—of which Heidegger speaks. It could be thought that this latter Difference, which simultaneously opens and conceals truth, and in fact distinguishes nothing—the invisible accomplice of all speech—is furtive power itself, if this were not to confuse the metaphysical and metaphorical category of the furtive with that which makes it possible. If the "destruction"[42] of the history of metaphysics, in the rigorous sense understood by Heidegger, is not a simple surpassing of this history, one could then, sojourning in a place which is neither within nor without this history, wonder about what links the concept of madness to the concept of metaphysics in general: the metaphysics which Artaud destroys and which he is still furiously determined to construct or to preserve within the same movement of destruction. Artaud keeps himself at the limit, and we have attempted to read him at this limit. One entire side of his discourse destroys a tradition which lives *within* difference, alienation, and negativity without seeing their origin and necessity. To reawaken this tradition, Artaud, in sum, recalls it to its own motifs: self-presence, unity, self-identity, the proper, etc. In this sense, Artaud's "metaphysics," at its most critical moments, fulfills the most profound and permanent ambition of Western metaphysics. But through another twist of his text, the most difficult one, Artaud affirms the *cruel* (that is to say, in the sense in which he takes this word, necessary) law of difference; a law that this time is raised to the level of consciousness and is no longer experienced within metaphysical naïveté. This duplicity of Artaud's text, simultaneously more and less than a stratagem, has unceasingly obliged us to pass over to the other side of the limit, and thereby to demonstrate the closure of the presence in which he had to enclose himself in order to denounce the naïve implications within difference. At this point, different things ceaselessly and rapidly pass into each other, and the *critical* experience of *difference resembles* the naïve and *metaphysical* implications *within difference,* such that to an inexpert scrutiny, we could appear to be criticizing Artaud's metaphysics from the standpoint of metaphysics itself, when we are actually delimiting a fatal complicity. Through this complicity is articulated a necessary dependency of all destructive discourses: they must inhabit the structures they demolish, and within them they must shelter an indestructible desire for full presence, for nondifference: simultaneously life and death. Such is the question that we have attempted to *pose,* in the sense in which one poses a net, surrounding the limit of an entire textual network, forcing the substitution of *discourse,* the detour made obligatory by sites, for the punctuality of the *position.* Without the necessary duration and traces of this text, each position immediately veers into its opposite. This too obeys a law. The transgression of metaphysics through the "thought" which, Artaud tells us, has not yet begun, always risks returning to metaphysics. Such is the question in which *we are posed.* A question which is still and always enveloped each time that speech, protected by the limits of a field, lets itself be provoked from afar by the enigma of flesh which wanted properly to be named Antonin Artaud.*

* Long after having written this text, I read in a letter of Artaud's to P. Loeb (cf. *Lettres Nouvelles*, no. 59, April 1958):
   this hole of the hollow between two bellows [*soufflets*]
                       of force
  which were not . . .
(September 1969)

This text is the fragment of a lecture given at the *Institut de psychanalyse* (Dr. Green's seminar). At that time we were concerned with opening a debate around certain propositions advanced in previous of my essays, notably, *Grammatology* ("De la grammatologie," *Critique* 223–24).

Could these propositions—which here will remain present in the background—have a place within the field of psychoanalytic questioning? Regarding such a field, where were these propositions to be maintained, as concerns their concepts and syntax?

The first part of the lecture touched upon this question in its greater generality. The central concepts of this section were those of *presence* and of *archi-trace*. We will indicate cursorily, by their general headings, the principal stages of this first part.

1. Despite appearances, the deconstruction of logocentrism is not a psychoanalysis of philosophy.

These appearances: the analysis of a historical repression and suppression of writing since Plato. This repression constitutes the origin of philosophy as *epistēmē*, and of truth as the unity of *logos* and *phonē*.

Repression, not forgetting; repression, not exclusion. Repression, as Freud says, neither repels, nor flees, nor excludes an exterior force; it contains an interior representation, laying out within itself a space of repression. Here, that which represents a force in the form of the writing interior to speech and essential to it has been contained outside speech.

An unsuccessful repression, on the road to historical dismantling. It is this dismantling that interests us, this unsuccessfulness which confers upon its becoming a certain legibility and limits its historical opaqueness. "Repressions that have failed will of course have more claim on our interest than those that may have been successful; for the latter will for the most part escape our examination" (*Standard Edition of the Complete Psychological Works of Sigmund Freud,* hereafter *SE,* XIV, 153).

The *symptomatic* form of the return of the repressed: the metaphor of writing which haunts European discourse, and the systematic contradictions of the onto-theological exclusion of the trace. The repression of writing as the repression of that which threatens presence and the mastering of absence.

The enigma of presence "pure and simple": as duplication, original repetition, auto-affection, and *différance.* The distinction between the mastering of absence as speech and the mastering of absence as writing. The writing within speech. Hallucination as speech and hallucination as writing.

The relationship between *phonē* and consciousness. The Freudian concept of verbal representation as preconsciousness. Logo-phonocentrism is not a philosophical or historical error which the history of philosophy, of the West, that is, of the world, would have rushed into pathologically, but is rather a necessary, and necessarily finite, movement and structure: the history of the possibility of symbolism *in general* (before the distinction between man and animal, and even before the distinction between the living and the nonliving); the history of *différance,* history as *différance* which finds in philosophy as *epistēmē,* in the European form of the metaphysical or onto-theological project, the privileged manifestation, with worldwide dominance, of dissimulation, of general censorship of the text in general.

2. An attempt to justify a theoretical reticence to utilize Freudian concepts, otherwise than in quotation marks: all these concepts, without exception, belong to the history of metaphysics, that is, to the system of logocentric repression which was organized in order to exclude or to lower (to put outside or below), the body of the written trace as a didactic and technical metaphor, as servile matter or excrement.

For example, logocentric repression is not comprehensible on the basis of the Freudian concept of repression; on the contrary, logocentric repression permits an understanding of how an original and individual repression became possible within the horizon of a culture and a historical structure of belonging.

Why it is a question neither of following Jung, nor of following the Freudian concept of the hereditary mnemic trace. Certainly, Freudian discourse—in its syntax, or, if you will, its labor—is not to be confused with these necessarily metaphysical and traditional concepts. Certainly it is not exhausted by belonging to them. Witness the precautions and the "nominalism" with which Freud manipulates what he calls conventions and conceptual hypotheses. And a conception of difference is attached less to concepts than to discourse. But Freud never reflected upon the historical and theoretical sense of these precautions.

The necessity of an immense labor of deconstruction of the metaphysical concepts and phrases that are condensed and sedimented within Freud's precautions. The metaphysical complications of psychoanalysis and the so-called human (or social) sciences (the concepts of presence, perception, reality, etc.). Linguistic phonologism.

The necessity of an explicit question concerning the meaning of presence in general: a comparison of the undertakings of Heidegger and of Freud. The epoch of presence, in the Heideggerian sense, and its central support, from Descartes to Hegel: presence as consciousness, self-presence conceived within the opposition of consciousness to unconsciousness. The concepts of archi-trace and of *différance:* why they are neither Freudian nor Heideggerian.

Différance, the pre-opening of the ontic-ontological difference (cf. *De la grammatologie,* p. 1029), and of all the differences which furrow Freudian conceptuality, such that they may be organized, and this is only an example, around the difference between "pleasure" and "reality," or may be derived from this difference. The difference between the pleasure principle and the reality principle, for example, is not uniquely, nor primarily, a distinction, an exteriority, but rather the original possibility, within life, of the detour, of deferral (*Aufschub*) and the original possibility of the economy of death (cf. *Beyond the Pleasure Principle, SE* XVIII).

Différance and identity. *Différance* within the economy of the same. The necessity of withdrawing the concepts of trace and of *différance* from all classical conceptual oppositions. Necessity of the concept of archi-trace and the erasure of the archia. This erasure, which maintains the legibility of the archia, signifies a *conceived* relationship of belonging to the history of metaphysics (*De la grammatologie,* 2:32).

In what ways would the Freudian concepts of writing and trace still be threatened by metaphysics and positivism? The complicity of these two menaces within Freud's discourse.

> Worin die Bahnung sonst besteht
> bleibt dahingestellt [In what
> pathbreaking consists remains
> undetermined]. (*Project for a
> Scientific Psychology,* 1895)

Our aim is limited: to locate in Freud's text several points of reference, and to isolate, on the threshhold of a systematic examination, those elements of psychoanalysis which can only uneasily be contained within logocentric closure, as this closure limits not only the history of philosophy but also the orientation of the "human sciences," notably of a certain linguistics. If the Freudian break-through has an historical originality, this originality is not due to its peaceful coexistence or theoretical complicity with this linguistics, at least in its congenital phonologism.[1]

It is no accident that Freud, at the decisive moments of his itinerary, has recourse to metaphorical models which are borrowed not from spoken language or from verbal forms, nor even from phonetic writing, but from a script which is never subject to, never exterior and posterior to, the spoken word. Freud invokes signs which do not transcribe living, full speech, master of itself and self-present. In fact, and this will be our problem, Freud *does not simply use* the metaphor of nonphonetic writing; he does not deem it expedient to manipulate scriptural metaphors for didactic ends. If such metaphors are indispensable, it is perhaps because they illuminate, inversely, the meaning of a trace in general, and eventually, in articulation with this meaning, may illuminate the meaning of writing in the popular sense. Freud, no doubt, is not manipulating metaphors, if to manipulate a metaphor means to make of the known an allusion to the unknown. On the contrary, through the insistence of his metaphoric investment he makes what we believe we know under the name of writing enigmatic. A movement unknown to classical philosophy is perhaps undertaken here, somewhere between the implicit and the explicit. From Plato and Aristotle on, scriptural images have regularly been used to *illustrate* the relationship between reason and experience, perception and memory. But a certain confidence has never stopped taking its assurance from the meaning of the well-known and familiar term: writing. The gesture sketched out by Freud interrupts that assurance and opens up a new kind of question about metaphor, writing, and spacing in general.

We shall let our reading be guided by this metaphoric investment. It will eventually invade the entirety of the psyche. Psychical *content* will be *represented* by a text whose essence is irreducibly graphic. The *structure* of the psychical *apparatus* will be *represented* by a writing machine. What questions will these representations impose upon us? We shall not have to ask if a writing apparatus—for example, the one described in the "Note on the Mystic Writing Pad"—is a *good* metaphor for representing the working of the psyche, but rather what apparatus we must create in order to represent psychical writing; and we shall have to ask what the imitation, projected and liberated in a machine, of something like psychical writing might mean. And not if the psyche is indeed a kind of text, but: what is a text, and what must the psyche be if it can be represented by a text? For if there is neither machine nor text without psychical origin, there is no domain of the psychic without text. Finally, what must be the relationship between psyche, writing, and spacing for such a metaphoric transition to be possible, not only, nor primarily, within theoretical discourse, but within the history of psyche, text, and technology?

Breaching and Difference

From the *Project* (1895) to the "Note on the Mystic Writing-Pad" (1925), a strange progression: a problematic of breaching[2] is elaborated only to conform increasingly to a metaphorics of the written trace. From a system of traces functioning according to a model which Freud would have preferred to be a natural one, and from which writing is entirely absent, we proceed toward a configuration of traces which can no longer be represented except by the structure and functioning of writing. At the same time, the structural model of writing, which Freud invokes immediately after the *Project,* will be persistently differentiated and refined in its originality. All the mechanical models will be tested and abandoned, until the discovery of the *Wunderblock,* a writing machine of marvelous complexity into which the whole of the psychical apparatus will be projected. The solution to all the previous difficulties will be presented in the *Wunderblock,* and the "Note," indicative of an admirable tenacity, will answer precisely the questions of the *Project.* The *Wunderblock,* in each of its parts, will realize the apparatus of which Freud said, in the *Project:* "We cannot off-hand imagine an apparatus capable of such complicated functioning" (*SE,* I, 299), and which he replaced at that time with a neurological fable whose framework and intention, in certain respects, he will never abandon.

In 1895, the question was to explain memory in the manner of the natural sciences, in order "to furnish a psychology that shall be a natural science: that is, to represent psychical processes as quantitatively determined states of specifiable material particles" (I, 295). Now, a "main characteristic of nervous tissue is memory: that is, quite generally, a capacity for being permanently altered by single occurrences" (I, 299). And a "psychological theory deserving any consideration must furnish an explanation of 'memory' " (ibid.). The crux of such an explanation, what makes such an apparatus almost unimaginable, is the necessity of accounting simultaneously, as the "Note" will do thirty years later, for the permanence of the trace and for the virginity of the receiving substance, for the engraving of furrows and for the perennially intact bareness of the perceptive surface: in this case, of the neurones. "It would seem, therefore, that neurones must be both influenced and also unaltered, unprejudiced (*unvoreingenommen*)" (ibid.). Rejecting a distinction, which was common in his day, between "sense cells" and "memory cells," Freud then forges the hypothesis of "contact-barriers" and "breaching" (*Bahnung,* lit. pathbreaking), of the breaking open of a path (*Bahn*). Whatever may be thought of the continuities and ruptures to come, this hypothesis is remarkable as soon as it is considered as a metaphorical model and not as a neurological description. Breaching, the tracing of a trail, opens up a conducting path. Which presupposes a certain violence and a certain resistance to effraction. The path is broken, cracked, *fracta,* breached. Now there would be two kinds of neurones: the permeable neurones (ϕ), which offer no resistance and thus retain no trace of impression, would be the perceptual neurones; other neurones (ψ), which would oppose contact-barriers to the quantity of excitation, would thus retain the printed trace: they "thus afford a possibility of representing *(darzustellen)* memory" (ibid.). This is the first representation, the first staging of memory. *(Darstellung* is representation in the weak sense of the word, but also frequently in the sense of visual depiction, and sometimes of theatrical performance. Our translation will vary with the inflection of the context.) Freud attributes psychical quality only to these latter neurones. They are the "vehicles of memory and so probably of psychical processes in general" (I, 300). Memory, thus, is not a psychical property among others; it is the very essence of the psyche: resistance, and precisely, thereby, an opening to the effraction of the trace.

Now assuming that Freud here intends to speak only the language of full and present quantity, assuming, as at least appears to be the case, that he intends to situate his work within the simple opposition of quantity and quality (the latter being reserved for the pure transparency of a perception without memory), we find that the concept of breaching shows itself intolerant of this intention. An equality of resistance to breaching, or an equivalence of the breaching forces, would eliminate any *preference* in the choice of itinerary. Memory would be paralyzed. It is the difference between breaches which is the true origin of memory, and thus of the psyche. Only this difference enables a "pathway to be preferred *(Wegbevorzugung)*": "Memory is represented *(dargestellt)* by the differences in the facilitations of the ψ-neurones" (I, 300). We then must not say that breaching without difference is insufficient for memory; it must be stipulated that there is no pure breaching without difference. Trace as memory is not a pure breaching that might be reappropriated at any time as simple presence; it is rather the ungraspable and invisible difference between breaches. We thus already know that psychic life is neither the transparency of meaning nor the opacity of force but the difference within the exertion of forces. As Nietzsche had already said.[3]

That quantity becomes *psychē* and *mnēmē* through differences rather than through plenitudes will be continuously confirmed in the *Project* itself. *Repetition* adds no quantity of present force, no *intensity;* it reproduces the same impression—yet it has the power of breaching. "The memory of an experience (that is, its continuing operative power) depends on a factor which is called the magnitude of the impression and on the frequency with which the same impression is repeated" (I, 300). The number of repetitions is thus added to the quantity ($Q\eta$) of the excitation, and these two quantities are of two absolutely heterogeneous types. There are only discrete repetitions, and they can act as such only through the diastem which maintains their separation. Finally, if breaching can supplement a quantity presently at work, or can be added to it, it is because breaching is certainly analogous to quantity, but is other than it as well: "*quantity* plus *facilitation* resulting from $Q\eta$ are at the same time something that can replace $Q\eta$'' (I, 300–301). Let us not hasten to define this other of pure quantity as quality: for in so doing we would be transforming the force of memory into present consciousness and the translucid perception of present qualities. Thus, neither the difference between full quantities, nor the interval between repetitions of the identical, nor breaching itself, may be thought of in terms of the opposition between quantity and quality.[4] Memory cannot be derived from this opposition, and it escapes the grasp of "naturalism" as well as of "phenomenology."

All these differences in the production of the trace may be reinterpreted as moments of deferring. In accordance with a motif which will continue to dominate Freud's thinking, this movement is described as the effort of life to protect itself by *deferring* a dangerous cathexis, that is, by constituting a reserve (*Vorrat*). The threatening expenditure or presence are deferred with the help of breaching or repetition. Is this not already the detour (*Aufschub*, lit. delay) which institutes the relation of pleasure to reality (*Beyond* . . . , *SE*, XVIII)? Is it not already death at the origin of a life which can defend itself against death only through an *economy* of death, through deferment, repetition, reserve? For repetition does not *happen to* an initial impression; its possibility is already there, in the resistance offered *the first time* by the psychical neurones. Resistance itself is possible only if the opposition of forces lasts and is repeated at the beginning. It is the very idea of a *first time* which becomes enigmatic. What we are advancing here does not seem to contradict what Freud will say further on: "Facilitation is probably the result of the single (*einmaliger*) passage of a large quantity." Even assuming that his affirmation does not lead us little by little to the problem of phylogenesis and of hereditary breaches, we may still maintain that in the *first time* of the contact between *two* forces, repetition has begun. Life is already threatened by the origin of the memory which constitutes it, and by the breaching which it resists, the effraction which it can contain only by repeating it. It is because breaching breaks open that Freud, in the *Project*, accords a privilege to pain. In a certain sense, there is no breaching without a beginning of pain, and "pain leaves behind it particularly rich breaches." But beyond a certain quantity, pain, the threatening origin of the psyche, must be deferred, like death, for it can "ruin" psychical "organization." Despite the enigmas of the "first time" and of originary repetition (needless to say, before any distinction between "normal" and "pathological" repetition), it is important that Freud attributes all this work to the primary function, and that he excludes any possible derivation of it. Let us observe this nonderivation, even if it renders only more dense the difficulty of the concepts of "primariness" and of the timelessness of the primary process, and even if this difficulty does not cease to intensify in what is to come. "Here we are almost involuntarily reminded of the endeavor of the nervous system, maintained through every modification, to avoid being burdened by a $Q\eta$ or to keep the burden as small as possible. Under the compulsion of the exigencies of life, the nervous system was obliged to lay up a store of $Q\eta$. This necessitated an increase in the number of its neurones, and these had to be impermeable. It now avoids, partly at least, being *filled* with $Q\eta$ (cathexis), by setting up *facilitations*. It will be seen, then, that *facilitations serve the primary function''* (I, 301).

No doubt life protects itself by repetition, trace, *différance* (deferral). But we must be wary of this formulation: there is no life present *at first* which would *then* come to protect, postpone, or reserve itself in *différance*. The latter constitutes the essence of life. Or rather: as *différance* is not an essence, as it is not anything, it *is not* life, if Being is determined as *ousia,* presence, essence/existence, substance or subject. Life must be thought of as trace before Being may be determined as presence. This is the only condition on which we can say that life *is* death, that repetition and the beyond of the pleasure principle are native and congenital to that which they transgress. When Freud writes in the *Project* that "facilitations serve the primary function," he is forbidding us to be surprised by *Beyond the Pleasure Principle.* He complies with a dual necessity: that of recognizing *différance* at the origin, and at the same time that of crossing out the concept of *primariness:* we will not, then, be surprised by the *Traumdeutung,* which defines primariness as a "theoretical fiction" in a paragraph on the "delaying" *(Verspätung)* of the secondary process. It is thus the delay which is in the beginning.[5] Without which, *différance* would be the lapse which a consciousness, a self-presence of the present, accords itself. To defer *(différer)* thus cannot mean to retard a present possibility, to postpone an act, to put off a perception already now possible. That possibility is possible only through a *différance* which must be conceived of in other terms than those of a calculus or mechanics of decision.[6] To say that *différance* is originary is simultaneously to erase the myth of a present origin. Which is why "originary" must be understood as having been *crossed out,* without which *différance* would be derived from an original plenitude. It is a non-origin which is originary.

Rather than abandon it, we ought perhaps then to rethink the concept of *différer*. This is what we should like to do, and this is possible only if *différance* is determined outside any teleological or eschatological horizon. Which is not easy. Let us note in passing that the concepts of *Nachträglichkeit* and *Verspätung,* concepts which govern the whole of Freud's thought and determine all his other concepts, are already present and named in the *Project.* The irreducibility of the "effect of deferral"—such, no doubt, is Freud's discovery. Freud exploits this discovery in its ultimate consequences, beyond the psychoanalysis of the individual, and he thought that the history of culture ought to confirm it. In *Moses and Monotheism* (1937), the efficacy of delay and of action subsequent to the event is at work over large historical intervals. The problem of latency, moreover, is in highly significant contact with the problem of oral and written tradition in this text.

Although "breaching" is not named writing at any time in the *Project,* the contradictory requirements which the *Mystic Writing Pad* will fulfill are already formulated in terms which are literally identical: "an unlimited receptive capacity and a retention of permanent traces" (*SE* XIX, 227).

Differences in the work of breaching concern not only forces but also locations. And Freud already wants to think force and place simultaneously.[7] He is the first not to believe in the descriptive value of his hypothetical representation of breaching. The distinction between the categories of neurones "has no recognized foundation, at least insofar as morphology (i.e., histology) is concerned." It is, rather, the index of a topographical description which external space, that is, familiar and constituted space, the exterior space of the natural sciences, cannot contain. This is why, under the heading of "the biological standpoint," a "difference in essence" (*Wesensverschiedenheit*) between the neurones is "replaced by a difference in the environment to which they are destined" (*Schicksals-Milieuverschiedenheit*) (I, 304): these are pure differences, differences of situation, of connection, of localization, of structural relations more important than their supporting terms; and they are differences for which the relativity of outside and inside is always to be determined. The thinking of difference can neither dispense with topography nor accept the current models of spacing.

This difficulty becomes more acute when it becomes necessary to explain those differences that are pure par excellence: differences of quality, that is, for Freud, differences of consciousness. He must provide an explanation for "what we are aware of, in the most puzzling fashion (*rätselhaft*), through our 'consciousness' " (I, 307). And "since this consciousness knows nothing of what we have so far been assuming—quantities and neurones—it [the theory] should explain this lack of knowledge to us as well" (I, 308). Now qualities are clearly pure differences: "Consciousness gives us what are called *qualities*—sensations which are *different* (*anders*) and whose difference (*Anders*, lit. otherness) is distinguished (*unterschieden wird,* lit. is differentiated) according to its relations with the external world. Within this difference there are series, similarities, and so on, but there are in fact no quantities in it. It may be asked *how* qualities originate and *where* qualities originate" (I, 308).

Neither outside nor inside. They cannot be in the external world, where the physicist recognizes only quantities, "masses in motion and nothing else" (I, 308). Nor in the interiority of the psyche (i.e., of memory), for "reproducing or remembering" are "without quality (*qualitätslos*)" (ibid.). Since rejection of the topographical model is out of the question, "we must summon up courage to assume that there is a third system of neurones—ω perhaps [perceptual neurones]—which is excited along with perception, but not along with reproduction, and whose states of excitation give rise to the various qualities—are, that is

to say, *conscious sensations''* (I, 309). Foreshadowing the interpolated sheet of
the mystic writing-pad, Freud, annoyed by this "jargon," tells Fliess (letter 39,
1 Jan. 1896) that he is inserting, "slipping" *(schieben)* the perceptual neurones
(ω) between the ϕ- and ψ-neurones.

This last bit of daring results in "what seems like an immense difficulty": we
have just encountered a permeability and a breaching which proceed from no
quantity at all. From what then? From pure time, from pure temporalization in its
conjunction with spacing: from periodicity. Only recourse to temporality and to a
discontinuous or periodic temporality will allow the difficulty to be resolved, and
we must patiently consider its implications. "I can see only one way out . . . . So
far I have regarded it [the passage of quantity] only as the transference of $Q\eta$
from one neurone to another. It must have another characteristic, of a temporal
nature" (I, 310).

If the discontinuity hypothesis "goes further," Freud emphasizes, than the
"physical clarification" due to its insistence on periods, it is because in this case
differences, intervals, and discontinuity are registered, "appropriated" without
their quantitative support. Perceptual neurones, "incapable of receiving $Q\eta$
[quantities], appropriate the *period* of the excitation" (ibid.). Pure difference,
again, and difference between diastems. The concept of a *period in general*
precedes and conditions the opposition between quantity and quality, and everything governed by this opposition. For "ψ-neurones too have their period, of
course; but it is without quality, or more correctly, monotonous" (ibid.). As we
shall see, this insistence on discontinuity will faithfully become the occupation of
the "Note on the Mystic Writing Pad": as in the *Project,* it will be a last bold
move resolving a final logical difficulty.

The rest of the *Project* will depend in its entirety upon an incessant and
increasingly radical invocation of the principle of difference. Beneath an indicial
neurology, which plays the representational role of an aritficial model, we repeatedly find a persistent attempt to account for the psyche in terms of spacing, a
topography of traces, a map of breaches; and we repeatedly find an attempt to
locate consciousness or quality in a space whose structure and possibility must be
rethought, along with an attempt to describe the "functioning of the apparatus"
in terms of pure differences and locations, an attempt to explain how "quantity
of excitation is expressed in ψ by complexity and quality by topography." It is
because the nature of this system of differences and of this topography is radically new and must not allow any ommissions that Freud, in his setting up of the
apparatus, multiplies "acts of boldness," "strange but indispensable hypotheses" (concerning "secreting" neurones or "key" neurones). And when he
renounces neurology and anatomical localizations, it will be not in order to
abandon his topographical preoccupations, but to transform them. Trace will
become *gramme;* and the region of breaching a ciphered spacing.

The Print and the
Original Supplement

A few weeks after the *Project* is sent to Fliess, during a "night of work," all the elements of the system arrange themselves into a "machine." It is not yet a writing machine: "Everything fell into place, the cogs meshed, the thing really seemed to be a machine which in a moment would run of itself." [8] In a moment: in thirty years. By itself: almost.

A little more than a year later, the trace starts to become writing. In letter 52 (6 Dec. 1896), the entire system of the *Project* is reconstituted in terms of a graphic conception as yet unknown in Freud. It is not surprising that this coincides with the transition from the neurological to the psychical. At the heart of the letter: the words "sign" (*Zeichen*), registration (*Niederschrift*), transcription (*Umschrift*). Not only is the communication between trace and delay (i.e., a present which does not constitute but is originally reconstituted from "signs" of memory) explicitly defined in this letter, but verbal phenomena are assigned a place within a system of stratified writing which these phenomena are far from dominating: "As you know, I am working on the assumption that our psychic mechanism has come into being by a process of stratification (*Aufeinanderschichtung*); the material present in the form of memory-traces (*Errinerungsspuren*) being subjected from time to time to a *rearrangement* (*Umordnung*) in accordance with fresh circumstances to a *retranscription* (*Umschrift*). Thus, what is essentially new about my theory is the thesis that memory is present not once but several times over, that it is laid down (*niederlegt*) in various species of indications [*Zeichen*, lit. signs] . . . . I cannot say how many of these registrations (*Niederschriften*) there are: at least three, probably more . . . . The different registrations are also separated (not necessarily topographically) according to the neurones which are their vehicles . . . . *Perception*. These are neurones in which perceptions originate, to which consciousness attaches, but which in themselves retain no trace of what has happened. *For consciousness and memory are mutually exclusive. Indication of perception:* the first registration of the perceptions; it is quite incapable of consciousness and arranged according to associations by simultaneity . . . . *Unconscious* is a second registration . . . . *Preconscious* is the third transcription, attached to word-presentations and corresponding to our official ego . . . . This secondary *thought-consciousness* is subsequent in time and probably linked to the hallucinatory activation of word-presentations" (I, 235).

This is the first move toward the "Note." From now on, starting with the *Traumdeutung* (1900), the metaphor of writing will *appropriate simultaneously the problems of the psychic apparatus in its structure and that of the psychic text in its fabric*. The solidarity of the two problems should make us that much more attentive: the two series of metaphors—text and machine—do not come on stage at the same time.

"Dreams generally follow old facilitations," said the *Project*. Topographical, temporal, and formal regression in dreams must thus be interpreted, henceforth, as a path back into a landscape of writing. Not a writing which simply transcribes, a stony echo of muted words, but a lithography before words: metaphonetic, nonlinguistic, alogical. (Logic obeys consciousness, or preconsciousness, the site of verbal images, as well as the principle of identity, the founding expression of a philosophy of presence. "It was only a logical contradiction, which does not have much import," we read in *The Wolf-Man*.) With dreams displaced into a forest of script, the *Traumdeutung,* the interpretation of dreams, no doubt, on the first approach will be an act of reading and decoding. Before the analysis of the Irma dream, Freud engages in considerations of method. In one of his familiar gestures, he opposes the old popular tradition to so-called scientific psychology. As always, it is in order to justify the profound intention which inspires the former. Popular tradition may err, of course, when according to a "symbolical" procedure, it treats dream content as an indivisible and unarticulated whole, for which a second, possibly prophetic whole may be substituted. But Freud is not far from accepting the "other popular method": "It might be described as the 'decoding' method (*Chiffriermethode*), since it treats dreams as a kind of cryptography *(Geheimschrift)* in which each sign can be translated into another sign having a known meaning, in accordance with a fixed key *(Schlüssel)*" (IV, 97). Let us retain the allusion to a permanent code: it is the weakness of a method to which Freud attributes, nevertheless, the merit of being analytic and of spelling out the elements of meaning one by one.

A strange example, the one chosen by Freud to illustrate this traditional procedure: a text of phonetic writing is cathected and functions as a discrete, specific, translatable and unprivileged element in the overall writing of the dream. Phonetic writing as writing within writing. Assume, for example, says Freud, that I have dreamed of a letter (*Brief / epistola*), then of a burial. Open a *Traumbuch,* a book in which the keys to dreams are recorded, an encyclopedia of dream signs, the dream dictionary which Freud will soon reject. It teaches us that letter must be translated (*übersetzen*) by spite, and burial by engagement to be married. Thus a letter (*epistola*) written with letters (*litterae*), a document composed of phonetic signs, the transcription of verbal discourse, may be translated by a nonverbal signifier which, inasmuch as it is a determined affect, belongs to the overall syntax of dream writing. The verbal is cathected, and its phonetic transcription is bound, far from the center, in a web of silent script.

Freud then borrows another example from Artemidorous of Daldis (second century), the author of a treatise on the interpretation of dreams. Let it be a pretext for recalling that in the eighteenth century an English theologian, known to Freud, had already invoked Artemidorus with an intention that is doubtless worthy of comparison.[9] Warburton describes the system of hieroglyphics, and discerns in it (rightly or wrongly—it is of no concern to us here) various

structures (hieroglyphics strictly speaking or symbolical ones, each type being
either curiological or tropological, the relation here being of analogy or of part to
whole) which ought to be systematically confronted with the mechanisms of
dream-work (condensation, displacement, overdetermination). Now Warburton,
interested, for reasons of self-justification, in demonstrating, against Father
Kircher, "the high antiquity of Egyptian learning," chooses the example of an
Egyptian science which draws all its resources from hieroglyphic writing. That
science is *Traumdeutung,* also known as oneirocriticism. When all is said and
done, it was only a science of writing in priestly hands. God, the Egyptians
believed, had made man a gift of writing just as he inspired dreams. Interpreters,
like dreams themselves, then had only to draw upon the curiological or tropological storehouse. They would readily find there the key to dreams, which they
would then pretend to divine. The hieroglyphic code itself served as a *Traumbuch.* An alleged gift of God, in fact constructed historically, it had become the
common source from which was drawn oneiric discourse: the setting and the text
of the dream's mise en scène. Since dreams are constructed like a form of
writing, the kinds of transposition in dreams correspond to condensations and
displacements already performed and enregistered in the system of hieroglyphics. Dreams would only manipulate elements (*stoicheia,* says Warburton,
elements or letters) contained in the storehouse of hieroglyphics, somewhat as
written speech would draw on a written language: "So that the question will be,
on what grounds or rules of interpretation the Onirocritics proceded, when, if a
man dreamt of a dragon, the Interpreter assured him it signified *majesty;* if of a
serpent, a *disease;* a viper, *money;* frogs, *impostors.*"[10] What then did the
hermeneuts of that age do? They consulted writing itself:

> Now the early *Interpreters of dreams* were not juggling impostors; but, like
> the early judicial *Astrologers,* more superstitious than their neighbors; and so
> the first who fell into their own delusions. However, suppose them to have
> been as arrant cheats as any of their successors, yet at their first setting up
> they must have had materials proper for their trade; which could never be the
> wild workings of each man's private fancy. Their customers would look to
> find a known analogy, become venerable by long application to mysterious
> wisdom, for the groundwork of their deciphering; and the Decipherers them-
> selves would as naturally fly to some confessed authority, to support their
> pretended Science. But what ground or authority could this be, if not the
> mysterious learning of *symbolic characters?* Here we seem to have got a
> solution of the difficulty. The *Egyptian* priests, the first interpreters of
> dreams, took their rules for this species of DIVINATION, from their
> *symbolic* riddling, in which they were so deeply read: A ground of
> interpretation which would give the strongest credit to the Art; and equally
> satisfy the diviner and the Consulter: for by this time it was generally be-
> lieved that their Gods have given them *hieroglyphic writing.* So that nothing

was more natural than to imagine that these Gods, who in their opinion gave
dreams likewise, had employed the same mode of expression in both revelations.[11]

It is here that the Freudian break occurs. Freud doubtless conceives of the dream
as a displacement similar to an original form of writing which puts words on
stage without becoming subservient to them; and he is thinking here, no doubt, of
a model of writing irreducible to speech which would include, like hieroglyphics,
pictographic, ideogrammatic, and phonetic elements. But he makes of psychical
writing so originary a production that the writing we believe to be designated by
the proper sense of the word—a script which is coded and visible "in the
world"—would only be the metaphor of psychical writing. This writing, for
example the kind we find in dreams which "follow old facilitations," a simple
moment in a regression toward a "primary" writing, cannot be read in terms of
any code. It works, no doubt, with a mass of elements which have been codified
in the course of an individual or collective history. But in its operations, lexicon,
and syntax a purely idiomatic residue is irreducible and is made to bear the
burden of interpretation in the communication between unconsciousnesses. The
dreamer invents his own grammar. No meaningful material or prerequisite text
exists which he might *simply use,* even if he never deprives himself of them.
Such, despite their interest, is the limitation of the *Chiffriermethode* and the
Traumbuch. As much as it is a function of the generality and the rigidity of the
code, this limitation is a function of an excessive preoccupation with *content,* and
an insufficient concern for relations, locations, processes, and differences: "My
procedure is not so convenient as the popular decoding method which translates
any given piece of a dream's content by a fixed key. I, on the contrary, am
prepared to find that the same piece of content may conceal a different meaning
when it occurs in various people or in various contexts" (*SE* IV, 105).
Elsewhere, in support of that statement, Freud thinks it proper to adduce the case
of Chinese writing: "They [the dream symbols] frequently have more than one or
even several meanings, and, as with Chinese script, the correct interpretation can
only be arrived at on each occasion from the context" (V, 353).

The absence of an exhaustive and absolutely infallible code means that in
psychic writing, which thus prefigures the meaning of writing in general, the
difference between signifier and signified is never radical. Unconscious experience, prior to the dream which "follows old facilitations," does not borrow but
produces its own signifiers; does not create them in their materiality, of course,
but produces their status-as-meaningful (*signifiance*). Henceforth, they are no
longer, properly speaking, signifiers. And the possibility of translation, if it is far
from being eliminated—for experience perpetually creates distances between the
points of identity or between the adherence of signifier to signified—is nevertheless in principle and by definition limited. Such, perhaps, is Freud's understand-

ing, from another standpoint, in the article on "Repression" : "Repression acts, therefore, in a *highly individual* manner" (XIV, 150). (Individuality, here does not refer primarily to the repression practiced by individuals but to that of each "derivative of the repressed, which may have its own special vicissitude.") Translation, a system of translation, is possible only if a permanent code allows a substitution or transformation of signifiers while retaining the same signified, always present, despite the absence of any specific signifier. This fundamental possibility of substitution would thus be implied by the coupled concepts signified/signifier, and would consequently be implied by the concept of the sign itself. Even if, along with Saussure, we envisage the distinction between signified and signifier only as the two sides of a sheet of paper, nothing is changed. Originary writing, if there is one, must produce the space and the materiality of the sheet itself.

It will be said: and yet Freud translates all the time. He believes in the generality and the fixity of a specific code for dream writing: "When we have become familiar with the abundant use made by symbolism for representing sexual material in dreams, the question is bound to arise of whether many of these symbols do not occur with a permanently fixed meaning, like the 'grammalogues' in short; and we shall feel tempted to draw up a new 'dream-book' on the decoding principle" (V:351). And, in fact, Freud never stopped proposing codes, rules of great generality. And the substitution of signifiers seems to be the essential activity of psychoanalytic interpretation. Certainly, Freud nevertheless stipulates an essential limitation on this activity. Or, rather, a double limitation.

If we consider first verbal expression, as it is circumscribed in the dream, we observe that its sonority, the materiality of the expression, does not disappear before the signified, or at least cannot be traversed and transgressed as it is in conscious speech. It acts as such, with the efficacy Artaud assigned it on the stage of cruelty.[12] The materiality of a word cannot be translated or carried over into another language. Materiality is precisely that which translation relinquishes. To relinquish materiality: such is the driving force of translation. And when that materiality is reinstated, translation becomes poetry. In this sense, since the materiality of the signifier constitutes the idiom of every dream scene, dreams are untranslatable: "Indeed, dreams are so closely related to linguistic expression that Ferenczi has truly remarked that every tongue has its own dream-language. It is impossible as a rule to translate a dream into a foreign language, and this is equally true, I fancy, of a book such as the present one" (IV, 99, n. 1). What is valid for a specific national language is a fortiori valid for a private grammar.

Moreover, this horizontal impossibility of translation without loss has its basis in a vertical impossibility. We are speaking here of the way in which unconscious thoughts become conscious. If a dream cannot be translated into another lan-

guage, it is because within the psychical apparatus as well there is never a
relation of simple translation. We are wrong, Freud tells us, to speak of translation or transcription in describing the transition of unconscious thoughts through
the preconscious toward consciousness. Here again the metaphorical concept of
translation *(Übersetzung)* or transcription *(Umschrift)* is dangerous, not because
it refers to writing, but because it presupposes a text which would be already
there, immobile: the serene presence of a statue, of a written stone or archive
whose signified content might be harmlessly transported into the milieu of a
different language, that of the preconscious or the conscious. It is thus not
enough to speak of writing in order to be faithful to Freud, for it is then that we
may betray him more than ever.

This is what the last chapter of the *Traumdeutung* explains. An entirely and
conventionally topographical metaphor of the psychical apparatus is to be completed by invoking the existence of force and of two kinds of processes of excitation or modes of its discharge: "So let us try to correct some conceptions
[intuitive illustrations: *Anschauungen*] which might be misleading so long as we
looked upon the two systems in the most literal and crudest sense as two
localities in the mental apparatus—conceptions which left their traces in the
expressions 'to repress' and 'to force a way through.' Thus, we may speak of an
unconscious thought seeking to convey itself into the preconscious so as to be
able then to force its way through into consciousness. What we have in mind here
is not the forming of a second thought situated in a new place, like a transcription
(Umschrift) which continues to exist alongside the original; and the notion of
forcing a way through into consciousness must be kept carefully free from any
idea of a change of locality" (V, 610).[13]

Let us interrupt our quotation for a moment. The conscious text is thus not a
transcription, because there is no text *present elsewhere* as an unconscious one to
be transposed or transported. For the value of presence can also dangerously
affect the concept of the unconscious. There is then no unconscious truth to be
rediscovered by virtue of having been written elsewhere. There is no text written
and present elsewhere which would then be subjected, without being changed in
the process, to an operation and a temporalization (the latter belonging to consciousness if we follow Freud literally) which would be external to it, floating on
its surface. There is no present text in general, and there is not even a past present
text, a text which is past as having been present. The text is not conceivable in an
originary or modified form of presence. The unconscious text is already a weave
of pure traces, differences in which meaning and force are united—a text
nowhere present, consisting of archives which are *always already* transcriptions.
Originary prints. Everything begins with reproduction. Always already: re-
positories of a meaning which was never present, whose signified presence is
always reconstituted by deferral, *nachträglich,* belatedly, *supplementarily:* for
the *nachträglich* also means *supplementary.* The call of the supplement is pri-

mary, here, and it hollows out that which will be reconstituted by deferral as the present. The supplement, which seems to be added as a plenitude to a plenitude, is equally that which compensates for a lack (*qui supplée*). "*Suppléer:* 1. To add what is missing, to supply a necessary surplus," says Littré, respecting, like a sleepwalker, the strange logic of that word. It is within its logic that the possibility of deferred action should be conceived, as well as, no doubt, the relationship between the primary and the secondary on all levels.[14] Let us note: *Nachtrag* has a precise meaning in the realm of letters: appendix, codicil, postscript. The text we call present may be deciphered only at the bottom of the page, in a footnote or postscript. Before the recurrence, the present is only the call for a footnote.[15] That the present in general is not primal but, rather, reconstituted, that it is not the absolute, wholly living form which constitutes experience, that there is no purity of the living present—such is the theme, formidable for metaphysics, which Freud, in a conceptual scheme unequal to the thing itself, would have us pursue. This pursuit is doubtless the only one which is exhausted neither within metaphysics nor within science.

Since the transition to consciousness is not a derivative or repetitive writing, a transcription duplicating an unconscious writing, it occurs in an original manner and, in its very secondariness, is originary and irreducible. Since consciousness for Freud is a surface exposed to the external world, it is here that instead of reading through the metaphor in the usual sense, we must, on the contrary, understand the possibility of a writing advanced as conscious and as acting in the world (the visible exterior of the graphism, of the literal, of the literal becoming literary, etc.) in terms of the labor of the writing which circulated like psychical energy between the unconscious and the conscious. The "objectivist" or "worldly" consideration of writing teaches us nothing if reference is not made to a space of psychical writing. (We might say: of transcendental writing in the event that, along with Husserl, we would see the psyche as a region of the world. But since this is also the case for Freud, who wants to respect simultaneously the Being-in-the-world of the psyche, its Being-situated, and the originality of its topology, which is irreducible to any ordinary intraworldliness, we perhaps should think that what we are describing here as the labor of writing erases the transcendental distinction between the origin of the world and Being-in-the-world. Erases it while producing it: the medium of the dialogue and misunderstanding between the Husserlian and Heideggerian concepts of Being-in-the-world.)

Concerning this nontranscriptive writing, Freud adds a fundamental specification. This specification will reveal: (1) the danger involved in immobilizing or freezing energy within a naive metaphorics of place; (2) the necessity not of abandoning but of rethinking the space or topology of this writing; (3) that Freud, who still insists on *representing* the psychical apparatus in an artificial model, has not yet discovered a mechanical model adequate to the graphematic conceptual scheme he is already using to describe the psychical text.

Again, we may speak of a preconscious thought being repressed or driven out and then taken over by the unconscious. These images, derived from a set of ideas (*Vorstellungskreis*) relating to a struggle for a piece of ground, may tempt us to suppose that it is literally true that a mental grouping (*Anordnung*) in one locality has been brought to an end and replaced by a fresh one in another locality. Let us replace these metaphors by something that seems to correspond better to the real state of affairs, and let us say that some particular mental grouping has had a cathexis of energy (*Energiebesetzung*) attached to it or withdrawn from it, so that the structure in question has come under the sway of a particular agency or been withdrawn from it. What we are doing here is once again to replace a topographical way of representing things by a dynamic one. What we regard as mobile (*das Bewegliche*) is not the psychical structure itself but its innervation [V, 610–611].

Let us once more interrupt our quotation. The metaphor of translation as the transcription of an original text would separate force and extension, maintaining the simple exteriority of the translated and the translating. This very exteriority, the static and topological bias of the metaphor, would assure the transparency of a neutral translation, of a phoronomic and nonmetabolic process. Freud emphasizes this: psychic writing does not lend itself to translation because it is a single energetic system (however differentiated it may be), and because it covers the entirety of the psychical apparatus. Despite the difference of agencies, psychical writing in general is not a displacement of meanings within the limidity of an immobile, pregiven space and the blank neutrality of discourse. A discourse which might be coded without ceasing to be diaphanous. Here energy cannot be reduced; it does not limit meaning, but rather produces it. The distinction between force and meaning is derivative in relation to an archi-trace; it belongs to the metaphysics of consciousness and of presence, or rather of presence in the word, in the hallucination of a language determined on the basis of the word or of verbal representation. The metaphysics of preconsciousness, Freud might say, since the preconscious is the place he assigns to the verbal. Without that, would Freud have taught us anything new?

Force produces meaning (and space) through the power of "repetition" alone, which inhabits it originarily as its death. This power, that is, this lack of power, which opens and limits the labor of force, institutes translatability, makes possible what we call "language," transforms an absolute idiom into a limit which is always already transgressed: a pure idiom is not language; it becomes so only through repetition; repetition always already divides the point of departure of the first time. Despite appearances, this does not contradict what we said earlier about untranslatability. At that time it was a question of recalling the origin of the movement of transgression, the origin of repetition, and the becoming- language of the idiom. If one limits oneself to the *datum or the effect of repetition,* to translation, to the obviousness of the distinction between force and meaning, not only does one miss the originality of Freud's aim, but one effaces the intensity of the relation to death as well.

We ought thus to examine closely—which we cannot do here—all that Freud invites to think concerning writing as "breaching" in the *psychical* repetition of this previously *neurological* notion: opening up of its own space, effraction, breaking of a path against resistances, rupture and irruption becoming a route *(rupta, via rupta),* violent inscription of a form, tracing of a difference in a nature or a matter which are conceivable as such only in their *opposition* to writing. The route is opened in nature or matter, forest or wood *(hyle),* and in it acquires a reversibility of time and space. We should have to study together, genetically and structurally, the history of the road and the history of writing.[16] We are thinking here of Freud's texts on the work of the memory-trace *(Erinnerungsspur)* which, though no longer the neurological trace, is not yet "conscious memory," ("The Unconscious," *SE* XIV, 188), and of the *itinerant* work of the trace, producing and following its route, the trace which traces, the trace which breaks open its own path. The metaphor of pathbreaking, so frequently used in Freud's descriptions, is always in communication with the theme of the *supplementary delay* and with the reconstitution of meaning through deferral, after a mole-like progression, after the subterranean toil of an impression. This impression has left behind a laborious trace which has never been *perceived,* whose meaning has never been lived in the present, i.e., has never been lived consciously. The postscript which constitutes the past present as such is not satisfied, as Plato, Hegel, and Proust perhaps thought, with reawakening or revealing the present past in its truth. It produces the present past. Is sexual deferral the best example or the essence of this movement? A false question, no doubt: the (presumably known) *subject* of the question—sexuality—is determined, limited, or unlimited only through inversion and through the answer itself. Freud's answer, in any event, is decisive. Take the Wolf-Man. It is by deferral that the perception of the primal scene—whether it be reality or fantasy hardly matters—is lived in its meaning, and sexual maturation is not the accidental form of this delay. "At age one and a half, he received impressions the deferred understanding of which became possible for him at the time of the dream through his development, exaltation and sexual investigations." Already in the *Project,* concerning repression in hysteria: "We invariably find that a memory is repressed which has become a trauma only after the event *(nur nachträglich).* The reason for this state of things is the retardation *(Verspätung)* of puberty as compared with the remainder of the individual's development." That should lead, if not to the solution, at least to a new way of posing the formidable problem of the temporalization and the so-called "timelessness" of the unconscious. Here, more than elsewhere, the gap between Freud's intuition and his concepts is apparent. The timelessness of the unconscious is no doubt determined only in opposition to a common concept of time, a traditional concept, the metaphysical concept: the time of mechanics or the time of consciousness. We ought perhaps to read Freud the way Heidegger read Kant: like the *cogito,* the unconscious is no doubt timeless only from the standpoint of a certain vulgar conception of time.[17]

Dioptrics and
Hieroglyphics

Let us not hasten to conclude that by invoking an energetics, as opposed to a topography, of translation Freud abandoned his efforts at localization. If, as we shall see, he persists in giving a projective and spatial—indeed, purely mechanical—representation of energetic processes, it is not simply for didactic reasons: a certain spatiality, inseparable from the very idea of system, is irreducible; its nature is all the more enigmatic in that we can no longer consider it as the homogeneous and serene milieu of dynamic and economic processes. In the *Traumdeutung,* the metaphoric machine is not yet adapted to the scriptural analogy which already governs—as shall soon be clear—Freud's entire descriptive presentation. It is an *optical machine.*

Let us return to our quotation. Freud does not want to abandon the topographical model against which he has just warned us: "Nevertheless, I consider it expedient and justifiable to continue to make use of the figurative image (*anschauliche Vorstellung:* intuitive representation, metaphor) of the two systems. We can avoid any possible abuse of this method of representation (*mode de mise en scène; Darstellungsweise*) by recollecting that ideas (*Vorstellungen:* representations), thoughts and psychical structures in general must never be regarded as localized in organic elements of the nervous system but rather, as one might say, *between* them, where resistance and facilitations provide the corresponding correlates. Everything that can be an object (*Gegenstand*) of our internal perception is *virtual,* like the image produced in a telescope by the passage of light rays. But we are justified in assuming the existence of the systems (*which are not in any way psychical entities themselves* [my italics] and can never be accessible to our psychical perception) like the lenses of the telescope, which cast the image. And, if we pursue this analogy, we compare the censorship between two systems to the refraction [the breaking of the ray: *Strahlenbrechung*] which takes place when a ray of light passes into a new medium" (V, 611)

This representation already cannot be understood in terms of the spatiality of a simple, homogenous structure. The change in medium and the movement of refraction indicate this sufficiently. Later, in a further reference to the same machine, Freud proposes an interesting differentiation. In the same chapter, in the section on "Regression," he attempts to explain the relation between memory and perception in the memory trace.

> What is presented to us in these words is the idea of *psychical locality*. I shall entirely disregard the idea that the mental apparatus with which we are here concerned is also known to us in the form of an anatomical preparation [*Preparat:* laboratory preparation], and I shall carefully avoid the temptation to determine psychical locality in any anatomical fashion. I shall remain upon psychological ground, and I propose simply to follow the suggestion that we should picture the instrument which carries out our mental functions as resembling a compound microscope, or a photographic apparatus, or something of the kind. On that basis, psychical locality will correspond to a place (*Ort*) inside the apparatus at which one of the preliminary stages of an image comes into being. In the microscope and telescope, as we know, these occur in part at ideal points, regions in which no tangible component of the apparatus is situated. I see no necessity to apologize for the imperfections of this or of any similar imagery [V, 536].

Beyond its pedagogical value, this illustration proves useful for its distinction between *system* and *psyche:* the psychical system is not psychical, and in this description only the system is in question. Next, it is the operation of the apparatus which interests Freud, how it runs and in what order, the regulated timing of its movements as it is *caught* and localized in the parts of the mechanism: "Strictly speaking, there is no need for the hypothesis that the psychical systems are actually arranged in a *spatial* order. It would be sufficient if a fixed order were established by the fact that in a given psychical process the excitation passes through the systems in a particular *temporal* sequence" (V, 537). Finally, these optical instruments *capture* light; in the example of photography they register it.[18] Freud wants to account for the photographic negative or inscription of light, and this is the differentiation (*Differenzierung*) which he introduces. It will reduce the "imperfections" of his analogy and perhaps "excuse" them. Above all it will throw into relief the apparently contradictory requirement which has haunted Freud since the *Project* and will be satisfied only by a writing machine, the "Mystic Pad":

> Next, we have grounds for introducing a first differentiation at the sensory end [of the apparatus]. A trace (*Spur*) is left in our psychical apparatus of the perceptions which impinge upon it. This we may describe as a "memory-trace" (*Errinerungsspur*); and to the function relating to it we give the name of "memory." If we are in earnest over our plan of attaching psychical processes to systems, memory-traces can only consist in permanent modifications of the elements of the systems. But, as has already been pointed out elsewhere, there are obvious difficulties involved in supposing that one and the same system can accurately retain modifications of its elements and yet remain perpetually open to the reception of fresh occasions for modification [V, 538].

Two systems will thus be necessary in a single machine. This double system, combining freshness of surface and depth of retention, could only distantly and "imperfectly" be represented by an optical machine. "By analysing dreams we can take a step forward in our understanding of the composition of that most marvelous and most mysterious of all instruments. Only a small step no doubt; but a beginning." Thus do we read in the final pages of the *Traumdeutung* (V, 608). Only a small step. The graphic representation of the (nonpsychical) system of the psychical is not yet ready at a time when such a representation of the psychical has already occupied, in the *Traumdeutung* itself, a large area. Let us measure this delay.

We have already defined elsewhere the fundamental property of writing, in a difficult sense of the word, as *spacing:* diastem and time becoming space; an unfolding as well, on an original site, of meanings which irreversible, linear consecution, moving from present point to present point, could only tend to repress, and (to a certain extent) could only fail to repress. In particular in so-called phonetic writing. The latter's complicity with logos (or the time of logic), which is dominated by the principle of noncontradiction, the cornerstone of all metaphysics or presence, is profound. Now in every silent or not wholly phonic spacing out of meaning, concatenations are possible which no longer obey the linearity of logical time, the time of consciousness or preconsciousness, the time of "verbal representations." The border between the non-phonetic space of writing (even "phonetic" writing) and the space of the stage (*scène*) of dreams is uncertain.

We should not be surprised then, if Freud, in order to suggest the strangeness of the logico-temporal relations in dreams, constantly adduces writing, and the spatial synopses of pictograms, rebuses, hieroglyphics and nonphonetic writing in general. Synopsis and not stasis: scene and not tableau. The laconic, lapidary quality of dreams is not the impassive presence of petrified signs.[19]

Interpretation has spelled out the elements of dreams. It has revealed the work of condensation and displacement. It is still necessary to account for the synthesis which composes and stages the whole. The resources of the mise en scène (*die Darstellungsmittel*) must be questioned. A certain polycentrism of dream representation is irreconcilable with the apparently linear unfolding of pure verbal representations. The logical and ideal structure of conscious speech must thus submit to the dream system and become subordinate to it, like a part of its machinery.

> The different portions of this complicated structure stand, of course, in the most manifold logical relations to one another. They can represent foreground and background, digressions and illustrations, conditions, chains of evidence and counter-arguments. When the whole mass of these dream-thoughts is brought under the pressure of the dream-work, and its elements are turned about, broken into fragments and jammed together—almost like pack-ice—the question arises of what happens to the logical connections

which have hitherto formed its framework. What representation (*mise en scène*) do dreams provide for "if," "because," "just as," "although," "either–or," and all the other conjunctions without which we cannot understand sentences or speeches?"[V, 312].

This type of representation (*mise en scène*) may at first be compared to those forms of expression which are like the writing within speech: the painting or sculpture of signifiers which inscribe in a common space elements which the spoken chain must suppress. Freud sets them off against poetry, "which can make use of speech (*Rede*)." But may the dream as well not use spoken language? "In dreams we see but we do not hear," said the *Project*. In point of fact, Freud, like Artaud later on, meant less the absence than the subordination of speech on the dream-stage.[20] Far from disappearing, speech then changes purpose and status. It is situated, surrounded, invested (in all senses of the word),[21] constituted. It figures in dreams much as captions do in comic strips, those picto-hieroglyphic combinations in which the phonetic text is secondary and not central in the telling of the tale: "Before painting became acquainted with the laws of expression by which it is governed . . . in ancient paintings small labels were hung from the mouths of the persons represented, containing in written characters (*als Schrift*) the speeches which the artist despaired of representing pictorially" (V, 312).

The overall writing of dreams exceeds phonetic writing and puts speech back in its place. As in hieroglyphics or rebuses, voice is circumvented. From the very beginning of the chapter on "The Dream-Work," we are left in no doubt on this subject, although Freud still uses the concept of translation on which he will later cast suspicion. "The dream-thoughts and the dream-content (the latent and manifest) are presented to us like two versions (*mises en scène*) of the same subject-matter in two different languages. Or, more properly, the dream-content seems like a transcript (*Übertragung*) of the dream-thoughts into another mode of expression, whose characters and syntactic laws it is our business to discover by comparing the original and the translation. The dream-thoughts are immediately comprehensible, as soon as we have learnt them. The dream-content, on the other hand, is expressed as it were in a pictographic script (*Bilderschrift*), the characters of which have to be transposed individually into the language of the dream-thoughts" (IV, 277). *Bilderschrift:* not an inscribed image but a figurative script, an image inviting not a simple, conscious, present perception of the thing itself—assuming it exists—but a reading. "If we attempted to read these characters according to their symbolic relation (*Zeichenbeziehung*), we should clearly be led into error. . . . A dream is a picture puzzle (*Bilderrätsel*) of this sort and our predecessors in the field of dream-interpretation have made the mistake of treating the rebus as a pictorial composition" (IV, 277–78). The figurative content is then indeed a form of writing, a signifying chain in scenic form. In that sense, of course, it summarizes a discourse, it is the *economy of speech*. The entire chapter on "Representability" (*Aptitude à la mise en scène; Darstellbar-keit*) shows this quite well. But the reciprocal economic transformation, the total reassimilation into discourse, is, in principle, impossible or limited. This is first of all because words are also and "primarily" things. Thus, in dreams they are absorbed, "caught" by the primary process. It is then not sufficient to say that in dreams, words are condensed by "things"; and that inversely, nonverbal signifiers may be interpreted to a certain degree in terms of verbal representations. It must be seen that insofar as they are attracted, lured into the dream, toward the fictive limit of the primary process, words tend to become things pure and simple. An equally fictive limit, moreover. Pure words and pure things are thus, like the idea of the primary process, and consequently, the secondary process, "theoretical fictions" (V, 603). The interval in "dreams" and the interval in "wakefulness" may not be. distinguished *essentially* insofar as the nature of language is concerned. "Words are often treated as things in dreams and thus undergo the same operations as thing presentations."[22] In the *formal regression* of dreams, words are not *overtaken* by the spatialization of representation (*mise en scène*). Formal regression could not even succeed, moreover, if words had not always been subject in their materiality to the mark of their inscription or scenic capacity, their *Darstellbarkeit* and all the forms of their spacing. This last factor could only have been repressed by so-called living, vigilant speech, by consciousness, logic, the history of language, etc. Spatialization does not surprise the time of speech or the ideality of meaning, it does not happen to them like an accident. Temporalization presupposes the possibility of symbolism, and every symbolic synthesis, even before it falls into a space "exterior" to it, includes within itself spacing as difference. Which is why the pure phonic chain, to the extent that it implies differences, is itself not a pure continuum or flow of time. Difference is the articulation of space and time. The phonic chain or the chain of phonetic writing are always already distended by that minimum of essential spacing upon which the dream-work and any formal regression in general can begin to operate. It is not a question of a negation of time, of a cessation of time in a present or a simultaneity, but of a different structure, a different stratification of time. Here, once more, a comparison with writing—phonetic writing this time—casts light on writing as well as on dreams:

> They [dreams] reproduce *logical connection* by *simultaneity in time*. Here they are acting like the painter who, in a picture of the School of Athens or of Parnassus, represents in one group all the philosophers or all the poets who were never, in fact, assembled in a single hall or on a single mountain-top. . . . Dreams carry this mode of reproduction (*mise en scène*) down to details. Whenever they show us two elements close together, this guarantees that there is some specially intimate connection between what corresponds to them among the dream-thoughts. In the same way, in our system of writing, *"ab"* means that the two letters are to be pronounced in a single syllable. If

a gap is left between the "*a*" and the "*b,*" it means that the "*a*" is the last
letter of one word and the "*b*" is the first of the next one [IV, 314].

The model of heiroglyphic writing assembles more strikingly—though we find it
in every form of writing—the diversity of the modes and functions of signs in
dreams. Every sign—verbal or otherwise—may be used at different levels, in
configurations and functions which are never prescribed by its "essence," but
emerge from a play of differences. Summarizing all these possibilities, Freud
concludes: "Yet, in spite of all this ambiguity, it is fair to say that the productions *(mises en scène)* of the dream-work, which, it must be remembered, *are
not made with the intention of being understood,* present no greater difficulties to
their translators than do the ancient hieroglyphic scripts to those who seek to read
them" (V, 341).

More than twenty years separate the first edition of the *Traumdeutung* from the
"Note on the Mystic Writing-Pad." If we continue to follow the two series of
metaphors—those concerning the nonpsychical system of the psychical and those
concerning the psychical itself—what happens?

On the one hand, the *theoretical* import of the *psychographic* metaphor will be
increasingly refined. A methodological inquiry will, to a certain extent, be devoted to it. It is with a graphematics still to come, rather than with a linguistics
dominated by an ancient phonologism, that psychoanalysis sees itself as destined
to collaborate. Freud recommends this *literally* in a text from 1913, and in this
case we have nothing to add, interpret, alter.[23] The interest which psychoanalysis
brings to linguistics presupposes an "overstepping of the habitual meaning of the
word 'speech.' For in what follows 'speech' must be understood not merely to
mean the expression of thought in words, but to include the speech of gesture and
every other method, such, for instance, as writing, by which mental activity can
be expressed" (XIII, 176). And having recalled the archaic character of expression in dreams, which accepts contradiction[24] and valorizes visibility, Freud
specifies:

> It seems to us more appropriate to compare dreams with a system of writing
> than with a language. In fact, the interpretation of a dream is completely
> analogous to the decipherment of an ancient pictographic script such as
> Egyptian hieroglyphics. In both cases there are certain elements which are
> not intended to be interpreted (or read, as the case may be) but are only
> designed to serve as "determinatives," that is to establish the meaning of
> some other element. The ambiguity of various elements of dreams finds a
> parallel in these ancient systems of writing . . . . If this conception of the
> method of representation in dreams *(mise en scène)* has not yet been fol-
> lowed up, this, as will be readily understood, must be ascribed to the fact
> that psycho-analysts are entirely ignorant of the attitude and knowledge with
> which a philologist would approach such a problem as that presented by
> dreams [XIII, 177].

On the other hand, the same year, in the article on "The Unconscious," the problematic of the *apparatus* itself will begin to be taken up in terms of scriptural concepts: neither, as in the *Project,* in a topology of traces without writing, nor, as in the *Traumdeutung,* in the operations of optical mechanisms. The debate between the functional hypothesis and the topographical hypothesis concerns the locations of an *inscription* (*Niederschrift*): "When a psychical act (let us confine ourselves here to one which is in the nature of an idea [*Vorstellung,* lit. representation] is transposed from the systems Ucs. into the system Cs. (or Pcs.), are we to suppose that this transposition involves a fresh record—as it were, a second registration—of the idea in question which may thus be situated as well in a fresh psychical locality, and alongside of which the original unconscious registration continues to exist? Or are we rather to believe that the transposition consists in a change in the state of the idea, a change involving the same material and occurring in the same locality?" (XIV, 174) The discussion which follows does not directly concern us here. Let us simply recall that the economic hypothesis and the difficult concept of anticathexis (*Gegenbesetzung:* "the sole mechanism of primal repression," XIV, 181) which Freud introduces after refusing to decide on the last question, do not eliminate the topographical difference of the two inscriptions.[25] And let us note that the concept of inscription still remains simply the graphic *element* of an apparatus which is not itself a writing machine. The difference between the system and the psychical is still at work: the graphism itself is reserved for the description of psychical content or of an element in the machine. We might think that the machine itself is subject to another principle of organization, another destination than writing. This is perhaps the case as well, for the main thread of the article on "The Unconscious," its *example,* as we have emphasized, is the fate of a *representation* after it is first registered. When perception—the apparatus which originally enregistered and inscribes—is described, the "perceptual apparatus" can be nothing but a writing machine. The "Note on the Mystic Writing Pad," twelve years later, will describe the perceptual apparatus and the origin of memory. Long disjointed and out of phase, the two series of metaphors will then be united.

*Freud's Piece of Wax
and the Three Analogies
of Writing*

In this six-page text, the analogy between a certain writing apparatus and the perceptual apparatus is demonstrated in progressive steps. Three stages in the description result each time in an increase in rigor, inwardness, and differentiation.

As has always been done—at least since Plato—Freud first considers writing as a technique subservient to memory, an external, auxiliary technique of psychical memory which is not memory itself: *hypomnesis* rather than *mneme* said the

Phaedrus. [26] But here—something not possible for Plato—the psychical is caught up in an apparatus, and what is written will be more readily represented as a part extracted from the apparatus and "materialized." Such is the *first analogy:*

> If I distrust my memory—neurotics, as we know, do so to a remarkable extent, but normal people have every reason for doing so as well—I am able to supplement and guarantee (*ergänzen und versichern*) its working by making a note in writing (*schriftliche Anzeichnung*). In that case the surface upon which this trace is preserved, the pocket-book or sheet of paper, is as it were a materialized portion (*ein materialisiertes Stück*) of my mnemic apparatus (*des Erinnerungsapparates*), the rest of which I carry about with me invisible. I have only to bear in mind the place where this "memory" has been deposited and I can then "reproduce" it at any time I like, with the certainty that it will have remained unaltered and so have escaped the possible distortions to which it might have been subjected in my actual memory" [XIX, 227].

Freud's theme here is not the absence of memory or the primal and normal finitude of the powers of memory; even less is it the structure of the temporalization which grounds that finitude, or this structure's essential relation to censorship and repression; nor is it the possibility and the necessity of the *Ergänzung*, the *hypomnemic supplement* which the psychical must project "into the world"; nor is it that which is called for, as concerns the nature of the psyche, in order for this supplementation to be possible. At first, it is simply a question of considering the conditions which customary writing surfaces impose on the operation of mnemic supplementation. Those conditions fail to satisfy the double requirement defined since the *Project:* a potential for indefinite preservation and an unlimited capacity for reception. A sheet of paper preserves indefinitely but is quickly saturated. A slate, whose virginity may always be reconstituted by erasing the imprints on it, does not conserve its traces. All the classical writing surfaces offer only one of the two advantages and always present the complementary difficulty. Such is the *res extensa* and the intelligible surface of classical writing apparatuses. In the processes which they substitute for our memory, "an unlimited receptive capacity and a retention of permanent traces seem to be mutually exclusive" (XIX, 227). Their extension belongs to classical geometry and is intelligible in its terms as pure exterior without relation to itself. A different writing space must be found, a space which writing has always claimed for itself.

Auxiliary apparatuses (*Hilfsapparate*), which, as Freud notes, are always constituted on the model of the organ to be supplemented (e.g., spectacles, camera, ear trumpet) thus seem particularly deficient when memory is in question. This remark makes even more suspect the earlier reference to optical apparatuses. Freud recalls, nevertheless, that the contradictory requirement he is presenting had already been recognized in 1900. He could have said in 1895. "As long ago as in 1900 I gave expression in *The Interpretation of Dreams* to a suspicion that

this unusual capacity was to be divided between two different systems (or organs
of the mental apparatus). According to this view, we possess a system *Pcpt.-Cs.*,
which receives perceptions but retains no permanent trace of them, so that it can
react like a clean sheet to every new perception; while the permanent traces of the
excitations which have been received are preserved in 'mnemic systems' lying
behind the perceptual system. Later, in *Beyond the Pleasure Principle* (1920), I
added a remark to the effect that the inexplicable phenomenon of consciousness
arises in the perceptual system *instead of* the permanent traces" (XIX, 228).[27]

A double system contained in a single differentiated apparatus: a perpetually
available innocence and an infinite reserve of traces have at last been reconciled
by the "small contrivance" placed "some time ago upon the market under the
name of the Mystic Writing-Pad," and which "promises to perform more than
the sheet of paper or the slate." Its appearance is modest, "but if it is examined
more closely, it will be found that its construction shows a remarkable agreement
with my hypothetical structure of our perceptual apparatus." It offers both advantages: "an ever-ready receptive surface and permanent traces of the inscriptions that have been made on it" (ibid.). Here is its description:

> The Mystic Pad is a slab of dark brown resin or wax with a paper edging;
> over the slab is laid a thin transparent sheet, the top end of which is firmly
> secured to the slab while its bottom end rests upon it without being fixed to
> it. This transparent sheet is the more interesting part of the little device. It
> itself consists of two layers which can be detached from each other except at
> their two ends. The upper layer is a transparent piece of celluloid; the lower
> layer is made of thin translucent waxed paper. When the apparatus is not in
> use, the lower surface of the waxed paper adheres lightly to the upper sur-
> face of the wax slab.
>   To make use of the Mystic Pad, one writes upon the celluloid portion of
> the covering-sheet which rests upon the wax slab. For this purpose no pencil
> or chalk is necessary, since the writing does not depend on material being
> deposited upon the receptive surface. It is a return to the ancient method of
> writing upon tablets of clay or wax: a pointed stilus scratches the surface,
> the depressions upon which constitute the "writing." In the case of the
> Mystic Pad this scratching is not effected directly, but through the medium
> of the covering-sheet. At the points which the stilus touches, it presses the
> lower surface of the waxed paper on to the wax slab, and the grooves are
> visible as dark writing upon the otherwise smooth whitish-gray surface of
> the celluloid. If one wishes to destroy what has been written, all that is
> necessary is to raise the double covering-sheet from the wax slab by a light
> pull, starting from the free lower end.[28] The close contact between the
> waxed paper and the wax slab at the places which have been scratched (upon
> which the visibility of the writing depended) is thus brought to an end and it
> does not recur when the two surfaces come together once more. The Mystic
> Pad is now clear of writing and ready to receive fresh inscriptions [XIX,
> 228–29].

Let us note that the *depth* of the Mystic Pad is simultaneously a depth without
bottom, an infinite allusion, and a perfectly superficial exteriority: a stratification
of surfaces each of whose relation to itself, each of whose interior, is but the
implication of another similarly exposed surface. It joins the two empirical
certainties by which we are constituted: infinite depth in the implication of
meaning, in the unlimited envelopment of the present, and, simultaneously, the
pellicular essence of being, the absolute absence of any foundation.

Neglecting the device's "slight imperfections," interested only in the analogy, Freud insists on the essentially protective nature of the celluloid sheet.
Without it, the fine waxed paper would be scratched or ripped. There is no
writing which does not devise some means of protection, *to protect against itself,*
against the writing by which the "subject" is himself threatened as he lets
himself be written: *as he exposes himself.* "The layer of celluloid thus acts as a
protective sheath for the waxed paper." It shields the waxed paper from "injuri-
ous effects from without." "I may at this point recall that in *Beyond the Pleasure
Principle,*[29] I showed that the perceptual apparatus of our mind consists of two
layers, of an external protective shield against stimuli whose task it is to diminish
the strength of excitations coming in, and of a surface behind it which receives
the stimuli, namely the system *Pcpt.-Cs*" (XIX, 230).

But this still concerns only reception or perception, the most superficial surface's openness to the incision of a scratch. There is as yet no writing in the
flatness of this *extensio*. We must account for writing as a trace which survives
the scratch's present, punctuality, and *stigmē*. "This analogy," Freud continues,
"would not be of much value if it could not be pursued further than this." This is
the *second analogy:* "If we lift the entire covering-sheet—both the celluloid
and the waxed paper—off the wax slab, the writing vanishes, and, as I have
already remarked, does not re-appear again. The surface of the Mystic Pad is
clear of writing and once more capable of receiving impressions. But it is easy to
discover that the permanent trace of what was written is retained upon the wax
slab itself and is legible in suitable lights" (ibid.). The contradictory requirements are satisfied by this double system, and "this is precisely the way in
which, according to the hypothesis which I mentioned just now, our psychical
apparatus performs its perceptual function. The layer which receives the
stimuli—the system *Pcpt.-Cs.*—forms no permanent traces; the foundations of
memory come about in other, supplementary, systems" (ibid.). Writing supple-
ments perception before perception even appears to itself [is conscious of itself].
"Memory" or writing is the opening of that process of appearance itself. The
"perceived" may be read only in the past, beneath perception and after it.[30]

Whereas other writing surfaces, corresponding to the prototypes of slate or
paper, could represent only a materialized part of the mnemic system in the
psychical apparatus, an abstraction, the Mystic Pad represents the apparatus in its
entirety, not simply in its perceptual layer. The wax slab, in fact, represents the

unconscious: "I do not think it is too far-fetched to compare the wax slab with the unconscious behind the system Pcpt.-Cs." (XIX, 230–31). The becoming-visible which alternates with the disappearance of what is written would be the flickering-up (*Aufleuchten*) and passing-away (*Vergehen*) of consciousness in the process of perception.

This introduces the *third and final analogy*. It is certainly the most interesting. Until now, it has been a question only of the space of writing, its extension and volume, reliefs and depressions. But there is as well a *time of writing,* and this time of writing is nothing other than the very structure of that which we are now describing. We must come to terms with the temporality of the wax slab. For it is not outside the slab, and the Mystic Pad includes in its structure what Kant describes as the three modes of time in the *three analogies of experience:* permanence, succession, simultaneity. Descartes, when he wonders *quaenam vero est haec cera,* can reduce its essence to the timeless simplicity of an intelligible object.[31] Freud, reconstructing an *operation,* can reduce neither time nor the multiplicity of sensitive layers. And he will link a discontinuist conception of time, as the periodicity and spacing of writing, to a whole chain of hypotheses which stretch from the *Letters to Fliess* to *Beyond the Pleasure Principle,* and which, once again, are constructed, consolidated, confirmed, and solidified in the Mystic Pad. Temporality as spacing will be not only the horizontal discontinuity of a chain of signs, but also will be writing as the interruption and restoration of contact between the various depths of psychical levels: the remarkably heterogeneous temporal fabric of psychical work itself. We find neither the continuity of a line nor the homogeneity of a volume; only the differentiated duration and depth of a stage, and its spacing:

> But I must admit that I am inclined to press the comparison still further. On the Mystic Pad the writing vanished every time the close contact is broken between the paper which receives the stimulus and the wax slab which preserves the impression. This agrees with a notion which I have long had about the method in which the perceptual apparatus of our mind functions, but which I have hitherto kept to myself [XIX, 231].

This hypothesis posits a discontinuous distribution—through rapid periodic impulses—of "cathectic innervations" (*Besetzungsinnervationen*), from within toward the outside, toward the permeability of the system Pcpt.-Cs. These movements are then "withdrawn" or "removed." Consciousness fades each time the cathexis is withdrawn in this way. Freud compares this movement to the feelers which the *unconscious* would stretch out toward the external world, and which it would withdraw when these feelers had sampled the excitations coming from the external world in order to warn the unconscious of any threat. (Freud had no more reserved the image of the feeler for the unconscious—we find it in chapter 4 of *Beyond the Pleasure Principle* [32]—than he had reserved the notion of cathectic periodicity, as we noted above.) The "origin of our concept of time" is attributed to this "periodic non-excitability" and to this "discontinuous method of functioning of the system Pcpt.-Cs." Time is the economy of a system of writing.

The machine does not run by itself. It is less a machine than a tool. And it is not held with only one hand. This is the mark of its temporality. Its *maintenance* is not simple. The ideal virginity of the present (*maintenant*) is constituted by the work of memory. At least two hands are needed to make the apparatus function, as well as a system of gestures, a coordination of independent initiatives, an organized multiplicity of origins. It is at this stage that the "Note" ends: "If we imagine one hand writing upon the surface of the Mystic Writing-Pad while another periodically raises its covering sheet from the wax slab, we shall have a concrete representation of the way in which I tried to picture the functioning of the perceptual apparatus of our mind" (XIX, 232).

Traces thus produce the space of their inscription only by acceding to the period of their erasure. From the beginning, in the "present" of their first impression, they are constituted by the double force of repetition and erasure, legibility and illegibility. A two-handed machine, a multiplicity of agencies or origins—is this not the original relation to the other and the original temporality of writing, its "primary" complication: an originary spacing, deferring, and erasure of the simple origin, and polemics on the very threshhold of what we persist in calling perception? The stage of dreams, "which follow old facilitations," was a stage of writing. But this is because "perception," the first relation of life to its other, the origin of life, had always already prepared representation. We must be several in order to write, and even to "perceive." The *simple* structure of maintenance and manuscription, like every intuition of an origin, is a myth, a "fiction" as "theoretical" as the idea of the primary process. For that idea is contradicted by the theme of primal repression.

Writing is unthinkable without repression. The condition for writing is that there be neither a permanent contact nor an absolute break between strata: the vigilance and failure of censorship. It is no accident that the metaphor of censorship should come from the area of politics concerned with the deletions, blanks, and disguises of writing, even if, at the beginning of the *Traumdeutung,* Freud seems to make only a conventional, didactic reference to it. The apparent exteriority of political censorship refers to an essential censorship which binds the writer to his own writing.

If there were only perception, pure permeability to breaching, there would be no breaches. We would be written, but nothing would be recorded; no writing would be produced, retained, repeated as legibility. But pure perception does not exist: we are written only as we write, by the agency within us which always already keeps watch over perception, be it internal or external. The "subject" of writing does not exist if we mean by that some sovereign solitude of the author.

The subject of writing is a *system* of relations between strata: the Mystic Pad, the psyche, society, the world. Within that scene, on that stage, the punctual simplicity of the classical subject is not to be found. In order to describe the structure, it is not enough to recall that one always writes for someone; and the oppositions sender-receiver, code-message, etc., remain extremely coarse instruments. We would search the "public" in vain for the first reader: i.e., the first author of a work. And the "sociology of literature" is blind to the war and the ruses perpetrated by the author who reads and by the first reader who dictates, for at stake here is the origin of the work itself. The *sociality* of writing as *drama* requires an entirely different discipline.

That the machine does not run by itself means something else: a mechanism without its own energy. The machine is dead. It is death. Not because we risk death in playing with machines, but because the origin of machines is the relation to death. In a letter to Fliess, it will be recalled, Freud, evoking his representation of the psychical apparatus, had the impression of being faced with a machine which would soon run by itself. But what was to run by itself was the psyche and not its imitation or mechanical representation. For the latter does not live. Representation is death. Which may be immediately transformed into the following proposition: death is (only) representation. But it is bound to life and to the living present which it repeats originarily. A pure representation, a machine, never runs by itself. Such at least is the limitation which Freud recognizes in his analogy with the Mystic Pad. Like the first section of the "Note," his gesture at this point is extremely Platonic. Only the writing of the soul, said the *Phaedrus,* only the psychical trace is able to reproduce and to represent itself spontaneously. Our reading had skipped over the following remark by Freud: "There must come a point at which the analogy between an auxiliary apparatus of this kind and the organ which is its prototype will cease to apply. It is true, too, that once the writing has been erased, the Mystic Pad cannot 'reproduce' it from within; it would be a mystic pad indeed if, like our memory, it could accomplish that" (XIX, 230). Abandoned to itself, the multiplicity of layered surfaces of the apparatus is a dead complexity without depth. Life as depth belongs only to the wax of psychical memory. Freud, like Plato, thus continues to oppose hypomnemic writing and writing *en tei psychei,* itself woven of traces, empirical memories of a present truth outside of time. Henceforth, the Mystic Pad, separated from psychical responsibility, a representation abandoned to itself, still participates in Cartesian space and mechanics: *natural* wax, exteriority of the *memory aid*.

All that Freud had thought about the unity of life and death, however, should have led him to ask other questions here. And to ask them explicitly. Freud does not explicitly examine the status of the "materialized" supplement which is necessary to the alleged spontaneity of memory, even if that spontaneity were differentiated in itself, thwarted by a censorhsip or repression which, moreover, could not act on a perfectly spontaneous memory. Far from the machine being a pure absence of spontaneity, its *resemblance* to the psychical apparatus, its existence and its necessity bear witness to the finitude of the mnemic spontaneity which is thus supplemented. The machine—and, consequently, representation— is death and finitude *within* the psyche. Nor does Freud examine the possibility of this machine, which, in the world, has at least begun to *resemble* memory, and increasingly resembles it more closely. Its resemblance to memory is closer than that of the innocent Mystic Pad: the latter is no doubt infinitely more complex than slate or paper, less archaic than a palimpsest; but, compared to other machines for storing archives, it is a child's toy. This resemblance—i.e., necessarily a certain Being-in-the-world of the psyche—did not happen to memory from without, any more than death surprises life. It founds memory. Metaphor—in this case the analogy between two apparatuses and the possibility of this representational relation—raises a question which, despite his premises, and for reasons which are no doubt essential, Freud failed to make explicit, at the very moment when he had brought this question to the threshold of being thematic and urgent. Metaphor as a rhetorical or didactic device is possible here only through the solid metaphor, the "unnatural," historical production of a *supplementary* machine, *added to* the psychical organization in order to supplement its finitude. The very idea of finitude is derived from the movement of this supplementarity. The historico-technical production of this metaphor which survives individual (that is, generic) psychical organization, is of an entirely different order than the production of an intrapsychical metaphor, assuming that the latter exists (to speak about it is not enough for that), and whatever bond the two metaphors may maintain between themselves. Here the question of *technology* (a new name must perhaps be found in order to remove it from its traditional problematic) may not be derived from an assumed opposition between the psychical and the nonpsychical, life and death. Writing, here, is *techne* as the relation between life and death, between present and representation, between the two apparatuses. It opens up the question of technics: of the apparatus in general and of the analogy between the psychical apparatus and the nonpsychical apparatus. In this sense writing is the stage of history and the play of the world. It cannot be exhausted by psychology alone. That which, in Freud's discourse, opens itself to the theme of writing results in psychoanalysis being not simply psychology—nor simply psychoanalysis.

Thus are perhaps augured, in the Freudian breakthrough, a beyond and a beneath of the closure we might term "Platonic." In that moment of world history "subsumed" by the name of Freud, by means of an unbelievable mythology (be it neurological or metapsychological: for we never dreamed of taking it seriously, outside of the question which disorganizes and disturbs its literalness, the metapsychological fable, which marks perhaps only a minimal advance beyond the neurological tales of the *Project*), a relationship to itself of the historico-transcendental stage of writing was spoken without being said, thought without being thought: was written and simultaneously erased, metaphorized; designating itself while indicating intrawordly relations, it *was represented.*

This may perhaps be recognized (*as an example and let this be understood prudently*) insofar as Freud too, with admirable scope and continuity, *performed for us the scene of writing.* But we must think of this scene in other terms than those of individual or collective psychology, or even of anthropology. It must be thought in the horizon of the scene/stage of the world, as the history of that scene/stage. Freud's language is *caught up* in it.

Thus Freud performs for us the scene of writing. Like all those who write. And like all who know how to write, he let the scene duplicate, repeat, and betray itself within the scene. It is Freud then whom we will allow to say what scene he has played for us. And from him that we shall borrow the hidden epigraph which has silently governed our reading.

In following the advance of the metaphors of path, trace, breach, of the march treading down a track which was opened by effraction through neurone, light or wax, wood or resin, in order violently to inscribe itself in nature, matter, or matrix; and in following the untiring reference to a dry stilus and a writing without ink; and in following the inexhaustible inventiveness and dreamlike renewal of mechanical models—the metonymy perpetually at work on the same metaphor, obstinately substituting trace for trace and machine for machine—we have been wondering just what Freud was doing.

And we have been thinking of those texts where, better than anywhere else, he tells us *worin die Bahnung sonst besteht.* In what pathbreaking consists.

Of the *Traumdeutung:* "It is highly probable that all complicated machinery and apparatuses occurring in dreams stand for the genitals (and as a rule male ones), in describing which dream-symbolism is as indefatigable as the joke-work (*Witzarbeit*)" (V, 356).

Then, of *Inhibitions, Symptoms, and Anxiety:* "As soon as writing, which entails making a liquid flow out of a tube onto a piece of white paper, assumes the significance of copulation, or as soon as walking becomes a symbolic substitute for treading upon the body of mother earth, both writing and walking are stopped because they represent the performance of a forbidden sexual act" (XX, 90).

The last part of the lecture concerned the archi-trace as erasure: erasure of the present and thus of the subject, of that which is proper to the subject and of his proper name. The concept of a (conscious or unconscious) subject necessarily refers to the concept of substance—and thus of presence—out of which it is born.

Thus, the Freudian concept of trace must be radicalized and extracted from the metaphysics of presence which still retains it (particularly in the concepts of consciousness, the unconscious, perception, memory, reality, and several others).

The trace is the erasure of selfhood, of one's own presence, and is constituted by the threat or anguish of its irremediable disappearance, of the disappearance of its disappearance. An unerasable trace is not a trace, it is a full presence, an immobile and uncorruptible substance, a son of God, a sign of parousia and not a seed, that is, a mortal germ.

This erasure is death itself, and it is within its horizon that we must conceive not only the "present," but also what Freud doubtless believed to be the indelibility of certain traces in the unconscious, where "nothing ends, nothing happens, nothing is forgotten." This erasure of the trace is not only an accident that can occur here or there, nor is it even the necessary structure of a determined censorship threatening a given presence; it is the very structure which makes possible, as the movement of temporalization and pure *auto-affection,* something that can be called repression in general, the original synthesis of original repression and secondary repression, repression "itself."

Such a radicalization of the *thought of the trace* (a *thought* because it escapes binarism and makes binarism possible on the basis of *nothing*), would be fruitful not only in the deconstruction of logocentrism, but in a kind of reflection exercised more positively in different fields, at different levels of writing in general, at the point of articulation of writing in the current sense and of the trace in general.

These fields, whose specificity thereby could be opened to a thought fecundated by psychoanalysis, would be numerous. The problem of their respective limits would be that much more formidable to the extent that this problem could not be subsumed by any authorized conceptual opposition.

In question, first, would be:

1. A *psychopathology of everyday life* in which the study of writing would not be limited to the interpretation of the *lapsus calami,* and, moreover, would be more attentive to this latter and to its originality than Freud himself ever was. "*Slips of the pen,* to which I now pass, are so closely akin to slips of the tongue that we have nothing new to expect from them" (XV, 69). This did prevent Freud from raising the fundamental juridical problem of responsibility, before the tribunal of psychoanalysis, as concerns, for example, the murderous *lapsus calami* (ibid.).

2. A *history of writing,* an immense field in which only preparatory work has been done up to now; however admirable this work has been, it still gives way, beyond its empirical discoveries, to unbridled speculation.

3. A *becoming-literary of the literal.* Here, despite several attempts made by Freud and certain of his successors, a psychoanalysis of literature respectful of the *originality of the literary signifier* has not yet begun, and this is surely not an accident. Until now, only the analysis of literary *signifieds,* that is, *nonliterary* signified meanings, has been undertaken. But such questions refer to the entire history of literary forms themselves, and to the history of everything within them which was destined precisely to authorize this disdain of the signifier.

4. Finally, to continue designating these fields according to traditional and problematic boundaries, what might be called a new *psychoanalytic graphology,* which would take into account the contributions of the three kinds of research we have just outlined roughly. Here, Melanie Klein perhaps opens the way. As concerns the forms of signs, even within phonetic writing, the cathexes of gestures, and of movements, of letters, lines, points, the elements of the writing apparatus (instrument, surface, substance, etc.), a text like *The Role of the School in the Libidinal Development of the Child* (1923) indicates the direction to be taken (cf. also, Strachey, *Some Unconscious Factors in Reading*).

Melanie Klein's entire thematic, her analysis of the constitution of good and bad objects, her genealogy of morals could doubtless begin to illuminate, if followed prudently, the entire problem of the archi-trace, not in its essence (it does not have one), but in terms of valuation and devaluation. Writing as sweet nourishment or as excrement, the trace as seed or mortal germ, wealth or weapon, detritus and/or penis, etc.

How, for example, on the stage of history, can writing as excrement separated from the living flesh and the sacred body of the hieroglyph (Artaud), be put into communication with what is said in *Numbers* about the parched woman drinking the inky dust of the law; or what is said in *Exekiel* about the son of man who fills his entrails with the scroll of the law which has become sweet as honey in his mouth?

The Theater of
Cruelty and
the Closure of
Representation

for Paule Thévenin

Unique fois au monde, parce
qu'en raison d'un événement
toujours que j'expliquerai,
il n'est pas de Présent, non
—un présent n'existe pas.
(Mallarmé, *Quant au livre*)

. . . as for my forces,
they are only a supplement,
the supplement of an acutal
    state,
it is that there has never been
    an origin.
(Artaud, 6 June 1947)

'' . . . Dance / and consequently the theater / have not yet begun to exist.'' This is what one reads in one of Antonin Artaud's last writings (Le théâtre de la cruauté, in *84*, 1948). And in the same text, a little earlier, the theater of cruelty is defined as ''the affirmation / of a terrible / and, moreover, implacable necessity.'' Artaud, therefore, does not call for destruction, for a new manifestation of negativity. Despite everything that it must ravage in its wake, ''the theater of cruelty / is not the symbol of an absent void.'' It *affirms*, it produces affirmation itself in its full and necessary rigor. But also in its most hidden sense, the sense most often buried, most often diverted from itself: ''implacable'' as it is, this affirmation has ''not yet begun to exist.''

It is still to be born. Now a necessary affirmation can be born only by being reborn to itself. For Artaud, the future of the theater—thus, the future in general—is opened only by the anaphora which dates from the eve prior to birth. Theatricality must traverse and restore ''existence'' and ''flesh'' in each of their aspects. Thus, whatever can be said of the body can be said of the theater. As we know, Artaud lived the morrow of a dispossession: his proper body, the property and propriety of his body, had been stolen from him at birth by the thieving god who was born in order ''to pass himself off / as me.''[1] Rebirth doubtless occurs through—Artaud recalls this often—a kind of reeducation of the organs. But this reeducation permits the access to a life before birth and after death (". . . through dying / I have finally achieved real immortality," p. 110), and not to a death before birth and after life. This is what distinguishes the affirmation of cruelty from romantic negativity; the difference is slight and yet decisive. Lichtenberger: "I cannot rid myself of this idea that I was *dead* before I was born, and that through death I will return to this very state. . . . To die and to be reborn with the memory of one's former existence is called fainting; to awaken with other organs which must first be reeducated is called birth." For Artaud, the primary concern is not to die in dying, not to let the thieving god divest him of his life. "And I believe that there is always someone else, at the extreme moment of death, to strip us of our own lives" (*AA*, p. 162).

Similarly, Western theater has been separated from the force of its essence, removed from its *affirmative* essence, its *vis affirmativa*. And this dispossession occurred from the origin on, is the very movement of origin, of birth as death.

This is why a "place" is "left on all the stages of stillborn theater" ("Le théâtre et l'anatomie," in *La rue,* July 1946). The theater is born in its own disappearance, and the offspring of this movement has a name: man. The theater of cruelty is to be born by separating death from birth and by erasing the name of man. The theater has always been made to do that for which it was not made: "The last word on man has not been said. . . . The theater was never made to describe man and what he does. . . . *Et le théâtre est ce patin dégingandé, qui musique de troncs par barbes métalliques de barbelés nous maintient en état de guerre contre l'homme qui nous corsetait . . . .* Man is quite ill in Aeschylus, but still thinks of himself somewhat as a god and does not want to enter the membrane, and in Euripides, finally, he splashes about in the membrane, forgetting where and when he was a god" (ibid.).

Indeed, the eve of the origin of this declining, decadent, and negative Western theater must be reawakened and reconstituted in order to revive the implacable necessity of affirmation on its Eastern horizon. This is the implacable necessity of an as yet inexistent stage, certainly, but the affirmation is not to be elaborated *tomorrow,* in some "new theater." Its implacable necessity operates as a permanent force. Cruelty is always at work. The void, the place that is empty and waiting for this theater which has not yet "begun to exist," thus measures only the strange distance which separates us from implacable necessity, from the *present* (or rather the contemporary, *active*) work of affirmation. Within the space of the unique opening of this distance, the stage of cruelty rears its enigma for us. And it is into this opening that we wish to enter here.

If throughout the world today—and so many examples bear witness to this in the most striking fashion—all theatrical audacity declares its fidelity to Artaud (correctly or incorrectly, but with increasing insistency), then the question of the theater of cruelty, of its present inexistence and its implacable necessity, has the value of a *historic* question. A historic question not because it could be inscribed within what is called the history of theater, not because it would be epoch-making within the becoming of theatrical forms, or because it would occupy a position within the succession of models of theatrical representation. This question is historic in an absolute and radical sense. It announces the limit of representation.

The theater of cruelty is not a *representation*. It is life itself, in the extent to which life in unrepresentable. Life is the nonrepresentable origin of representation. "I have therefore said 'cruelty' as I might have said 'life' " (*TD*, p. 114). This life carries man along with it, but is not primarily the life of man. The latter is only a representation of life, and such is the limit—the humanist limit—of the metaphysics of classical theater. "The theater as we practice it can therefore be reproached with a terrible lack of imagination. The theater must make itself the equal of life—not an individual life, that individual aspect of life in which CHARACTERS triumph, but the sort of liberated life which sweeps away human individuality and in which man is only a reflection" (*TD*, p. 116).

Is not the most naïve form of representation *mimesis?* Like Nietzsche—and the affinities do not end there—Artaud wants to have done with the *imitative* concept of art, with the Aristotelean aesthetics[2] in which the metaphysics of Western art comes into its own. "Art is not the imitation of life, but life is the imitation of a transcendental principle which art puts us into communication with once again" (*OC* 4:310).

Theatrical art should be the primordial and privileged site of this destruction of imitation: more than any other art, it has been marked by the labor of total representation in which the affirmation of life lets itself be doubled and emptied by negation. This representation, whose structure is imprinted not only on the art, but on the entire culture of the West (its religions, philosophies, politics), therefore designates more than just a particular type of theatrical construction. This is why the question put to us today by far exceeds the bounds of theatrical technology. Such is Artaud's most obstinate affirmation: technical or theatrological reflection is not to be treated marginally. The decline of the theater doubtless begins with the possibility of such a dissociation. This can be emphasized without weakening the importance or interest of theatrological problems, or of the revolutions which may occur within the limits of theatrological problems, or of the revolutions which may occur within the limits of theatrical technique. But Artaud's intention indicates these limits. For as long as these technical and intratheatrical revolutions do not penetrate the very foundations of Western theater, they will belong to the history and to the stage that Antonin Artaud wanted to explode.

What does it mean to break this structure of belonging? Is it possible to do so? Under what conditions can a theater today legitimately invoke Artaud's name? It is only a fact that so many directors wish to be acknowledged as Artaud's heirs, that is (as has been written), his "illegitimate sons." The question of justification and legality must also be raised. With what criteria can such a claim be recognized as unfounded? Under what conditions could an authentic "theater of cruelty" "begin to exist"? These simultaneously technical and "metaphysical" questions (metaphysical in the sense understood by Artaud), arise spontaneously from the reading of all the texts in *The Theater and Its Double,* for these texts are more *solicitations* than a sum of precepts, more a system of critiques *shaking the entirety* of Occidental history than a treatise on theatrical practice.

The theater of cruelty expulses God from the stage. It does not put a new atheist discourse on stage, or give atheism a platform, or give over theatrical space to a philosophizing logic that would once more, to our greater lassitude, proclaim the death of God. The theatrical practice of cruelty, in its action and structure, inhabits or rather *produces* a nontheological space.

The stage is theological for as long as it is dominated by speech, by a will to speech, by the layout of a primary logos which does not belong to the theatrical site and governs it from a distance. The stage is theological for as long as its structure, following the entirety of tradition, comports the following elements: an author-creator who, absent and from afar, is armed with a text and keeps watch over, assembles, regulates the time or the meaning of representation, letting this latter *represent* him as concerns what is called the content of his thoughts, his intentions, his ideas. He lets representation represent him through representatives, directors or actors, enslaved interpreters who represent characters who, primarily through what they say, more or less directly represent the thought of the "creator." Interpretive slaves who faithfully execute the providential designs of the "master." Who moreover—and this is the ironic rule of the representative structure which organizes all these relationships—creates nothing, has only the illusion of having created, because he only transcribes and makes available for reading a text whose nature is itself necessarily representative; and this representative text maintains with what is called the "real" (the existing real, the "reality" about which Artaud said, in the "Avertissement" to *Le moine,* that it is an "excrement of the mind") an imitative and reproductive relationship. Finally, the theological stage comports a passive, seated public, a public of spectators, of consumers, of "enjoyers"—as Nietzsche and Artaud both say— attending a production that lacks true volume or depth, a production that is level, offered to their voyeuristic scrutiny. (In the theater of cruelty, pure visibility is not exposed to voyeurism.) This general structure in which each agency is linked to all the others by representation, in which the irrepresentability of the living present is dissimulated or dissolved, suppressed or deported within the infinite chain of representations—this structure has never been modified. All revolutions have maintained it intact, and most often have tended to protect or restore it. And it is the phonetic text, speech, transmitted discourse—eventually transmitted by the prompter whose hole is the hidden but indispensable center of representative structure—which ensures the movement of representation. Whatever their importance, all the pictorial, musical and even gesticular forms introduced into Western theater can only, in the best of cases, illustrate, accompany, serve, or decorate a text, a verbal fabric, a logos which *is said* in the beginning. "If then, the author is the man who arranges the language of speech and the director is his slave, there is merely a question of words. There is here a confusion over terms, stemming from the fact that, for us, and according to the sense generally attributed to the word *director,* this man is merely an artisan, an adapter, a kind of translator eternally devoted to making a dramatic work pass from one language into another; this confusion will be possible and the director will be forced to play second fiddle to the author only so long as there is a tacit agreement that the language of words is superior to others and that the theater admits none other than this one language" (*TD,* p. 119). This does not imply, of course, that to be faithful to Artaud it suffices to give a great deal of importance and responsibility to the "director" while maintaining the classical structure.

By virtue of the word (or rather the unity of the word and the concept, as we will say later—and this specification will be important) and beneath the theological ascendancy both of the "verb [which] is the measure of our impotency" (*OC* 4:277) and of our fear, it is indeed the stage which finds itself threatened throughout the Western tradition. The Occident—and such is the energy of its essence—has worked only for the erasure of the stage. For a stage which does nothing but illustrate a discourse is no longer entirely a stage. Its relation to speech is its malady, and "we repeat that the epoch is sick" (*OC* 4:280). To reconstitute the stage, finally to put on stage and to overthrow the tyranny of the text is thus one and the same gesture. "The triumph of pure mise en scène" (*OC* 4:305).

This classical forgetting of the stage is then confused with the history of theater and with all of Western culture; indeed, it even guaranteed their unfolding. And yet, despite this "forgetting," the theater and its arts have lived richly for over twenty-five centuries: an experience of mutations and perturbations which cannot be set aside, despite the peaceful and impassive immobility of the fundamental structures. Thus, in question is not only a forgetting or a simple surface concealment. A certain stage has maintained with the "forgotten," but, in truth, violently erased, stage a secret communication, a certain relationship of *betrayal,* if to betray is at once to denature through infidelity, but also to let oneself be evinced despite oneself, and to manifest the foundation of force. This explains why classical theater, in Artaud's eyes, is not simply the absence, negation, or forgetting of theater, is not a nontheater: it is a mark of cancellation that lets what it covers be read; and it is corruption also, a "perversion," a *seduction,* the margin of an aberration whose meaning and measure are visible only beyond birth, at the eve of theatrical representation, at the origin of tragedy. Or, for example, in the realm of the "Orphic Mysteries which subjugated Plato," or the

"Mysteries of Eleusis" stripped of the interpretations with which they have been covered, or the "pure beauty of which Plato, at least once in this world, must have found the complete, sonorous, streaming naked realization" (*TD,* p. 52). Artaud is indeed speaking of perversion and not of forgetting, for example, in this letter to Benjamin Crémieux:

> The theater, an independent and autonomous art, must, in order to *revive or simply to live,* realize what differentiates it from text, pure speech, literature, and all other fixed and written means. We can perfectly well continue to conceive of a theater based upon the authority of the text, and on a text more and more wordy, diffuse, and boring, to which the esthetics of the stage would be subject. But this conception of theater, which consists of having people sit on a certain number of straight-backed or overstuffed chairs placed in a row and tell each other stories, however marvelous, is, if not the absolute negation of theater—which does not absolutely require movement in order to be what it should—certainly its *perversion* [*TD,* p. 106; *my italics*].

Released from the text and the author-god, mise en scène would be returned to its creative and founding freedom. The director and the participants (who would no longer be actors *or* spectators) would cease to be the instruments and organs of representation. Is this to say that Artaud would have refused the name *representation* for the theater of cruelty? No, provided that we clarify the difficult and equivocal meaning of this notion. Here, we would have to be able to play upon all the German words that we indistinctly translate with the unique word representation. The stage, certainly, *will no longer represent,* since it will not operate as an addition, as the sensory illustration of a text already written, thought, or lived outside the stage, which the stage would then only repeat but whose fabric it would not constitute. The stage will no longer operate as the repetition of a *present,* will no longer re-present a present that would exist elsewhere and prior to it, a present that would exist elsewhere and prior to it, a present whose plenitude would be older than it, absent from it, and rightfully capable of doing without it: the being-present-to-itself of the absolute Logos, the living present of God. Nor will the stage be a representation, if representation means the surface of a spectacle displayed for spectators. It will not even offer the presentation of a present, if present signifies that which is maintained *in front* of me. Cruel representation must permeate me. And nonrepresentation is, thus, original representation, if representation signifies, also, the unfolding of a volume, a multidimensional milieu, an experience which produces its own space. *Spacing* [*espacement*], that is to say, the production of a space that no speech could condense or comprehend (since speech primarily presupposes this spacing), thereby appeals to a time that is no longer that of so-called phonic linearity, appeals to "a new notion of space" and "a specific idea of time" (*TD,* p. 124). "We intend to base the theater upon spectacle before everything else, and we shall introduce into the spectacle a new notion of space utilized on all possible levels and in all degrees of perspective in depth and height, and within this notion a specific idea of time will be added to that of movement . . . . Thus, theater space will be utilized not only in its dimensions and volume but, so to speak, in its undersides *(dans ses dessous)''* (*TD*, p. 124).

Thus, the closure of classical representation, but also the reconstitution of a closed space of original representation, the archi-manifestation of force or of life. A closed space, that is to say a space produced from within itself and no longer organized from the vantage of an other absent site, an illocality, an alibi or invisible utopia. The end of representation, but also original representation; the end of interpretation, but also an original interpretation that no master-speech, no project of mastery will have permeated and leveled in advance. A visible representation, certainly, directed against the speech which eludes sight—and Artaud insists upon the productive images without which there would be no theater (*theaomai*)—but whose visibility does not consist of a spectacle mounted by the discourse of the master. Representation, then, as the autopresentation of pure visibility and even pure sensibility.[3]

It is this extreme and difficult sense of spectacular representation that another passage from the same letter attempts to delimit: "So long as the *mise en scène* remains, even in the minds of the boldest directors, a simple means of presentation, an accessory mode of expressing the work, a sort of spectacular intermediary with no significance of its own, it will be valuable only to the degree it succeeds in hiding itself behind the works it is pretending to serve. And this will continue as long as the major interest in a performed work is in its text, as long as literature takes precedence over the kind of performance improperly called spectacle, with everything pejorative, accessory, ephemeral and external that that term carries with it" (*TD*, pp. 105–6). Such, on the stage of cruelty, would be "spectacle acting not as reflection, but as force" (*OC* 4:297). The return to original representation thus implies, not simply but above all, that theater or life must cease to "represent" an other language, must cease to let themselves be derived from an other art, from literature, for example, be it poetic literature. For in poetry, as in literature, verbal representation purloins scenic representation. Poetry can escape Western "illness" only by becoming theater. "We think, precisely, that there is a notion of poetry to be dissociated, extracted from the forms of written poetry in which an epoch at the height of disorder and illness wants to keep all poetry. And when I say that the epoch wants, I am exaggerating, for in reality it is incapable of wanting anything; it is the victim of a formal habit which it absolutely cannot shake. It seems to us that the kind of diffuse poetry which we identify with natural and spontaneous energy (but all natural energies are not poetic) must find its integral expression, its purest, sharpest and most truly separated expression, in the theater" (*OC*, 4:280).

Thus, we can distinguish the sense of *cruelty* as *necessity* and *rigor*. Artaud certainly invites us to think only of "rigor, implacable intention and decision," and of "irreversible and absolute determination" (*TD*, p. 101), of "determinism," "submission to necessity" (*TD*, p. 102), etc., under the heading of cruelty, and not necessarily of "sadism," "horror," "bloodshed," "crucified enemies" (ibid.), etc. (And certain productions today inscribed under Artaud's name are perhaps violent, even bloody, but are not, for all that, cruel.) Nevertheless, there is always a murder at the origin of cruelty, of the necessity named cruelty. And, first of all, a parricide. The origin of theater, such as it must be restored, is the hand lifted against the abusive wielder of the logos, against the father, against the God of a stage subjugated to the power of speech and text.[4]

> In my view no one has the right to call himself author, that is to say creator, except the person who controls the direct handling of the stage. And exactly here is the vulnerable point of the theater as it is thought of not only in France but in Europe and even in the Occident as a whole: Occidental theater recognizes as language, assigns the faculties and powers of a language, permits to be called language (with that particular intellectual dignity generally ascribed to this word) only articulated language, grammatically articulated language, i.e., the language of speech, and of written speech, speech which, pronounced or unpronounced, has no greater value than if it is merely written. In the theater as we conceive it, the text is everything [*TD*, p. 117].

What will speech become, henceforth, in the theater of cruelty? Will it simply have to silence itself or disappear?

In no way. Speech will cease to govern the stage, but will be present upon it. Speech will occupy a rigorously delimited place, will have a function within a system to which it will be coordinated. For it is known that the representations of the theater of cruelty had to be painstakingly determined in advance. The absence of an author and his text does not abandon the stage to dereliction. The stage is not forsaken, given over to improvisatory anarchy, to "chance vaticination" (*OC* 4:234), to "Copeau's improvisations" (*TD*, p. 109), to "Surrealist empiricism" (*OC* 4:313), to *commedia dell'arte*, or to "the capriciousness of untrained inspiration" (ibid.). Everything, thus, will be *prescribed* in a writing and a text whose fabric will no longer resemble the model of classical representation. To what place, then, will speech be assigned by this necessary prescription called for by cruelty itself?

Speech and its notation—phonetic speech, an element of classical theater—speech and *its* writing will be erased on the stage of cruelty only in the extent to which they were allegedly *dictation:* at once citations or recitations and orders. The director and the actor will no longer take dictation: "Thus we shall renounce the theatrical superstition of the text and the dictatorship of the writer" (*TD*, p. 124). This is also the end of the *diction* which made theater into an exercise of reading. The end of the fact that for "certain theatrical amateurs this means that a play read affords just as definite and as great a satisfaction as the same play performed" (*TD*, p. 118).

How will speech and writing function then? They will once more become *gestures;* and the *logical* and discursive intentions which speech ordinarily uses in order to ensure its rational transparency, and in order to purloin its body in the direction of meaning, will be reduced or subordinated. And since this theft of the body by itself is indeed that which leaves the body to be strangely concealed by the very thing that constitutes it as diaphanousness, then the deconstitution of diaphanousness lays bare the flesh of the word, lays bare the word's sonority, intonation, intensity—the shout that the articulations of language and logic have not yet entirely frozen, that is, the aspect of oppressed gesture which remains in all speech, the unique and irreplaceable movement which the generalities of concept and repetition have never finished rejecting. We know what value Artaud attributed to what is called—in the present case, quite incorrectly—onomatopoeia. Glossopoeia, which is neither an imitative language nor a creation of names, takes us back to the borderline of the moment when the word has not yet been born, when articulation is no longer a shout but not yet discourse, when repetition is *almost* impossible, and along with it, language in general: the separation of concept and sound, of signified and signifier, of the pneumatical and the grammatical, the freedom of translation and tradition, the movement of interpretation, the difference between the soul and the body, the master and the slave, God and man, author and actor. This is the eve of the origin of languages, and of the dialogue between theology and humanism whose inextinguishable reoccurrence has never not been maintained by the metaphysics of Western theater.[5]

Thus, it is less a question of constructing a mute stage than of constructing a stage whose clamor has not yet been pacified into words. The word is the cadaver of psychic speech, and along with the language of life itself the "speech before words"[6] must be found again. Gesture and speech have not yet been separated by the logic of representation. "I am adding another language to the spoken language, and I am trying to restore to the language of speech its old magic, its essential spellbinding power, for its mysterious possibilities have been forgotten. When I say I will perform no written play, I mean that I will perform no play based on writing and speech, that in the spectacles I produce there will be a preponderant physical share which could not be captured and written down in the customary language of words, and that even the spoken and written portions will be spoken and written in a new sense" (*TD,* p. 111).

What of this "new sense"? And first, what of this new theatrical writing? This latter will no longer occupy the limited position of simply being the notation of words, but will cover the entire range of this new language: not only phonetic writing and the transcription of speech, but also hieroglyphic writing, the writing in which phonetic elements are coordinated to visual, pictorial, and plastic elements. The notion of hieroglyphics is at the center of the *First Manifesto:* "Once aware of this language in space, language of sounds, cries, lights, onomatopoeia, the theater must organize it into veritable hieroglyphs, with the help of characters and objects, and make use of their symbolism and interconnections in relation to all organs and on all levels" (TD, p. 90).

On the stage of the dream, as described by Freud, speech has the same status. This analogy requires patient meditation. In *The Interpretation of Dreams* and in the *Metapsychological Supplement to the Theory of Dreams* the place and functioning of writing are delimited. Present in dreams, speech can only behave as an element among others, sometimes like a "thing" which the primary process manipulates according to its own economy. "In this process thoughts are transformed into images, mainly of a visual sort; that is to say, word presentations are taken back to the thing-presentations which correspond to them, as if, in general the process were dominated by considerations of *representability* (*Darstellbarkeit*)." "It is very noteworthy how little the dream-work keeps to word-presentations; it is always ready to exchange one word for another till it finds the expression which is most handy for plastic representation" (*SE* 14:228). Artaud too, speaks of a "visual and plastic materialization of speech" (*TD*, p. 69) and of making use of speech "in a concrete and spatial sense" in order to "manipulate it like a solid object, one which overturns and disturbs things" (*TD*, p. 72). And when Freud, speaking of dreams, invokes sculpture and painting, or the primitive painter who, in the fashion of the authors of comic strips, hung "small labels . . . from the mouths of the persons represented, containing in written characters the speeches which the artist despaired of representing pictorially" (*SE* 4:312), we understand what speech can become when it is but an element, a circumscribed site, a circumvented writing within both general writing and the space of representation. This is the structure of the rebus or the hieroglyphic. "The dream-content, on the other hand, is expressed as it were in a pictographic script" (*SE* 4:227). And in an article from 1913: "For in what follows 'speech' must be understood not merely to mean the expression of thought in words but to include the speech of gesture and every other method, such, for instance, as writing, by which mental activity can be expressed . . . . If we reflect that the means of representation in dreams are principally visual images and not words, we shall see that it is even more appropriate to compare dreams with a system of writing than with a language. In fact the interpretation of dreams is completely analogous to the decipherment of an ancient pictographic script such as Egyptian hieroglyphs" (*SE* 13:176–77).[7]

It is difficult to know the extent to which Artaud, who often referred to psychoanalysis, had approached the text of Freud. It is in any event remarkable that he describes the play of speech and of writing on the stage of cruelty according to Freud's very terms, a Freud who at the time was hardly elucidated. Already in the *First Manifesto:*

THE LANGUAGE OF THE STAGE: It is not a question of suppressing the spoken language, but of giving words approximately the importance they have in dreams. Meanwhile new means of recording this language must be found, whether these means belong to musical transcription or to some kind of code. As for ordinary objects, or even the human body, raised to the dignity of signs, it is evident that one can draw one's inspiration from hieroglyphic characters [*TD*, p. 94] . . . . Eternal laws, those of all poetry and all viable language, and, among other things, of Chinese ideograms and ancient Egyptian hieroglyphs. Hence, far from restricting the possibilities of theater and language, on the pretext that I will not perform written plays, I extend the language of the stage and multiply its possibilities [*TD*, p. 111].

As concerns psychoanalysis and especially psychoanalysts, Artaud was no less careful to indicate his distance from those who believe that they can retain discourse with the aid of psychoanalysis, and thereby can wield its initiative and powers of initiation.

For the theater of cruelty is indeed a theater of dreams, but of *cruel* dreams, that is to say, absolutely necessary and determined dreams, dreams calculated and given direction, as opposed to what Artaud believed to be the empirical disorder of spontaneous dreams. The ways and figures of dreams can be mastered. The surrealists read Hervey de Saint-Denys.[8] In this theatrical treatment of dreams, "poetry and science must henceforth be identical" (*TD*, p. 140). To make them such, it is certainly necessary to proceed according to the modern magic that is psychoanalysis. "I propose to bring back into the theater this elementary magic idea, taken up by modern psychoanalysis" (*TD*, p. 80). But no concession must be made to what Artaud believes to be the faltering of dreams and of the unconscious. It is the *law* of dreams that must be produced or reproduced: "I propose to renounce our empiricism of imagery, in which the unconscious furnishes images at random, and which the poet arranges at random too" (ibid.).

Because he wants "to see sparkle and triumph on stage" "whatever is part of the illegibility and magnetic fascination of dreams" (*CW* 2:23), Artaud therefore rejects the psychoanalyst as interpreter, second-remove commentator, hermeneut, or theoretician. He would have rejected a psychoanalytic theater with as much rigor as he condemned psychological theater. And for the same reasons: his rejection of any secret interiority, of the reader, of directive interpretations or of psychodramaturgy. "The *subconscious* will not play any true rule on stage. We've had enough of the confusion engendered between author and audience through the medium of producers and actors. Too bad for analysts, students of the soul and surrealists . . . . We are determined to safeguard the plays we put on against any secret commentary" (*CW* 2:39).[9] By virtue of his situation and his status, the psychoanalyst would belong to the structure of the classical stage, to its societal form, its metaphysics, its religion, etc.

The theater of cruelty thus would not be a theater of the unconscious. Almost the contrary. Cruelty is consciousness, is exposed lucidity. "There is no cruelty without consciousness and without the application of consciousness" (*TD*, p.

102). And this consciousness indeed lives upon a murder, is the consciousness of this murder, as we suggested above. Artaud says this in "The First Letter on Cruelty": "It is consciousness that gives to the exercise of every act of life its blood-red color, its cruel nuance, since it is understood that life is always someone's death" (TD, p. 102).

Perhaps Artaud is also protesting against a certain Freudian description of dreams as the substitutive fulfillment of desire, as the function of vicariousness: through the theater, Artaud wants to return their dignity to dreams and to make of them something more original, more free, more *affirmative* than an activity of displacement. It is perhaps against a certain image of Freudian thought that he writes in the *First Manifesto:* "To consider the theater as a second-hand psychological or moral function, and to believe that dreams themselves have only a substitute function, is to diminish the profound poetic bearing of dreams as well as of the theater" (TD, p. 92).

Finally, a psychoanalytic theater would risk being a desacralizing theater, and thereby would confirm the West in its project and its trajectory. The theater of cruelty is a hieratic theater. Regression toward the unconscious (cf. TD, p. 47) fails if it does not reawaken the sacred, if it is not both the "mystic" experience of "revelation" and the manifestation of life in their first emergence.[10] We have seen the reasons why hieroglyphics had to be substituted for purely phonic signs. It must be added that the latter communicate less than the former with the imagination of the sacred. "And through the hieroglyph of a breath I am able to recover an idea of the sacred theater" (TD, p. 141). A new epiphany of the supernatural and the divine must occur within cruelty. And not despite but thanks to the eviction of God and the destruction of the theater's theological machinery. The divine has been ruined by God. That is to say, by man, who in permitting himself to be separated from Life by God, in permitting himself to be usurped from his own birth, became man by polluting the divinity of the divine. "For far from believing that man invented the supernatural and the divine, I think it is man's age-old intervention which has ultimately corrupted the divine within him" (TD, p. 8). The restoration of divine cruelty, hence, must traverse the murder of God, that is to say, primarily the murder of the man-God.[11]

Perhaps we now can ask, not about the conditions under which a modern theater could be faithful to Artaud, but in what cases it is surely unfaithful to him. What might the themes of infidelity be, even among those who invoke Artaud in the militant and noisy fashion we all know? We will content ourselves with naming these themes. Without a doubt, foreign to the theater of cruelty are:

1. All non-sacred theater.

2. All theater that privileges speech or rather the verb, all theater of words, even if this privilege becomes that of a speech which is self-destructive, which once more becomes gesture of hopeless reoccurrence, a *negative* relation of speech to itself, theatrical nihilism, what is still called the theater of the absurd.

Such a theater would not only be consumed by speech, and would not destroy the functioning of the classical stage, but it also would not be, in the sense understood by Artaud (and doubtless by Nietzsche), an *affirmation*.

3. All *abstract* theater which excludes something from the totality of art, and thus, from the totality of life and its resources of signification: dance, music, volume, depth of plasticity, visible images, sonority, phonicity, etc. An abstract theater is a theater in which the totality of sense and the senses is not consumed. One would incorrectly conclude from this that it suffices to accumulate or to juxtapose all the arts in order to create a total theater addressed to the "total man"[12] (cf. *TD,* p. 123). Nothing could be further from addressing total man than an assembled totality, an artificial and exterior mimicry. Inversely, certain apparent exhaustions of stage technique sometimes more rigorously pursue Artaud's trajectory. Assuming, which we do not, that there is some sense in speaking of a fidelity to Artaud, to something like his "message" (this notion already betrays him), then a rigorous, painstaking, patient and implacable sobriety in the work of destruction, and an economical acuity aiming at the master parts of a still quite solid machine, are more surely imperative, today, than the general mobilization of art and artists, than turbulence or improvised agitation under the mocking and tranquil eyes of the police.

4. All theater of alienation. Alienation only consecrates, with didactic insistence and systematic heaviness, the nonparticipation of spectators (and even of directors and actors) in the creative act, in the irruptive force fissuring the space of the stage. The *Verfremdungseffekt*[13] remains the prisoner of a classical paradox and of "the European ideal of art" which "attempts to cast the mind into an attitude distinct from force but addicted to exaltation" (*TD,* p. 10). Since "in the 'theater of cruelty' the spectator is in the center and the spectacle surrounds him" (*TD,* p. 81), the distance of vision is no longer pure, cannot be abstracted from the totality of the sensory milieu; the infused spectator can no longer *constitute* his spectacle and provide himself with its object. There is no longer spectator or spectacle, but *festival* (cf. *TD,* p. 85). All the limits furrowing classical theatricality (represented/representer, signified/signifier, author/director/actors/spectators, stage/audience, text/interpretation, etc.) were ethico-metaphysical prohibitions, wrinkles, grimaces, rictuses—the symptoms of fear before the dangers of the festival. Within the space of the festival opened by transgression, the distance of representation should no longer be extendable. The festival of cruelty lifts all footlights and protective barriers before the "absolute danger" which is "without foundation": "I must have actors who are first of all beings, that is to say, who on stage are not afraid of the true sensation of the touch of a knife and the convulsions—*absolutely* real for them—of a supposed birth. Mounet-Sully believes in what he does and gives the illusion of it, but he knows that he is behind a protective barrier, me—I suppress the protective barrier" (letter to Roger Blin, Spetember 1945). As regards the festival, as

invoked by Artaud, and the menace of that which is "without foundation," the "happening" can only make us smile: it is to the theater of cruelty what the carnival of Nice might be to the mysteries of Eleusis. This is particularly so due to the fact that the happening substitutes political agitation for the total revolution prescribed by Artaud. The festival must be a political *act*. And the *act* of political revolution is *theatrical*.

5. All nonpolitical theater. We have indeed said that the festival must be a political *act* and not the more or less eloquent, pedagogical, and superintended transmission of a concept or a politico-moral vision of the world. To reflect—which we cannot do here—the political sense of this act and this festival, and the image of society which fascinates Artaud's desire, one should come to invoke (in order to note the greatest difference within the greatest affinity) all the elements in Rousseau which establish communication between the critique of the classical spectacle, the suspect quality of *articulation* in language, the ideal of a public festival substituted for representation, and a certain model of society perfectly present to itself in small communities which render both useless and nefarious all recourse to *representation* at the decisive moments of social life. That is, all recourse to political as well as to theatrical representation, replacement, or delegation. It very precisely could be shown that it is the "representer" that Rousseau suspects in *The Social Contract*, as well as in the *Letter to M. d'Alembert*, where he proposes the replacement of theatrical representations with public festivals lacking all exhibition and spectacle, festivals without "anything to see" in which the spectators themselves would become actors: "But what then will be the objects of these entertainments? . . . Nothing, if you please . . . . Plant a stake crowned with flowers in the middle of a square; gather the people together there, and you will have a festival. Do better yet; let the spectators become an entertainment to themselves; make them actors themselves." [14]

6. All ideological theater, all cultural theater, all communicative, *interpretive* (in the popular and not the Nietzschean sense, of course) theater seeking to transmit a content, or to deliver a message (of whatever nature: political, religious, psychological, metaphysical, etc.) that would make a discourse's meaning intelligible for its listeners;[15] a message that would not be totally exhausted in the *act* and *present tense* of the stage, that would not coincide with the stage, that could be repeated without it. Here we touch upon what seems to be the profound essence of Artaud's project, his historico-metaphysical decision. *Artaud wanted to erase repetition in general.*[16] For him, repetition was evil, and one could doubtless organize an entire reading of his texts around this center. Repetiton separates force, presence, and life from themselves. This separation is the economical and calculating gesture of that which defers itself in order to maintain itself, that which reserves expenditure and surrenders to fear. This power of repetition governed everything that Artaud wished to destroy, and it has several names: God, Being, Dialectics. God is the eternity whose death goes on indef-

initely, whose death, as difference and repetition within life, has never ceased to menace life. It is not the living God, but the Death-God that we should fear. God is Death. "For even the infinite is dead, / infinite is the name of a dead man / who is not dead" (*84*). As soon as there is repetition, God is there, the present holds on to itself and reserves itself, that is to say, eludes itself. "The absolute is not a being and will never be one, for there can be no being without a crime committed against myself, that is to say, without taking from me a being who wanted one day to be god when this is not possible, God being able to manifest himself only all at once, given that he manifests himself an infinite number of times during all the times of eternity as the infinity of times and eternity, which creates perpetuity" (September 1945). Another name of repetition: Being. Being is the form in which the infinite diversity of the forms and forces of life and death can indefinitely merge and be repeated in the word. For there is no word, nor in general a sign, which is not constituted by the possibility of repeating itself. A sign which does not repeat itself, which is not already divided by repetition in its "first time," is not a sign. The signifying referral therefore must be ideal—and ideality is but the assured power of repetition—in order to refer to the same thing each time. This is why Being is the key word of eternal repetition, the victory of God and of Death over life. Like Nietzsche (for example in *The Birth of Philosophy*), Artaud refuses to subsume Life to Being, and inverses the genealogical order: "First to live and to be according to one's soul; the problem of being is only their consequence" (September 1945) "There is no greater enemy of the human body than being." (September 1947) Certain other unpublished texts valorize what Artaud properly calls "the beyond of being" (February 1947), manipulating this expression of Plato's (whom Artaud did not fail to read) in a Nietzschean style. Finally, Dialectics is the movement through which expenditure is reappropriated into presence—it is the economy of repetition. The economy of truth. Repetition *summarizes* negativity, gathers and maintains the past present as truth, as ideality. The truth is always that which can be repeated. Nonrepetition, expenditure that is resolute and without return in the unique time consuming the present, must put an end to fearful discursiveness, to unskirtable ontology, to dialectics, "dialectics [a certain dialectics] being that which finished me" (September 1945)[17]

Dialectics is always that which has finished us, because it is always that which *takes into account* our rejection of it. As it does our affirmation. To reject death as repetition is to affirm death as a present expenditure without return. And inversely. This is a schema that hovers around Nietzsche's repetition of affirmation. Pure expenditure, absolute generosity offering the unicity of the present to death in order to make the present appear *as such,* has already begun to want to maintain the presence of the present, has already opened the book and memory, the thinking of Being as memory. Not to want to maintain the present is to want to preserve that which constitutes its irreplaceable and mortal presence, that within it which cannot be repeated. To consume pure difference with pleasure.

Such, reduced to its bloodless framework, is the matrix of the history of thought conceptualizing itself since Hegel.[18]

The possibility of the theater is the obligatory focal point of this thought which reflects tragedy as repetition. The menace of repetition is nowhere else as well organized as in the theater. Nowhere else is one so close to the stage as the origin of repetition, so close to the primitive repetition which would have to be erased, and only by detaching it from itself as if from its double. Not in the sense in which Artaud spoke of *The Theater and its Double,*[19] but as designating the fold, the interior duplication which steals the simple presence of its present act from the theater, from life, etc., in the irrepressible movement of repetition. "One time" is the enigma of that which has no meaning, no presence, no legibility. Now, for Artaud, the festival of cruelty could take place only *one time:* "Let us leave textual criticism to graduate students, formal criticism to esthetes, and recognize that what has been said is not still to be said; that an expression does not have the same value twice, does not live two lives; that all words, once spoken, are dead and function only at the moment when they are uttered, that a form, once it has served, cannot be used again and asks only to be replaced by another, and that the theater is the only place in the world where a gesture, once made, can never be made the same way twice" (*TD,* p. 75). This is indeed how things appear: theatrical representation is finite, and leaves behind it, behind its actual presence, no trace, no object to carry off. It is neither a book nor a work, but an energy, and in this sense it is the only art of life. "The theater teaches precisely the uselessness of the action which, once done, is not to be done, and the superior use of the state unused by the action and which, *restored,* produces a purification" (*TD,* p. 82). In this sense the theater of cruelty would be the art of difference and of expenditure without economy, without reserve, without return, without history. Pure presence as pure difference. Its act must be forgotten, actively forgotten. Here, one must practice the *aktive Vergesslichkeit* which is spoken of in the second dissertation of *The Genealogy of Morals,* which also explicates "festivity" and "cruelty" (*Grausamkeit*).

Artaud's disgust with nontheatrical writing has the same sense. What inspires this disgust is not, as in the *Phaedrus,* the gesture of the body, the sensory and mnemonic, the hypomnesiac mark exterior to the inscription of truth in the soul, but, on the contrary, writing as the site of the inscription of truth, the other of the living body, writing as ideality, repetition. Plato criticizes writing as a body; Artaud criticizes it as the erasure of the body, of the living gesture which takes place only once. Writing is space itself and the possibility of repetition in general. This is why "We should get rid of our superstitious valuation of texts and written poetry. Written poetry is worth reading once, and then should be destroyed" (*TD,* p. 78).

In thus enumerating the themes of infidelity, once comes to understand very quickly that fidelity is impossible. There is no theater in the world today which fulfills Artaud's desire. And there would be no exception to be made for the attempts made by Artaud himself. He knew this better than any other: the "grammar" of the theater of cruelty, of which he said that it is "to be found," will always remain the inaccessible limit of a representation which is not repetition, of a *re*-presentation which is full presence, which does not carry its double within itself as its death, of a present which does not repeat itself, that is, of a present outside time, a nonpresent. The present offers itself as such, appears, presents itself, opens the stage of time or the time of the stage only by harboring its own intestine difference, and only in the interior fold of its original repetition, in representation. In dialectics.

Artaud knew this well: "a certain dialectics . . . " For if one appropriately conceives the *horizon* of dialectics—outside a conventional Hegelianism—one understands, perhaps, that dialectics is the indefinite movement of finitude, of the unity of life and death, of difference, of original repetition, that is, of the origin of tragedy as the absence of a simple origin. In this sense, dialectics is tragedy, the only possible affirmation to be made against the philosophical or Christian idea of pure origin, against "the spirit of beginnings": "But the spirit of beginnings has not ceased to make me commit idiocies, and I have not ceased to dissociate myself from the spirit of beginnings which is the Christian spirit" (September 1945). What is tragic is not the impossibility but the necessity of repetition.

Artaud knew that the theater of cruelty neither begins nor is completed within the purity of simple presence, but rather is already within representation, in the "second time of Creation," in the conflict of forces which could not be that of a simple origin. Doubtless, cruelty could begin to be practiced within this conflict, but thereby it must also let itself be *penetrated*. The origin is always *penetrated*. Such is the alchemy of the theater.

Perhaps before proceeding further I shall be asked to define what I mean by the archetypal, primitive theater. And we shall thereby approach the very heart of the matter. If in fact we raise the question of the origins and *raison d'être* (or primordial necessity) of the theater, we find, metaphysically, the materialization or rather the exteriorization of a kind of essential drama, already *disposed* and *divided,* not so much as to lose their character as principles, but enough to comprise, in a substantial and active fashion (i.e. resonantly), an infinite perspective of conflicts. To analyze such a drama philosophically is impossible; only poetically . . . . And this essential drama, we come to realize, exists, and in the image of something subtler than Creation itself, something which must be represented as the result of one Will alone—and *without conflict.* We must believe that the essential drama, the one at the root of all the Great Mysteries, is associated with the second phase of Creation, that of difficulty and of the Double, that of matter and the materialization of the idea. It seems indeed that where simplicity and order reign, there can be no theater nor drama, and the true theater, like poetry as

well, though by other means, is born out of a kind of organized anarchy
[*TD,* pp. 50–51].

Primitive theater and cruelty thus also begin by repetition. But if the idea of a
theater without representation, the idea of the impossible, does not help us to
regulate theatrical practice, it does, perhaps, permit us to conceive its origin, eve
and limit, and the horizon of its death. The energy of Western theater thus lets
itself be encompassed within its own possibility, which is not accidental and
serves as a constitutive center and structuring locus for the entire history of the
West. But repetition steals the center and the locus, and what we have just said of
its possibility should prohibit us from speaking both of death as a horizon and of
birth as a past *opening.*

Artaud kept himself as close as possible to the limit: the possibility and
impossibility of pure theater. Presence, in order to be presence and self-presence,
has always already begun to represent itself, has always already been penetrated.
Affirmation itself must be penetrated in repeating itself. Which means that the
murder of the father which opens the history of representation and the space of
tragedy, the murder of the father that Artaud, in sum, wants to repeat at the
greatest proximity to its origin but *only a single time*—this murder is endless and
is repeated indefinitely. It begins by penetrating its own commentary and is
accompanied by its own representation. In which it erases itself and confirms the
transgressed law. To do so, it suffices that there be a sign, that is to say, a
repetition.

Underneath this side of the limit, and in the extent to which he wanted to save
the purity of a presence without interior difference and without repetition (or,
paradoxically amounting to the same thing, the purity of a pure difference),[20]
Artaud also desired the impossibility of the theater, wanted to erase the stage, no
longer wanted to see what transpires in a locality always inhabited or haunted by
the father and subjected to the repetition of murder. Is it not Artaud who wants to
reduce the archi-stage when he writes in the *Here-lies:* "I Antonin Artaud, am
my son, / my father, my mother, / and myself" (*AA,* p. 238)?

That he thereby kept himself at the limit of theatrical possibility, and that he
simultaneously wanted to produce and to annihilate the stage, is what he knew in
the most extreme way. December 1946:

And now I am going to say something which, perhaps,
is going to stupify many people.
I am the enemy
of theater.
I have always been.
As much as I love the theater,
I am, for this very reason, equally its enemy.

We see him immediately afterward: he cannot resign himself to theater as
repetition, and cannot renounce theater as nonrepetition:

The theater is a passionate overflowing
a frightful transfer of forces
   from body
   to body.
This transfer cannot be reproduced twice.
Nothing more impious than the system of the Balinese which consists,
after having produced this transfer one time,
instead of seeking another,
in resorting to a system of particular enchantments
in order to deprive astral photography of the gestures thus obtained.

Theater as repetition of that which does not repeat itself, theater as the original repetition of difference within the conflict of forces in which "evil is the permanent law, and what is good is an effort and already a cruelty added to the other cruelty"—such is the fatal limit of a cruelty which begins with its own representation.

Because it has always already begun, representation therefore has no end. But one can conceive of the closure of that which is without end. Closure is the circular limit within which the repetition of difference infinitely repeats itself. That is to say, closure is its *playing* space. This movement is the movement of the world as play. "And for the absolute life itself is a game" (*OC* 4:282) This play is cruelty as the unity of necessity and chance. "It is chance that is infinite, not god" (*Fragmentations*). This play of life is artistic.[21]

To think the closure of representation is thus to think the cruel powers of death and play which permit presence to be born to itself, and pleasurably to consume itself through the representation in which it eludes itself in its deferral. To think the closure of representation is to think the tragic: not as the representation of fate, but as the fate of representation. Its gratuitous and baseless necessity.

And it is to think why it is *fatal* that, in its closure, representation continues.

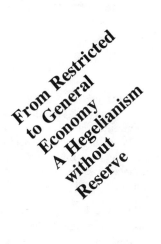

Nine

From Restricted
to General
Economy
A Hegelianism
without
Reserve

He [Hegel] did not know to what extent he was right.

(Georges Bataille)

"Often Hegel seems to me self-evident, but the self-evident is a heavy burden" (*Le coupable*). Why today—even today—are the best readers of Bataille among those for whom Hegel's self-evidence is so lightly borne? So lightly borne that a murmured allusion to given fundamental concepts—the pretext, sometimes, for avoiding the details—or a complacent conventionality, a blindness to the text, an invocation of Bataille's complicity with Nietzsche or Marx, suffice to undo the constraint of Hegel. Perhaps the self-evident would be too heavy to bear, and so a shrug of the shoulders is preferred to discipline. And, contrary to Bataille's experience, this puts one, without seeing or knowing it, *within* the very self-evidence of Hegel one often thinks oneself unburdened of. Misconstrued, treated lightly, Hegelianism only extends its historical domination, finally unfolding its immense enveloping resources without obstacle. Hegelian self-evidence seems lighter than ever at the moment when it finally bears down with its full weight. Bataille had feared this too: heavy, "it will be even more so in the future." And if Bataille considered himself closer to Nietzsche than anyone else, than to anyone else, to the point of identification with him, it was not, in this case, as a motive for simplification:

251

Nietzsche knew of Hegel only the usual vulgarization. The *Genealogy of Morals* is the singular proof of the state of general ignorance in which remained, and remains today, the dialectic of the master and the slave, whose lucidity is blinding.... no one knows anything of him*self* if he has not grasped this movement which determines and limits the successive possibilities of man [*L'experience intérieure* (hereafter *EI*), p. 140, n. 1].

To bear the self-evidence of Hegel, today, would mean this: one must, in every sense, go through the "slumber of reason," the slumber that engenders monsters and then puts them to sleep; this slumber must be effectively traversed so that awakening will not be a ruse of dream. That is to say, again, a ruse of reason. The slumber of reason is not, perhaps, reason put to sleep, but slumber in the form of reason, the vigilance of the Hegelian logos. Reason keeps watch over a deep slumber in which it has an interest. Now, if "evidence received in the slumber of reason loses or will lose the characteristics of wakefulness" (ibid.), then it is necessary, in order to open our eyes (and did Bataille ever want to do otherwise, correctly certain that he was thereby risking death: "the condition in which I *would see* would be to die"), to have spent the night with reason, to have kept watch and to have slept with her: and to have done so throughout the night, until morning, until the other dawn which resembles, even to the point of being taken for it—like daybreak for nightfall—the hour when the philosophical animal can also finally open its eyes. That morning and none other. For at the far reaches of this night something was contrived, blindly, I mean in a discourse, by means of which philosophy, in completing itself, could both include within itself and anticipate all the figures of its beyond, all the forms and resources of its exterior; and could do so in order to keep these forms and resources close to itself by simply taking hold of their enunciation. Except, perhaps, for a certain laughter. And yet.

To laugh at philosophy (at Hegelianism)—such, in effect, is the form of the awakening—henceforth calls for an entire "discipline," an entire "method of meditation" that acknowledges the philosopher's byways, understands his techniques, makes use of his ruses, manipulates his cards, lets him deploy his strategy, appropriates his texts. Then, thanks to this work which has prepared it—and philosophy is work *itself* according to Bataille—but quickly, furtively, and unforeseeably breaking with it, as betrayal or as detachment, drily, laughter bursts out. And yet, in privileged moments that are less moments than the always rapidly sketched movements of experience; rare, discreet and light movements, without triumphant stupidity, far from public view, very close to that at which laughter laughs: close to anguish, first of all, which must not even be called the negative of laughter for fear of once more being sucked in by Hegel's discourse. And one can already foresee, in this prelude, that the *impossible* meditated by Bataille will always have this form: how, after having exhausted the discourse of philosophy, can one inscribe in the lexicon and syntax of a language, our language, which was also the language of philosophy, that which nevertheless exceeds the oppositions of concepts governed by this communal logic? Necessary and impossible, this excess had to fold discourse into strange shapes. And, of course, constrain it to justify itself to Hegel indefinitely. Since more than a century of ruptures, of "surpassings" with or without "overturnings," rarely has a relation to Hegel been so little definable: a complicity without reserve accompanies Hegelian discourse, "takes it seriously" up to the end, without an objection in philosophical form, while, however, a certain burst of laughter exceeds it and destroys its sense, or signals, in any event, the extreme point of "experience" which makes Hegelian discourse dislocate *itself;* and this can be done only through close scrutiny and full knowledge of what one is laughing at.

Bataille, thus, took Hegel seriously, and took absolute knowledge seriously.[1] And to take such a system seriously, Bataille knew, was to prohibit oneself from extracting concepts from it, or from manipulating isolated propositions, drawing effects from them by transportation into a discourse foreign to them: "Hegel's thoughts are interdependent to the point of it being impossible to grasp their meaning, if not in the necessity of the movement which constitutes their coherence" (*EI,* p. 193). Bataille doubtless put into question the idea or meaning of the chain in Hegelian reason, but did so by thinking the chain as such, in its totality, without ignoring its internal rigor. One could describe as a scene, but we will not do so here, the history of Bataille's relations to Hegel's different faces: the one that assumed "absolute rending";[2] the one who "thought he would go mad";[3] the one who, between Wolff and Comte and "the clouds of professors" at the "village wedding" that is philosophy, asks himself no questions, while "alone, his head aching, Kierkegaard questions";[4] the one who "towards the end of his life," "no longer put the problem to himself," "repeated his courses and played cards;" the "portrait of the aged Hegel" before which, as "in reading the *Phenomenology of the Mind,*" "one cannot help being seized by freezing impression of completion."[5] Finally, the Hegel of the "small comic recapitulation."[6]

But let us leave the stage and the players. The drama is first of all textual. In his interminable explication with Hegel, Bataille doubtless had only a restricted and indirect access to the texts themselves.[7] This did not prevent him from bringing his reading and his question to bear on the crucial point of the decision. Taken one by one and immobilized outside their syntax, all of Bataille's concepts are Hegelian. We must acknowledge this without stopping here. For if one does not grasp the rigorous effect of the trembling to which he submits these concepts, the new configuration into which he displaces and reinscribes them, barely reaching it however, one would conclude, according to the case at hand, that Bataille is Hegelian or anti-Hegelian, or that he has muddled Hegel. One would be deceived each time. And one would miss the formal law which, necessarily enunciated by Bataille in a nonphilosophical mode, has constrained the relationship of all his concepts to those of Hegel, and through Hegel's concepts to the concepts of the entire history of metaphysics. All of Bataille's concepts, and not only those to which we must limit ourselves here, in order to reconstitute the enunciation of this law.

The Epoch of Meaning: Lordship and Sovereignty

To begin with, does not *sovereignty,* at first glance, translate the *lordship* (*Herrschaft*) of the *Phenomenology?*[8] The operation of lordship indeed consists in, writes Hegel, "showing that it is fettered to determinate existence, that it is not bound at all by the particularity everywhere characteristic of existence as such, and is not tied up with life" (Hegel, p. 232). Such an "operation" (this word, constantly employed by Bataille to designate the privileged moment or the act of sovereignty, was the current translation of the word *Tun,* which occurs so frequently in the chapter on the dialectic of the master and the slave) thus amounts to risking, putting at stake (*mettre en jeu, wagen, daransetzen; mettre en jeu* is one of Bataille's most fundamental and frequently used expressions) the entirety of one's own life. The servant is the man who does not put his life at stake, the man who wants to conserve his life, wants to be conserved (*servus*). By raising oneself above life, by looking at death directly, one acceeds to lordship: to the for-itself [*pour soi, für sich*], to freedom, to recognition. Freedom must go through the putting at stake of life (*Daransetzen des Lebens*). The lord is the man who has had the strength to endure the anguish of death and to maintain the work of death. Such, according to Bataille, is the center of Hegelianism. The "principal text" would be the one, in the *Preface* to the *Phenomenology,* which places knowledge "at the height of death."[9]

The rigorous and subtle corridors through which the dialectic of master and slave passes are well known. They cannot be summarized without being mistreated. We are interested, here, in the essential displacements to which they are submitted as they are reflected in Bataille's thought. And we are interested, first of all, in the difference between lordship and sovereignty. It cannot even be said that this difference has a sense: it is the *difference of sense,* the *unique* interval which separates meaning from a certain non-meaning. Lordship has a meaning. The putting at stake of life is a moment in the constitution of meaning, in the presentation of essence and truth. It is an obligatory stage in the history of self-consciousness and phenomenality, that is to say, in the presentation of meaning. For history—that is, meaning—to form a continuous chain, to be woven, the master must *experience his truth.* This is possible only under two conditions which cannot be separated: the master must stay alive in order to enjoy what he has won by risking his life; and, at the end of this progression so admirably described by Hegel, the "truth of the independent consciousness is

accordingly the consciousness of the bondsman'' (Hegel, p. 237). And when
servility becomes lordship, it keeps within it the trace of its repressed origin,
''being a consciousness within itself (*zurückgedrängtes Bewusstsein*), it will
enter into itself, and change round into real and true independence'' (ibid.). It is
this dissymmetry, this absolute privilege given to the slave, that Bataille did not
cease to meditate. The truth of the master is in the slave; and the slave become a
master remains a ''repressed'' slave. Such is the condition of meaning, of history
of discourse, of philosophy, etc. The master is in relation to himself, and self-
consciousness is constituted, only through the mediation of servile consciousness
in the movement of recognition; but simultaneously through the mediation of the
thing, which for the slave is initially the essentiality that he cannot immediately
negate in pleasurable consumption, but can only work upon, ''elaborate'' (*bear-
beiten*); which consists in inhibiting (*hemmen*) his desire, in delaying (*aufhalten*)
the disappearance of the thing. To stay alive, to maintain oneself in life, to work,
to defer pleasure, to limit the stakes, to have *respect* for death at the very moment
when one looks *directly* at it—such is the servile condition of mastery and of the
entire history it makes possible.

Hegel clearly had proclaimed the necessity of the master's retaining the life
that he exposes to risk. Without this economy of life, the ''trial by death, however, cancels both the truth which was to result from it, and therewith the
certainty of self altogether'' (Hegel, p. 233). To rush headlong into death pure
and simple is thus to risk the absolute loss of meaning, in the extent to which
meaning necessarily traverses the truth of the master and of self-consciousness.
One risks losing the effect and profit of meaning which were the very *stakes* one
hoped *to win*. Hegel called this mute and nonproductive death, this death pure
and simple, *abstract negativity,* in opposition to ''the negation characteristic of
consciousness, which cancels in such a way that it preserves and maintains what
is sublated (*Die Negation des Bewusstseins welches so* aufhebt, *dass es das
Aufgehobene* aufbewahrt *und* erhält), and thereby survives its being sublated
(und hiermit sein Aufgehobenwerden überlebt). In this experience self-consciousness becomes aware that *life* is as essential to it as pure self-consciousness''
(Hegel, p. 234).

Burst of laughter from Bataille. Through a ruse of life, that is, of reason, life
has thus stayed alive. Another concept of life had been surreptitiously put in its
place, to remain there, never to be exceeded, any more than reason is ever
exceeded (for, says *L'erotisme,* ''by definition, the *excess* is outside reason'').
This life is not natural life, the biological existence put at stake in lordship, but an
essential life that is welded to the first one, holding it back, making it work for
the constitution of self-consciousness, truth, and meaning. Such is the truth of
life. Through this recourse to the *Aufhebung,* which conserves the stakes, remains
in control of the play, limiting it and elaborating it by giving it form and meaning
(*Die Arbeit* ... *bildet*), this economy of life restricts itself to conservation, to

circulation and self-reproduction as the reproduction of meaning; henceforth, everything covered by the name lordship collapses into comedy. The independence of self-consciousness[10] becomes laughable at the moment when it liberates itself by enslaving itself, when it starts to *work,* that is, when it enters into dialectics. Laughter alone exceeds dialectics and the dialectician: it bursts out only on the basis of an absolute renunciation of meaning, an absolute risking of death, what Hegel calls abstract negativity. A negativity that never takes place, that never *presents* itself, because in doing so it would start to work again. A laughter that literally never *appears,* because it exceeds phenomenality in general, the absolute possibility of meaning. And the word ''laughter'' itself must be read in a burst, as its nucleus of meaning bursts in the direction of the *system* of the sovereign operation (''drunkenness, erotic effusion, sacrificial effusion, poetic effusion, heroic behavior, anger, absurdity,'' etc., cf. *Méthode de meditation*). This burst of laughter makes the difference between lordship and sovereignty shine, without *showing* it however and, above all, without saying it. Sovereignty, as we shall verify, is more and less than lordship, more or less free than it, for example; and what we are saying about the predicate ''freedom'' can be extended to every characteristic of lordship. Simultaneously more and less a lordship than lordship, sovereignty is totally other. Bataille pulls it out of dialectics. He withdraws it from the horizon of meaning and knowledge. And does so to such a degree that, despite the characteristics that make it resemble lordship, sovereignty is no longer a figure in the continuous chain of phenomenology. Resembling a phenomenological figure, trait for trait, sovereignty is the absolute alteration of all of them. And this difference would not be produced if the analogy was limited to a given abstract characteristic. Far from being an abstract negativity, sovereignty (the absolute degree of putting at stake), rather, must make the seriousness of meaning appear as an abstraction inscribed in play. Laughter, which constitutes sovereignty in its relation to death, is not a negativity, as has been said.[11] And it laughs at itself, a ''major'' laughter laughs at a ''minor'' laughter, for the sovereign operation also needs life—the life that welds the two lives together—in order to be in relation to itself in the pleasurable consumption of itself. Thus, it must simulate, after a fashion, the absolute risk, and it must laugh at this simulacrum. In the comedy that it thereby plays for itself, the burst of laughter is the almost-nothing into which meaning sinks, absolutely. ''Philosophy,'' which ''is work,''[12] can do or say nothing about this laughter, for it should have ''considered laughter *first*'' (ibid.). This is why laughter is absent from the Hegelian system, and not in the manner of a negative or abstract side of it. ''In the 'system' poetry, laughter, ecstasy are nothing. Hegel hastily gets rid of them: he knows no other aim than knowledge. To my eyes, his immense fatigue is linked to his horror of the blind spot'' (*EI,* p. 142). What is laughable is the *submission* to the self-evidence of meaning, to the force of this imperative: that there must be meaning, that nothing must be definitely lost in death, or further, that death should receive the signification of "abstract negativity," that a work must always be possible which, because it defers enjoyment, confers meaning, seriousness, and truth upon the "putting at stake." This submission is the essence and element of philosophy, of Hegelian ontologics. Absolute comicalness is the anguish experienced when confronted by expenditure on lost funds, by the absolute sacrifice of meaning: a sacrifice without return and without reserves. The notion of *Aufhebung* (the speculative concept par excellence, says Hegel, the concept whose untranslatable privilege is wielded by the German language)[13] is laughable in that it signifies the *busying* of a discourse losing its breath as it reappropriates all negativity for itself, as it works the "putting at stake" into an *investment,* as it *amortizes* absolute expenditure; and as it gives meaning to death, thereby simultaneously blinding itself to the baselessness of the nonmeaning from which the basis of meaning is drawn, and in which this basis of meaning is exhausted. To be indifferent to the comedy of the *Aufhebung,* as was Hegel, is to blind oneself to the experience of the sacred, to the heedless sacrifice of presence and meaning. Thus is sketched out a figure of experience—but can one still use these two words?—irreducible to any phenomenology, a figure which finds itself *displaced* in phenomenology, like laughter in philosophy of the mind, and which mimes through sacrifice the absolute risk of death. Through this mime it simultaneously produces the risk of absolute death, the feint through which this risk can be lived, the impossibility of reading a sense or a truth in it, and the laughter which is confused, in the simulacrum, with the opening of the sacred. Describing this simulacrum, unthinkable for philosophy, philosophy's blind spot, Bataille must, of course, say it, feign to say it, in the Hegelian logos:

> I will speak later about the profound differences between the man of sacrifice, who operates ignorant (unconscious) of the ramifications of what he is doing, and the Sage (Hegel), who surrenders to a knowledge that, in his own eyes, is absolute. Despite these differences, it is always a question of manifesting the Negative (and always in a concrete form, that is, at the heart of the Totality whose constitutive elements are inseparable). The privileged manifestation of Negativity is death, but death, in truth, reveals nothing. In principle, death reveals to Man his natural, animal being, but the revelation never takes place. For once the animal being that has supported him is dead, the human being himself has ceased to exist. For man finally to be revealed to himself he would have to die, but he would have to do so while living— while watching himself cease to be. In other words, death itself would have to become (self) consciousness at the very moment when it annihilates conscious being. In a sense this is what takes place (or at least is on the point of taking place, or which takes place in a fugitive, ungraspable manner) by means of a subterfuge. In sacrifice, the sacrificer identifies with the animal struck by death. Thus he dies while watching himself die, and even, after a fashion, dies of his own volition, as one with the sacrificial arm. But this is

a comedy! Or at least it would be a comedy if there were some other method of revealing the encroachment of death upon the living; this completion of the finite being, which alone accomplishes and can alone accomplish *his* Negativity which kills him, *finishes* him and definitively suppresses him . . . . Thus it is necessary, at any cost, for man to live at the moment when he truly dies, or it is necessary for him to live with the impression of truly dying. This difficulty foreshadows the necessity of *spectacle,* or generally of *representation,* without the repetition of which we could remain foreign to and ignorant of death, as animals apparently remain. In effect, nothing is less animal than the fiction, more or less removed from reality, of death.[14]

Only the accent on simulacrum and subterfuge interrupt the Hegelian continuity of this text. Further on, gaiety marks the difference:

In juxtaposing it with sacrifice and thereby with the primary theme of *representation* (art, festivals, spectacles), I have wanted to show that Hegel's reaction is the fundamental human behavior . . . it is par excellence the expression that tradition has repeated infinitely . . . . It was essential for Hegel to *become conscious* of Negativity as such, to grasp its horror, in this case the horror of death, while supporting the work of death and looking at it full in the face. In this fashion, Hegel is opposed less to those who "draw back" than to those who say: "it is nothing." He seems most removed from those who react gaily. I am insisting upon the opposition of the naïve attitude to that of the *absolute* wisdom of Hegel, wanting to make the opposition between them emerge as clearly as possible, after their apparent similarity. I am, in effect, not sure that the least *absolute* of the two attitudes is the naive one. I will cite a paradoxical example of a gay reaction before the work of death. The Irish and Welsh custom of the wake is little known, but was still observed at the end of the last century. It is the subject of Joyce's last work, *Finnegan's Wake,* Finnegan's funeral vigil (but the reading of this famous novel is at least uneasy). In Wales, the coffin was placed *open* and upright in the place of honor of the house. The dead person was dressed in his Sunday best and his top hat. His family invited all his friends, who increasingly honored the one who had left them as they danced on and drank stronger toasts to his health. In question is the death of an *other,* but in such cases the death of the other is always the image of one's own death. No one could enjoy himself thus, if he did not accept one condition: the dead man, who is an other, is assumed to be in agreement, and thus the dead man that the drinker will become, in turn, will have no other meaning than the first one [*Hegel, la mort,* p. 38].

This gaiety is not part of the economy of life, does not correspond "to the desire to deny the existence of death," although it is as close to this desire as possible. Gaiety is not the convulsion that follows anguish, the minor laugh which melts away at the moment when one has had "a close call," and which is in relation to anguish along the lines of the relationship of positive to negative:

On the contrary, gaiety, tied to the work of death, fills me with anguish, is accentuated by an anguish and, in exchange, exasperates this anguish: finally, gay anguish, anguished gaiety present me with "absolute rending" in an aspic in which it is my joy that finally rends me asunder, but in which abatement would follow if I was totally torn apart, without measure [*Hegel, la mort,* p. 39].

The blind spot of Hegelianism, *around* which can be organized the representation of meaning, is the *point* at which destruction, suppression, death and sacrifice constitute so irreversible an expenditure, so radical a negativity—here we would have to say an expenditure and a negativity *without reserve*—that they can no longer be determined as negativity in a process or a system. In discourse (the unity of process and system), negativity is always the underside and accomplice of positivity. Negativity cannot be spoken of, nor has it ever been except in this fabric of meaning. Now, the sovereign operation, the *point of nonreserve,* is neither positive nor negative. It cannot be inscribed in discourse, except by crossing out predicates or by practicing a contradictory superimpression that then exceeds the logic of philosophy.[15] Even while taking into account their value as ruptures, it could be shown, in this respect, that the immense revolutions of Kant and Hegel only reawakened or revealed the most permanent philosophical determination of negativity (with all the concepts systematically entwined around it in Hegel: ideality, truth, meaning, time, history, etc.). The immense revolution consisted—it is almost tempting to say consisted *simply*—in taking the negative *seriously.* In giving meaning to its labor. Now, Bataille does not take the negative seriously. But he must mark his discourse to show that he is not, to that extent, returning to the positive and pre-Kantian metaphysics of full presence. In his discourse he must mark the point of no return of destruction, the instance of an expenditure without reserve which no longer leaves us the resources with which to think of this expenditure as negativity. For negativity is a *resource.* In naming the without-reserve of absolute expenditure "abstract negativity," Hegel, through *precipitation,* blinded himself to that which he had laid bare under the rubric of negativity. And did so through precipitation toward the seriousness of meaning and the security of knowledge. This is why "he did not know to what extent he was right." And was wrong for being right, for having triumphed over the negative. To go "to the end" both of "absolute rending" and of the negative without "measure," without reserve, is not progressively to pursue *logic* to the point at which, *within discourse,* the *Aufhebung* (discourse itself) makes logic collaborate with the constitution and interiorizing memory of meaning, with *Erinnerung.* On the contrary, it is convulsively to tear apart the negative side, that which makes it the reassuring *other* surface of the positive; and it is to exhibit within the negative, in an instant, that which can no longer be called negative. And can no longer be called negative precisely because it has no reserved underside, because it can no longer permit itself to be converted into positivity, because it can no longer *collaborate* with the continuous linking-up of meaning, concept, time and truth in discourse; because it literally can no longer *labor* and let itself be interrogated as the "work of the negative." Hegel saw this without seeing it, showed it while concealing it. Thus, he must be followed to the end, without reserve, to the point of agreeing with him against himself and of wresting his discovery from the too *conscientious* interpretation he gave of it. No more than any other, the Hegelian text is not made of a piece. While respecting its faultless coherence, one can decompose its strata and show that it *interprets itself:* each proposition is an interpretation submitted to an interpretive decision. The necessity of *logical* continuity is the decision or interpretive milieu of all Hegelian interpretations. In interpreting negativity as labor, in betting for discourse, meaning, history, etc., Hegel has bet against play, against chance. He has blinded himself to the possibility of his own bet, to the fact that the conscientious suspension of play (for example, the passage through the certitude of oneself and through lordship as the independence of self-consciousness) was itself a phase of play; and to the fact that play *includes* the work of meaning or the meaning of work, and includes them not in terms of *knowledge,* but in terms of *inscription:* meaning is a *function* of play, is inscribed in a certain place in the configuration of a meaningless play.

Since no logic governs, henceforth, the meaning of interpretation, because logic is an interpretation, Hegel's own interpretation can be reinterpreted—against him. This is what Bataille does. Reinterpretation is a simulated repetition of Hegelian discourse. In the course of this repetition a barely perceptible displacement disjoints all the articulations and penetrates all the points welded together by the imitated discourse. A trembling spreads out which then makes the entire old shell crack.

> In effect, if Hegel's attitude opposes scientific consciousness and an endless ordering of discursive thought to the naïveté of sacrifice, this consciousness and this ordering still have a point of obscurity: it could not be said that Hegel misconstrued the "moment" of sacrifice: this "moment" is included, implied in the entire movement of the *Phenomenology,* in which it is the Negativity of death, insofar as man assumes it, that makes a man of the human animal. But not having seen that sacrifice by itself bore witness to the *entire* movement of death, the Preface to the *Phenomenology* was first of all *initial* and *universal*—he did not know to what extent he was right— with what exactitude he described the movement of Negativity [*Hegel, la mort,* pp. 35–36].

In *doubling* lordship, sovereignty does not *escape* dialectics. It could not be said that it extracts itself from dialectics like a morsel of dialectics which has suddenly become independent through a process of decision and tearing away. Cut off from dialectics in this way, sovereignty would be made into an abstract negation, and would consolidate ontologics. Far from interrupting dialectics, history, and the movement of meaning, sovereignty provides the economy of reason with its

element, its milieu, its unlimiting boundaries of non-sense. Far from suppressing
the dialectical synthesis,[16] it inscribes this synthesis and makes it function within
the sacrifice of meaning. It does not suffice to risk death if the putting at stake is
not permitted to take off, as chance or accident, but is rather invested as the work
of the negative. Sovereignty must still sacrifice lordship and, thus, the *presentation* of the meaning of death. For meaning, when lost to discourse, is absolutely
destroyed and consumed. For the meaning of meaning, the dialectic of the senses
and sense, of the sensory and the concept, the meaningful unity of the word
"sense," to which Hegel was so attentive,[17] has always been linked to the
possibility of discursive signification. In sacrificing meaning, sovereignty sub-
merges the possibility of discourse: not simply by means of an interruption, a
caesura, or an interior wounding of discourse (an abstract negativity), but,
through such an opening, by means of an irruption suddenly uncovering the limit
of discourse and the beyond of absolute knowledge.

To be sure, Bataille sometimes opposes poetic, ecstatic sacred speech to
"significative discourse" ("But intelligence, the *discursive thought* of Man,
developed as a function of servile work. Only sacred, poetic speech, limited to
the level of impotent beauty, kept the power of manifesting full sovereignty.
Sacrifice is a *sovereign,* autonomous way of being only in the extent to which it is
not informed by *significative* discourse." *Hegel, la mort,* p. 40), but this sovereign
speech is not *another* discourse, another chain unwound alongside significative
discourse. There is only one discourse, it is significative, and here one cannot get
around Hegel. The poetic or the ecstatic is that *in every discourse* which can open
itself up to the absolute loss of its sense, to the (non-)base of the sacred, of
nonmeaning, of un-knowledge or of play, to the swoon from which it is reawakened by a throw of the dice. What is poetic in sovereignty is announced in "the
moment when poetry renounces *theme* and meaning" (*EI,* p. 239). It is only
announced in this renunciation, for, given over to "play without rules," poetry
risks letting itself be domesticated, "subordinated," better than ever. This risk is
properly *modern.* To avoid it, poetry must be "accompanied by an affirmation of
sovereignty" "which provides," Bataille says in an admirable, untenable formulation which could serve as the heading for everything we are attempting to
reassemble here as the form and torment of his writing, "the commentary on its
absence of meaning." Without which poetry would be, in the worst of cases,
subordinated and, in the best of cases, *"inserted."* For then, "laughter, drunkenness, sacrifice and poetry, eroticism itself, subsist autonomously, in a reserve, *inserted* into a sphere, *like children in a house.* Within their limits they are
minor sovereigns who cannot contest the *empire* of activity" (ibid.). It is within
the interval between *subordination, insertion,* and *sovereignty* that one should
examine the relations between literature and revolution, such as Bataille conceived them in the course of his explication with Surrealism. The apparent
ambiguity of his judgments on poetry is included within the configuration of

these three concepts. The poetic image is not *subordinated* to the extent that it "leads from the known to the unknown;" but poetry is almost entirely fallen poetry in that it retains, in order to maintain itself within them, the metaphors that it has certainly torn from the "servile domain," but has immediately "refused to the inner ruination which is the access to the unknown." "It is unfortunate to possess no more than ruins, but this is not any longer to possess nothing; it is to keep in one hand what the other gives."[18] An operation that is still Hegelian.

As a manifestation of meaning, discourse is thus the loss of sovereignty itself. Servility is therefore only the desire for meaning: a *proposition* with which the history of philosophy is confused; a proposition that determines work as the meaning of meaning, and *techne* as the unfolding of truth; a proposition powerfully reassembled in the Hegelian moment, and a proposition that Bataille, in the wake of Nietzsche, wanted to bring to the point of enunciation, and whose denunciation he wished to wrest from the non-basis of an inconceivable nonsense, finally placing it within major play. The minor play consisting in still attributing a meaning, within discourse, to the absence of meaning.[19]

The Two Forms of Writing

These judgments should lead to silence yet I write. This is not paradoxical (*EI*, p. 89)

But we must speak. "The inadequation of all speech ... at least, must be said,"[20] in order to maintain sovereignty, which is to say, after a fashion, in order to lose it, in order still to reserve the possibility not of its meaning but of its nonmeaning; in order to distinguish it, through this impossible "commentary," from all negativity. We must find a speech which maintains silence. Necessity of the impossible: to say in language—the language of servility—that which is not servile. "That which is not servile is unspeakable . . . . The idea of silence (which is the inaccessible) is disarming! I cannot speak of an absence of meaning, except by giving it a meaning it does not have. Silence is broken because I have spoken. Some *lamma sabachtani* always ends history, and cries out our total inability to keep still: I must give a meaning to that which does not have one: in the end, being is given to us as impossible" (*EI*, p. 215). If the word *silence* "among all words," is "the most perverse or the most poetic," it is because in pretending to silence meaning, it *says* nonmeaning, it slides and it erases itself, does not maintain itself, silences *itself,* not as silence, but as speech. This sliding simultaneously betrays discourse and nondiscourse. It can be imposed upon us, but sovereignty can also play upon it in order rigorously to betray the meaning within meaning, the discourse within discourse. "We must find," Bataille explains to us, in choosing "*silence*" as "an example of a sliding word," "words" and "objects" which "make us slide" ... (*EI*, p. 29). Toward what? Toward other words, other objects, of course, which announce sovereignty.

This sliding is risky. But since it has this orientation, what it risks is meaning and the loss of sovereignty in the figure of discourse. It risks *making sense,* risks agreeing to the reasonableness of reason, of philosophy, of Hegel, who is always right, as soon as one opens one's mouth in order to articulate meaning. In order to run this risk within language, in order to save that which does not want to be saved—the possibility of play and of absolute risk—we must redouble language and have recourse to ruses, to stratagems, to simulacra.[21] To masks: "That which is not servile is unspeakable: a reason for laughing, for . . . : the same holds for ecstasy. Whatever is not useful must be hidden (under a mask)" (*EI,* p. 214). In speaking "at the limit of silence," we must organize a strategy and "find [words] which reintroduce—at a point—the sovereign silence which interrupts articulated language."

Since it excludes articulated language, sovereign silence is therefore, *in a certain fashion,* foreign to difference as the source of signification. It seems to erase discontinuity, and this is how we must, in effect, understand the necessity of the *continuum* which Bataille unceasingly invokes, just as he does *communication.*[22] The *continuum* is the privileged experience of a sovereign operation transgressing the limit of discursive difference. But—and here we are touching upon, as concerns the movement of sovereignty, the point of greatest ambiguity and greatest instability—this *continuum* is not the plenitude of meaning or of presence, as this plenitude is *envisaged* by metaphysics. Pushing itself toward the nonbasis of negativity and of expenditure, the experience of the *continuum* is also the experience of absolute difference, of a difference which would no longer be the one that Hegel had conceived more profoundly than anyone else: the difference in the service of presence, at work for (the) history (of meaning). The difference between Hegel and Bataille is the difference between these two differences. This enables one to dispel the equivocality which might weigh upon the concepts of *communication, continuum,* or *instant.* These concepts, which *seem to be identical to* each other like the accomplishing of presence, in fact mark and sharpen the incision of difference. "A fundamental principle is expressed as follows: 'communication' cannot take place from one full and intact being to another: it requires beings who have put the being within themselves *at stake,* have placed it at the limit of death, of nothingness" (*Sur Nietzsche*). And the *instant*—the temporal mode of the sovereign operation—is not a *point* of full and unpenetrated presence: it slides and *eludes* us between two presences; it is difference as the affirmative elusion of presence. It does not give itself but is *stolen,* carries itself off in a movement which is simultaneously one of violent effraction and of vanishing flight. The instant is the *furtive:* "Un-knowledge implies at once fundamentally anguish, but also the suppression of anguish. Henceforth, it becomes possible furtively to undergo the furtive experience that I call the experience of the instant" (*Conférences sur le Non-savoir*).

Words, therefore, we must "find which reintroduce—at a point—the sovereign silence which interrupts articulated language." Since it is a certain *sliding* that is in question, as we have seen, what must be found, no less than the word, is the point, the *place in a pattern* at which a word drawn from the old language will start, by virtue of having been placed there and by virtue of having received such an impulsion, to slide and to make the entire discourse slide. A certain strategic twist must be imprinted upon language; and this strategic twist, with a violent and sliding, furtive, movement must inflect the old corpus in order to relate its syntax and its lexicon to major silence. And to the privileged moment of the sovereign *operation*, "even if it took place only once," rather than to the concept or meaning of sovereignty.

An absolutely *unique relation:* of a language to a sovereign silence which *tolerates no relations*, tolerates no symmetry with that which tilts itself and slides in order to be related to it. A relation, however, which must rigorously, *scientifically*, place into a common syntax both the subordinated significations and the operation which is nonrelation, which has no signification and freely keeps itself outside syntax. Relations must scientifically be related to nonrelations, knowledge to unknowledge. "The sovereign operation, even if it were possible only once, the science relating objects of thought to sovereign moments is possible" (*Méthode de méditation*). "Henceforth, an ordered reflection, founded on the abandoning of knowledge, begins" (*Conférences*).

This will be even more difficult, if not impossible, in that sovereignty, since it is not lordship, cannot govern this scientific discourse in the manner of a founding basis or a principle of responsibility. Like lordship, sovereignty certainly makes itself independent through the putting at stake of life; it is attached to nothing and conserves nothing. But, differing from Hegelian lordship, it does not even want to maintain itself, collect itself, or collect the profits from itself or from its own risk; it "cannot even be defined as a possession." "I hold to it, but would I hold to it as much if I was not certain that I could just as well laugh at it?" (*Méthode de méditation*). At stake in the operation, therefore, is not a self-consciousness, an ability to be near oneself, to maintain and to watch oneself. We are not in the element of phenomenology. And this can be recognized in the primary characteristic—illegible within philosophical logic—that sovereignty *does not govern itself.* And does not govern in general: it governs neither others, nor things, nor discourses in order to produce meaning. This is the first obstacle in the way of this science which, according to Bataille, must relate its objects to sovereign moments and which, like every science, requires order, relatedness and the difference between the original and the derivative. The *Méthode de méditation* does not hide the "obstacle" (the expression is Bataille's): "Not only is the sovereign operation not subordinate to anything, but it makes nothing subordinate to itself, is indifferent to any possible results; if afterward I wish to pursue the reduction of subordinate thought to sovereign thought, I may do so, but whatever is authentically sovereign is not concerned with this, and at every moment disposes of me otherwise" (p. 283).

Once sovereignty has to attempt to make someone or something subordinate to itself, we know that it would be retaken by dialectics, would be subordinate to the slave, to the thing and to work. It would fail for having wanted to be victorious, and for having alleged that it kept the upper hand. Lordship, on the contrary, becomes sovereign when it ceases to fear failure and is lost as the absolute victim of its own sacrifice.[23] Master and sovereign thus fail equally,[24] and both succeed in their failure, the one by giving it meaning through subjugation to the mediation of the slave—which is also to fail for having lost failure— and the other by failing absolutely, which is simultaneously to lose the very meaning of failure by gaining nonservility. This almost imperceptible difference, which is not even the symmetry of an upper and a lower side, should regulate all the "slidings" of sovereign writing. It should *cut into* the *identity* of sovereignty which is *always in question*. For sovereignty has no identity, is not *self, for itself, toward itself, near itself*. In order not to govern, that is to say, in order not to be subjugated, it *must* subordinate nothing (direct object), that is to say, be subordinated to *nothing or no one* (servile mediation of the indirect object): it must expend itself without reserve, lose itself, lose consciousness, lose all memory of itself and all the interiority of itself; as opposed to *Erinnerung,* as opposed to the avarice which assimilates meaning, it must *practice forgetting,* the *aktive Vergesslichkeit* of which Nietzsche speaks; and, as the ultimate subversion of lordship, it must no longer seek to be recognized.[25]

The renunciation of recognition simultaneously prescribes and prohibits writing. Or rather, discerns *two* forms of *writing*. It forbids the form that *projects* the trace, and through which, as the writing of lordship, the will seeks to maintain itself within the trace, seeks to be recognized within it and to reconstitute the presence of itself. This is servile writing as well; Bataille, therefore, scorned it. But this scorned servility of writing is not the servility condemned by tradition since Plato. The latter has in mind servile writing as an irresponsible *techne,* because the presence of the person who pronounced discourse has disappeared within it.[26] Bataille, on the contrary, has in mind the servile project of serving life—the phantom of life—in presence. In both cases, it is true, a certain death is feared, and this complicity demands consideration. The problem is even more difficult in that sovereignty simultaneously assigns itself another form of writing: the one that produces the trace as trace. This latter is a trace only if presence is irremediably eluded in it, from its initial promise, and only if it constitutes itself as the possibility of absolute erasure. An unerasable trace is not a trace. We would thus have to reconstruct the *system of Bataille's propositions on writing,* his propositions on these two relations—let us call them minor and major—to the trace.

1. In one whole group of texts, the sovereign renunciation of recognition enjoins the erasure of the written text. For example, the erasure of poetic writing

as minor writing:

> This sacrifice of reason is apparently imaginary, it has neither a bloody con-
> sequence, nor anything analogous. It nevertheless differs from poetry in that
> it is total, holds back no enjoyment, except through arbitrary sliding, which
> cannot be maintained, or through abandoned laughter. If it leaves behind a
> chance survivor, it does so unbeknownst to itself, like the flower of the
> fields after the harvest. This strange sacrifice which supposes an advanced
> state of megalomania—we feel ourselves become God—nonetheless has or-
> dinary consequences in one case: if enjoyment is concealed by sliding, and
> megalomania is not entirely consumed, we remain condemned to make our-
> selves "recognized," to want to be a God for the crowd; a condition favor-
> able to madness, but to nothing else . . . . If one goes to the end, one must
> erase oneself, undergo solitude, suffer harshly from it, renounce being *rec-
> ognized:* one must be there as if absent, deranged, and submit without will
> or hope, being elsewhere. Thought (because of what it has at its base) must
> be buried alive. I publish this knowing it misconstrued in advance, necessar-
> ily so . . . . I can do nothing, and it along with me, but sink into non-sense to
> this degree. Thought ruins, and its destruction is incommunicable to the
> crowd; it is addressed to the least weak [*EI,* p. 199].

The sovereign operation *engages* these developments: they are the
residues both of a trace left in memory and of the subsistence of functions;
but to the extent that it occurs, the sovereign operation is indifferent, and
defies these residues [*EI,* p. 235].

or, further:

> The survival of that which is written is the survival of the mummy [*Le
> coupable* p. 146].

2. But there is a sovereign form of writing which, on the contrary, must interrupt
the servile complicity of speech and meaning. "I write in order to annihilate the
play of subordinate operations within myself" (*EI,* p. 242).

The putting at stake, the one which exceeds lordship, is therefore the *space of
writing;* it is played out between minor writing and major writing, both unknown
to the master, the latter more than the former, the major play more than the
minor play ("For the master, play was nothing, neither minor nor major" *Conférences*).

Why is this uniquely the space of writing?

Sovereignty is absolute when it is absolved of every relationship, and keeps
itself in the night of the secret. The *continuum* of sovereign communication has
as its milieu this night of secret difference. One would understand nothing about
it in thinking that there was some contradiction between these two requisites. In
fact, one would understand only that which is understood in the logic of
philosophical lordship: because for this logic, on the contrary, one must con-

ciliate the desire for recognition, the breaking of secrecy, discourse, collabora-
tion, etc., with discontinuity, articulation, and negativity. The opposition of the
continuous and the discontinuous is constantly displaced from Hegel to Bataille.

But this displacement is powerless to transform the nucleus of predicates. All
the attributes ascribed to sovereignty are borrowed from the (Hegelian) logic of
"lordship." We cannot, and Bataille neither could, nor should dispose of any
other concepts or any other signs, any other unity of word and meaning. The sign
"sovereignty" itself, in its opposition to servility, was issued from the same
stock as that of "lordship." Considered outside its functioning, nothing distinguishes it from "lordship." One could even abstract from Bataille's text an
entire zone throughout which sovereignty remains inside a classical philosophy
of the *subject* and, above all, inside the *voluntarism*[27] which Heidegger has shown
still to be confused, in Hegel and Nietzsche, with the essence of metaphysics.

Since the space which separates the logic of lordship and, if you will, the
nonlogic of sovereignty neither can nor may be inscribed in the nucleus of the
concept itself (for what is discovered here is that there is no nucleus of meaning,
no conceptual atom, but that the concept is produced within the tissue of differences); it will have to be inscribed within the continuous chain (or functioning)
of a form of writing. *This*—major—writing will be called *writing* because it
exceeds the *logos* (of meaning, lordship, presence etc.). Within this writing—the
one sought by Bataille—the *same* concepts, apparently unchanged in themselves,
will be subject to a mutation of meaning, or rather will be struck by (even though
they are apparently indifferent), the loss of sense toward which they slide,
thereby ruining themselves immeasurably. To blind oneself to this rigorous precipitation, this pitiless sacrifice of philosophical concepts, and to continue to
read, interrogate, and judge Bataille's text *from within* "significative discourse"
is, perhaps, to hear something within it, but it is assuredly not to read it. Which
can always be done—and has it not been?—with great agility, resourcefulness
occasionally, and philosophical security. Not to read, is, here, to ignore the
formal necessity of Bataille's text, to ignore its own fragmentation, its relationship to the narratives whose adventure cannot simply be juxtaposed with
aphorisms or with "philosophical" discourses which erase their signifiers in
favor of their signified contents. Differing from logic, such as it is understood in
its classical concept, even differing from the Hegelian *Book* which was Kojève's
theme, Bataille's writing, in its major instance, does not tolerate the distinction
of form and content.[28] Which makes it writing, and a requisite of sovereignty.

This writing (and without concern for instruction, this is the example it provides for us, what we are interested in here, today) folds itself in order to link up
with classical concepts—insofar as they are inevitable ("I could not avoid expressing my thought in a philosophical mode. But I do not address myself to
philosophers" *Méthode*)—in such a way that these concepts, through a certain
twist, apparently obey their habitual laws; but they do so while relating them-

selves, at a certain point, to the moment of sovereignty, to the absolute loss of their meaning, to expenditure without reserve, to what can no longer even be called negativity or loss of meaning except on its philosophical side; thus, they relate themselves to a nonmeaning which is beyond absolute meaning, beyond the closure or the horizon of absolute knowledge. Carried away in this calculated sliding,[29] concepts become nonconcepts, they are unthinkable, they become *untenable*. ("I introduce untenable concepts," *Le petit*). The philosopher is blind to Bataille's text because he is a philosopher only through the desire to hold on to, to *maintain* his certainty of himself and the security of the concept as security against this sliding. For him, Bataille's text is full of traps: it is, in the initial sense of the word, a *scandal*.

The transgression of meaning is not an access to the immediate and indeterminate *identity* of a nonmeaning, nor is it an access to the possibility of *maintaining* nonmeaning. Rather, we would have to speak of an *epochē* of the epoch of meaning, of a—written—putting between brackets that suspends the epoch of meaning: the opposite of a phenomenological *epochē*, for this latter is carried out *in the name and in sight of* meaning. The phenomenological *epochē* is a reduction that pushes us back toward meaning. Sovereign transgression is a reduction of this reduction: not a reduction to meaning, but a reduction of meaning. Thus, while exceeding the *Phenomenology of the Mind*, this transgression at the same time exceeds phenomenology in general, in its most modern developments (cf. *EI*, p. 19).

Will this new writing *depend* upon the agency of sovereignty? Will it *obey* the imperatives of sovereignty? Will it subordinate itself to that which subordinates nothing? (And does so, one might say, by essence, if sovereignty had an essence.) The answer is, not at all; and this is the unique paradox of the relation between discourse and sovereignty. To relate the major form of writing to the sovereign operation is to institute a relation in the form of a nonrelation, to inscribe rupture in the text, to place the chain of discursive knowledge in relation to an unknowledge which is not a moment of knowledge: an absolute unknowledge from whose nonbasis is launched chance, or the wagers of meaning, history, and the horizons of absolute knowledge. The inscription of such a relation will be "scientific," but the word "science" submits to a radical alteration: without losing any of its proper norms, it is made to tremble, simply by being placed in relation to an absolute unknowledge. One can call it science only within the transgressed closure, but to do so one will have to answer to all the requirements of this denomination. The unknowledge exceeding science itself, the unknowledge that *will know* where and how to exceed science *itself*, will not have scientific qualification ("Who will ever know what it is to know nothing?" *Le petit*). It will not be a determined unknowledge, circumscribed by the history of knowledge as a figure taken from (or leading toward) dialectics, but will be the absolute excess of every *epistemē*, of every philosophy and every science. Only a

double position can account for this unique relation, which belongs neither to
"scientism" nor "mysticism."[30]

As the affirmative reduction of sense, rather than the position of non-sense,
sovereignty therefore is not the *principle* or foundation of this inscription. A
nonprinciple and a nonfoundation, it definitively eludes any expectation of a
reassuring *archia,* a condition of possibility or transcendental of discourse. Here,
there are no longer any philosophical preliminaries. The *Méthode de méditation*
teaches us that the disciplined itinerary of writing must rigorously take us to the
point at which there is no longer any method or any meditation, the point at
which the sovereign operation breaks with method and meditation because it
cannot be conditioned by anything that precedes or even prepares it. Just as it
seeks neither to be applied nor propagated, neither to last nor to instruct (and this
is also why, according to Blanchot's expression, its authority *expiates itself*), and
just as it does not seek recognition, so too it has no movement of recognition for
the discursive and prerequisite labor that it could not do without. Sovereignty
must be ungrateful. "My sovereignty . . . gives me no thanks for my work"
(*Méthode*). The conscientious concern for preliminaries is precisely philosophical and Hegelian.

> The criticism addressed by Hegel to Schelling (in the preface to the
> *Phenomenology*) is no less decisive. The preliminary efforts of the operation
> are not within the reach of an unprepared intelligence (as Hegel says: it
> would be similarly senseless, if one were not a shoemaker, to make a shoe).
> These efforts, through the mode of application which belongs to them,
> nevertheless inhibit the sovereign operation (the being which goes as far as it
> possibly can). Sovereign behavior precisely demands a refusal to submit its
> operation to the condition of preliminaries. The operation takes place only if
> the urgency for it appears: and if the operation does become urgent, it is no
> longer time to undertake efforts whose essence is to be subordinate to ends
> exterior to them, whose essence is not to be ends themselves [*Méthode*].

Now, if one muses upon the fact that Hegel is doubtless the first to have demonstrated the ontological unity of method and historicity, it must indeed be concluded that what is *exceeded* by sovereignty is not only the "subject" (*Méthode,*
p. 75), but history itself. Not that one returns, in classical and pre-Hegelian
fashion, to an ahistorical sense which would constitute a figure of the
Phenomenology of the Mind. Sovereignty transgresses the entirety of the history
of meaning and the entirety of the meaning of history, and the project of knowledge which has always obscurely welded these two together. Unknowledge is,
then, superhistorical,[31] but only because it takes its responsibilities from the
completion of history and from the closure of absolute knowledge, having first
taken them seriously and having then betrayed them by exceeding them or by
simulating them in play.[32] In this simulation, I conserve or anticipate the entirety
of knowledge, I do not limit myself to a determined and abstract kind of knowl-

edge or unknowledge, but I rather absolve myself of absolute knowledge, putting it back in its place as such, situating it and inscribing it within a space which it no longer dominates. Bataille's writing thus relates all semantemes, that is, philosophemes, to the sovereign operation, to the consummation, without return, of meaning. It draws upon, in order to exhaust it, the resource of meaning. With minute audacity, it will acknowledge the rule which constitues that which it efficaciously, economically must deconstitute.

Thus proceeding along the lines of what Bataille calls the *general economy*.

*Writing and General
Economy*

The writing of sovereignty conforms to general economy by at least two characteristics: (1) it is a science; (2) it relates its objects to the destruction, without reserve, of meaning.

The *Méthode de méditation* announces *la Part maudite* in this way:

> The science of relating the object of thought to sovereign moments, in fact,
> is only a *general economy* which envisages the meaning of these objects
> in relation to each other and finally in relation to the loss of meaning.
> The question of this *general economy* is situated on the level of *political
> economy,* but the science designated by this name is only a restricted econ-
> omy, (restricted to commercial values). In question is the essential problem
> for the science dealing with the use of wealth. The *general economy,* in
> the first place, makes apparent that excesses of energy are produced, and
> that by definition, these excesses cannot be utilized. The excessive energy
> can only be lost without the slightest aim, consequently without any mean-
> ing. It is this useless, senseless loss that *is* sovereignty. [*EI,* p. 233].[33]

Insofar as it is a scientific form of writing, general economy is certainly not sovereignty itself. Moreover, there is no sovereignty *itself.* Sovereignty dissolves the values of meaning, truth and a *grasp-of-the-thing-itself.* This is why the discourse that it opens above all is not true, truthful or "sincere."[34] Sovereignty is the impossible, therefore it *is not,* it *is*—Bataille writes this word in italics— "this loss." The writing of sovereignty places discourse *in relation* to absolute non-discourse. Like general economy, it is not the loss of meaning, but, as we have just read, the "relation to this loss of meaning." It opens the question of meaning. It does not describe unknowledge, for this is impossible, but only the effect of unknowledge. "In sum, it would be impossible to speak of unknowl-edge, while we can speak of its effects."[35]

To this extent, we do not return to the usual order of knowledge-gathering science. The writing of sovereignty *is neither sovereignty in its operation nor current scientific discourse.* This latter has as its *meaning* (as its discursive content and direction) the relation oriented from the unknown to the known or knowable, to the always already known or to anticipated knowledge. Although general writing also has a meaning, *since it is only a relation* to nonmeaning this order is reversed within it. And the relation to the absolute possibility of knowledge is suspended within it. The known is related to the unknown, meaning to nonmeaning. "This knowledge, which might be called liberated (but which I prefer to call neutral), is the usage of a function detached (liberated) from the servitude from whence it springs: the function in question related the unknown to the known (the solid), while, dating from the moment it is detached, it relates the known to the unknown" (*Méthode*). A movement that is only sketched, as we have seen, in the "poetic image."

Not that the phenomenology of the mind, which proceeded within the horizon of absolute knowledge or according to the circularity of the Logos, is thus *overturned*. Instead of being simply overturned, it is comprehended: not comprehended by knowledge-gathering comprehension, but inscribed within the opening of the general economy along with its horizons of knowledge and its figures of meaning. General economy folds these horizons and figures so that they will be related not to a basis, but to the nonbasis of expenditure, not to the *telos* of meaning, but to the *indefinite* destruction of value. Bataille's atheology[36] is also an a-teleology and an aneschatology. Even in its discourse, which already must be distinguished from sovereign affirmation, this atheology does not, however, proceed along the lines of negative theology; lines that could not fail to fascinate Bataille, but which, perhaps, still reserved, beyond all the rejected predicates, and even "beyond being," a "superessentiality;"[37] beyond the categories of beings, a supreme being and an indestructible meaning. Perhaps: for here we are touching upon the limits and the greatest audacities of discourse in Western thought. We could demonstrate that the distances and proximities do not differ among themselves.

Since it relates the successive figures of phenomenality to a knowledge of meaning that always already has been anticipated, the phenomenology of the mind (and phenomenology in general) corresponds to a restricted economy: restricted to commercial values, one might say, picking up on the terms of the definition, a "science dealing with the utilization of wealth," limited to the meaning and the established value of objects, and to their *circulation*. The *circularity* of absolute knowledge could dominate, could comprehend only this circulation, only the *circuit of reproductive consumption*. The absolute production and destruction of value, the exceeding energy as such, the energy which "can only be lost without the slightest aim, consequently without any meaning"—all this escapes phenomenology as restricted economy. The latter can determine difference and negativity only as facets, moments, or conditions of meaning: as work. Now the nonmeaning of the sovereign operation is neither the negative of, nor the condition for, meaning, even if it is this *also,* and even if this is what its name gives us to understand. It is not a reserve of meaning. It keeps itself beyond the opposition of the positive and the negative, for the act of consumption, although it induces the loss of sense, is not the *negative* of presence, presence maintained or looked on in the *truth* of its meaning (its *bewahren*). Such a rupture of symmetry must propagate its effects throughout the entire chain of discourse. The concepts of general writing can be *read* only on the condition that they be deported, shifted outside the symmetrical alternatives from which, however, they seem to be taken, and in which, after a fashion, they must also remain. Strategy plays upon this origin and "backwardation." For example, if one takes into account this *commentary on nonmeaning,* then that which *indicates itself* as nonvalue, within the closure of metaphysics, *refers* beyond the opposition of value and nonvalue, even beyond the concept of value, as it does beyond the concept of meaning. That which *indicates itself* as mysticism, in order to shake the security of discursive knowledge, refers beyond the opposition of the mystic and the rational.[38] Bataille above all is not a new mystic. That which *indicates itself* as interior experience is not an experience, because it is related to no presence, to no plentitude, but only to the "impossible" it "undergoes" in torture. This experience above all is not interior: and if it seems to be such because it is related to nothing else, to no exterior (except in the modes of nonrelation, secrecy, and rupture), it is also completely *exposed*—to torture—naked, open to the exterior, with no interior reserve or feelings, profoundly superficial.

One could submit all the concepts of general writing (those of science, the unconscious, materialism, etc.) to this schematization. The predicates are not there in order to *mean* something, to enounce or to signify, but in order to make sense slide, to denounce it or to deviate from it. This writing does not necessarily produce new conceptual unities; and its concepts are not necessarily distinguished from classical concepts by marked characteristics in the form of essential predicates, but rather by qualitative differences of force, height, etc., which themselves are qualified in this way only by metaphor. Tradition's names are maintained, but they are struck with the differences between the *major* and the *minor,* the *archaic* and the *classic.*[39] This is the only way, within discourse, to mark that which separates discourse from its excess.

However, the writing within which these stratagems operate does not consist in subordinating conceptual moments to the totality of a system in which these moments would finally take on meaning. It is not a question of subordinating the slidings and differences of discourse, the play of syntax, to the entirety of an anticipated discourse. On the contrary. If the play of difference is indispensable for the correct reading of the general economy's concepts, and if each notion must be reinscribed within the law of its own sliding and must be related to the sovereign operation, one must not make of these requirements the subordinate moment of a structure. The reading of Bataille must pass through these two dangerous straits. It must not isolate notions as if they were their own context, as if one could immediately understand what the content of words like "experience," "interior," "mystic," "word," "material," "sovereign," etc. *means.* Here, the error would consist in taking as an immediate given of reading the blindness to a traditional culture which itself wishes to be taken as the natural element of discourse. But inversely, one must not submit contextual attentiveness and differences of signification to a *system of meaning* permitting or promising an absolute formal mastery. This would amount to erasing the excess of nonmeaning and to falling back into the closure of knowledge: would amount, once more, to not reading Bataille.

On this point the dialogue with Hegel is again decisive. An example: Hegel, and following him, whoever installs himself within the sure element of philosophical discourse, would have been unable to read, in its regulated sliding, a sign like that of "experience." In *l'Erotisme,* Bataille notes, without explaining any further: "In Hegel's mind, what is immediate is bad, and Hegel certainly would have related what I call experience to the immediate." Now, if in its major moments, interior experience breaks with mediation, interior experience is not, however, immediate. It does not pleasurably consume an absolutely close presence, and, above all, it cannot enter into the movement of mediation, as can the Hegelian immediate. Immediacy and mediacy, such as they are presented in the elements of philosophy, in Hegel's logic, or in phenomenology, are *equally* "subordinated." It is thus that they can pass one into the other. The sovereign operation therefore also suspends subordination in the form of immediacy. In order to understand that it does not, at this point, enter into work and phenomenology, one must exit from the philosophical logos and think the unthinkable. How can mediacy and immediacy be transgressed simultaneously? How can "subordination," in the sense of the (philosophical) logos be exceeded in its totality? *Perhaps* through major writings: "I write in order to annihilate the play of subordinate operations within myself (which is, after all, superfluous)" (*Méthode*). Only *perhaps,* and this is "after all, superfluous," for this writing must assure us of nothing, must give us no certitude, no result, no profit. It is absolutely adventurous, is a chance and not a technique.

The Transgression of the
Neutral and the Displace-
ment of the Aufhebung

Beyond the classical oppositions, is the writing of sovereignty blank or neutral? One might think so, because the writing of sovereignty can enounce nothing, except in the form of *neither this, nor that.* Is this not one of the affinities between the thought of Bataille and that of Blanchot? And does not Bataille propose a neutral knowledge? "This knowledge, which might be called liberated (but which I prefer to call neutral), is the usage of a function detached (liberated) from the servitude from whence it springs.... It relates the known to the unknown'' (cited above).

But here, we must attentively consider the fact that it is not the sovereign operation, but discursive knowledge that is *neutral*. Neutrality has a negative essence (*ne-uter*), is the negative side of transgression. Sovereignty is not neutral even if it neutralizes, *in its discourse,* all the contradictions and all the oppositions of classical logic. Neutralization is produced within knowledge and within the syntax of writing, but it is related to a sovereign and transgressive affirmation. The sovereign operation is not content with neutralizing the classical operations *in discourse;* in the major form of experience it transgresses the law or prohibitions that form a system with discourse, *and even with the work of neutralization.* Twenty pages after having proposed a ''neutral knowledge'': ''I am establishing the possibility of neutral knowledge? my sovereignty welcomes it in me as the bird sings, and gives me no thanks for my work.''

Also the destruction of discourse is not simply an erasing neutralization. It multiplies words, precipitates them one against the other, engulfs them too, in an endless and baseless substitution whose only rule is the sovereign affirmation of the play outside meaning. Not a reserve or a withdrawal, not the infinite murmur of a blank speech erasing the traces of classical discourse, but a kind of potlatch of signs that burns, consumes, and wastes words in the gay affirmation of death: a sacrifice and a challenge.[40] Thus, for example:

> Previously, I designated the sovereign operation under the names of *interior experience* or *extremity of the possible.* Now, I am also designating it under the name of *meditation.* The change of words signifies the bothersomeness of using any words at all (*sovereign operation* is the most loathsome of all the names: in a sense, *comic operation* would be less deceptive); I prefer *meditation,* but it has a pious appearance [*EI,* p. 237].

What has happened? In sum, nothing has been said. We have not stopped at any word; the chain rests on nothing; none of the concepts satisfies the demand, all are determined by each other and, at the same time, destroy or neutralize each other. But the rule of the game or, rather, the game as rule has been *affirmed;* as has been the necessity of transgressing both discourse and the negativity of the bothersomeness of using any word at all in reassuring identity of its meaning.

But this transgression of discourse (and consequently of law in general, for discourse establishes itself only by establishing normativity or the value of meaning, that is to say, the element of legality in general) must, in some fashion, and like every transgression, conserve or confirm that which it exceeds.[41] This is the only way for it to affirm itself *as transgression* and thereby to accede to the sacred, which ''is presented in the violence of an infraction.'' Now, describing ''the contradictory experience of prohibition and transgression,'' in *L'erotisme,* Bataille adds a note to the following sentence: ''But transgression differs from the 'return to nature': it dispels the prohibition without suppressing it." Here is the note: "It is useless to insist upon the Hegelian character of this operation, which corresponds to the moment of dialectics expressed by the untranslatable German verb *Aufheben* (to surpass while maintaining)."

Is it "useless to insist"? Can one, as Bataille says, understand the movement of transgression under the Hegelian concept of *Aufhebung,* which, we have seen often enough, represents the victory of the slave and the constitution of meaning?

Here, we must interpret Bataille against Bataille, or rather, must interpret one stratum of his work from another stratum.[42] By protesting against what, for Bataille, seems to go without saying in this note, we will perhaps sharpen the figure of displacement to which the entire Hegelian discourse is submitted here. In which Bataille is even less Hegelian than he thinks.

The Hegelian *Aufhebung* is produced entirely from within discourse, from within the system or the work of signification. A determination is negated and conserved in another determination which reveals the truth of the former. From infinite indetermination one passes to infinite determination, and this transition, produced by the anxiety of the infinite, continuously links meaning up to itself. The *Aufhebung* is included *within* the circle of absolute knowledge, never exceeds its closure, never suspends the totality of discourse, work, meaning, law, etc. Since it never dispels the veiling form of absolute knowledge, even by maintaining this form, the Hegelian *Aufhebung* in all its parts belongs to what Bataille calls "the world of work," that is, the world of the prohibition not perceived as such, in its totality. "And the human collectivity, in part devoted to work, is just as much defined by *prohibitions,* without which it would not have become the *world of work* that it essentially is" (*L'erotisme*). The Hegelian *Aufhebung* thus belongs to restricted economy, and is the form of the passage from one prohibition to another, the *circulation* of prohibitions, history as the truth of the prohibition.

Bataille, thus, can only utilize the *empty* form of the *Aufhebung,* in an analogical fashion, in order to designate, *as was never done before,* the transgressive relationship which links the world of meaning to the world of nonmeaning. This displacement is paradigmatic: within a form of writing, an intraphilosophical concept, the speculative concept par excellence, is forced to designate a movement which properly constitutes the excess of every possible philosopheme. This movement then makes philosophy appear as a form of natural or naïve consciousness (which in Hegel also means cultural consciousness). For as long as the *Aufhebung* remains within restricted economy, it is a prisoner of this natural consciousness. The "we" of the *Phenomenology of the Mind* presents itself in vain as the knowledge of what the naïve consciousness, embedded in its history and in the determinations of its figures, does not yet know; the "we" remains natural and vulgar because it conceives the *passage* from one figure to the next and the *truth* of this passage only as the circulation of meaning and value. It develops the sense, or the desire for sense, of natural consciousness, the consciousness that encloses itself in the circle in order to *know sense;* which is always where it comes from, and where it is going to.[43] It does not *see* the nonbasis of play upon which (the) history (of meaning) is launched. To this extent, philosophy, Hegelian speculation, absolute knowledge and everything that they govern, and will govern endlessly in their closure, remain determinations of natural, servile and vulgar consciousness. Self-consciousness is servile.

> Between extreme knowledge and vulgar knowledge—the most generally disposed of—the difference is nil. In Hegel, the knowledge of the world is that of the firstcomer (the firstcomer, not Hegel, decides upon the key question for Hegel: touching upon the difference between madness and reason: on this point "absolute knowledge" confirms the vulgar notion, is founded on it, is one of its forms). Vulgar knowledge is in us like another *tissue!*
> ... In a sense, the condition in which *I would* see would be to get out of, to emerge from the "tissue"! And doubtless I must immediately say: the condition in which I *would see* would be to die. At no moment would I have the chance *to see!* [*EI,* p. 222].

If the entire history of meaning is reassembled and *represented,* at a point of the canvas, by the figure of the slave, if Hegel's discourse, Logic, and the Book of which Kojève speaks are the slave('s) language, that is, the worker('s) language, then they can be read from left to right or from right to left, as a reactionary movement or as a revolutionary movement, or both at once. It would be absurd for the transgression of the Book by writing to be legible only in a determined sense. It would be at once absurd, given the form of the *Aufhebung* which is maintained in transgression, *and* too full of meaning for a transgression of meaning. From right to left or left to right: these two contradictory and too-meaningful propositions equally lack pertinence. At a certain determined point.

A very determined point. Thus, the effects of ascertaining nonpertinence would have to be watched as closely as possible. One understands nothing about general strategy if one absolutely renounces any regulation of ascertaining nonpertinence. If one loans it, abandons it, puts it into any hands: the right or the left.

. . . .
. . . .
. . . .

the condition in which I *would see* would be to get out of, to emerge from the "tissue"! And doubtless I must immediately say: the condition in which I *would see* would be to die. At no moment would I have the chance *to see!*

Thus, there is the *vulgar* tissue of absolute knowledge and the mortal opening of an *eye.* A text and a vision. The servility of meaning and the awakening to death. A minor writing and a major illumination.

From one to the other, totally other, a certain text. Which in silence traces the structure of the eye, sketches the opening, ventures to contrive "absolute rending," absolutely rends its own tissue once more become "solid" and servile in once more having been read.

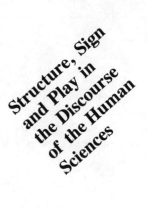

Ten

We need to interpret interpretations more than to interpret things. (Montaigne)

Perhaps something has occurred in the history of the concept of structure that could be called an "event," if this loaded word did not entail a meaning which it is precisely the function of structural—or structuralist—thought to reduce or to suspect. Let us speak of an "event," nevertheless, and let us use quotation marks to serve as a precaution. What would this event be then? Its exterior form would be that of a *rupture* and a redoubling.

It would be easy enough to show that the concept of structure and even the word "structure" itself are as old as the *epistēmē*—that is to say, as old as Western science and Western philosophy—and that their roots thrust deep into the soil of ordinary language, into whose deepest recesses the *epistēmē* plunges in order to gather them up and to make them part of itself in a metaphorical displacement. Nevertheless, up to the event which I wish to mark out and define, structure—or rather the structurality of structure—although it has always been at work, has always been neutralized or reduced, and this by a process of giving it a center or of referring it to a point of presence, a fixed origin. The function of this center was not only to orient, balance, and organize the structure—one cannot in fact conceive of an unorganized structure—but above all to make sure that the organizing principle of the structure would limit what we might call the *play* of the structure. By orienting and

278

organizing the coherence of the system, the center of a structure permits the play
of its elements inside the total form. And even today the notion of a structure
lacking any center represents the unthinkable itself.

Nevertheless, the center also closes off the play which it opens up and makes
possible. As center, it is the point at which the substitution of contents, elements,
or terms is no longer possible. At the center, the permutation or the transformation of elements (which may of course be structures enclosed within a structure)
is forbidden. At least this permutation has always remained *interdicted* (and I am
using this word deliberately). Thus it has always been thought that the center,
which is by definition unique, constituted that very thing within a structure which
while governing the structure, escapes structurality. This is why classical thought
concerning structure could say that the center is, paradoxically, *within* the
structure and *outside it*. The center is at the center of the totality, and yet, since
the center does not belong to the totality (is not part of the totality), the totality
has its center elsewhere. The center is not the center. The concept of centered
structure—although it represents coherence itself, the condition of the *epistēmē*
as philosophy or science—is contradictorily coherent. And as always, coherence
in contradiction expresses the force of a desire.[1] The concept of centered
structure is in fact the concept of a play based on a fundamental ground, a play
constituted on the basis of a fundamental immobility and a reassuring certitude,
which itself is beyond the reach of play. And on the basis of this certitude anxiety
can be mastered, for anxiety is invariably the result of a certain mode of being
implicated in the game, of being caught by the game, of being as it were at stake
in the game from the outset. And again on the basis of what we call the center
(and which, because it can be either inside or outside, can also indifferently be
called the origin or end, *archē* or *telos*), repetitions, substitutions, transformations, and permutations are always *taken* from a history of meaning [*sens*]—that
is, in a word, a history—whose origin may always be reawakened or whose end
may always be anticipated in the form of presence. This is why one perhaps
could say that the movement of any archaeology, like that of any eschatology, is an
accomplice of this reduction of the structurality of structure and always attempts
to conceive of structure on the basis of a full presence which is beyond play.

If this is so, the entire history of the concept of structure, before the rupture of
which we are speaking, must be thought of as a series of substitutions of center
for center, as a linked chain of determinations of the center. Successively, and in
a regulated fashion, the center receives different forms or names. The history of
metaphysics, like the history of the West, is the history of these metaphors and
metonymies. Its matrix—if you will pardon me for demonstrating so little and for
being so elliptical in order to come more quickly to my principal theme—is the
determination of Being as *presence* in all senses of this word. It could be shown
that all the names related to fundamentals, to principles, or to the center have
always designated an invariable presence—*eidos, archē, telos, energeia, ousia*

(essence, existence, substance, subject) *alētheia,* transcendentality, consciousness, God, man, and so forth.

The event I called a rupture, the disruption I alluded to at the beginning of this paper, presumably would have come about when the structurality of structure had to begin to be thought, that is to say, repeated, and this is why I said that this disruption was repetition in every sense of the word. Henceforth, it became necessary to think both the law which somehow governed the desire for a center in the constitution of structure, and the process of signification which orders the displacements and substitutions for this law of central presence—but a central presence which has never been itself, has always already been exiled from itself into its own substitute. The substitute does not substitute itself for anything which has somehow existed before it. Henceforth, it was necessary to begin thinking that there was no center, that the center could not be thought in the form of a present-being, that the center had no natural site, that it was not a fixed locus but a function, a sort of nonlocus in which an infinite number of sign-substitutions came into play. This was the moment when language invaded the universal problematic, the moment when, in the absence of a center or origin, everything became discourse—provided we can agree on this word—that is to say, a system in which the central signified, the original or transcendental signified, is never absolutely present outside a system of differences. The absence of the transcendental signified extends the domain and the play of signification infinitely.

Where and how does this decentering, this thinking the structurality of structure, occur? It would be somewhat naïve to refer to an event, a doctrine, or an author in order to designate this occurrence. It is no doubt part of the totality of an era, our own, but still it has always already begun to proclaim itself and begun to *work.* Nevertheless, if we wished to choose several "names," as indications only, and to recall those authors in whose discourse this occurrence has kept most closely to its most radical formulation, we doubtless would have to cite the Nietzschean critique of metaphysics, the critique of the concepts of Being and truth, for which were substituted the concepts of play, interpretation, and sign (sign without present truth); the Freudian critique of self-presence, that is, the critique of consciousness, of the subject, of self-identity and of self-proximity or self-possession; and, more radically, the Heideggerean destruction of metaphysics, of onto-theology, of the determination of Being as presence. But all these destructive discourses and all their analogues are trapped in a kind of circle. This circle is unique. It describes the form of the relation between the history of metaphysics and the destruction of the history of metaphysics. There is no sense in doing without the concepts of metaphysics in order to shake metaphysics. We have no language—no syntax and no lexicon—which is foreign to this history; we can pronounce not a single destructive proposition which has not already had to slip into the form, the logic, and the implicit postulations of precisely what it

seeks to contest. To take one example from many: the metaphysics of presence is
shaken with the help of the concept of *sign*. But, as I suggested a moment ago, as
soon as one seeks to demonstrate in this way that there is no transcendental or
privileged signified and that the domain or play of signification henceforth has no
limit, one must reject even the concept and word "sign" itself—which is precisely what cannot be done. For the signification "sign" has always been understood and determined, in its meaning, as sign-of, a signifier referring to a
signified, a signifier different from its signified. If one erases the radical difference between signifier and signified, it is the word "signifier" itself which
must be abandoned as a metaphysical concept. When Lévi-Strauss says in the
preface to *The Raw and the Cooked* that he has "sought to transcend the opposition between the sensible and the intelligible by operating from the outset at the
level of signs," [2] the necessity, force, and legitimacy of his act cannot make us
forget that the concept of the sign cannot in itself surpass this opposition between
the sensible and the intelligible. The concept of the sign, in each of its aspects,
has been determined by this opposition throughout the totality of its history. It
has lived only on this opposition and its system. But we cannot do without the
concept of the sign, for we cannot give up this metaphysical complicity without
also giving up the critique we are directing against this complicity, or without the
risk of erasing difference in the self-identity of a signified reducing its signifier
into itself or, amounting to the same thing, simply expelling its signifier outside
itself. For there are two heterogenous ways of erasing the difference between the
signifier and the signified: one, the classic way, consists in reducing or deriving
the signifier, that is to say, ultimately in *submitting* the sign to thought; the other,
the one we are using here against the first one, consists in putting into question
the system in which the preceding reduction functioned: first and foremost, the
opposition between the sensible and the intelligible. For the *paradox* is that the
metaphysical reduction of the sign needed the opposition it was reducing. The
opposition is systematic with the reduction. And what we are saying here about
the sign can be extended to all the concepts and all the sentences of metaphysics,
in particular to the discourse on "structure." But there are several ways of being
caught in this circle. They are all more or less naïve, more or less empirical,
more or less systematic, more or less close to the formulation—that is, to the
formalization—of this circle. It is these differences which explain the multiplicity of destructive discourses and the disagreement between those who elaborate
them. Nietzsche, Freud, and Heidegger, for example, worked within the inherited concepts of metaphysics. Since these concepts are not elements or atoms,
and since they are taken from a syntax and a system, every particular borrowing
brings along with it the whole of metaphysics. This is what allows these de-
stroyers to destroy each other reciprocally—for example, Heidegger regarding
Nietzsche, with as much lucidity and rigor as bad faith and misconstruction, as
the last metaphysician, the last "Platonist." One could do the same for Heideg-

ger himself, for Freud, or for a number of others. And today no exercise is more widespread.

What is the relevance of this formal schema when we turn to what are called the "human sciences"? One of them perhaps occupies a privileged place—ethnology. In fact one can assume that ethnology could have been born as a science only at the moment when a decentering had come about: at the moment when European culture—and, in consequence, the history of metaphysics and of its concepts—had been *dislocated,* driven from its locus, and forced to stop considering itself as the culture of reference. This moment is not first and foremost a moment of philosophical or scientific discourse. It is also a moment which is political, economic, technical, and so forth. One can say with total security that there is nothing fortuitous about the fact that the critique of ethnocentrism—the very condition for ethnology—should be systematically and historically contemporaneous with the destruction of the history of metaphysics. Both belong to one and the same era. Now, ethnology—like any science—comes about within the element of discourse. And it is primarily a European science employing traditional concepts, however much it may struggle against them. Consequently, whether he wants to or not—and this does not depend on a decision on his part—the ethnologist accepts into his discourse the premises of ethnocentrism at the very moment when he denounces them. This necessity is irreducible; it is not a historical contingency. We ought to consider all its implications very carefully. But if no one can escape this necessity, and if no one is therefore responsible for giving in to it, however little he may do so, this does not mean that all the ways of giving in to it are of equal pertinence. The quality and fecundity of a discourse are perhaps measured by the critical rigor with which this relation to the history of metaphysics and to inherited concepts is thought. Here it is a question both of a critical relation to the language of the social sciences and a critical responsibility of the discourse itself. It is a question of explicitly and systematically posing the problem of the status of a discourse which borrows from a heritage the resources necessary for the deconstruction of that heritage itself. A problem of *economy* and *strategy*.

If we consider, as an example, the texts of Claude Lévi-Strauss, it is not only because of the privilege accorded to ethnology among the social sciences, nor even because the thought of Lévi-Strauss weighs heavily on the contemporary theoretical situation. It is above all because a certain choice has been declared in the work of Lévi-Strauss and because a certain doctrine has been elaborated there, and precisely, in a *more or less explicit manner,* as concerns both this critique of language and this critical language in the social sciences.

In order to follow this movement in the text of Lévi-Strauss, let us choose as one guiding thread among others the opposition between nature and culture. Despite all its rejuvenations and disguises, this opposition is congenital to philosophy. It is even older than Plato. It is at least as old as the Sophists. Since the statement of the opposition *physis/nomos, physis/technē,* it has been relayed to us by means of a whole historical chain which opposes "nature" to law, to education, to art, to technics—but also to liberty, to the arbitrary, to history, to society, to the mind, and so on. Now, from the outset of his researches, and from his first book (*The Elementary Structures of Kinship*) on, Lévi-Strauss simultaneously has experienced the necessity of utilizing this opposition and the impossibility of accepting it. In the *Elementary Structures,* he begins from this axiom or definition: that which is *universal* and spontaneous, and not dependent on any particular culture or on any determinate norm, belongs to nature. Inversely, that which depends upon a system of *norms* regulating society and therefore is capable of *varying* from one social structure to another, belongs to culture. These two definitions are of the traditional type. But in the very first pages of the *Elementary Structures* Lévi-Strauss, who has begun by giving credence to these concepts, encounters what he calls a *scandal,* that is to say, something which no longer tolerates the nature/culture opposition he has accepted, something which *simultaneously* seems to require the predicates of nature and of culture. This scandal is the *incest prohibition.* The incest prohibition is universal; in this sense one could call it natural. But it is also a prohibition, a system of norms and interdicts; in this sense one could call it cultural:

> Let us suppose then that everything universal in man relates to the natural order, and is characterized by spontaneity, and that everything subject to a norm is cultural and is both relative and particular. We are then confronted with a fact, or rather, a group of facts, which, in the light of previous definitions, are not far removed from a scandal: we refer to that complex group of beliefs, customs, conditions and institutions described succinctly as the prohibition of incest, which presents, without the slightest ambiguity, and inseparably combines, the two characteristics in which we recognize the conflicting features of two mutually exclusive orders. It constitutes a rule, but a rule which, alone among all the social rules, possesses at the same time a universal character.[3]

Obviously there is no scandal except within a system of concepts which accredits the difference between nature and culture. By commencing his work with the *factum* of the incest prohibition, Lévi-Strauss thus places himself at the point at which this difference, which has always been assumed to be self-evident, finds itself erased or questioned. For from the moment when the incest prohibition can no longer be conceived within the nature/culture opposition, it can no longer be said to be a scandalous fact, a nucleus of opacity within a network of transparent significations. The incest prohibition is no longer a scandal one meets with or comes up against in the domain of traditional concepts; it is something which escapes these concepts and certainly precedes them—probably as the condition of their possibility. It could perhaps be said that the whole of philosophical conceptualization, which is systematic with the nature/culture opposition, is designed to leave in the domain of the unthinkable the very thing that makes this conceptualization possible: the origin of the prohibition of incest.

This example, too cursorily examined, is only one among many others, but nevertheless it already shows that language bears within itself the necessity of its own critique. Now this critique may be undertaken along two paths, in two "manners." Once the limit of the nature/culture opposition makes itself felt, one might want to question systematically and rigorously the history of these concepts. This is a first action. Such a systematic and historic questioning would be neither a philological nor a philosophical action in the classic sense of these words. To concern oneself with the founding concepts of the entire history of philosophy, to deconstitute them, is not to undertake the work of the philologist or of the classic historian of philosophy. Despite appearances, it is probably the most daring way of making the beginnings of a step outside of philosophy. The step "outside philosophy" is much more difficult to conceive than is generally imagined by those who think they made it long ago with cavalier ease, and who in general are swallowed up in metaphysics in the entire body of discourse which they claim to have disengaged from it.

The other choice (which I believe corresponds more closely to Lévi-Strauss's manner), in order to avoid the possibly sterilizing effects of the first one, consists in conserving all these old concepts within the domain of empirical discovery while here and there denouncing their limits, treating them as tools which can still be used. No longer is any truth value attributed to them; there is a readiness to abandon them, if necessary, should other instruments appear more useful. In the meantime, their relative efficacy is exploited, and they are employed to destroy the old machinery to which they belong and of which they themselves are pieces. This is how the language of the social sciences criticizes *itself*. Lévi-Strauss thinks that in this way he can separate *method* from *truth*, the instruments of the method and the objective significations envisaged by it. One could almost say that this is the primary affirmation of Lévi-Strauss; in any event, the first words of the *Elementary Structures* are: "Above all, it is beginning to emerge that this distinction between nature and society ('nature' and 'culture' seem preferable to us today), while of no acceptable historical significance, does contain a logic, fully justifying its use by modern sociology as a methodological tool."[4]

Lévi-Strauss will always remain faithful to this double intention: to preserve as an instrument something whose truth value he criticizes.

On the one hand, he will continue, in effect, to contest the value of the nature/culture opposition. More than thirteen years after the *Elementary Structures, The Savage Mind* faithfully echoes the text I have just quoted: "The opposition between nature and culture to which I attached much importance at one time ... now seems to be of primarily methodological importance.'' And this methodological value is not affected by its ''ontological'' nonvalue (as might be said, if this notion were not suspect here): ''However, it would not be enough to reabsorb particular humanities into a general one. This first enterprise opens the way for others which ... are incumbent on the exact natural sciences: the reintegration of culture in nature and finally of life within the whole of its physico-chemical conditions.''[5]

On the other hand, still in *The Savage Mind,* he presents as what he calls *bricolage* what might be called the discourse of this method. The *bricoleur,* says Lévi-Strauss, is someone who uses ''the means at hand,'' that is, the instruments he finds at his disposition around him, those which are already there, which had not been especially conceived with an eye to the operation for which they are to be used and to which one tries by trial and error to adapt them, not hesitating to change them whenever it appears necessary, or to try several of them at once, even if their form and their origin are heterogenous—and so forth. There is therefore a critique of language in the form of *bricolage,* and it has even been said that *bricolage* is critical language itself. I am thinking in particular of the article of G. Genette, ''Structuralisme et critique littéraire,'' published in homage to Lévi-Strauss in a special issue of *L'Arc* (no. 26, 1965), where it is stated that the analysis of *bricolage* could ''be applied almost word for word'' to criticism, and especially to ''literary criticism.''

If one calls *bricolage* the necessity of borrowing one's concepts from the text of a heritage which is more or less coherent or ruined, it must be said that every discourse is *bricoleur.* The engineer, whom Lévi-Strauss opposes to the *bricoleur,* should be the one to construct the totality of his language, syntax, and lexicon. In this sense the engineer is a myth. A subject who supposedly would be the absolute origin of his own discourse and supposedly would construct it ''out of nothing,'' ''out of whole cloth,'' would be the creator of the verb, the verb itself. The notion of the engineer who supposedly breaks with all forms of *bricolage* is therefore a theological idea; and since Lévi-Strauss tells us elsewhere that *bricolage* is mythopoetic, the odds are that the engineer is a myth produced by the *bricoleur.* As soon as we cease to believe in such an engineer and in a discourse which breaks with the received historical discourse, and as soon as we admit that every finite discourse is bound by a certain *bricolage* and that the engineer and the scientist are also species of *bricoleurs,* then the very idea of *bricolage* is menaced and the difference in which it took on its meaning breaks down.

This brings us to the second thread which might guide us in what is being contrived here.

Lévi-Strauss describes *bricolage* not only as an intellectual activity but also as a mythopoetical activity. One reads in *The Savage Mind,* ''Like *bricolage* on the technical plane, mythical reflection can reach brilliant unforeseen results on the intellectual plane. Conversely, attention has often been drawn to the mytho-poetical nature of *bricolage*."[6]

But Lévi-Strauss's remarkable endeavor does not simply consist in proposing, notably in his most recent investigations, a structural science of myths and of mythological activity. His endeavor also appears—I would say almost from the outset—to have the status which he accords to his own discourse on myths, to what he calls his "mythologicals." It is here that his discourse on the myth reflects on itself and criticizes itself. And this moment, this critical period, is evidently of concern to all the languages which share the field of the human sciences. What does Lévi-Strauss say of his "mythologicals"? It is here that we rediscover the mythopoetical virtue of *bricolage*. In effect, what appears most fascinating in this critical search for a new status of discourse is the stated abandonment of all reference to a *center*, to a *subject*, to a privileged *reference*, to an origin, or to an absolute *archia*. The theme of this decentering could be followed throughout the "Overture" to his last book, *The Raw and the Cooked*. I shall simply remark on a few key points.

1. From the very start, Lévi-Strauss recognizes that the Bororo myth which he employs in the book as the "reference myth" does not merit this name and this treatment. The name is specious and the use of the myth improper. This myth deserves no more than any other its referential privilege: "In fact, the Bororo myth, which I shall refer to from now on as the key myth, is, as I shall try to show, simply a transformation, to a greater or lesser extent, of other myths originating either in the same society or in neighboring or remote societies. I could, therefore, have legitimately taken as my starting point any one representative myth of the group. From this point of view, the key myth is interesting not because it is typical, but rather because of its irregular position within the group."[7]

2. There is no unity or absolute source of the myth. The focus or the source of the myth are always shadows and virtualities which are elusive, unactualizable, and nonexistent in the first place. Everything begins with structure, configuration, or relationship. The discourse on the acentric structure that myth itself is, cannot itself have an absolute subject or an absolute center. It must avoid the violence that consists in centering a language which describes an acentric structure if it is not to shortchange the form and movement of myth. Therefore it is necessary to forego scientific or philosophical discourse, to renounce the *epistēmē* which absolutely requires, which is the absolute requirement that we go back to the source, to the center, to the founding basis, to the principle, and so on. In opposition to *epistemic* discourse, structural discourse on myths—*mythological* discourse—must itself be *mythomorphic*. It must have the form of that of which it speaks. This is what Lévi-Strauss says in *The Raw and the Cooked*, from which I would now like to quote a long and remarkable passage:

The study of myths raises a methodological problem, in that it cannot be carried out according to the Cartesian principle of breaking down the difficulty into as many parts as may be necessary for finding the solution. There is no real end to methodological analysis, no hidden unity to be grasped once the breaking-down process has been completed. Themes can be split up *ad infinitum*. Just when you think you have disentangled and separated them, you realize that they are knitting together again in response to the operation of unexpected affinities. Consequently the unity of the myth is never more than tendential and projective and cannot reflect a state or a particular moment of the myth. It is a phenomenon of the imagination, resulting from the attempt at interpretation; and its function is to endow the myth with synthetic form and to prevent its disintegration into a confusion of opposites. The science of myths might therefore be termed "anaclastic," if we take this old term in the broader etymological sense which includes the study of both reflected rays and broken rays. But unlike philosophical reflection, which aims to go back to its own source, the reflections we are dealing with here concern rays whose only source is hypothetical . . . . And in seeking to imitate the spontaneous movement of mythological thought, this essay, which is also both too brief and too long, has had to conform to the requirements of that thought and to respect its rhythm. It follows that this book on myths is itself a kind of myth.[8]

This statement is repeated a little farther on: "As the myths themselves are based on secondary codes (the primary codes being those that provide the substance of language), the present work is put forward as a tentative draft of a tertiary code, which is intended to ensure the reciprocal translatability of several myths. This is why it would not be wrong to consider this book itself as a myth: it is, as it were, the myth of mythology."[9] The absence of a center is here the absence of a subject and the absence of an author: "Thus the myth and the musical work are like conductors of an orchestra, whose audience becomes the silent performers. If it is now asked where the real center of the work is to be found, the answer is that this is impossible to determine. Music and mythology bring man face to face with potential objects of which only the shadows are actualized . . . . Myths are anonymous."[10] The musical model chosen by Lévi-Strauss for the composition of his book is apparently justified by this absence of any real and fixed center of the mythical or mythological discourse.

Thus it is at this point that ethnographic *bricolage* deliberately assumes its mythopoetic function. But by the same token, this function makes the philosophical or epistemological requirement of a center appear as mythological, that is to say, as a historical illusion.

Nevertheless, even if one yields to the necessity of what Lévi-Strauss has done, one cannot ignore its risks. If the mythological is mythomorphic, are all discourses on myths equivalent? Shall we have to abandon any epistemological requirement which permits us to distinguish between several qualities of dis-

course on the myth? A classic, but inevitable question. It cannot be answered—
and I believe that Lévi-Strauss does not answer it—for as long as the problem of
the relations between the philosopheme or the theorem, on the one hand, and the
mytheme or the mythopoem, on the other, has not been posed explicitly, which is
no small problem. For lack of explicitly posing this problem, we condemn
ourselves to transforming the alleged transgression of philosophy into an unnoticed fault within the philosophical realm. Empiricism would be the genus of
which these faults would always be the species. Transphilosophical concepts
would be transformed into philosophical naïvetés. Many examples could be
given to demonstrate this risk: the concepts of sign, history, truth, and so forth.
What I want to emphasize is simply that the passage beyond philosophy does not
consist in turning the page of philosophy (which usually amounts to philosophizing badly), but in continuing to read philosophers *in a certain way*. The risk I
am speaking of is always assumed by Lévi-Strauss, and it is the very price of this
endeavor. I have said that empiricism is the matrix of all faults menacing a
discourse which continues, as with Lévi-Strauss in particular, to consider itself
scientific. If we wanted to pose the problem of empiricism and *bricolage* in
depth, we would probably end up very quickly with a number of absolutely
contradictory propositions concerning the status of discourse in structural ethnology. On the one hand, structuralism justifiably claims to be the critique of
empiricism. But at the same time there is not a single book or study by Lévi-
Strauss which is not proposed as an empirical essay which can always be
completed or invalidated by new information. The structural schemata are always
proposed as hypotheses resulting from a finite quantity of information and which
are subjected to the proof of experience. Numerous texts could be used to
demonstrate this double postulation. Let us turn once again to the "Overture" of
The Raw and the Cooked, where it seems clear that if this postulation is double, it
is because it is a question here of a language on language:

> If critics reproach me with not having carried out an exhaustive inventory of
> South American myths before analyzing them, they are making a grave mis-
> take about the nature and function of these documents. The total body of
> myth belonging to a given community is comparable to its speech. Unless
> the population dies out physically or morally, this totality is never complete.
> You might as well criticize a linguist for compiling the grammar of a lan-
> guage without having complete records of the words pronounced since the
> language came into being, and without knowing what will be said in it dur-
> ing the future part of its existence. Experience proves that a linguist can
> work out the grammar of a given language from a remarkably small number
> of sentences. . . . And even a partial grammar or an outline grammar is a
> precious acquisition when we are dealing with unknown languages. Syntax
> does not become evident only after a (theoretically limitless) series of events
> has been recorded and examined, because it is itself the body of rules gover-

ning their production. What I have tried to give is an outline of the syntax of
South American mythology. Should fresh data come to hand, they will be
used to check or modify the formulation of certain grammatical laws, so that
some are abandoned and replaced by new ones. But in no instance would I
feel constrained to accept the arbitrary demand for a total mythological pattern, since, as has been shown, such a requirement has no meaning.[11]

Totalization, therefore, is sometimes defined as *useless,* and sometimes as *impossible.* This is no doubt due to the fact that there are two ways of conceiving
the limit of totalization. And I assert once more that these two determinations
coexist implicitly in Lévi-Strauss's discourse. Totalization can be judged impossible in the classical style: one then refers to the empirical endeavor of either a
subject or a finite richness which it can never master. There is too much, more
than one can say. But nontotalization can also be determined in another way: no
longer from the standpoint of a concept of finitude as relegation to the empirical,
but from the standpoint of the concept of *play.* If totalization no longer has any
meaning, it is not because the infiniteness of a field cannot be covered by a finite
glance or a finite discourse, but because the nature of the field—that is, language
and a finite language—excludes totalization. This field is in effect that of *play,*
that is to say, a field of infinite substitutions only because it is finite, that is to
say, because instead of being an inexhaustible field, as in the classical
hypothesis, instead of being too large, there is something missing from it: a
center which arrests and grounds the play of substitutions. One could say—
rigorously using that word whose scandalous signification is always obliterated in
French—that this movement of play, permitted by the lack or absence of a center
or origin, is the movement of *supplementarity.* One cannot determine the center
and exhaust totalization because the sign which replaces the center, which sup-
plements it, taking the center's place in its absence—this sign is added, occurs as
a surplus, as a *supplement.*[12] The movement of signification adds something,
which results in the fact that there is always more, but this addition is a floating
one because it comes to perform a vicarious function, to supplement a lack on the
part of the signified. Although Lévi-Strauss in his use of the word ''supplementary'' never emphasizes, as I do here, the two directions of meaning which are so
strangely compounded within it, it is not by chance that he uses this word twice
in his ''Introduction to the Work of Marcel Mauss,'' at one point where he is
speaking of the ''overabundance of signifier, in relation to the signifieds to which
this overabundance can refer'':

> In his endeavor to understand the world, man therefore always has at his
> disposal a surplus of signification (which he shares out amongst things ac-
> cording to the laws of symbolic thought—which is the task of ethnologists
> and linguists to study). This distribution of a *supplementary* allowance [*ra-
> tion supplémentaire*]—if it is permissible to put it that way—is absolutely

necessary in order that on the whole the available signifier and the signified it aims at may remain in the relationship of complementarity which is the very condition of the use of symbolic thought."[13]

(It could no doubt be demonstrated that this *ration supplémentaire* of signification is the origin of the *ratio* itself.) The word reappears a little further on, after Lévi-Strauss has mentioned "this floating signifier, which is the servitude of all finite thought";

> In other words—and taking as our guide Mauss's precept that all social phenomena can be assimilated to language—we see in *mana, Wakau, oranda* and other notions of the same type, the conscious expression of a semantic function, whose role it is to permit symbolic thought to operate in spite of the contradiction which is proper to it. In this way are explained the apparently insoluble antinomies attached to this notion . . . . At one and the same time force and action, quality and state, noun and verb; abstract and concrete, omnipresent and localized—*mana* is in effect all these things. But is it not precisely because it is none of these things that *mana* is a simple form, or more exactly, a symbol in the pure state, and therefore capable of becoming charged with any sort of symbolic content whatever? In the system of symbols constituted by all cosmologies, *mana* would simply be a zero symbolic value, that is to say, a sign marking the necessity of a symbolic content *supplementary* [my italics] to that with which the signified is already loaded, but which can take on any value required, provided only that this value still remains part of the available reserve and is not, as phonologists put it, a group-term"

Lévi-Strauss adds the note:
"Linguists have already been led to formulate hypotheses of this type. For example: 'A zero phoneme is opposed to all the other phonemes in French in that it entails no differential characters and no constant phonetic value. On the contrary, the proper function of the zero phoneme is to be opposed to phoneme absence.' (R. Jakobson and J. Lutz, "Notes on the French Phonemic Pattern," *Word* 5, no. 2 [August 1949]: 155). Similarly, if we schematize the conception I am proposing here, it could almost be said that the function of notions like *mana* is to be opposed to the absence of signification, without entailing by itself any particular signification."[14]

The *overabundance* of the signifier, its *supplementary* character, is thus the result of a finitude, that is to say, the result of a lack which must be *supplemented*.

It can now be understood why the concept of play is important in Lévi-Strauss. His references to all sorts of games, notably to roulette, are very frequent, especially in his *Conversations,*[15] in *Race and History,*[16] and in *The Savage Mind*. Further, the reference to play is always caught up in tension.

Tension with history, first of all. This is a classical problem, objections to

which are now well worn. I shall simply indicate what seems to me the formality
of the problem: by reducing history, Lévi-Strauss has treated as it deserves a
concept which has always been in complicity with a teleological and eschatological metaphysics, in other words, paradoxically, in complicity with that philosophy of presence to which it was believed history could be opposed. The thematic of historicity, although it seems to be a somewhat late arrival in philosophy,
has always been required by the determination of Being as presence. With or
without etymology, and despite the classic antagonism which opposes these
significations throughout all of classical thought, it could be shown that the
concept of *epistémé* has always called forth that of *historia,* if history is always
the unity of a becoming, as the tradition of truth or the development of science
or knowledge oriented toward the appropriation of truth in presence and self-
presence, toward knowledge in consciousness-of-self. History has always been
conceived as the movement of a resumption of history, as a detour between two
presences. But if it is legitimate to suspect this concept of history, there is a risk,
if it is reduced without an explicit statement of the problem I am indicating here,
of falling back into an ahistoricism of a classical type, that is to say, into a
determined moment of the history of metaphysics. Such is the algebraic formality
of the problem as I see it. More concretely, in the work of Lévi-Strauss it must be
recognized that the respect for structurality, for the internal originality of the
structure, compels a neutralization of time and history. For example, the appearance of a new structure, of an original system, always comes about—and this is
the very condition of its structural specificity—by a rupture with its past, its
origin, and its cause. Therefore one can describe what is peculiar to the structural
organization only by not taking into account, in the very moment of this description, its past conditions: by omitting to posit the problem of the transition from
one structure to another, by putting history between brackets. In this
"structuralist" moment, the concepts of chance and discontinuity are indispensable. And Lévi-Strauss does in fact often appeal to them, for example, as concerns that structure of structures, language, of which he says in the "Introduction to the Work of Marcel Mauss" that it "could only have been born in one fell
swoop":

> Whatever may have been the moment and the circumstances of its appear-
> ance on the scale of animal life, language could only have been born in one
> fell swoop. Things could not have set about acquiring signification pro-
> gressively. Following a transformation the study of which is not the concern
> of the social sciences, but rather of biology and psychology, a transition
> came about from a stage where nothing had a meaning to another where
> everything possessed it.[17]

This standpoint does not prevent Lévi-Strauss from recognizing the slowness, the
process of maturing, the continuous toil of factual transformations, history (for

example, *Race and History*). But, in accordance with a gesture which was also Rousseau's and Husserl's, he must "set aside all the facts" at the moment when he wishes to recapture the specificity of a structure. Like Rousseau, he must always conceive of the origin of a new structure on the model of catastrophe—an overturning of nature in nature, a natural interruption of the natural sequence, a setting aside *of* nature.

Besides the tension between play and history, there is also the tension between play and presence. Play is the disruption of presence. The presence of an element is always a signifying and substitutive reference inscribed in a system of differences and the movement of a chain. Play is always play of absence and presence, but if it is to be thought radically, play must be conceived of before the alternative of presence and absence. Being must be conceived as presence or absence on the basis of the possibility of play and not the other way around. If Lévi-Strauss, better than any other, has brought to light the play of repetition and the repetition of play, one no less perceives in his work a sort of ethic of presence, an ethic of nostalgia for origins, an ethic of archaic and natural innocence, of a purity of presence and self-presence in speech—an ethic, nostalgia, and even remorse, which he often presents as the motivation of the ethnological project when he moves toward the archaic societies which are exemplary societies in his eyes. These texts are well known.[18]

Turned towards the lost or impossible presence of the absent origin, this structuralist thematic of broken immediacy is therefore the saddened, *negative,* nostalgic, guilty, Rousseauistic side of the thinking of play whose other side would be the Nietzschean *affirmation,* that is the joyous affirmation of the play of the world and of the innocence of becoming, the affirmation of a world of signs without fault, without truth, and without origin which is offered to an active interpretation. *This affirmation then determines the noncenter otherwise than as loss of the center.* And it plays without security. For there is a *sure* play: that which is limited to the *substitution* of *given* and *existing, present,* pieces. In absolute chance, affirmation also surrenders itself to *genetic* indetermination, to the *seminal* adventure of the trace.

There are thus two interpretations of interpretation, of structure, of sign, of play. The one seeks to decipher, dreams of deciphering a truth or an origin which escapes play and the order of the sign, and which lives the necessity of interpretation as an exile. The other, which is no longer turned toward the origin, affirms play and tries to pass beyond man and humanism, the name of man being the name of that being who, throughout the history of metaphysics or of ontotheology—in other words, throughout his entire history—has dreamed of full presence, the reassuring foundation, the origin and the end of play. The second interpretation of interpretation, to which Nietzsche pointed the way, does not seek in ethnography, as Lévi-Strauss does, the "inspiration of a new humanism" (again citing the "Introduction to the Work of Marcel Mauss").

There are more than enough indications today to suggest we might perceive that these two interpretations of interpretation—which are absolutely irreconcilable even if we live them simultaneously and reconcile them in an obscure economy—together share the field which we call, in such a problematic fashion, the social sciences.

For my part, although these two interpretations must acknowledge and accentuate their difference and define their irreducibility, I do not believe that today there is any question of *choosing*—in the first place because here we are in a region (let us say, provisionally, a region of historicity) where the category of choice seems particularly trivial; and in the second, because we must first try to conceive of the common ground, and the *différance* of this irreducible difference. Here there is a kind of question, let us still call it historical, whose *conception, formation, gestation,* and *labor* we are only catching a glimpse of today. I employ these words, I admit, with a glance toward the operations of childbearing—but also with a glance toward those who, in a society from which I do not exclude myself, turn their eyes away when faced by the as yet unnamable which is proclaiming itself and which can do so, as is necessary whenever a birth is in the offing, only under the species of the nonspecies, in the formless, mute, infant, and terrifying form of monstrosity.

Eleven

Ellipsis

for Gabriel Bounore

Here or there we have discerned writing: a nonsymmetrical division designated on the one hand the closure of the book, and on the other the opening of the text. On the one hand the theological encyclopedia and, modeled upon it, the book of man. On the other a fabric of traces marking the disappearance of an exceeded God or of an erased man. The question of writing could be opened only if the book was closed. The joyous wandering of the *graphein* then became wandering without return. The opening into the text was adventure, expenditure without reserve.

And yet did we not know that the closure of the book was not a simple limit among others? And that only in the book, coming back to it unceasingly, drawing all our resources from it; could we indefinitely designate the writing beyond the book?

Which brings us to consider *Le retour au livre*[1] (The Return to the Book). Under this heading, Edmond Jabès first tells us what it is "to abandon the book." If closure is not end, we protest or deconstruct in vain,

God succeeds God and the Book succeeds the Book.

But within this movement of succession, writing keeps its vigil, between God and God, between the Book and the Book. And if writing takes shape on the basis of both this vigil and the beyond of the closure, then the return to the book does not enclose us within the book. The return is a moment of wandering, it repeats the *epoch* of the book, its totality suspended between two forms of writing, its withdrawal, and that which is reserved within it.

A book which is the interfacing of a risk....

... My life, from the book on, will have been a vigil of writing in the interval of limits.

Repetition does not reissue the book but describes its origin from the vantage of a writing which does not yet belong to it, or no longer belongs to it, a writing which feigns, by repeating the book, inclusion in the book. Far from letting itself be oppressed or enveloped within the volume, this repetition is the first writing. The writing of the origin, the writing that retraces the origin, tracking down the signs of its disappearance, the lost writing of the origin.

To write is to have the passion of the origin.

But what disposes it in this way, we now know, is not the origin, but that which takes its place; which is not, moreover, the opposite of an origin. It is not absence instead of presence, but a trace which replaces a presence which has never been present, an origin by means of which nothing has begun. Now, the book has lived on this lure: to have given us to believe that passion, having originally been impassioned by *something,* could in the end be appeased by the return of that something. Lure of the origin, the end, the line, the ring, the volume, the center.

As in the first *Book of Questions,* imaginary rabbis answer each other, in the Song on *The Ring.*

The line is the lure
Reb Séab

One of my greatest anxieties, said Reb Aghim, was to see, without being able to stop it, my life curve itself to form a ring.

Once the circle turns, once the volume rolls itself up, once the book is repeated, its identification with itself gathers an imperceptible difference which permits us efficaciously, rigorously, that is, discreetly, to exit from closure. In redoubling the closure of the book, one cuts it in half. One then furtively escapes from it, between two passageways through the same book, the same line, along the same ring, *"vigil of writing in the interval of limits."* This exit from the identical into the same[2] remains very slight, weighs nothing itself, thinks and weighs the book *as such.* The return to the book is then the abandoning of the book; it has slipped in between God and God, the Book and the Book, in the neutral space of succession, in the suspense of the interval. The return, at this point, does not retake possession of something. It does not reappropriate the origin. The latter is no longer in itself. Writing, passion of the origin, must also be understood through the subjective genetive. It is the origin itself which is impassioned, passive, and past, in that it is written. Which means inscribed. The inscription of the origin is doubtless its Being-as-writing, but it is also its Being-as-inscribed in a system in which it is only a function and a locus.

Thus understood, the return to the book is of an *elliptical* essence. Something invisible is missing in the grammar of this repetition. As this lack is invisible and undeterminable, as it completely redoubles and consecrates the book, once more passing through each point along its circuit, nothing has budged. And yet all meaning is altered by this lack. Repeated, the same line is no longer exactly the same, the ring no longer has exactly the same center, *the origin has played.* Something is missing that would make the circle perfect. But within the *elleipsis,* by means of simple redoubling of the route, the solicitation of closure, and the jointing of the line, the book has let itself be thought as such.

And Yukel said:
The circle is acknowledged. Break the curve. The route doubles the route.
The book consecrates the book.

The return to the book here announces the form of the eternal return.[3] The return of the same does not alter itself—but does so absolutely—except by amounting to the same. Pure repetition, were it to change neither thing nor sign, carries with it an unlimited power of perversion and subversion.

This repetition is writing because what disappears in it is the self-identity of the origin, the self-presence of so-called living speech. That is the center. The first book, the mythic book, the eve prior to all repetition, has lived on the deception that the center was sheltered from play: irreplaceable, withdrawn from metaphor and metonymy, a kind of *invariable first name* that could be invoked, but not repeated. The center of the first book should not have been repeatable in its own representation. Once it lends itself a single time to such a representation—that is to say, once it is written—when one can read a book in the book, an origin in the origin, a center in the center, it is the abyss, is the bottomlessness of infinite redoubling. The other is in the same,

The Elsewhere within . . .

The center is the well . . .

"Where is the center?" screamed Reb Madies. *"The scorned water permits*
*   the falcon to pursue his prey."*
The center, perhaps, is the displacement of the question.
No center there where the circle is impossible.
"May my death come from myself," said Reb Bekri.
"For I would then be, all at once, both the servitude of the ring and the
*   caesura."*

As soon as a sign emerges, it begins by repeating itself. Without this, it would not be a sign, would not be what it is, that is to say, the non-self-identity which regularly refers to the same. That is to say, to another sign, which itself will be born of having been divided. The grapheme, repeating itself in this fashion, thus has neither natural site nor natural center. But did it ever lose them? Is its excentricity a decentering? Can one not affirm the nonreferral to the center, rather than bemoan the absence of the center? Why would one mourn for the center? Is not the center, the absence of play and difference, another name for death? The death which reassures and appeases, but also, with tis hole, creates anguish and puts at stake?

The passage through negative excentricity is doubtless necessary; but only liminary.

> *The center is the threshold.*
> *Reb Naman said: "God is the center; this is why great minds have pro-claimed that He did not exist, for if the center of an apple or the star is the heart of the heavenly body or of the fruit, which is the true middle of the orchard and the night?"*

> *And Yukel said:*
> *The center is failure.*
> *"Where is the center?* [Où est le centre?]
> *—Under ashes.* [Sous la cendre]*'*
>   *Reb Selah*

> *"The center is mourning."*

Just as there is a negative theology, there is a negative atheology. An ac-complice of the former, it still pronounces the absence of a center, when it is play that should be affirmed. But is not the desire for a center, as a function of play itself, the indestructible itself? And in the repetition or return of play, how could the phantom of the center not call to us? It is here that the hesitation between writing as decentering and writing as an affirmation of play is infinite. This hesitation is part of play and links it to death. Hesitation occurs within a "who knows?" without subject or knowledge.

> *The last obstacle, the ultimate limit is, who knows? the center.*
> *For then everything comes to us from the end of the night, from childhood.*

If the center is indeed *"the displacing of the question,"* it is because the un-namable bottomless well whose sign the center was, has always been *surnamed;* the center as the sign of a hole that the book attempted to fill. The center was the name of a hole; and the name of man, like the name of God, pronounces the force of that which has been raised up in the hole in order to operate as a work in the form of a book. The volume, the scroll of parchment, was to have insinuated itself into the dangerous hole, was to have furtively penetrated into the menacing dwelling place with an animal-like, quick, silent, smooth, brilliant, sliding motion, in the fashion of a serpent or a fish. Such is the anxious desire of the book. It is tenacious too, and parasitic, loving and breathing through a thousand mouths that leave a thousand imprints on our skin, a marine monster, a *polyp*.

> *Ridiculous, this position on your belly. You are crawling. You are boring a*
> *hole through the wall at its base. You hope to escape, like a rat. Like*
> *shadows, in the morning, on a road.*
> *And this will to*
> *stand upright, despite fatigue and hunger?*
> *A hole, it was only a hole,*
> *the chance for a book.*
>> *(A hole-octopus, your work? [Un trou-pieuvre, ton oeuvre?]*
>> *The octopus was hung from the ceiling and his tentacles began to*
>> *sparkle.)*
> *It was only a hole*
> *in the wall*
> *so narrow that you never*
> *could have gotten into it*
> *to flee.*
> *Beware of dwellings. They are not always hospitable.*

The strange serenity of such a return. Rendered hopeless by repetition, and yet joyous for having affirmed the abyss, for having inhabited the labyrinth as a poet, for having written the hole, *"the chance for a book"* into which one can only plunge, and that one must maintain while destroying it. The dwelling is inhospitable because it seduces us, as does the book, into a labyrinth. The labyrinth, here is an abyss: we plunge into the horizontality of a pure surface, which itself represents itself from detour to detour.

> *The book is the labyrinth. You think you have left it, you are plunged into*
> *it. You have no chance to get away. You must destroy the work. You cannot*
> *resolve yourself to do so. I notice the slow but sure rise of your anguish.*
> *Wall after wall. Who waits for you at the end?—No one . . . . Your name has*
> *folded over on itself, like the hand on the white arm.*

In the serenity of this *third* volume, *The Book of Questions* is fulfilled. Fulfilled as it should be, by remaining open, by pronouncing nonclosure, simultaneously infinitely open and infinitely reflecting on itself, *"an eye in an eye,"* a commentary infinitely accompanying the *"book of the rejected and called-for book,"* the book ceaselessly begun and taken up again on a site which is neither in the book nor outside it, articulating itself as the very opening which is reflection without exit, referral, return, and detour of the labyrinth. The latter is a way which encloses in itself the ways out of itself, which includes its own exits, which itself opens its own doors, that is to say, opening them onto itself, closes itself by thinking its own opening.

This contradiction is thought as such in the third book of questions. This is why triplicity is its figure and the key to its serenity. To its composition, too: the third book says,

> *I am the first book in the second.*
> *. . .*
> *And Yukel said:*
> *Three questions have*
> *seduced the book*
> *and three questions*
> *will finish it.*
> *That which ends*
> *three times begins.*
> *The book is three.*
> *The world is three*
> *And God, for man,*
> *the three answers.*

Three: not because the equivocality, the duplicity of everything and nothing, of absent presence, of the black sun, of the open ring, of the eluded center, of the elliptical return, finally would be summarized and reduced in some dialectic, in some conciliating final term. The *pas* and the *pacte* of which Yukel speaks at *Midnight or the third question,* are another name for the death affirmed since *Dawn or the first question* and *Midday or the second question.*

> *And Yukel said:*
> *"The book has led me*
> *from dawn to twilight,*
> *from death to death,*
> *with your shadow* [avec ton ombre], *Sarah,*
> *within the number* [dans le nombre], *Yukel,*
> *at the end of my questions,*
> *at the foot of the three questions . . . .*

Death is at the dawn because everything has begun with repetition. Once the center or the origin have begun by repeating themselves, by redoubling themselves, the double did not only add itself to the simple. It divided it and supplemented it. There was immediately a double origin plus its repetition. Three is the first figure of repetition. The last too, for the abyss of representation always remains dominated by its rhythm, infinitely. The infinite is doubtless neither one, nor empty, nor innumerable. It is of a ternary essence. Two, like the second *Book of questions (The Book of Yukel),* like Yukel, remains the indispensable and useless articulater of the book, the sacrificed mediator without which triplicity would not be, and without which meaning would not be what it is, that is to say, different from itself: in play, at stake. To articulate is to joint. One could say of the *second* book what is said of *Yukel* in the second part of the *Return to the book:*

> "*He was liana and lierne in the book, before being expelled from it.*"

If nothing has preceded repetition, if no present has kept watch over the trace, if, after a fashion, it is the "void which reempties itself and marks itself with imprints,"[4] then the time of writing no longer follows the line of modified present tenses. What is to come is not a future present, yesterday is not a past present. The beyond of the closure of the book is neither to be awaited nor to be refound. It is *there,* but out there, *beyond,* within repetition, but eluding us there. It is there like the shadow of the book, the third party between the hands holding the book, the deferral within the now of writing, the distance between the book and the book, that other hand.

Opening the third part of the third *Book of Questions,* thus begins the song on *distance and accent:*

> "*Tomorrow is the shadow and reflexibility of our hands.*"
> > Reb Derissa

Notes

For abbreviations used in text and notes, see chapter 4, note 1; chapter 6, note 8; chapter 7, note 2; and chapter 9, note 6. Translator's notes are indicated at the beginning of each such note by the abbreviation TN. Translator's interpolations in author's notes are enclosed in brackets.

One   **Force and Signification**

1. In *L'univers imaginaire de Mallarmé* (Paris: Editions du Seuil, 1961, p. 30, n. 27), Jean-Pierre Richard writes: "We would be content if our work could provide some new materials for a future history of imagination and affectivity; this history, not yet written for the nineteenth century, would probably be an extension of the works of Jean Rousset on the baroque, Paul Hazard on the eighteenth century, André Monglond on preromanticism."

2. In his *Anthropology* (New York: Harcourt, Brace and World, 1948, p. 325) A. L. Kroeber notes: " 'Structure' appears to be just a yielding to a word that has a perfectly good meaning but suddenly becomes fashionably attractive for a decade or so—like 'streamlining'—and during its vogue tends to be applied indiscriminately because of the pleasurable connotations of its sound."

To grasp the profound necessity hidden beneath the incontestable phenomenon of fashion, it is first necessary to operate negatively: the choice of a word is first an ensemble—a structural ensemble, of course—of exclusions. To know why one says "structure" is to know why one no longer wishes to say *eidos*, "essence," form, *Gestalt*, "ensemble," "composition," "complex," "construction," "correlation," "totality," "Idea," "organism," "state," "system," etc. One must understand not only why each of these words showed itself to be insufficient but also why the notion of structure continues to borrow some implicit signification from them and to be inhabited by them.

3. TN. The most consistently difficult sections of Derrida's texts are his "prefatory" remarks, for reasons that he has explained in "Hors-livre," the preface to *La dissémination* (Paris: Seuil, 1972). The question hinges upon the classical difference between a philosophical text and its preface, the preface usually being a recapitulation of the truth presented by the text. Since Derrida challenges the notion that a *text* can *present* a *truth*, his prefaces—in which this challenge is anticipated—must especially mark that which makes a text explode the classical ideas of truth and

presence. And they must do so without letting the preface anticipate this "conclusion" as a single, clear, luminous truth. Thus the *complication* of these prefaces. One way of complicating a preface is to leave as a knot that which will later become several strands. Here, the relationship between history, somnambulism, the "question" and the difference between almost-everything and almost-nothing is not explained, for the unraveling of this question touches at least on the topics of the relationship between history and philosophy (cf. below, "Violence and Metaphysics"), and the relation of both of these, as writing or texts, to Freud's analysis of the "text of somnambulism," i.e., *The Interpretation of Dreams* (cf. below, "Freud and the Scene of Writing").

4. On the theme of the *separation* of the writer, cf. particularly chapter 3 of Jean Rousset's introduction of his *Forme et Signification*. Delacroix, Diderot, Balzac, Baudelaire, Mallarmé, Proust, Valéry, Henry James, T. S. Eliot, Virginia Woolf are called upon to bear witness to the fact that separation is diametrically opposed to critical impotency. By insisting upon this separation between the critical act and creative force, we are only designating the most banally essential—others might say, structural—necessity attached to these two actions and moments. Impotence, here, is a property not of the critic but of criticism. The two are sometimes confused. Flaubert does not deny himself this confusion. This is brought to light in the admirable collection of letters edited by Geneviève Bollème and entitled *Préface à la vie d'écrivain* (Paris: Seuil, 1963). Attentive to the fact that the critic takes his material from the work rather than bringing anything to it, Flaubert writes: "One writes criticism when one cannot create art, just as one becomes a spy when one cannot be a soldier.... Plautus would have laughed at Aristotle had he known him! Corneille resisted him all he could! Voltaire himself was belittled by Boileau! We would have been spared much evil in modern drama without Schlegel. And when the translation of Hegel is finished, Lord knows where we will end up!" (Bollème, p. 42). The translation of Hegel hasn't been finished, thank the Lord, thus explaining Proust, Joyce, Faulkner and several others. The difference between Mallarmé and these authors is perhaps the reading of Hegel. Or that Mallarmé chose, at least, to approach Hegel. In any event, genius still has some respite, and translations can be left unread. But Flaubert was right to fear Hegel: "One may well hope that art will continue to advance and perfect itself, but its form has ceased to be the highest need of the spirit. In all these relationships art is and remains for us, on the side of its highest vocation, something past" ("Vorlesungen über die Aesthetik," in Martin Heidegger: *Poetry, Language, Thought,* trans. Albert Hofstadter [New York: Harper and Row, 1971]). The citation continues: "It [art] has lost, for us, its truth and its life. It invites us to a philosophical reflection which does not insure it any renewal, but rigorously recognizes its essence."

5. Richard, *L'univers imaginaire de Mallarmé,* p. 14.

6. Cf. Gérard Genette, "Une poétique structurale," *Tel Quel,* no. 7, Autumn 1961, p. 13.

7. Cf. Jean Rousset, *La littérature de l'âge baroque en France,* vol. 1: *Circe et le paon* (Paris: José Corti, 1954). In particular, the following passage à propos of a German example, can be read: "Hell is a world in pieces, a pillage that the poem imitates closely through its disordered shouts, bristling with scattered tortures in a torrent of exclamations. The sentence is reduced to its disordered elements, the framework of the sonnet is broken: the lines are too short or too long, the quatrains unbalanced; the poem bursts" (ibid., p. 194).

8. TN. The play is on the etymology of the word *critic,* which comes from the Greek verb *krinein,* meaning both "to separate, to cut into" and "to discern, to judge."

9. Jean Rousset, *Forme et Signification: Essais sur les structures littéraires de Corneille à Claudel* (Paris: José Corti, 1962).

10. After citing (ibid., p. vii) this passage of Picon: "Before modern art, the work seems to be the expression of a previous experience..., the work says what has been conceived or seen; so much so that from the experience to the work there is only the transition to the techniques of execution. For modern art the work is not expression but creation: it makes visible what was not visible before it, it forms instead of reflecting," Rousset makes this idea more specific with this distinction: "An important difference and, in our eyes, an important conquest of modern art, *or rather of the consciousness of the creative process achieved by this art...*" (my italics; according to Rousset, we are

becoming conscious *today* of the *creative process in general*). For Picon, the mutation affects art and not only the modern consciousness of art. He wrote elsewhere: "The history of modern poetry is entirely that of the substitution of a language of creation for a language of expression. . . . Language must now produce the world that it can no longer express" (*Introduction à une esthétique de la littérature*, vol. 1: *L'écrivain et son ombre* [Paris: Gallimard, 1953], p. 195).

11. *Critique of Pure Reason*, translated by Norman Kemp Smith (London: Macmillan and Co., 1929). The texts of Kant to which we will refer—and numerous other texts which we will call upon later—are not utilized by Rousset. It will be our rule to refer directly to the page numbers of *Forme et Signification* each time that a citation presented by Rousset is in question.

12. Ibid.

13. *The Critique of Judgment*, trans. James Creed Meridith (London: Oxford University Press, 1952), p. 212.

14. Ibid., p. 176.

15. Ibid., p. 88.

16. Ibid., p. 43.

17. *Critique of Pure Reason*.

18. TN. On the nonmetaphoricity of the verb *to be* and the philosophical implications of tracing a word's genealogy through its etymology, cf. "Violence and Metaphysics," III, 1, B, and "Of Ontological Violence." In question is the notion of metaphor, which implies the transfer of the name of a thing to another thing with a different name. In a sense, any application of a name to a thing is always metaphorical, and for many philosophies (e.g., those of Rousseau and Condillac) metaphor is the origin of language. The question, then, is whether there is an *origin* of metaphor, an absolutely nonmetaphorical concept, as, for example, the verb *to be*, or the notion of breathing, for which Nietzsche says the notion of Being is a metaphor (in *Greek Philosophy during the Tragic Age*). If it could be shown that there is no absolute origin of metaphor, the separation or space implied in metaphor as transfer would become problematical, as it would then be nonreducible.

19. TN. The reference is to Descartes, for whom everything perceived clearly and distinctly had to be something understandable, could not be nothing. Cf. *Meditations*.

20. Cited by Maurice Blanchot in *L'Arche*, nos. 27–28 (August–September, 1948), p. 133. Is not the same situation described in *l'Introduction à la méthode de Léonard de Vinci?*

21. Is it not constituted by this requirement? Is it not a kind of privileged representation of inscription?

22. TN. The play is on the etymology of *anguish*, from the Latin *angustia*, meaning narrowness or distress.

23. Also, the anguish of a breath that cuts itself off in order to reenter itself, to aspirate itself and return to its original source. Because to speak is to know that thought *must* become alien to itself in order to be pronounced and to appear. It wishes, then, to take itself back by offering itself. This is why one senses the gesture of withdrawal, of retaking possession of the exhaled word, beneath the language of the authentic writer, the writer who wishes to maintain the greatest proximity to the origin of his act. This too is inspiration. One can say of original language what Feuerbach says of philosophical language: "Philosophy emerges from mouth or pen only in order to return immediately to its proper *source;* it does not speak for the pleasure of speaking—whence its antipathy for fine phrases—but in order not to speak, in order *to think*. . . . To demonstrate is simply to show that what I *say* is *true;* simply to grasp once more the alienation (*Entäusserung*) of thought at the *original source* of thought. Thus the signification of the demonstration cannot be conceived without reference to the signification of language. Language is nothing other than the *realization of the species*, the mediation between the I and the thou which is to represent the unity of the species by means of the suppression (*Aufhebung*) of their individual isolation. This is why the element of speech is air, the most spiritual and most universal vital medium" (*Zur Kritik der Hegelschen Philosophie,*1839, in L. Feuerbach, *Sämtliche Werke*, vol. 2 [Stuttgart–Bad Canstatt, 1959], pp. 169–70).

But did Feuerbach muse upon the fact that *vaporized* language forgets itself? That air is not the element in which history develops if it does not rest (itself) on earth? Heavy, serious, solid earth. The earth that is worked upon, scratched, written upon. The no less universal element in which meaning is engraved so that it will last.

Hegel would be of more assistance here. For even though he too, in a spiritual metaphorization of natural elements, thinks that "air is the unchanging factor, purely universal and transparent; water, the reality that is forever being resolved and given up; fire, their animating unity," he nevertheless posits that "earth is the tightly compact knot of this articulated whole, the subject in which these realities *are*, where their processes take effect, that which they start from and to which they return" (*Phenomenology of the Mind*, trans. J. B. Baillie [London: George Allen & Unwin, 1931], p. 518.

The problem of the relation between writing and the earth is also that of the possibility of such a metaphorization of the elements. Of its origin and meaning.

24. TN. The Hebrew *ruah*, like the Greek *pneuma*, means both wind or breath and soul or spirit. Only in God are breath and spirit, speech and thought, absolutely identical; man can always be duplicitous, his speech can be other than his thought.

25. G. W. Leibniz, *Theodicy: Essays on the Goodness of God, the Freedom of Man, and the Origin of Evil*, trans. E. M. Huggard (New Haven: Yale University Press, 1952), pp. 370–72. [At issue again is the distinction between the divine and the human, the Book and books. For Leibniz, God's thought is his action and he is not in the world; but for man, whose action is limited but whose thoughts are not, being in the world means that he must always choose between alternatives. Man's will, the power to choose between alternatives as a function of their merits, implies that he is finite, that his actions do not always equal his thought. God is infinite *because* his thought and his action are coextensive, because he is extraworldly, transcendent.—Trans.]

26. Stéphane Mallarmé, *Selected Poems, Essays and Letters*, trans. Bradford Cook (Baltimore: Johns Hopkins University Press, 1956), p. 15.

27. ". . . à illuminer ceci—que, plus ou moins, tous les livres contiennent la fusion des quelques redites complètes: même il n'en serait qu'un—au monde sa loi—bible comme la simulent les nations. La différence, d'un ouvrage à l'autre, offrant autant de leçons proposées dans un immense councours pour le texte véridique, entre les âges dits civilisés—ou lettrés." Ibid., pp. 41–42.

28. TN. The *Livre de raison* was the journal kept by the head of a family during the Middle Ages.

29. "Réflexions sur la création artistique selon Alain," *Revue de métaphysique et de morale*, April–June 1952, p. 171. This analysis makes evident that the *Système des beaux-arts*, written during the First World War, does more than foretell the most apparently original themes of "modern" aesthetics. Particularly through a certain anti-Platonism which does not exclude, as Canguilhem demonstrates, a profound alliance with Plato, beyond Platonism "understood without malice."

30. TN. According to Leibniz, each monad—the spiritual (nonmaterial) building blocks of the universe—is the representation of the entire universe as preordained by God. Cf. *Monadology*.

31. Maurice Merleau-Ponty, "An Unpublished Text," trans. Arleen B. Ballery, in *The Primacy of Perception*, ed. James M. Edie (Evanston: Northwestern University Press, 1964), pp. 8–9. The text was first published in the *Revue de metaphysique et de morale*, October–December, 1962.

32. "Problèmes actuels de la phénoménologie," in *Actes du colloque internationale de phénoménologie* (Paris, 1952), p. 97.

33. Saint John Chrysostom, *Homilies on the Gospel of Saint Matthew*, vol. 10 of the *Select Library of the Nicene and Post-Nicene Fathers of the Christian Church*, ed. Philip Schaff (Grand Rapids: William B. Eerdman, 1956), p. 1.

34. TN. In his translation of the Old Testament, Buber attempted to restore as much as possible the polysemantic structure of certain key words upon which he based his interpretations. Derrida here is attempting to examine the presuppositions of construing certain words or ideas as the source of the play of difference implied in linguistic multivalence. The idea that seems to support the next few sentences (in the text) is that if there is no source of "Being," "Being" must then be understood like a game, that is, only in function of itself. Language would then most accurately "approximate" Being

when it, too, functions only in relation to itself—"poetry"—without attempting to adequate itself to any particular existent. One could then be led to speak of language as having no reference to signified meanings but rather as creating these meanings through the play of signifiers. The signifier is always that which is inscribed or written.

35. TN. Finitude: empiricity and historicity. Derrida's vocabulary here is Heideggerean—which is not to say that he is simply adopting Heidegger's ideas, but is rather gradually putting Heidegger into question. To suggest that the hidden essence of the empirical is historicity, to deal with affectivity as the index of finitude—these are all Heideggerean themes related to the problem of transcendence as discussed at length, and unreproduceably, in Heidegger's *Kant and the Question of Metaphysics,* trans. James S. Churchill (Bloomington: Indiana University Press, 1962).

36. "Brief über den 'Humanismus,' " in *Wegmarken* (Frankfurt, 1967), p. 158.

37. Rousset, *Forme et Signification,* p. xviii, "For this very reason, Georges Poulet has little interest in *art,* in the work as a reality incarnated in a language and in formal structures; he suspects them of 'objectivity': the critic runs the risk of grasping them from without."

38. "Jean-Pierre Richard's analyses are so intelligent, his results so new and so convincing that one must agree with him, regarding his own questions. But in conformity with his own perspectives, he is primarily interested in the imaginary world of the poet, in the latent work, rather than in the work's morphology and style."

39. Guez de Balzac, book 8, letter 15.

40. Vaugelas, *Rem.,* vol. 2, p. 101.

41. Claude Lévi-Strauss, *Structural Anthropology,* trans. C. Jacobson and B. G. Schoepf (New York: Basic Books, 1963), p. 283.

42. G. W. Leibniz, *Discourse on Metaphysics, Correspondence with Arnauld and Monadology,* trans. George R. Montgomery (LaSalle, Ill.: Open Court Publishing Co., 1968), pp. 18–19.

43. Let us at least reproduce the synthesizing conclusion, the resumé of the essay: "An itinerary and a metamorphosis, we said after the analysis of the first and fifth acts, as concerns their symmetry and variants. We must now affix to this another essential characteristic of Corneillean drama: the movement it describes is an ascending movement toward a center situated in infinity." (In this spatial schema, what happens to infinity, which is here the essential, that is, is not only the irreducible *specificity* of the "movement," but also its *qualitative* specificity?) "Its nature can be further specified. An upward movement of two rings is a helical ascent; two ascending lines separate, cross, move away from and rejoin each other in a common profile beyond the play itself . . . " (the structural meaning of the expression "beyond the play itself?") " . . . Pauline and Polyeucte meet and separate in the first act; they meet again, closer to each other and on a higher plane, in the third act, only to separate again; they climb up another level and reunite in the fifth act, the culminating phase of the ascension, from whence they jump forth in a final leap which will unite them definitively, at the supreme point of freedom and triumph, in God" (Rousset, *Forme et Signification,* p. 6).

44. Leibniz, *Discourse on Metaphysics,* p. 10.

45. Ibid.

46. Cf., for example, Maurice Leenhardt, *L'art océanien: Gens de la grande terre,* p. 99; *Do kamo,* pp. 19–21.

47. TN. I.e., of structure as a metaphor for locality, site.

48. TN. This is the question of the closure of metaphysics, for metaphysics contains every discourse that attempts to emerge from it. According to Derrida, metaphysics can only be destroyed from within, by making its own language—which is the only language we have—work against it.

49. Here are several formulations of this "permanent structure": "where is the true play? It is in the superimposing and interweaving of the two levels, in the separations and exchanges established between them, offering us the subtle pleasure of binocular viewing and double reading" (Rousset, *Forme et Signification,* p. 56) "From this point of view, all of Marivaux's plays could be defined as

an organism existing on two levels whose designs gradually approach until they are completely joined. The play is over when the two levels are indistinguishable, that is, when the group of heroes watched by the spectators sees itself as the spectator-characters saw them. The real resolution is not the marriage promised to us at the fall of the curtain but the encounter of heart and vision'' (ibid., p. 58) "We are invited to follow the development of the play in two registers, which offer us two parallel curves that are separated, however, different in their importance, their language, and their function: the one rapidly sketched, the other fully drawn in all its complexity, the first letting us guess the direction that the second will take, the second deeply echoing the first, providing its definitive meaning. This play of interior reflections contributes to the imparting of a rigorous and supple geometry to Marivaux's play, while at the same time closely linking the two registers, even up to the movements of love'' (ibid., p. 59)

50. TN. In the *Phenomenology* Hegel takes the reader on a "voyage of discovery" that Hegel himself has already made. The dialectical turning points of the *Phenomenology* are always marked by the reader's being brought to a point where he can grasp what Hegel has already grasped, the concept in question becoming true "for us," the distance between subject and object having been annihilated. Hegel defines the structure of the *Phenomenology* as circular, a return to its point of departure.

51. Cited in *Forme et Signification,* p. 189. And Rousset, in fact, comments: "Not isolated, such a declaration is valid for all orders of reality. Everything obeys the law of *composition,* which is the law of the artist as it is of the Creator. For the universe is a simultaneity, by virtue of which things at a remove from each other lead a concerted existence and form a harmonic solidarity; to the metaphor that unites them corresponds, in the relations between beings, love, the link between separated souls. It is thus natural for Claudel's thought to admit that two beings severed from each other by distance can be conjoined in their simultaneity, henceforth resonating like two notes of a chord, like Prouhèze and Rodrigue in their inextinguishable relationship.''

52. Bergson, *Essai sur les données immédiates de la conscience.*

53. For the man of literary structuralism (and perhaps of structuralism in general), the letter of books—movement, infinity, lability, and instability of meaning rolled up in itself in the wrapping, the volume—has not yet replaced (but can it ever?) the letter of the flattened, established Law: the commandment on the Tables.

54. On this "identification with itself" of the Mallarmean book, cf. Jacques Scherer, *Le 'Livre' de Mallarmé,* p. 95 and leaf 94, and p. 77 and leaves 129–30.

55. We will not insist upon this type of question, banal but difficult to get around, and posing itself, moreover, at each step of Rousset's work, whether he is concerned with an author taken by himself or with an isolated work. Is there only one fundamental structure each time? How is it to be recognized and given its privilege? The criterion can be neither an empirical-statistical accumulation, nor an intuition of an essence. It is the problem of induction which presents itself to a structuralist science concerned with works, that is to say, with things whose structure is not apriorical. Is there a material a priori of the work? But the intuition of a material a priori poses formidable preliminary problems.

56. TN. This is a reference to Levinas and his attempted pacification of philosophy through the notion of the Other as face. For Derrida, philosophy, metaphysics, is irreducibly violent, practices an economy of violence. Cf. "Violence and Metaphysics."

57. TN. The reference is to Nietzsche's opposition of the Apollonian and the Dionysian (sculpture/music, individuation/unification of the many with the one, tranquility/bacchanal) in *The Birth of Tragedy.*

58. TN. This explication is to be found in the chapter of the *Phenomenology* entitled "Force and Understanding." The title of that chapter alone demonstrates its relationship to this essay.

59. TN. Cf. above, note 18.

60. TN. Derrida here is specifying several characteristics of metaphysics without demonstrating their interrelatedness. 1. "Heliocentric metaphysics" refers to the philosophical language founded

on metaphors of light and dark, e.g., truth as light, error as dark, etc. 2. This language always implies a privileged position of "acoustics," i.e., a privilege accorded to a phonological, spoken model of the *presence* of truth in living, spoken discourse, and a concomitant abasement of the silent work of the "force" of differentiation. This abasement is typically revealed in the philosophical treatment of writing. 3. This system is set in motion by Platonism, whose doctrine of the *eidos* implies both points just mentioned.

61. Friedrich Nietzsche, *The Twilight of the Idols*, translated by Anthony M. Ludovici (New York: Russell and Russell, 1964), p. 67.

62. Flaubert, *Préface à la vie d'écrivain*, p. 111.

63. Friedrich Nietzsche, "Nietzsche contra Wagner," in *The Case of Wagner*, trans. Anthony M. Ludovici (New York: Russell and Russell, 1964) p. 116. [In Nietzsche's text the French is left untranslated: "Flaubert is always despicable, the man is nothing, the work everything."] It is not without interest, perhaps, to juxtapose this barb of Nietzsche's with the following passage from *Forme et Signification:* "Flaubert's correspondence is precious, but in Flaubert the letter writer I cannot find Flaubert the novelist; when Gide states that he prefers the former I have the feeling that he chooses the lesser Flaubert or, at least, the Flaubert that the novelist did everything to eliminate" (Rousset, p. xx).

64. Nietzsche, *The Twilight of the Idols,* p. 59.

65. Ibid., p. 6.

66. Friedrich Nietzsche, *Thus Spake Zarathrustra,* trans. Thomas Common (New York: Russell and Russell, 1964), p. 239.

67. Ibid., p. 242, slightly modified.

Two	**Cogito and the**
	History of Madness

1. With the exception of several notes and a short passage (in brackets), this paper is the reproduction of a lecture given 4 March 1963 at the Collège Philosophique. In proposing that this text be published in the *Revue de métaphysique et de morale,* M. Jean Wahl agreed that it should retain its first form, that of the spoken word, with all its requirements and, especially, its particular weaknesses: if in general, according to the remark in the *Phaedrus,* the written word is deprived of "the assistance of its father," if it is a fragile "idol" fallen from "living and animated discourse" unable to "help itself," then is it not more exposed and disarmed than ever when, miming the improvisation of the voice, it must give up even the resources and lies of style?

2. Michel Foucault, *Folie et déraison: Histoire de la folie à l'âge classique* (Paris: Plon, 1961); trans. Richard Howard *Madness and Civilization: A History of Insanity in the Age of Reason* (New York: Pantheon, 1965). [Howard has translated the abridged version of Foucault's book. Whenever possible I have used Howard's translations of passages cited by Derrida. All nonfootnoted translations of Foucault are my own.]

3. In *The Interpretation of Dreams* (trans. and ed. James Strachey in *The Standard Edition of the Complete Psychological Works of Sigmund Freud,* vol. 4 London: Hogarth Press, 1955, p. 99, n.1), speaking of the link between dreams and verbal expression, Freud recalls Ferenczi's remark that every language has its own dream language. The latent content of a dream (and of any behavior or consciousness in general) communicates with the manifest content only through the unity of a language—a language that the analyst must thus speak as well as possible. (On this subject cf. Daniel Lagache, "Sur le polyglottisme dans l'analyse," in *La psychanalyse,* vol. 1 [Paris: 1956], pp. 167–78.) *As well as possible:* progress in the knowledge and practice of a language being by nature infinitely open (*first* by virtue of the original and essential equivocality of the signifier, at least in the language of "everyday life," its indeterminateness and playing-space being precisely that which liberates the difference between hidden and stated meaning; *then,* by virtue of the original and

essential communication between different languages throughout history; *finally,* by virtue of the play, the relation to itself, or "sedimentation," of every language), are not the insecurities and insufficiencies of analysis axiomatic or irreducible? And does not the historian of philosophy, whatever his method or project, abandon himself to the same dangers? Especially if one takes into account a certain embedding of philosophical language in nonphilosophical language.

4. That all history can only be, in the last analysis, the history of meaning, that is, of Reason in general, is what Foucault could not fail to experience—we shall come to this in a moment. What he could not fail to experience is that the general meaning of a difficulty he attributes to the "classical experience" is valid well beyond the "classical age." Cf., for example: "And when it was a question, in seeking it in its most withdrawn essence, of peeling it away to its last structure, we would discover, in order to formulate it, only the *very language of reason* employed in the impeccable logic of delirium; precisely that which made it accessible counterfeited it as madness." The very language of reason . . . but what is a language that would not be one of reason *in general?* And if there is no history, except of rationality and meaning in general, this means that philosophical language, as soon as it speaks, reappropriates negativity—or forgets it, which is the same thing—even when it allegedly affirms or recognizes negativity. More surely then, perhaps. The history of truth is therefore the history of this *economy* of the negative. It is necessary, and it is perhaps time to come back to the ahistorical in a sense radically opposed to that of classical philosophy: not to misconstrue negativity, but this time to affirm it—silently. It is negativity and not positive truth that is the nonhistorical capital of history. In question then would be a negativity so negative that it could not even be called such any longer. Negativity has always been determined by dialectics—that is to say, by metaphysics—as *work* in the service of the constitution of meaning. To affirm negativity in silence is to gain access to a nonclassical type of dissociation between thought and language. And perhaps to a dissociation of thought and philosophy as discourse, if we are conscious of the fact that this schism cannot be enunciated, thereby erasing itself, except within philosophy.

5. Foucault, *Folie et déraison,* pp. x–xi. [I have modified Howard's translation of this sentence to include the "on" whose double sense was played upon above, p. 34.]

6. TN. I have consistently translated *œuvre* as "work" throughout this essay to avoid confusions that could be caused by translating it as "work of art," as Howard does. To translate Foucault's definition of madness, commented upon by Derrida, as "the absence of the work of art" (*l'absence d'œuvre*) does not convey Foucault's sense of the absence of a work governed by institutionalized rationalism.

7. TN. Derrida is making use of the fact that the word *éloge* (praise) is derived from the same word as "logos."

8. Foucault, *Folie et déraison,* p. xi.

9. Cf. also, for example, *Symposium* 217e/218b; *Phaedrus* 244b–c/245a/249/265a ff.; *Theatetus* 257e; *Sophist* 228d/229a; *Timeus* 86b; *Republic* 382c; *Laws* X 888a.

10. TN. Cf. note 7 above.

11. TN. *The Philosophical Works of Descartes,* translated by Elizabeth S. Haldane and G. R. T. Ross (Cambridge: The University Press, 1970), p. 146.

12. TN. Ibid., p. 146.

13. TN. Ibid., pp. 146–47.

14. TN. Ibid., p. 145.

15. *Madness, theme or index:* what is significant is that Descartes, at bottom, never speaks of madness itself in this text. Madness is not his theme. He treats it as the index of a question of principle, that is, of epistemological value. It will be said, perhaps, that this is the sign of a profound exclusion. But this silence on madness itself simultaneously signifies the opposite of an exclusion, since *it is not a question of madness* in this text, if only to exclude it. It is not in the *Meditations* that Descartes speaks of madness itself.

16. To underline this vulnerability and touch on the greatest difficulty, we would have to specify that

the expressions "sensory or corporeal fault" or "corporeal error" could have no meaning for Descartes. There is no corporeal error, particularly in illness: jaundice or melancholy are only the *occasions* of an error that itself is born only with the consent or affirmation of the will in judgment, when "one who is ill with jaundice judges everything to be yellow because his eye is tinged with yellow. So finally, too, when the imagination is diseased, as in cases of melancholia, and a man thinks that his own disorderly fancies represent real things" (*Rule XII*. Descartes emphasizes this point: the most abnormal sensory or imaginative experience, considered in and of itself, at its own level and at its proper moment, never deceives us; or never deceives understanding, "if it restrict its attention accurately to the object presented to it, just as it is given to it either firsthand or by means of an image; and if it moreover refrain from judging that the imagination faithfully reports the objects of the senses, or that the senses take on the true forms of things, or in fine that external things always are as they appear to be" [Haldane and Ross, p. 44].)

17. TN. The paragraph organization of Haldane and Ross does not correspond to the paragraph organization of the edition of Descartes cited by Derrida.

18. Haldane and Ross, p. 147.

19. Haldane and Ross, p. 148.

20. Ibid. It is a question here of the order of reasons, as it is followed in the *Meditations*. It is well known that in the *Discourse* (part 4) doubt very promptly attacks the "simplest geometrical questions" in which men sometimes "commit paralogisms."

21. Like Leibniz, Descartes has confidence in "scientific" or "philosophical" language, which is not necessarily the language taught in the Schools (*Rule III*) and which must also be carefully distinguished from the "terms of ordinary language" which alone can "deceive us" (*Meditations* II).

22. That is to say, as soon as, more or less implicitly, *Being* is *called upon* (even before its determination as essence and existence)—which can only mean, *to be called upon by Being*. Being would not be what it is if speech *simply* preceded or invoked it. Language's final protective barrier against madness is the meaning of Being.

23. Haldane and Ross, p. 101.

24. It is a question less of a *point* than of a temporal originality in general.

25. TN. The reference is to Plato's *Republic* 509b–c.

26. It risks erasing the excess by which every philosophy (of meaning) is related, in some region of its discourse, to the nonfoundation of unmeaning.

27. In the next to last paragraph of the sixth *Meditation,* the theme of normality communicates with the theme of memory, at the moment when the latter, moreover, is confirmed by absolute Reason as "divine veracity," etc.

Generally speaking, does not God's confirmation of the remembrance of obvious truths signify that only the positive infinity of divine reason can absolutely reconcile temporality and truth? In the infinite alone, beyond all determinations, negations, "exclusions" and "internments," is produced the reconciliation of time and thought (truth) which Hegel claimed was the task of nineteenth-century philosophy, while the reconciliation of thought and space was to have been the aim of the so-called "Cartesian" rationalisms. That this divine infinity is the proper location, condition, name, or horizon of these two reconciliations is what has never been contested by any *metaphysician,* neither by Hegel, nor by the majority of those, such as Husserl, who have attempted to think and to name the essential temporality or historicity of truth and meaning. For Descartes, the crisis of which we are speaking would finally have its intrinsic (that is, *intellectual*) origin in time itself, as the absence of a necessary link between its parts, as the contingency and discontinuity of the transition from instant to instant; which supposes that here we follow all the interpretations opposed to Laporte's on the question of the role of the instant in Descartes's philosophy. In the last resort, only continuous creation, uniting conservation and creation, which "differ only as concerns our way of thinking," reconciles temporality and truth. It is God who excludes madness and crisis, that is to say, embraces them in the presence that encompasses all traces and differences. Which amounts to saying that crisis, anomaly, negativity, etc. are irreducible within the experience of finitude, or of a finite moment, a *determination* of absolute reason, or of reason in general. To attempt to deny this, and allegedly to affirm positivity (the positivity of truth, meaning, norms, etc.) outside the horizon of this infinite reason (reason in general, beyond all its specific determinations), is to attempt to erase negativity, and is to forget finitude at the very moment when one allegedly denounces as mystification the theologism of the great classical rationalisms.

28. But God is the other name of the absolute of reason *itself,* of reason and meaning in general. And what could exclude, reduce, or—amounting to the same thing—*absolutely embrace* madness, if not reason in general, absolute and undetermined reason, whose other name is God, for the classical rationalists? One cannot accuse those, individuals or societies, who use God as a recourse against madness of seeking to *shelter themselves,* to be sure of having protections against madness—the safe boundaries of asylums—except by construing this shelter as a *finite* one, within the world, by making God a third party or finite power, that is, except by deceiving oneself; by deceiving oneself not concerning the content and effective finality of this gesture in history, but concerning the philosophical specificity of the idea and name of God. If philosophy has taken place—which can always be contested—it is only in the extent to which it has formulated the aim of thinking beyond the finite shelter. By describing the historical constitution of these finite protective barriers against madness within the movement of individuals, societies and all finite totalities in general—a legitimate, immense, and necessary task—one can finally describe everything except the philosophical project itself. And except the project of this description itself. One cannot allege that the philosophical project of the "infinitivist" rationalisms served as an instrument or as an alibi for a finite historico-politico-social violence (which is doubtless the case) without *first* having to acknowledge and respect the intentional meaning of this project itself. Now, within its own intentional meaning, this project presents itself as the conceptualization of the infinite, that is, of that which cannot be exhausted by any finite totality, by any function or by any instrumental, technical, or political determination. It will be said that this presentation of the philosophical project by itself as such is its greatest lie, its violence and its mystification—or, further, its bad faith. And, certainly, the structure which links this intention to exceed the world to the totality of history must be described rigorously, and its economy must be determined. But like all ruses, these economic ones are possible only for finite words and finite intentions, substituting one finitude for another. One cannot lie when one says *nothing* (that is finite or determined), or when one says God, Being, or Nothingness, or when one does not modify the finite by the declared meaning of one's words, or when one says the infinite, that is, when one lets the infinite (God, Being, or Nothingness, for part of the meaning of the infinite is its inability to be an ontic determination among others) be said and conceived. The theme of divine veracity and the difference between God and the evil genius are thus illuminated by a light which is only apparently indirect.

In short, Descartes knew that, without God, finite thought never had the *right* to exclude madness, etc. Which amounts to saying that madness is never excluded, except *in fact,* violently, in history; or rather that this exclusion, this *difference* between the fact and the principle is historicity, the possibility of history itself. Does Foucault say otherwise? *"The necessity of* madness . . . is linked to the *possibility of history"* (author's italics).

29. Haldane and Ross, p. 171.

30. Foucault, *Folie et déraison,* p. 199.

Three	Edmond Jabès and the Question of the Book

1. *Je bâtis ma demeure: Poèmes, 1943–1957* (Paris: Gallimard, 1959). This collection has been admirably prefaced by Gabriel Bounore. There have now been major studies devoted to Jabès: Maurice Blanchot, "L'interruption," *Nouvelle revue française,* May 1964; Gabriel Bounore, "Ed-

mond Jabès: la demeure et le livre," *Mercure de France,* January 1965; and "Edmond Jabès, ou la guérison par le livre," *Les lettres nouvelles,* July-September 1966.

2. TN. Jabès, *Le Livre des questions* (Paris: Gallimrd, 1963).

3. TN. The two interpretations of interpretation are again examined at the end of "Structure, Sign, and Play," this vol, chap. 10. The "rabbinical" interpretation of interpretation is the one which seeks a final truth, which sees interpretation as an unfortunately necessary road back to an original truth. The "poetical" interpretation of interpretation does not seek truth or origin, but affirms the play of interpretation.

4. TN. Cf. the end of "Force and Signification," this vol., chap. 1, for the broken tables in Nietzsche as they relate to writing as the mark of otherness, the "rupture" that "begins" history.

5. TN. Derrida is referring here to the moment of the unhappy consciousness in Hegel's *Phenomenology of the Mind.* Hegel's first model for the unhappy consciousness was Abraham.

6. TN. The silence and hiding of Being are Heideggerean themes, for they are, as Heidegger says, "the question of Nothing."

7. TN. "To leave speech" is to leave behind a *trace* which always means that the writer is not present.

8. TN. On the Leibnizian Book, cf. "Force and Signification," chap. 1 above, note 25.

9. TN. On these questions, cf. "Violence and Metaphysics."

10. TN. That Being is neither present nor outside difference are the themes of *Identity and Difference* by Heidegger.

11. TN. The ontological double genitive is also a theme of *Identity and Difference.*

| **Four** | **Violence and Metaphysics** |

1. Emmanuel Levinas, *Théorie de l'intuition dans la phénoménologie de Husserl* (1st ed., Paris: Alcan, 1930; 2d ed., Vrin, 1963); *De l'existence à l'existant* (Fontaine, 1947); *Le temps et l'autre,* in *Le Choix, le Monde, l'Existence,* Cahiers du Collège philosophique (Arthaud, 1949); *En découvrant l'existence, avec Husserl et Heidegger* (Vrin, 1949); *Totalité et infini, Essai sur l'extériorité* (The Hague: Martinus Nijhoff, 1961); *Difficile liberté, Essais sur le judaisme* (Albin Michel, 1963).

I shall also refer to several articles which I shall mention at the proper moment. The principal works will be designated by the initials of their titles: *Théorie de l'intuition . . . : THI; De l'existence à l'existant: EE; Le temps et l'autre: TA; En découvrant l'existence: EDE; Totalité et infini: TI* [see below]; *Difficile liberté: DL.*.

This essay was already written when two important texts by Emmanuel Levinas appeared: "La trace de l'autre", in *Tijdschrift voor Filosofie,* September 1963; and "La signification et le sens," *Revue de métaphysique et de morale,* 1964, no. 2. Unfortunately we can make but brief allusions to these texts here. [The major work referred to in this essay has appeared in English: *Totality and Infinity,* trans. Alphonso Lingis (Pittsburgh: Duquesne University Press, 1969). All page references to *TI* are to Lingis's translation.]

2. TN. On the double genitive cf. above, chap. 3, note 11.

3. After desiring to restore the properly ontological intention dormant within metaphysics, after having reawakened the "fundamental ontology" beneath "metaphysical ontology," Heidegger, faced by the tenacity of traditional ambiguity, finally proposes to abandon the terms "ontology" and "ontological" (*Introduction to Metaphysics*). The question of Being cannot be submitted to an ontology.

4. That is, to relativism: the truth of philosophy does not depend upon its relation to the actuality of the Greek or European event. On the contrary, we must gain access to the Greek or European *eidos* through an irruption or a call whose point of departure is variously determined by Husserl and Heidegger. It remains that, for both, "the irruption of philosophy" ("Aufbruch oder Einbruch der

Philosophie," Husserl, *Krisis* ...) is the "original" phenomenon "which characterizes Europe as a "spiritual figure" (ibid.). For both, the "word *philosophia* tells us that philosophy is something which, first of all, determines the existence of the Greek world. Not only that—*philosophia* also determines the innermost basic feature of our Western-European history, the often heard expression 'Western-European philosophy' is, in truth, a tautology. Why? Because philosophy is Greek in its nature; Greek, in this instance, means that in origin the nature of philosophy is of such a kind that it first appropriated the Greek world, and only it, in order to unfold." Heidegger, *What Is Philosophy?*, trans. William Kluback and Jean T. Wilde (London: Vision Press, 1958), pp. 29–31.

5. Husserl: "Reason does not suffer being distinguished into 'theoretical,' 'practical,' or 'esthetic,' etc." (*Verité et liberté,* trans. P. Ricoeur). Heidegger: "Terms such as 'logic,' 'ethics,' 'physics,' appear only at the moment when original thinking loses its hold" (*Brief über den "Humanismus,"* in *Wegmerken* [Frankfurt, 1967], p. 147).

6. TN. Lingis's note, *TI,* p. 24: "With the author's permission, we are translating '*autrui*' (the personal Other, the you) by 'Other,' and '*autre*' by 'other.' In doing so, we regrettably sacrifice the possibility of reproducing the author's use of capital or small letters with both these terms in the French text." I have followed Lingis's practice throughout this text.

7. Partial not only due to the point of view chosen, the amplitude of the works, the material and other limits of this essay. But also because Levinas's writing, which would merit an entire separate study itself, and in which stylistic gestures (especially in *Totality and Infinity*) can less than ever be distinguished from intention, forbids the prosaic disembodiment into conceptual frameworks that is the first violence of all commentary. Certainly, Levinas recommends the good usage of prose which breaks Dionysiac charm or violence, and forbids poetic rapture, but to no avail: in *Totality and Infinity* the use of metaphor, remaining admirable and most often—if not always—beyond rhetorical abuse, shelters within its pathos the most decisive movements of the discourse.

By too often omitting to reproduce these metaphors in our disenchanted prose, are we faithful or unfaithful? Further, in *Totality and Infinity* the thematic development is neither purely descriptive nor purely deductive. It proceeds with the infinite insistence of waves on a beach: return and repetition, always, of the same wave against the same shore, in which, however, as each return recapitulates itself, it also infinitely renews and enriches itself. Because of all these challenges to the commentator and the critic, *Totality and Infinity* is a work of art and not a treatise.

8. At the end of *Difficile liberté,* under the title "Signature," will be found the references for a philosophical biography of Levinas.

9. TN. The reference is to Hegel.

10. TN. "Glance" is the translation of *le regard.* Here, Derrida is playing on the visual metaphors in the Greek derivations of theory (from *theorein:* to look at, behold) and phenomenon (from *phainesthai:* to appear).

11. Cf. "La technique phénoménologique," in *Husserl: Cahiers de Royaumont,* and "Intentionnalité et métaphysique," *Revue philosophique,* 1959.

12. The other ancestor, the Latin one, will be Cartesian: the idea of Infinity announcing itself to thought as that which always overflows it. We have just named the only two philosophical gestures—their authors aside—totally acquitted, judged innocent by Levinas. Except for these two anticipations, tradition would only have known, under the name of infinity, the "false infinity" incapable of absolutely overflowing the Same: the infinite as indefinite horizon, or as the transcendence of the totality over its parts.

13. Cf. the philosophical and poetic examples given by Bachelard in *La terre et les rêveries du repos,* pp. 22ff.

14. This schema always regulates Levinas's relations to Husserl. Theoretism and objectivism would be its conclusion, the Husserlian letter betraying the spirit of intentional analysis and of phenomenology. Cf., for example, *Intentionalité et métaphysique:* "The great contribution of Husserlian phenomenology is in the idea that intentionality, or the relation to alterity, is not frozen by polariza-

tion into subject-object. Certainly the manner in which Husserl himself interprets this overflowing of objectifying intentionality by transcendental intentionality consists in reducing the former to other intuitions and as if to 'little perceptions.' " (Would Husserl have subscribed to this interpretation of his "interpretation?" We are not at all sure, but this is not the place for such a question.) There follows a description of the preobjective sphere of an intentional experience absolutely departing from itself toward the other (a description, however, which has never seemed to us to exceed a certain Husserlian literality.) Same schema in *Totality and Infinity:* Husserl's "essential teaching" is opposed to its "letter": "What does it matter if in the Husserlian phenomenology taken literally these unsuspected horizons are in their turn interpreted as thoughts aiming at objects?" (*TI*, p. 28).

15. A proposition that Husserl doubtless would not have accepted easily. Similarly, does the entire analysis devoted to the doxical thesis and to paragraph 117 of Ideas (*Theory of Intuition*, p. 192) take into account the extraordinary enlargement of the notions of *thesis* and *doxa* effected by Husserl, who is already showing such care in respecting the originality of the practical, the axiological, and the aesthetic? As for the meaning of the reduction, it is true that in 1930, and in his published works, Husserl had not yet made it into a theme. We will come back to this. For the moment we are not interested in Husserlian truth, but in Levinas's itinerary.

16. As concerns representation, an important motif in the divergence, as concerns its dignity and status in Husserlian phenomenology, Levinas, however, never seems to have stopped hesitating. But again, almost always, it is a hesitation between the spirit and the letter. Sometimes too between law and fact. This movement can be followed through the following passages: *THI*, pp. 90ff.; *EDE*, pp. 22–23, esp. p. 52; *La technique phénoménologique*, pp. 98–99; *TI*, pp. 95ff.

17. In *EDE*, at a time (1940–49) when the surprises in this area were no longer held in store, the theme of this criticism still will be central: "In Husserl the phenomenon of meaning has never been determined by history." (We do not mean to say, here, that this sentence is *finally* in contradiction with Husserl's then known intentions. But are not the latter, whatever the definitive heart of the matter, already more problematical than Levinas seems to believe?)

18. TN. The reference is to the structure of *Being-with* analyzed in *Being and Time*.

19. TN. Although, as noted in the introduction above, I have attempted to keep to the practice of translating *Sein* by "Being," and *Seiendes* by "being," I shall most often use "existent" for "being" (*Seiendes, étant*) throughout this essay in order to have my vocabulary conform to Levinas's. "Existent" has been maintained in the English translation of *Totality and Infinity*.

20. Hegel himself would not escape the rule. Contradiction would be ceaselessly, and at the end of ends, surmounted. Extreme audacity here would be to turn the accusation of formalism against Hegel, and to denounce speculative reflection as a logic of understanding, as tautological. One can imagine the difficulty of the task.

21. Another discomfort: Levinas never simply condemns technology. It can rescue from a worse violence, the "reactionary" violence of sacred ravishment, of taking root, of the natural proximity of landscape. "Technology takes us out of the Heideggerean world and the superstititons of Place." It offers the chance "to let the human face shine in its nudity" (*DL*). We will return to this. Here, we only wish to foreshadow that *within history*—but is it meaningful elsewhere?—every philosophy of nonviolence can only choose the lesser violence within an *economy of violence*.

22. TN. The reference is to the dialectic of the master and the slave in *The Phenomenology of the Mind:* the master enjoys and consumes the product of the slave's work. The slave defers this enjoyment in the experience of work and therefore, according to Hegel, negates reality in a more abstract, speculative fashion. The slave, thus, is the truth of the master. Cf. chap. 9, "From Restricted to General Economy."

23. TN. In Hegel's *Phenomenology* the model of the unhappy, split consciousness is Abraham, forced to choose between God's command to sacrifice his son Isaac and his love for Isaac. Cf. also the remarks at the beginning of *"Cogito* and the History of Madness," chap. 2 above.

24. "Liberté et commandment," *Revue de métaphysique et de morale,* 1933.

25. Among the numerous passages denouncing the impotence of so-called "formal logic" when confronted with naked experience, let us point out in particular *TI,* pp. 194, 260, 276, where the description of fecundity must acknowledge "a duality of the Identical." (One in two, one in three . . . Had not the Greek Logos already survived tremors of this nature? Had it not, rather, welcomed them?)

26. An affirmation at once profoundly faithful to Kant ("Respect is applied only to persons"— *Practical Reason*) and implicitly anti-Kantian, for without the formal element of universality, without the pure order of the law, respect for the other, respect and the other no longer escape empirical and pathological immediacy. Nevertheless, how do they escape according to Levinas? It is perhaps to be regretted that no systematic and patient confrontation has been organized with Kant in particular. To our knowledge, only an allusion is made to the "Kantian echos," and "to Kant's practical philosophy to which we feel particularly close,"—and this barely in passing—in one article ("L'ontologie est-elle fondamentale?" *Revue de métaphysique et de morale* 1951; reprinted in *Phénoménologie, Existence.*) This confrontation is called for not only because of the ethical themes but also because of the difference between totality and infinity, about which Kant, among others and perhaps more than others, had a number of thoughts.

27. Levinas often makes accusations against the Socratic mastery which teaches nothing, teaches only the already known, and makes everything arise from the self, that is from the Ego, or from the Same as Memory. Anamnesis too, would be a procession of the Same. On this point, at least, Levinas cannot oppose himself to Kierkegaard (cf., for example, J. Wahl, *Etudes Kierkegaardiennes,* pp. 308–9), for his critique of Platonism here is literally Kierkegaardian. It is true that Kierkegaard opposed Socrates to Plato each time that reminiscence was in question. The latter would belong to the Platonic "speculation" from which Socrates "separates" himself (*Post scriptum*).

28. G. W. F. Hegel, *The Philosophy of Fine Art,* trans. F. P. B. Osmaston (London: C. Bell and Sons, 1920) 1:206–7.

29. Ibid., 3:15.

30. Ibid.

31. Ibid., p. 341.

32. "A priori et subjectivité," *Revue de métaphysique et de morale,* 1962.

33. Ludwig Feuerbach, *Kleine philosophische Schriften* (Leipzig 1950), p. 191.

34. M. de Gondillac, *Introduction aux oeuvres choisies de Nicolas de Cues,* p. 35.

35. *Nouvelle revue française,* December 1961, "Connaissance de l'inconnu."

36. It is true that for Merleau-Ponty—differing from Levinas—the phenomenon of alterity was primordially, if not exclusively, that of the movement of temporalization.

37. While defending himself against "the ridiculous pretension of 'correcting' Buber" (*TI*), Levinas, in substance, reproaches the I-Thou relationship (1) for being reciprocal and symmetrical, thus committing violence against height, and especially against separateness, and secretiveness; (2) for being formal, capable of "uniting man to things, as much as Man to man" (*TI*); (3) for preferring preference, the "private relationship," the "clandestine nature" of the couple which is "self-sufficient and forgetful of the universe" (*TI*). For there is also in Levinas's thought, despite his protests against neutrality, a summoning of the third party, the universal witness, the face of the world which keeps us from the "disdainful spiritualism" of the I-Thou. Others will determine, perhaps, whether Buber would recognize himself in this interpretation. It can already be noted in passing that Buber seems to have foreseen these reservations. Did he not specify that the I-Thou relationship was neither referential nor exclusive in that it is previous to all empirical and eventual modifications? Founded by the absolute I-Thou, which turns us toward God, it opens up, on the contrary, the possibility of every relationship to Others. Understood in its original authenticity, it is neither detour nor diversion. Like many of the contradictions which have been used to embarrass Buber, this one yields, as the *Postscript to I-Thou* tells us, "to a superior level of judgment" and to "the paradoxical description of God as the absolute Person. . . . It is as the absolute Person that God

enters into a direct relation with us. . . . The man who turns to him therefore need not turn away from any other I-Thou relation; but he properly brings them to him, and lets them be fulfilled 'in the face of God' " (*I and Thou,* trans. Ronald Gregor Smith, New York: Scribner's, 1958).

38. On the theme of the height of God in its relation to the prone position of child or man (for example, on his sick bed or deathbed), on the relations between the *clinic* and *theology,* cf., for example, Feuerbach (see note 33 above), p. 233.

39. Here we ought to examine Malebranche too grappling with the problem of light and of the face of God (cf. especially 10th *Eclaircissement*).

40. We will not go beyond this schema. It would be useless to attempt, here, to enter into the descriptions devoted to interiority, economy, enjoyment, habitation, femininity, Eros, to everything suggested under the title *Beyond the Face,* matters that would doubtless deserve many questions. These analyses are not only an indefatiguable and interminable destruction of ''formal logic'' they are so acute and so free as concerns traditional conceptuality, that a commentary running several pages would betray them immeasurably. Let it suffice to state that they depend upon the conceptual matrix we have just outlined, without being deduced from it but ceaselessly regenerating it.

41. On these decisive themes of identity, ipseity and equality, and to confront Hegel and Levinas, cf. notably Jean Hyppolite, *Genèse et structure de la phénoménologie de l'esprit,* 1:147ff.; and Heidegger, *Identity and Difference.*

42. Here we are thinking of the distinction between discourse and violence particularly common to Levinas and to Eric Weil. It does not have the same meaning for both. Levinas notes this in passing and, while paying homage to Weil for his ''systematic and vigorous use of the term violence in its opposition to discourse,'' claims to give ''different meaning'' to this distinction (*DL*). We would be tempted to give a diametrically opposed meaning. The discourse which Weil acknowledges as nonviolent is ontology, the project of ontology. (Cf. *Logique de la philosophie,* e.g., pp. 28ff., ''La naissance de l'ontologie, le discours.'') ''Harmony between men will be established by itself if men are not concerned with themselves, but with what is;'' its polarity is infinite coherence, and its style, at least, is Hegelian. This coherence in ontology is violence itself for Levinas: the ''end of history'' is not absolute Logic, the absolute coherence of the Logos with itself in itself; nor is it harmony in the absolute System, but Peace in separation, the diaspora of absolutes. Inversely, is not peaceful discourse, according to Levinas, the discourse which respects separation and rejects the horizon of ontological coherence, violence itself for Weil? Let us schematize: according to Weil, violence will be, or rather would be, reduced only with the reduction of alterity, or the will to alterity. The reverse is true for Levinas. But for Levinas coherence is always finite (totality, in the meaning he gives to the word, rejecting any possible meaning for the notion of infinite totality). For Weil, it is the notion of alterity, on the contrary, which implies irreducible finitude. But for both, only the infinite is nonviolent, and it can be announced only in discourse. One should examine the common presuppositions of this convergence and divergence. One should ask whether the predetermination, common to these two systems, of violation and of pure logos, and, above all, the predetermination of their incompatability, refers to an absolute truth, or perhaps to an epoch of the history of thought, the history of Being. Let us note that Bataille too, in *Eroticism,* draws inspiration from Weil's concepts, and states this explicitly.

43. TN. Derrida is playing on the double sense of *regard* as ethical concern and as objectifying glance. Cf. note 10 above.

44. At bottom, it is the very notion of a ''constitution of an alter ego'' to which Levinas refuses any merit. He would probably say, with Sartre, ''One *encounters* the Other, one does not constitute it'' (*Being and Nothingness*). This is to understand the word ''constitution'' in a sense that Husserl often warns his reader against. Constitution is not opposed to encounter. It goes without saying that constitution creates, constructs, engenders, nothing: neither existence, nor the fact, which is evident, nor even meaning, which is less evident but equally certain, provided that one takes some patient precautions, and provided that one distinguishes the moments of passivity and activity within

intuition, in Husserl's sense, and the moment in which the distinction becomes impossible. That is, in which the entire problematic opposing "encounter" to "constitution" is no longer meaningful, or has only a derivative and dependent meaning. Unable to enter into these difficulties here, let us simply recall this warning of Husserl's, among so many others: "Here too, as concerns the alter ego, the 'constitution of consciousness' (*Bewusstseinleistung*) does not mean that I invent (*erfinde*) and that I *make* (*mache*) this supreme transcendence." (In question is God.)

Inversely, does not the notion of encounter—a notion to which one must refer, if one rejects all constitution, in the Husserlian sense of the term—aside from being prey to empiricism, let it be understood that there is a time and an experience without "other" *before* the encounter? The difficulties into which one is driven can be imagined. Husserl's philosophical prudence on this matter is exemplary. The *Cartesian Meditations* often emphasize that in *fact, really,* nothing precedes the experience of Others.

45. Or at least cannot *be,* or be anything; and it is indeed the authority of Being which Levinas profoundly questions. That his discourse must still submit to the contested agency is a necessity whose rule we must attempt to inscribe systematically in the text.

46. This connaturality of discourse and of violence does not appear to us to have *emerged in* history, nor to be tied to a given form of communication, or again to a given "philosophy." We wish to show here that this connaturality belongs to the very essence of history, to transcendental historicity, a notion which here can only be understood in the resonance of a speech common—in a way that still calls for clarification—to Hegel, Husserl, and Heidegger.

Historical or ethnosociological information here can only confirm or support, under the rubric of the factual example, the eidetic-transcendental evidence. Even if this information is manipulated (gathered, described, explicated) with the greatest philosophical or methodological prudence, that is, even if it is articulated correctly with the essential reading, and if it respects all levels of eidetic generality, in no case could it *found* or *demonstrate* any necessity of essence. For example, we are not sure that these technical, as well as transcendental precautions are taken by Claude Lévi-Strauss when, in *Tristes tropiques,* amongst many beautiful pages, he advances the "hypothesis" "that the primary function of written communication is to facilitate servitude." If writing—and, indeed, speech in general—retains within it an essential violence, this cannot be "demonstrated" or "verified" on the basis of "facts," whatever sphere they are borrowed from and even if the totality of the "facts" in this domain were available. One can often see in the descriptive practice of the "social sciences" the most *seductive* (in every sense of the word) confusion of empirical investigation, inductive hypothesis and intuition of essence, without any precautions as to the origin and function of the propositions advanced.

47. Alterity, difference, and time are not *suppressed* but *retained* by absolute knowledge in the form of the *Aufhebung.*

48. *Formale und transzendentale Logik* (Halle 1929), p. 209. Husserl's italics.

49. Ibid., pp. 209–10.

50. Ibid., p. 222.

51. Of course we cannot do so here. Far from thinking that this fifth of the *Cartesian Mediations* must be admired in silence as the last word on this problem, we have sought here only to begin to experience and to respect its power of resistance to Levinas's criticisms.

52. "Die Frage des Warum ist ursprünglich Frage nach der Geschichte." Husserl (unpublished E, III, 9, 1931.)

53. *Logische Untersuchungen* (Tübingen 1968), vol. 2, I, para. 4, p. 115.

54. Ibid., p. 124.

55. *L'ontologie est-elle fondamentale?*

56. *Brief über den 'Humanismus,'* p. 192.

57. "We go further, and at the risk of seeming to confuse theory and practice, we treat the one and

the other as modes of metaphysical transcendence. The apparent confusion is willful, and constitutes one of the theses of this book" (*TI*).

58. *Brief über den 'Humanismus,'* p. 192.

59. On this turning back to Being within the predicative, within the articulation essence–existence, etc., cf., among a thousand examples, *Kant and the Problem of Metaphysics,* pp. 40ff.

60. By the expression "Being of the existent," the source of so many confusions, we do not understand, here, as Heidegger does occasionally when the context is clear enough to prevent misunderstanding, the Being-existent of the existent, existenthood (*Seiendheit*), but rather the Being of existenthood, which Heidegger also calls the truth of Being.

61. "The thought which asks the question of the truth of Being ... is neither ethics nor ontology. This is why the question of the relationship between these two disciplines is henceforth without foundation in this domain." (*Humanismus* p. 188).

62. *L'ontologie est-elle fondamentale?*

63. An explicit theme in *Being and Time,* for example. Cf. the opposition of *Sorge, besorgen* and *Fürsorge* in section 26.

64. In the same problematical horizon, one may confront Heidegger's procedures (for example, in the *Introduction to Metaphysics,* "On the Grammar and Etymology of the Word 'Being'") with Benveniste's ("Etre et avoir dans leurs fonctions linguistiques," in *Problèmes de linguistique générale*).

65. Here we could refer to a hundred passages from Heidegger. Rather, let us cite Levinas, who had written, however: "For Heidegger, the comprehension of Being is not a purely theoretical act ... an act of knowledge like any other" (*EDE*).

66. It is not necessary to return to the pre-Socratics here. Aristotle already had rigorously demonstrated that Being is neither genre nor principle. (Cf. for example, *Metaphysics* B, 3, 998 b 20). Does not this demonstration, made at the same time as a critique of Plato, in truth confirm one of the *Sophist*'s intentions? There, Being was certainly defined as one of the "largest genres," and as the most universal of predicates, but also as that which permits all predication in general. As the origin and possibility of predication, it is not a predicate, not, at least, a predicate like any other, but a *transcendental* or *transcategorical* predicate. Further, the *Sophist*—and this is its theme—teaches us to think that Being—which is other than the other and other the same, is the same as itself, and is implied by all genres to the extent that they are—far from closing difference, on the contrary liberates it, and itself is what it is only by this liberation.

67. *Kant and the Problem of Metaphysics,* trans. James S. Churchill (Bloomington: Indiana University Press, 1962), p. 233.

On the nonconceptual character of the thought of Being, cf., among other places *Vom Wesen des Grundes (On the Essence of Reason)* in *Wegmarken* pp. 29ff.; *Humanismus,* pp. 168ff.; *Einführung in die Metaphysik (Introduction to Metaphysics)* pp. 30ff.; and *Holzwege.* And, primarily, section 1 of *Being and Time.*

68. The essential relations between the same and the other (difference) are such that even the hypothesis of a subsumption of the other by the same—violence, according to Levinas—has no meaning. The same is not a category, but the possibility of every category. Here, we should attentively compare Levinas's theses with Heidegger's text entitled *Identity and Difference* (1957). For Levinas, the same is the concept, just as Being and unity are concepts, and these three concepts immediately communicate among each other (cf. *TI* p. 274, for example). For Heidegger, the same is not the identical (cf. *Humanismus,* for example). And, mainly, because it is not a category. The same is not the negation of difference, nor is Being.

69. *Kant and the Problem of Metaphysics* pp. 235–36.

70. In his very fine study, *Heidegger et la pensée de la finitude,* Henri Birault shows how the theme of *Endlichkeit* is progressively abandoned by Heidegger, for "*the same reason* which had

motivated its use at a certain time'' due to ''concern for separating from the thought of Being not only the survivals and metamorphoses of Christian theology, but still the *theological* itself, which is absolutely constitutive of metaphysics as such. In effect, if the Heideggerean concept of *Endlichkeit* was never the Christian-theological concept of finitude, it nevertheless remains that the idea of finite Being is in itself *ontologically* theological and, as such, is incapable of satisfying a thought which draws back from Metaphysics only to meditate, in the light of the forgotten truth of Being, the still hidden unity of its onto-theological essence'' (*Revue internationale de philosophie,* 1960, no. 52). A thought which seeks to go to its very end in its language, to the end of what is envisages under the name of original finitude or finitude of Being, therefore should abandon not only the words and themes of the finite and the infinite, but also, which is doubtless *impossible,* everything that they govern in language, in the deepest sense of the word. This last impossibility does not signify that the beyond of metaphysics is impracticable; on the contrary, it confirms the necessity for this incommensurable overflow to take support from metaphysics. A necessity clearly recognized by Heidegger. Indeed, it marks that only difference is fundamental, and that Being is nothing outside the existent.

71. ''Liberté et commandement,'' *Revue de métaphysique et de morale,* 1953.

72. *Vom Wesen des Grundes* pp. 56ff. and *Einführung in die Metaphysik* p. 150.

73. *Humanismus,* p. 154.

74. Ibid.

75. Ibid., p. 133.

76. Ibid.

77. Rather, let us cite a passage from *Of Learned Ignorance* in which Nicholas of Cusa says: ''The creature comes from God, yet it cannot, in consequence of that, add anything to Him who is the Maximum [Being]. How are we going to be able to form an idea of creature as such?'' And in order to illustrate ''the double process of envelopment and development'' ''whose mode is absolutely unknown,'' he writes: ''It is as if a face were reproduced in its own image. With multiplication of the image we get distant and close reproductions of the face. (I do not mean distance in space but a gradual distance from the true face, since without that multiplication would be impossible.) In the many different images of that face one face would appear in many, different ways, but it would be an appearance that the senses would be incapable of recognizing and the mind of understanding.'' *Of Learned Ignorance,* trans. Father Germain Heron [London: Routledge and Kegan Paul, 1954], p. 79.

78. The thought of Being is what permits us to say, without naïveté, reduction, or blasphemy, ''God, for example.'' That is, to *think* God as what he is without making an object of him. This is what Levinas, here in agreement with all the most classical infinist metaphysics, would judge to be impossible, absurd, or purely verbal: how to think what one says when one proposes the expression, *God—or the infinite—for example*? But the notion of exemplariness would offer more than one piece of resistance to this objection.

79. In a violent article (*Heidegger, Gagarine et nous* in *Difficile liberté,* Heidegger is designated as the enemy of technology and classed among the ''enemies of industrial society,'' who ''most often are reactionaries.'' This is an accusation to which Heidegger has so frequently and so clearly responded that we can do no better than to refer to his writings, in particular to *La question de la technique,* which treats technology as a ''mode of unveiling'' (in *Essais et conférences*), to the *Letter on Humanism,* and to the *Introduction to Metaphysics* (*The Limitation of Being*), where a certain violence, of which we will speak in a moment, is linked in a nonpejorative and nonethical way to technology in the unveiling of Being (*dainon-techné*).

In any event, we can see the specificity of the accusation made by Levinas. Being (as concept) would be the violence of the neutral. The sacred would be the *neutralization* of the personal God. The ''reaction'' against technology would not have as its target the danger of technical depersonalization, but precisely that which liberates from ravishment by the Sacred and implantation in the Site.

80. Since we cannot unfold this debate here, we will refer to the clearest of Heidegger's texts on

this point: (*a*) *Sein und Zeit:* the themes of essential *Unheimlichkeit,* of the "nudity" of being-in-the-world, *"als Un-zuhause."* It is precisely this authentic condition that the *neutral* existence of the *One* flees from. (*b*) *Humanismus:* concerning Hölderlin's poem *Return,* Heidegger notes that in his commentary the word "country" is "thought in an essential sense, not at all a patriotic sense, nor a nationalist sense, but rather, from the point of view of the History of Being." (*c*) In the same location, Heidegger writes in particular: "On the metaphysical plane, every nationalism is an anthropologism, and as such, a subjectivism. Nationalism is not overcome by pure internationalism, but is rather enlarged and set up as a system." (*d*) Finally, as concerns the dwelling and the home (whose praises Levinas also understands himself to sing, but, it is true, as a moment of interiority, and precisely as economy), Heidegger indeed specifies that the home does not metaphorically determine Being on the basis of its economy but, on the contrary, can only be determined as such on the basis of the essence of Being. Cf. also . . . *L'homme habite en poète,* in which, let us note in passing, Heidegger distinguishes the Same and the Equal (*das Selbe–das Gleiche*): "The Same sets to one side any haste to resolve differences in the Equal," in *Essais et conférences.*

81. Cf., for example, *Erläuterungen zu Hölderlins Dichtung* (Frankfurt, 1963), p. 14.

82. Ibid.

83. Ibid., p. 27.

84. Cf. also *Vom Wesen des Grundes.* Theology, the thinking of the existent-God, of the essence and existence of God, thus would suppose the thinking of Being. Here we need not refer to Heidegger in order to understand this movement, but first to Duns Scotus, to whom Heidegger had devoted one of his first writings, as is well known. For Duns Scotus, the thought of common and uniform Being is necessarily prior to the thought of the determined existent (determined, for example, as finite or infinite, created or uncreated, etc.). Which does not mean:

First, that common and uniform Being is a genre, and that Duns Scotus revives the Aristotelian demonstration without nevertheless referring to the analogy. (On this subject, cf. notably Etienne Gilson, *Jean Duns Scot, Introduction à ses positions fondamentales,* pp. 104–5.)

Second, that the doctrine of the uniformity of Being is incompatible with the Aristotelian-Thomist doctrine and with the analogy which, as Gilson shows (ibid., pp. 84–115), is situated on another plane, and answers a different question. The problem which presents itself to Scotus—and which is the one which occupies us here, in the dialogue between Levinas and Heidegger—"is therefore posed on a terrain," writes Gilson, "which is no longer Aristotle's nor Aquinas's, because in order to penetrate it, one must first have emerged from the dilemma imposed by Aristotelianism between the universal and the singular, the 'first' and the 'second,' and thereby have escaped the necessity of choosing between the analogous and the uniform, which can only be accomplished by isolating a notion of Being in some way metaphysically pure of all determination" (ibid., p. 89). It follows that if the thought of Being (which Gilson, differing from Heidegger, here calls "metaphysics") is implied in all theology, it does not precede it, or govern it in any way, as would a principle or a concept. The relations of "first" and "second," etc., have no meaning here.

85. Sartre, like Levinas, had earlier interpreted the *Mitsein* in the sense of camaraderie, the team, etc. Here, we refer to *Being and Time.* Cf. also, *Le concept du monde chez Heidegger.* In this work, Walter Biemel, with much precision and clarity, confronts this interpretation with Heidegger's intentions (pp. 90ff). Let us add simply that the *with* of the *Mitsein originally* no more denotes the structure of a team animated by a neutral common task than does the *with* of the "language *with* God" (*TI*). The Being which can interpellate the *Mitsein* is not, as Levinas often gives us to understand, a third term, a common truth, etc. Finally, the notion of *Mitsein* describes an original structure of the relationship between *Da-Sein* and *Da-Sein* which is prior to every meaning of "encounter" or of "constitution," that is, to the debate which we mentioned above. (Cf. also *Being and Time:* "*With* and *also* must be understood as existentiales and not as categories.")

86. Cf. *Introduction to Metaphysics* (especially "The Limitation of Being").

87. We must specify here, that "ontology" does not refer to the concept of ontology which

Heidegger proposes to renounce (cf. above [note 4]), but to the unfindable expression by which it must be replaced. The word "historical" also must be modified in order to be understood in consonance with the word "ontological," of which it is not an attribute, and in relation to which it marks no derivation.

88. Nicholas of Cusa, *The Idiot,* translated (1650) from *Idiota* (1450), edited by P. Radin (San Francisco: California State Library Occasional Papers, Reprint Series no. 19, 1940), pp. 15–16.

89. *Entre deux mondes* ("Biographie spirituelle de Franz Rosenzweig" in *La conscience juive* [Paris: P.U.F. 1963], p. 126). This lecture, along with an article by A. Néher (*Cahiers de l'Institut de science économique appliqué,* 1959, is the only important text devoted to Rosenzweig, better known in France as the author of *Hegel und der Staat* than of *Der Stern der Erlösung* (*The Star of Redemption,* 1921). Rosenzweig's influence on Levinas seems to have been profound. "We were impressed by the opposition to the idea of totality in Franz Rosenzweig's *Stern der Erlösung,* a work too often present in this book to be cited" *TI,* p. 28.

90. In his *Exposition of Philosophical Empiricism* Schelling wrote: "Thus God would be Being enclosed in itself in an absolute manner, would be substance in the most elevated sense, free of every relation. But from the very fact that we consider these determinations as purely immanent, as relating to nothing external, one finds oneself in the necessity of having to conceive them by parting from *Him,* that is, to conceive him as the *prius,* that is as the absolute *prius.* And it is thus that, pushed to its final consequences, empiricism leads us to the supra-empirical." Naturally, by "enclosed" and "enfolded" one is not to understand finite closure and egoistic muteness, but rather absolute alterity, what Levinas calls the Infinite absolved of relation. An analogous movement is outlined in Bergson, who, in his *Introduction to Metaphysics,* criticizes the empiricist doctrines unfaithful to pure experience in the name of true empiricism, and concludes: "This true empiricism is the true metaphysics."

91. Pure difference is not absolutely different (from nondifference). Hegel's critique of the concept of pure difference is for us here, doubtless, the most uncircumventable theme. Hegel thought absolute difference, and showed that it can be pure only by being impure. In the *Science of Logic,* as concerns *Absolute Difference,* Hegel writes, for example: "This difference is difference in-and-for-itself, absolute difference, the difference of Essence. It is difference in-and-for-itself not by the effect of an external cause, but a difference in relation to itself, thus a simple difference. It is essential to see in absolute difference a simple difference . . . Difference in itself is difference in relation to itself; thus it is its own negativity, difference not in relation to an *other,* but in relation to itself . . . What differentiates difference is identity. Difference, thus, is both itself and identity. Both together make difference; difference is both the All and its own moment. It can just as much be said that difference, as simple, is not difference at all; it is such first in relation to identity; but as such, difference contains both itself and this relationship. Difference is the All and its own moment, just as identity is the All and its own moment" (*Wissenschaft der Logik,* [Leipzig O. J.], 2:48–49).

92. James Joyce, *Ulysses;* p. 622. But Levinas does not care for Ulysses, nor for the ruses of this excessively Hegelian hero, this man of *nostos* and the closed circle, whose adventure is always summarized in its totality. Levinas often reproaches him. "To the myth of Ulysses returning to Ithaca, we would prefer to oppose the story of Abraham leaving his country forever for an as yet unknown land, and forbidding his servant to take back even his son to the point of departure" (*La trace de l'autre*). The impossibility of the return doubtless was not overlooked by Heidegger: the original historicity of Being, the originality of difference, and irreducible wandering all forbid the return to Being *itself* which is nothing. Therefore, Levinas here is in agreement with Heidegger. Inversely, is the theme of the return as unhebraic as all that? While constructing Bloom and Stephen (Saint Stephen, the Hellenic-Jew), Joyce took great interest in the theses of Victor Bérard, who saw Ulysses as a Semite. It is true that "Jewgreek is greekjew" is a *neutral* proposition, anonymous in the sense execrated by Levinas, inscribed in Lynch's *headpiece.* "Language of no one," Levinas would say. Moreover, it is attributed to what is called "feminine logic": "Woman's reason. Jewgreek is greekjew." On this subject, let us note in passing that *Totality and Infinity* pushes the respect

for dissymmetry so far that it seems to us impossible, essentially impossible, that it could have been written by a woman. Its philosophical subject is man (*vir*). (Cf., for example, the *Phenomenology of Eros*, which occupies such an important place in the book's economy.) Is not this principled impossibility for a book to have been written by a woman unique in the history of metaphysical writing? Levinas acknowledges elsewhere that femininity is an "ontological category." Should this remark be placed in relation to the essential virility of metaphysical language? But perhaps metaphysical desire is essentially virile, even in what is called woman. It appears that this is what Freud (who would have misconstrued sexuality as the "relationship with what is absolutely other," *TI*), thought, not of desire, certainly, but of libido.

Five   **Genesis and Structure**

1. Husserl, *Formale und transzendentale Logik* (Halle, 1929), p. 76.
2. Husserl, *Logische Untersuchungen* (Tübingen, 1968), 2, I, sec. 21, p. 101. Husserl says at this time that it is a question of "preparing by a series of 'psychological and logical researches' the scientific foundations for a future structure on which to erect mathematics and philosophy" (*Philosophie der Arithmetik, Husserliana*, vol. 12 [The Hague, 1970], p. 5). In the *Logische Untersuchungen* he writes: "I set out from an absolute conviction that, like logic in general, the logic of deductive science awaited its philosophical clarification from psychology (ibid., vol. 1, p. vi). And an article written shortly after the *Philosophie der Arithmetik*, Husserl asserts again: "I believe it possible to maintain that no theory of judgment will ever be in agreement with the facts if it is not based upon a profound study of the descriptive and *genetic* relations between intuitions and representations" ("Psychologische Studien zur elementaren Logik," *Philosophische Monatshefte* 33 [Berlin, 1894]: 187 (my italics).
4. The *Philosophie der Arithmetik* is dedicated to Brentano.
5. Speaking of the attempt made in *Philosophie der Arithmetik*, Husserl notes, in the preface to the *Logische Untersuchungen*: "Correspondingly, the psychological researches occupy a very large place in the first (and only published) volume of my philosophy of arithmetic. This psychological foundation never seemed to me to suffice for certain developments. Whenever it was a question of the origin of mathematical determinations, or of the in fact psychologically determined shaping of practical methods, the results of psychological analysis appeared to me to be clear and instructive. But as soon as the transition from the psychological developments of thought to the logical unity of the content of thought (the unity of theory) was made, no real continuity or clarity was apparent" (ibid., vol. 1, p. vii).
6. Husserl writes: "I do not understand how he [Dilthey] believes that he has gained decisive grounds *against* skepticism on the basis of his very instructive analysis of the structure and typology of *Weltanschauungen*" (*Philosophie als strenge Wissenschaft* [Frankfurt 1965], p. 53). Naturally, historicism is condemned only to the extent that it is necessarily tied to an empirical history, to a history as *Tatsachenwissenschaft*. "History, the *empirical science* of the mind in general, is incapable of deciding by its own means whether or not religion should be distinguished as a particular form of culture from religion as idea, that is, as valid religion; or whether art should be distinguished as a form of culture from valid art, historical right from valid right, and finally, if philosophy in the historical sense should be distinguished from valid philosophy" (ibid.).
7. Cf. *Philosophie als strenge Wissenschaft*, p. 61.
8. The polemic will be pursued beyond *Philosophie als strenge Wissenschaft*. Cf. *Phänomenologische Psychologie: Vorlesungen Sommersemester, 1925*.
9. Speaking of the feeling of power which can ensure historical relativism, Husserl writes: "We insist upon the fact that the principles of such relative evaluations belong to the ideal sphere, and that the historian who evaluates, and does not only seek to understand pure developments [of facts], can only presuppose, but cannot, as a historian, ensure their foundation. The norm of mathematics is

found in the mathematical, that of logic in the logical, that of ethics in the ethical, etc.'' (*Philosophie als strenge Wissenschaft,* p. 54).

10. ''Wisdom or *Weltanschauung* . . . belong to the cultural community and to the times, and in relation to its most pronounced forms there is a correct sense in which one speaks not only of an individual's culture and *Weltanschauung,* but of an entire epoch's.'' It is this wisdom, Husserl continues, which gives ''the relatively most perfect answer to the enigmas of life and the world, that is, leads to a solution and satisfactory clarification, in the best possible way, of the theoretical, axiological, and practical disagreements of life, which experience, wisdom, and the pure apprehension of life and the world can resolve only imperfectly'' (*Philosophie als strenge Wissenschaft,* pp. 58–59). ''In the urgency of life, in the practical necessity to take a position, man cannot await—perhaps for millennia—that science be there, supposing that he already knows the idea of rigorous science'' (ibid., p. 64).

11. Cf. notably *Ideas,* trans. W. R. Boyce Gibson (London: Allen and Unwin, 1931), I, sec. 1, p. 51, n. 1.

12. Ibid., I, secs. 9 and 25.

13. Ibid., sec. 71, p. 202.

14. ''With the help of axioms, i.e., of primordial laws of Essential Being [*Wesengesetze*], it [geometry] is now in the position to infer deductively, and in the form of exact determining concepts which represent essences that remain as a rule estranged from our intuition, *all* forms that 'exist' [*existierenden*] in space, i.e., all spatial forms that are ideally possible and all the essential relations that concern them. The essential generic nature of the domain of geometry, and in relation thereto the pure essential nature of space, is so ordered that geometry can be fully certain of being able to control with exact precision, through its method, really all the possible cases. In other words, the variety of spatial formations generally has a remarkable logical basic property, to indicate which we introduce the name '*definite' manifold or 'mathematical manifold in the pregnant sense of the term.'* It has the following distinctive feature, that a *finite number of concepts and propositions . . . determines completely and unambiguously on lines of pure logical necessity the totality of all possible formations in the domain,* so that *in principle,* therefore, *nothing further remains open* within it'' (ibid., sec. 72, p. 204).

15. Cf. *Ideas,* notably third part, chaps. 2 and 4.

16. Ibid., sec. 85, p. 247.

17. In the paragraph devoted to *hylē* and *morphē* Husserl writes, most notably, ''At the level of discussion to which we have so far been limited, which stops short of descending into the obscure depths of the ultimate consciousness which constitutes the whole scheme of intentional experience'' (ibid., p. 246). Further on: ''At all events, in the whole phenomenological domain (in the whole, that is, within the stage of constituted temporality, as must always be borne in mind), this remarkable duality and unity of *sensile hylē* and *intentional morphē* plays a dominant part'' (p. 247). Previously, after having compared the spatial and temporal dimensions of the *hylē* Husserl indicated, while justifying them, the limits of static description and the necessity of making the transition to genetic description: ''For the rest, as will be apparent in the light of the studies to be undertaken later, Time is the name for a completely *self-contained sphere of problems* and one of exceptional difficulty. It will be seen that in a certain sense our previous exposition has been silent, and necessarily so, concerning a whole dimension, so as to maintain free of confusion what first becomes transparent from the phenomenological standpoint alone . . . The transcendental 'Absolute' which we have laid bare through the reductions is in truth not ultimate; it is something which in a certain profound and wholly unique sense constitutes itself, and has its primeval source [*Urquelle*] in what is ultimately and truly absolute'' (ibid., p. 236). Will this limitation ever disappear in the works elaborated later? One encounters reservations of this type in all the great later books, particularly in *Erfahrung und Urteil* (pp. 72, 116, 194, etc.) and every time that a ''transcendental aesthetic'' is announced (Conclusion of *Formale und transzendentale Logik* and *Cartesian Meditations,* sec. 61).

18. Notably this is the project of Köhler, for whom psychology must surrender to "phenomenological description," and of Koffka, a disciple of Husserl who seeks to show, in his *Principles of Gestalt Psychology,* that the "psychology of form" escapes the criticism of psychologism by means of its structuralism.

The conjunction of phenomenology and the "psychology of form" was readily foreseeable. Not at the moment when Husserl had to "return" to the "notion of 'configuration' and even of *Gestalt*" in the *Crisis,* as Merleau-Ponty suggests (*Phénoménologie de la perception,* p. 62, n. 1), but, on the contrary, because Husserl always alleged, and with some justification, that *Gestaltpsychologie* borrowed his own concepts, particularly the concept of "motivation" (cf. *Ideas,* sec. 47, and *Cartesian Meditations,* sec. 37) which had already appeared in the *Logische Untersuchungen,* and the concept of an organized totality, the unified plurality, already present in *Philosophie der Arithmetik* (1887–91). Concerning all these questions we refer to A. Gurwitsch's important work *Théorie du champ de la conscience.*

19. (Halle, 1913), pp. 564ff.

20. "Since the monadically concrete ego includes also the whole of actual and potential conscious life, it is clear that the problem of explicating this *monadic ego phenomenologically* (the problem of his constitution for himself) must include *all constitutional problems without exception.* Consequently, the phenomenology of this *self-constitution* coincides with *phenomenology as a whole.*" (*Cartesian Meditations,* trans. Dorian Cairns [The Hague: Martinus Nijhoff, 1960], sec. 33, p. 68).

21. "Now, however, we must call attention to a great gap in our exposition. The ego is himself *existent for himself* in continuous evidence; thus, in himself, he is *continuously constituting himself as existing.* Heretofore we have touched on only one side of this self-constitution, we have looked at only the *flowing cogito.* The ego grasps himself not only as a flowing life but also as *I,* who live this and that subjective process, who live through this and that cogito as the *same I.* Since we were busied up to now with the intentional relation of consciousness to object, cogito to cogitatum . . ." etc. (ibid., p. 66).

22. "Access to the ultimate universalities involved in problems of eidetic phenomenology is, however, very difficult. This is particularly true with respect to an *ultimate genesis.* The beginning phenomenologist is bound involuntarily by the circumstance that he takes himself as his initial example. Transcendentally he finds himself as the ego, then as generically an ego, who already has (in conscious fashion) a world—a world of our universally familiar ontological type, with Nature, with culture (sciences, fine art, mechanical art and so forth), with personalities of a higher order (state, church), and the rest. The phenomenology developed at first is merely 'static'; its descriptions are analogous to those of natural history, which concerns particular types and, at best, arranges them in their systematic order. Questions of universal genesis and the genetic structure of the ego in his universality, so far as that structure is more than temporal formation, are still far away; and, indeed, they belong to a higher level. But even when they are raised, it is with a restriction. At first, even eidetic observation will consider an ego as such with the restriction that a constituted world already exists for him. This, moreover, is a necessary level; only by laying open the law-forms of the genesis pertaining to this level can one see the possibilities of a *maximally universal* eidetic phenomenology" (ibid., pp. 76–77).

23. *The Crisis of European Sciences and Transcendental Phenomenology,* trans. David Carr (Evanston: Northwestern University Press, 1970), p. 378. [This citation is from "The Origin of Geometry," translated into French by Derrida.—Trans.]

24. *Cartesian Meditations,* sec. 37, p. 75.

25. TN. Auto-affection refers also to Heidegger's analysis of Kant's notion of time in *Kant and the Problem of Metaphysics.* As can be seen in the next few sentences the concept of auto-affection is concerned with time as the self-generating infinite series of *present* moments. Here Derrida is beginning the important analysis of speech as that which makes truth *present.* It is this analysis which will allow him to view the treatment of writing by philosophy as an index of the similar paradoxes

contained within the notions of speech and presence. Derrida's book on Husserl, *La voix et le phénomène* (Paris: P.U.F., 1967) contains an extended analysis of speech as auto-affection.

26. *Cartesian Meditations,* sec. 60, p. 139.

27. Ibid., sec. 64, p. 156.

28. These expressions from late Husserl are ordered as in Aristotelean metaphysics, where *eidos, logos,* and *telos* determine the transition from power to act. Certainly, like the name of God, which Husserl also calls Entelechy, these notions are designated by a transcendental index, and their metaphysical virtue is neutralized by phenomenological brackets. But, of course, the possibility of this neutralization, the possibility of its purity, its conditions, or its "immotivation," will never cease to be problematical. Nor did it ever cease to be so for Husserl himself, like the possibility of the transcendental reduction itself. The latter maintains an essential affinity with metaphysics.

29. *Die Krisis der europaischen Wissenschaften und die transzendentale Phänomenologie* (The Hague: Martinus Nijhoff, 1954), pp. 502–3.

Six   La parole soufflée

1. TN. On the question of madness and the work, cf. above, "Cogito and the History of Madness," in which Derrida examines at length Foucault's definition of madness as "the absence of the work."

2. Michel Foucault *"Le 'non' du père,"* *Critique,* March 1962, pp. 207–8. [Foucault's article is a review of Jean Laplanche's *Hölderlin et la question du père;* Paris: P.U.F., 1961.]

3. TN. Maurice Blanchot, *Le livre à venir* (Paris: Gallimard, 1959), p. 48.

4. TN. This is a pre-Hegelian concept of the relations between truth, error, and history because, for Hegel, historical "error" is dialectically intrinsic to historical truth, and individual experience is never isolated from historical process.

5. Blanchot, *Le livre à venir,* p. 48.

6. Ibid., p. 57.

7. TN. This is the figure of the "beautiful soul" from the *Phenomenology.* Hegel is generally considered to have been describing Novalis in his analysis of the "beautiful soul." Derrida seems to be saying here that just as Hegel makes Novalis an example of a transcendental structure without considering anything in Novalis that does not participate in this structure, so Blanchot is making an example of Artaud, inevitably reducing to the level of error that which is particular to Artaud.

8. This affirmation, whose name is "the theater of cruelty," is pronounced after the letters to Jacques Rivière and after the early works, but it already governs them. "The theater of cruelty / is not the symbol of an absent void, / or a horrifying inability to realize oneself within one's life / as a person, / it is the affirmation / of a terrifying / and, moreover, unavoidable necessity" (*Le théâtre de la cruauté, 84,* nos. 5–6 [1948], p. 124). [There is no complete translation of Artaud's work into English. References to *OC* are to the *Œuvres complètes* (Paris: Gallimard, 1970), by volume and page. *TD* refers to *The Theater and Its Double,* trans. Mary Caroline Richards (New York: Grove Press, 1958); *AA* refers to the *Artaud Anthology,* ed. Jack Hirschman (San Francisco: City Lights Books, 1965); *CW* refers to volume and page of the *Collected Works,* trans. Victor Corti (London: Calder & Boyars, 1971).]

9. Blanchot, *Le livre à venir,* p. 52.

10. Preface to Karl Jaspers' *Strindberg et Van Gogh, Hölderlin et Swedenborg* (Paris: Editions de Minuit, 1953). The same essentialist schema, even more bare this time, appears in another text of Blanchot's: "La cruelle raison poétique," in *Artaud et le Théâtre de notre temps* (Paris: Gallimard, 1958).

11. TN. Laplanche (see note 2 above), p. 11. Hellingrath was a Hölderlin scholar and editor of his collected works.

12. "Hölderlin's existence thus would be a particularly good example of poetic fate, which Blanchot links to the very essence of speech as the 'relation to absence.' " Laplanche, p. 10.

13. TN. The name of this essay is untranslatable because it plays on all the meanings of *souffler,* some of which Derrida is about to explain. We have chosen "spirited away" because it maintains the connections with theft, breath (from the Latin *spirare*), and the multiple meanings of in-*spir*-ation. The French word for "prompter" (*souffleur*) might best be rendered by the neologism "inspirator." Every use of a derivative of *souffler* in the original text has been indicated in brackets.

14. The public is not to exist outside, before or after the stage of cruelty, is not to await it, to contemplate it, or to survive it—is not even to exist as a public at all. Whence an enigmatic and lapidary formulation, in *The Theater and Its Double,* in the midst of abundant, inexhaustible definitions of "directing," the "language of the Stage," "musical instruments," "lighting," "costumes," etc. The problem of the public is thereby exhausted: *"The Public.* First of all this theater must exist" (*TD,* p. 99).

15. The word appears in *Nerve-Scales, CW* 1:72. [In the *Collected Works,* the original *impouvoir* which we have translated as "unpower," is translated as "powerlessness."]

16. TN. *Répétition* in French means both repetition and rehearsal.

17. TN. The reference to Poe's "The Purloined Letter" seems deliberate. This story was the focus of a seminar by Jacques Lacan in which he expounded his theory of the signifier, as does Derrida here.

18. TN. The excess in question may be construed as that which holds apart and unites multiple meanings in one signifier. That a historical system must be open at some point means that it must be founded on something like this excess. History begins with writing.

19. With the proper precautions we could speak of Artaud's Bergsonian vein. The continuous transition of his metaphysics of life into his theory of Language, and his critique of the word, dictated a great number of theoretical formulations and metaphors of energy that are rigorously Bergsonian. Cf., in particular, *OC* 5:15, 18, 56, 132, 141, etc.

20. Each time that it operates within the framework that we are attempting to restore here, Artaud's language has a precise resemblance, in its syntax and vocabulary, to that of the young Marx. In the first of the *Economic and Political Manuscripts of 1844,* the labor which produces the *work* and gives it value (*Verwertung*) proportionately increases the de-preciation (*Entwertung*) of its author. "Labor's realization is its objectification. In the sphere of political economy this realization of labor appears as *loss of realization* for the workers; objectification as *loss of the object* and *bondage to it;* appropriation as *estrangement,* as *alienation*" (Karl Marx, *Economic and Philosophic Manuscripts of 1844,* trans. Martin Milligan [New York: International Publishers, 1964], p. 41. This juxtaposition escapes the realms of intellectual puttering or of historical curiosity. Its necessity will appear later when the question of what belongs to that which we call the metaphysics of the proper (or of alienation) is posed.

21. It goes without saying that we have deliberately abstained from anything that could be called a "biographical reference." If it is precisely at this point that we recall that Artaud died of cancer of the rectum, we do not do so in order to have the exception prove the rule, but because we think that the status (still to be found) of this remark, and of other similar ones, must not be that of the so-called "biographical reference." The new status—to be found—is that of the relations between existence and the text, between these two forms of textuality and the generalized writing within whose play they are articulated.

22. In the Preface to his *Collected Wroks,* Artaud writes: "The cane of 'The New Revelations of Being' fell into the black cyst along with the little sword. I have got another cane ready to accompany my collected works in hand to hand combat, not with ideas, but with those monkeys who never stop riding them to death from one end of my conscious self to the other, as well as through my organism they have blighted . . . . My cane will be this furious book called forth by ancient peoples now dead, spotted throughout my nervous fibres like daughters shed." *CW* 1:21.

23. Friedrich Hölderlin, *Poems and Fragments,* trans. Michael Hamburger (Ann Arbor: University of Michigan Press, 1967), pp. 375–77.

24. Friedrich Nietzsche, *The Twilight of the Idols,* trans. Anthony M. Ludovici (New York: Russell and Russell, 1964), p. 59. "To seize the paternal lightning, itself, in one's own hands . . ." "To be able to dance with the pen . . ." "The cane . . . the little sword . . . another cane . . . . My cane will be this furious book." And in *The New Revelations of Being:* "Because, on the third of June, 1937, the five serpents appeared, who were already in the sword whose strength of decision is represented by a staff! What does this mean? It means that I who am speaking have a Sword and a Staff" (*AA,* p. 92). To be juxtaposed with this text by Genet: "All burglars will understand the dignity with which I was arrayed when I held my jimmy, my 'pen.' From its weight, material, and shape, and from its function too, emanated an authority that made me a man. I had always needed that steel penis in order to free myself completely from my faggotry, from my humble attitudes, and to attain the clear simplicity of manliness" (Jean Genet, *Miracle of the Rose,* trans. Bernard Frechtman [New York: Grove Press, 1966], p. 27).

25. Nietzsche, *Twilight of the Idols,* p. 6.

26. Let us acknowledge that Artaud is the first to attempt to reassemble, on a martyrological tree, the vast family of madmen of genius. He does so in *Van Gogh, le suicidé de la société* (1947), one of the rare texts in which Nietzsche is named, among other "suicides" (Baudelaire, Poe, Nerval, Nietzsche, Kierkegaard, Hölderlin, Coleridge). Artaud writes fruther on: "No, Socrates did not have this eye; perhaps the only one before Van Gogh was the unhappy Nietzsche who had the same power to undress the soul, to pluck the body from the soul, to lay the body of man bare, beyond the subterfuges of the mind" (*AA,* p. 160).

27. Martin Heidegger, *An Introduction to Metaphysics,* trans. Ralph Manheim (New Haven: Yale University Press, 1959), p. 64.

28. "I told you; no works, no language, no words, no mind, nothing. Nothing, except fine Nerve-Scales. A sort of impenetrable stop in the midst of everything in our minds" (*Nerve-Scales, CW* 1:75).

29. "For even the infinite is dead/infinity is the name of a dead man" (*84,* p. 118). Which means that God did not die at a given moment of history, but that God is Dead because he is the name of Death itself, the name of the death within me and the name of that which, *having stolen me from my birth,* has penetrated my life. As God-Death is difference within life, he has never ceased to die, that is to say, to live. "For even the infinite is dead/infinite is the name of a dead man, who is not dead" (ibid.). Only life without difference, life without death will vanquish death and God. But it will do so by negating itself as life, within death, and by becoming God himself. God, thus, is Death: infinite Life, Life without difference, as it is attributed to God by the classical ontotheology or metaphysics (with the ambiguous and remarkable exception of Hegel) to which Artaud still belongs. But just as death is the name of difference within life, of finitude as the essence of life, so the infinity of God, as Life and Presence, is the other name of finitude. But the other name of the same thing *does not mean* the same thing as the first name, is not *synonymous with it and this is the entirety of history.* [On this last point, cf. above, note 18.]

30. This is why poetry as such remains an abstract art in Artaud's eyes, whether poetic speech or writing are in question. Only the theater is the total art in which is produced, aside from poetry, music and dance, the "surrection" of the body itself. Also, when we *primarily* see in Artaud a poet, the central nerve of his thought escapes us. Unless, of course, we make poetry into an unlimited genre, that is, the theater with its real space. To what extent can one follow Maurice Blanchot when he writes, "Artaud has left us a major document which is nothing other than an *Ars poetica.* I acknowledge that he is speaking of the theater in this text, but what is in question are the demands of poetry such that poetry can be fulfilled only by rejecting limited genres and by affirming a more original language . . . . It is no longer a question of the real space presented by the stage, but of an *other* space"? To what extent does one have the right to add "of poetry" in brackets when one is citing a

sentence of Artaud's defining "the highest idea of theater"? (Cf. *La cruelle raison poétique*, p. 69.)

31. Again, the strange resemblance of Artaud to Nietzsche. The praise of the mysteries of Eleusis (cf. *TD*, p. 52) and a certain disdain of Latinity (*TD*, pp. 40–41) would further confirm this resemblance. However, a difference is hidden in this resemblance, as we said above rather lapidarily, and this is the place to specify it. In *The Birth of Tragedy*, at the moment when (div. 19) Nietzsche designates "Socratic culture" in its "intrinsic substance," and with its most "distinct" name, as the "culture of the opera" (p. 142), Nietzsche wonders about the birth of recitative and the *stilo rappresentativo*. This birth can only refer to unnatural instincts foreign to all aesthetics, be they Appollonian or Dionysian. Recitative, the subjection of music to libretto, finally corresponds to fear and to the need for security, to the "yearning for the idyll," to "the belief in the prehistoric existence of the artistic, good man" (p. 144). "The recitative was regarded as the rediscovered language of this primitive man" (p. 144). Opera was "a solace . . . found for the pessimism" inherent in a situation of "frightful uncertainty" (p. 145). And here, as in *The Theater and Its Double*, the place of the text is recognized as that of usurped mastery and as the proper, nonmetaphorical, practice of slavery. To have the text at one's disposition is to be a master. "Opera is the birth of the theoretical man, of the critical layman, not of the artist: one of the most surprising facts in the whole history of art. It was the demand of thoroughly unmusical hearers that the words must above all be understood, so that according to them a re-birth of music is only to be expected when some mode of singing has been discovered in which the text-word lords over the counterpoint as the master over the servant" (Friedrich Nietzsche, *The Birth of Tragedy*, trans. William A. Houssman [New York: Russell and Russell, 1964], p. 145). And elsewhere, à propos of the customary tendency to enjoy the text separately by reading it, of the relations between the scream and the concept, between "gesture-symbolism" and the "tone of the speaker" ("On Music and Words," in *Early Greek Philosophy*, trans. Maximilian A. Mugge [New York: Russell and Russell, 1964], p. 31), and à propos of the "heiroglyphic" relation between the text of a poem and music (ibid., p. 37), the musical illustration of the poem and the project of imparting to music an intelligible language ("What a perverted world! A task that appears to my mind like that of a son wanting to create his father!" ibid. p. 33)— numerous formulations announce Artaud. But here it is music, as elsewhere dance, that Nietzsche wants to liberate from the text and from recitation. Doubtless, an abstract liberation in Artaud's eyes. Only the theater, the total art including and utilizing music and dance among other forms of language, can accomplish this liberation. It must be noted that if Artaud, like Nietzsche, often supports dance, he never abstracts it from the theater. If one heedlessly takes dance literally, and not, as we said above, in an analogical sense, it would not be the entirety of theater. Artaud, perhaps, would not say, as Nietzsche did, "I can only believe in a God who would dance." Not only because God could not dance, as Nietzsche knew, but because dance alone is an impoverished theater. This specification was even more necessary in that Zarathustra condemns poets and poetic works as the alienation of the body into metaphor. *On Poets* begins thus: " 'Since I have known the body better,' said Zarathustra to one of his disciples—'the spirit hath only been to me symbolically spirit; and all that is "imperishable"—That is also but a simile.' 'So have I heard thee say once before,' answered the disciple 'and then thou addedst: "But the poets lie too much." Why didst thou say that the poets lie too much?' . . . 'And fain would they thereby prove themselves reconcilers: but mediaries and mixers are they unto me, and half-and-half, and impure! Ah, I cast indeed my net into their sea, and meant to catch good fish; but always did I draw up the head of some ancient God' " (Nietzsche, *Thus Spake Zarathustra*, vol. 2, trans. Thomas Common [New York: Russell and Russell, 1964], pp. 151, 154) Nietzsche also disdained spectacle ("Spectators, seeketh the spirit of the poet—should they even be buffaloes!" ibid., p. 155), and we know that for Artaud the visibility of the theater was to cease being an object of spectacle. In this confrontation we are not concerned with knowing whether it is Nietzsche or Artaud who went the furthest in destruction. To this question, which is foolish, we seem to answer Artaud. In another direction, we could also legitimately support the opposite.

32. In *Centre-Noeuds*, Rodez, April 1946. Published in *Juin*, no. 18.

33. Twenty years earlier, in *Umbilical Limbo:* "I suffer because the mind is not in life and life is not Mind. I suffer because the Mind is an organ, the Mind is an interpreter or the Mind intimidates things to accept them in the Mind." *CW* 1:49.

34. *Zarathustra: Reading and Writing:* "Of all that is written, I love only what a person hath written with his blood. Write with blood, and thou wilt find that blood is spirit. / It is no easy task to understand unfamiliar blood; I hate the reading idlers. / He who knoweth the reader, doeth nothing more for the reader. Another century of readers—and spirit itself will stink" (*Thus Spake Zarathustra,* p. 43).

35. Why not play the serious game of juxtaposed citations? It has been written since: "That the dream uses words (*la parole*) makes no difference since for the unconscious they are but one among several elements of the performance (*mise en scène*)" (Jacques Lacan, "The Insistence of the Letter in the Unconscious," trans. Jan Miel, *Yale French Studies,* October 1966).

36. "Thought underlies grammar, an infamy harder to conquer, an infinitely more shrewish maid, rougher to override when taken as an innate fact. / For thought is a matron who has not always existed. / But let my life's inflated words inflate themselves through living in the b-a-ba of composition (*de l'ecrit*). I am writing for illiterates" (*CW* 1:19–20).

37. Revolutionary in the full sense, and in particular the political sense. All of *The Theater and Its Double* could be read—this cannot be done here—as a political manifesto, and moreover a highly ambiguous one. Renouncing immediate political action, guerilla action, anything that would have been a waste of forces in the economy of his political intentions, Artaud intended the preparation of an unrealizable theater, without the destruction of the political structures of our society. "Dear friend, I did not say that I wanted to act directly on our times; I said that the theater I wanted to create assumed, in order to be possible, in order to be permitted by the times to exist, another form of civilization" (*TD,* pp. 116–17). Political revolution must first take power from literality and the world of letters. See, for example, the *Post-Script* to the *Manifesto for an Abortive Theater:* in the name of the revolution against *literature,* Artaud, aiming at the Surrealists, those "bog-paper revolutionaries" "with their bowing down to Communism," articulates his disdain for the "lazy man's revolution," for revolution as simple "transferring [of] power." "Bombs need to be thrown, but they need to be thrown at the root of the majority of present-day habits of thought, whether European or not. I can assure you, those gentlemen, the Surrealists, are far more affected by such habits than I . . . . the most urgently needed revolution is a sort of retro-action in time. We ought to return to the state of mind, or simply even the practices of the Middle Ages" (*CW* 2:24–25).

38. "True culture operates by exaltation and force, while the European ideal of art attempts to cast the mind into an attitude distinct from force but addicted to exaltation" (*TD,* p. 10).

39. A concern for universal writing appears beneath the surface of the *Lettres de Rodez.* Artaud alleged that he had written in "a language which was not French, but which everyone could read, regardless of his nationality" (to Henri Parisot).

40. Artaud did not only reintroduce the written work into his theory of the theater; he is, in the last analysis, the author of a body of works. And he knows it. In a letter from 1946 (cited by Maurice Blanchot in *l'Arche* 27–28 [1948], p. 133) he speaks of the "two very short books" (*The Umbilical* and *Nerve-Scales*) which "circulate around the profound, inveterate, endemic absence of any idea." "At the moment, they seemed to me to be full of cracks, gaps, platitudes and as if stuffed with spontaneous abortions . . . . But after twenty years gone by, they appear stupefying, not as my own triumphs, but in relation to the inexpressible. It is thus that works are bottled and all *lie* in relation to the author, constituting a bizarre truth by themselves . . . . Something inexpressible expressed by works which are only part debacles." Thinking then, of Artaud's convulsed rejection of the work, can one not say, with the same intonation, the opposite of what Blanchot says in *Le livre à venir*? Not "naturally, this is not a work" (p. 49), but "naturally, this is still but a work"? To this extent, the work authorizes the effraction of commentary and the violence of exemplification, the very violence which we could not avoid at the moment when we intended to proscribe it. But perhaps we can better comprehend, now, the necessity of this incoherence.

41. TN. This is a reaction to Foucault's definition of madness as "the absence of the work." Cf. chap. 2 above, "Cogito and the History of Madness," note 6.

42. And today, madness lets itself be "destroyed" by the same destruction as onto-theological metaphysics, the work and the book. We do not say the same of the text.

Seven	Freud and the Scene of Writing

1. TN. Phonologism is Derrida's abbreviated fashion of describing one of the metaphysical gestures inherent in most linguistics: the privilege given to a model of language based on speech, because speech is the most *present* form of language, is presence in language. This is equivalent to the metaphysical repression of writing, i.e., of difference. Here, too, Derrida might be challenging Jacques Lacan, whose statement about the unconscious being structured like a language seems to depend upon many of the linguistic conceptions which Derrida considers to be uncritically metaphysical.

2. TN. "Breaching" is the translation we have adopted for the German word *Bahnung. Bahnung* is derived from *Bahn,* road, and literally means pathbreaking. Derrida's translation of *Bahnung* is *frayage,* which has an idomatic connection to pathbreaking in the expression, *se frayer un chemin.* "Breaching" is clumsy, but it is crucial to maintain the sense of the *force* that breaks open a pathway, and the *space* opened by this force; thus, "breaching" must be understood here as a shorthand for these meanings. In the Standard Edition *Bahnung* has been translated as "facilitation," and we have, of course, maintained this in all citations from the Standard Edition. Citations from *The Standard Edition of the Complete Psychological Works of Sigmund Freud,* London: Hogarth Press (abbreviated as *SE*) are by volume and page number.

3. TN. Cf. the end of "Force and Signification," below for a discussion of differences of force in Nietzsche.

4. Here more than elsewhere, concerning the concepts of difference, quantity, and quality, a systematic confrontation between Nietzsche and Freud is called for. Cf., for example, among many others, this fragment from *The Will to Power:* "Our 'knowing' limits itself to establishing quantities; but we cannot help feeling these differences in quantity as qualities. Quality is a perspective truth for *us;* not an 'in-itself.' . . . If we sharpened or blunted our senses tenfold, we should perish; i.e., with regard to making possible our existence we sense even relations between magnitudes as qualities" (Nietzsche: *The Will to Power,* trans. Walter Kauffmann [New York: Random House, 1967], p. 304).

5. The concepts of originary *différance* and of delay are unthinkable within the authority of the logic of identity or even within the concept of time. The very absurdity betrayed *by the terms* provides the possibility—if organized in a certain manner—of thinking beyond that logic and that concept. The word "delay" must be taken to mean something other than a relation between two "presents"; and the following model must be avoided: what was to happen (should have happened) in a (prior) present A, occurs only in a present B. The concepts of originary *différance* and originary "delay" were imposed upon us by a reading of Husserl.

6. TN. In "Cogito and the History of Madness" (chap. 2 above), Derrida begins to elaborate on the metaphysical nature of the concept of decision. Decision in Greek is *krinein,* whence comes our "critic." The critic always *decides* on a meaning, which can be conceived only in terms of presence. Since *différance* subverts meaning and presence, it does not *decide.*

7. TN. On the relation of force and place (site, *topos*) see "Force and Signification" (chap. 2 above).

8. Letter 32 (10 Oct. 1895). The machine: "The three systems of neurones, the 'free' and 'bound' states of quantity, the primary and secondary processes, the main trend and the compromise trend of the nervous system, the two biological rules of attention and defence, the indications of quality, reality and thought, the state of the psycho-sexual group, the sexual determination of repression, and finally the factors determining consciousness as a perceptual function—the whole thing held together,

and still does. I can hardly contain myself with delight. If I had only waited a fortnight before setting it all down for you" (Freud: *The Origins of Psychoanalysis: Letters to Wilhelm Fliess, Drafts and Notes*, trans. Eric Mosbacher and James Strachey [New York: Basic Books, 1954], p. 129).

9. Warburton, the author of *The Divine Legation of Moses*. The fourth part of his work was translated in 1744 under the title: *Essai sur les hiéroglyphes des Egyptiens, ou l'on voit l'origine et le progrès du langage, l'antiquité des sciences en Egypte, et l'origine du culte des animaux*. This work, which we shall discuss elsewhere, had considerable influence. All of that era's reflections on language and signs bore its mark. The editors of the *Encyclopedia*, Condillac, and, through him, Rousseau all drew specific inspiration from it, borrowing in particular the theme of the originally metaphorical nature of language.

10. William Warburton: *The Divine Legation of Moses Demonstrated*, 10th ed., (London: Thomas Tegg, 1846) 2:220.

11. Ibid., p. 221.

12. TN. Derrida discusses Artaud's strikingly similar formulations about speech as but one element of language and representation among others in "The Theater of Cruelty and the Closure of Representation" (chap. 8 below), cf. especially note 7.

13. *The Ego and the Id* (*SE* XIX, chap. 2) also underscores the danger of a topographical representation of psychical facts.

14. TN. Derrida's fullest discussion of supplementarity is in *De la grammatologie*.

15. TN. Derrida fully develops the supplementary status of the footnote—*la greffe*—in *La double séance* in *La dissémination*.

16. TN. On roads, writing, and incest see "De la grammatologie," *Critique* 223–24, pp. 149ff. An English translation by Gayatri C. Spivak, *On Grammatology* (Baltimore: Johns Hopkins University Press, 1977), appeared after I had finished the present translation. All references are to the original French version.

17. TN. In *Being and Time*, and especially *Kant and the Problem of Metaphysics*, Heidegger "deconstructs" Kant's posited timelessness of the *cogito*, a position taken over from Descartes, in order to develop an "authentic" temporality.

18. The metaphor of a photographic negative occurs frequently. Cf. "The Dynamics of Transference" (*SE* XII). The notions of negative and copy are the principal means of the analogy. In the analysis of Dora, Freud defines the transference in terms of editions. In "Notes on the Concept of the Unconscious in Psychoanalysis," 1913 (*SE* XII, 264). Freud compares the relations between the conscious and the unconscious to a photographic process: "The first stage of the photograph is the 'negative'; every photographic picture has to pass through the 'negative process,' and some of these negatives which have held good in examination are admitted to the 'positive process' ending in the picture." Hervey de Saint-Denys devotes an entire chapter of his book to the same analogy. The intentions are the same. They suggest a precaution that we will find again in the "Note on the Mystic Writing Pad": "Memory, compared to a camera, has the marvelous superiority of natural forces: to be able to renew by itself its means of action."

19. "Dreams are parsimonious, indigent, laconic." Dreams are "stenographic" (cf. above).

20. TN. Cf. note 12 above.

21. TN. "Invested in all senses of the word" includes the specifically Freudian sense of *Besetzung* or libidinal investment, which has been translated into English as "cathexis." The French *investissement* is much closer to the original German.

22. The "Metapsychological Supplement to the Theory of Dreams," 1916 (*SE* XIV) devotes an important development to formal regression, which, according to the *Interpretation of Dreams*, entails the substitution of "primitive methods of expression and representation [which] takes the place of the usual ones" (V, 548). Freud insists above all on the role of verbal representations: "It is very noteworthy how little the dream-work keeps to the word-presentations; it is always ready to exchange one word for another till it finds the expression most handy for plastic representation"

(XIV, 228). This passage is followed by a comparison, from the point of view of word-representations and thing-representations, of the dreamer's language and the language of the schizophrenic. It should be analysed closely. We would perhaps find (against Freud?) that a rigorous determination of the anomaly is impossible. On the role of verbal representation in the preconscious and the (consequently) secondary character of visual elements, cf. *The Ego and the Id,* chap. 2.

23. "The Claim of Psychoanalysis to Scientific Interest" (*SE* XIII). The second part of this text, devoted to "non-psychological sciences," is concerned first of all with the science of language (p. 176)—before philosophy, biology, history, sociology, pedagogy.

24. As is known, the note on "The Antithetical Meaning of Primal Words," 1910 (*SE* XI) tends to demonstrate, after Abel, and with a great abundance of examples borrowed from hieroglyphic writing, that the contradictory or undetermined meaning of primal words could be determined, could receive its difference and its conditions of operation, only through gesture and writing. On this text and Abel's hypothesis, cf. Emile Benveniste, *Problèmes de linguistique générale* (Paris: Gallimard, 1964), chap. 7.

25. P. 228. This is the passage we quoted earlier, and in which the memory-trace was distinguished from "memory."

26. TN. For a complete discussion of *hypomnesis/mnesis* in Plato, cf. "La pharmacie de Platon", in *La dissémination.*

27. Cf. chapter 4 of *Beyond the Pleasure Principle.*

28. The *Standard Edition* notes here a slight infidelity in Freud's description. "The principle is not affected." We are tempted to think that Freud inflects his description elsewhere as well, in order to suit the analogy.

29. This is still in chapter 4 of *Beyond the Pleasure Principle.*

30. TN. In *La voix et le phénomène* (*The Voice and the Phenomenon*) trans. David Allison (Evanston: Northwestern University Press, 1973), there is a full "deconstruction" of perception as a past that was never present.

31. TN. "Now what is this wax . . .?" The reference is to the *Second Meditation,* and Derrida is playing upon the fact that Freud's piece of wax, the mystic writing-pad, is irreducibly temporal and differentiated, while the timelessness of Descartes's piece of wax is symptomatic of the metaphysical repression of writing and difference. Cf. note 17 above.

32. We find it again, the same year, in the article on "Negation" (*SE* XIX). In a passage which concerns us here for its recognition of the relation between negation in thought and *différance,* delay, detour (*Aufschub, Denkaufschub*) (*différance,* union of Eros and Thanatos), the sending out of feelers is attributed not to the unconscious but to the ego. On *Denkaufschub,* on thought as retardation, postponement, suspension, respite, detour, *différance* as opposed to—or rather *différante* (deferring, differing) from—the theoretical, fictive, and always already transgressed pole of the "primary process," cf. all of chapter 7 of the *Interpretation of Dreams.* The concept of the "circuitous path" (*Umweg*) is central to it. "Thought identity," entirely woven of memory, is an aim always already substituted for "perceptual identity," the aim of the "primary process," and *das ganze Denken ist nur ein Umweg* . . . ("All thinking is no more than a circuitous path," *SE* V, 602). Cf. also the "Umwege zum Tode" in *Beyond the Pleasure Principle.* "Compromise," in Freud's sense, is always *différance.* But there is nothing before the compromise.

Eight   **The Theater of Cruelty**
                                          and the Closure
                                          of Representation

1. *84,* p. 109. As in the preceding essay on Artaud, texts referred to by dates are unpublished. [For the abbreviations used to refer to the English translations of Artaud, cf. *La parole soufflée,* chap. 6 above, note 8.]

2. "The psychology of orgiasm conceived as the feeling of a superabundance of vitality and strength, within the scope of which even pain acts as a *stimulus,* gave me the key to the concept of *tragic* feeling, which has been misunderstood not only by Aristotle, but also even more by our pessimists" (Friedrich Nietzsche, *The Twilight of the Idols,* trans. Anthony Ludovici [New York: Russell and Russell, 1964], p. 119). Art, as the imitation of nature, communicates in an essential way with the theme of catharsis. "Not in order to escape from terror and pity, not to purify one's self of a dangerous passion by discharging it with vehemence—this is how Aristotle understood it—but to be far beyond terror and pity and to be the eternal lust of becoming itself—that lust which also involves the *lust of destruction.* And with this I once more come into touch with the spot from which I once set out—the 'Birth of Tragedy' was my first transvaluation of all values: with this again I take my stand upon the soil from out of which my will and my capacity spring—I, the last disciple of the philosopher Dionysus—I, the prophet of eternal recurrence" (ibid., p. 120).

3. TN. That *re*presentation is the auto-presentation of pure visibility and pure sensibility, amounts to postulating that presence is an effect of repetition.

4. TN. On the question of parricide and the "father of the Logos," cf. "La pharmacie de Platon," pp. 84ff. in *La dissémination.*

5. *The Theater and Its Double* would have to be confronted with *The Essay on the Origin of Languages, The Birth of Tragedy,* and all the connected texts of Rousseau and Nietzsche: the *System* of their analogies and oppositions would have to be reconstituted.

6. *TD,* pp. 60, 110. In this sense the word is a sign, a symptom of living speech's fatigue, of life's disease. The word, as clear speech subjected to transmission and to repetition is death in language. "One could say that the mind, able to go on no longer, resigned itself to the clarities of speech" (*CW* 4:289). On why it is necessary to "change the role of speech in the theater," cf. *TD* pp. 72–73, 94–95.

7. TN. On these questions, cf. "Freud and the Scene of Writing," chap. 7 above, note 12.

8. *Les rêves et les moyens de les diriger* (1867) is invoked at the opening of *Les vases communicants.*

9. "Miserable, improbable psyche that the cartel of psychological presuppositions has never ceased pinning into the muscles of humanity" (letter written from Espalion to Roger Blin, 25 March 1946.) "Only a very few highly contestable documents on the Mysteries of the Middle Ages remain. It is certain that they had, from the purely scenic point of view, resources that the theater has not contained for centuries, but one could also find on the repressed debates of the soul a science that modern psychoanalysis has barely rediscovered and in a much less efficacious and morally less fruitful sense than in the mystical dramas played on the parvis" (February 1945). This fragment multiplies aggressions against psychoanalysis.

10. *TD,* pp. 46–47, 60.

11. Against the pact of fear which gives birth to man and to God must be restored the unity of evil and life, of the Satanic and the divine: "I, M. Antonin Artaud, born in Marseilles 4 September 1896, I am Satan and I am god and I do not want anything to do with the Holy Virgin" (written from Rodez, September 1945).

12. On the integral spectacle, cf. *CW* 2:31. This theme is often accompanied by allusions to participation as an "interested emotion": the critique of esthetic experience as disinterestedness. It recalls Nietzsche's critique of Kant's philosophy of art. No more in Nietzsche than in Artaud must this theme contradict the value of gratuitous play in artistic creation. Quite to the contrary.

13. TN. Brecht is the major representative of the theater of alienation.

14. *Letter to M. d'Alembert,* trans. Allan Bloom (Glencoe: Free Press, 1960), p. 126. [These questions receive an extended treatment in *de la Grammatologie,* pp. 235ff.]

15. The theater of cruelty is not only a spectacle without spectators, it is speech without listeners. Nietzsche: "The man in a state of Dionysean excitement has a listener just as little as the orgiastic crowd, a listener to whom he might have something to communicate, a listener which the epic

narrator, and generally speaking the Apollonian artist, to be sure, presupposes. It is rather in the nature of the Dionysean art, that it has no consideration for the listener: the inspired servant of Dionysus is, as I said in a former place, understood only by his compeers. But if we now imagine a listener at those endemic outbursts of Dionysean excitement then we shall have to prophesy for him a fate similar to that which Pentheus the discovered eavesdropper suffered, namely, to be torn to pieces by the Maenads.... But now the *opera* begins, according to the clearest testimonies, with the *demand of the listener to understand the word.* What? The listener *demands?* The word is to be understood?'' (''On Music and Words,'' in *Early Greek Philosophy,* trans. Maximilian Mugge [New York: Russell and Russell, 1964], pp. 40–41).

16. TN. *Répétition* also means ''rehearsal'' in French.

17. TN. On the economy of dialectics, cf. below ''From Restricted to General Economy.'' On truth, repetition and the beyond of being, cf. ''La pharmacie de Platon,'' pp. 192–195 in *La dissémination.*

18. TN. Derrida seems to making a point here which is developed much more fully in ''From Restricted to General Economy'' (see this volume, chap. 9). He seems to be referring, if rather elliptically, to the Hegelian dialectic of the master and the slave, in which the master, who both risks death and *consumes* with pleasure, does not *maintain* the *present.* The slave is the truth of the master because he maintains the present through his relation to work, his deferred consumption of the present. Thus he is also the embodiment of the dialectical ''memory''—*Erinnerung.* Both master and slave are possibilities of metaphysics, of *presence,* and to confirm the one or the other—as happens inevitably—is to repeat a metaphysical gesture.

19. Letter to Jean Paulhan, 25 January 1936: ''I think I have a suitable title for my book. It will be *The Theater and Its Double,* for if theater doubles life, life doubles true theater.... This title corresponds to all the doubles of the theater that I believe to have found over the course of so many years: metaphysics, the plague, cruelty.... It is on the stage that the union of thought, gesture and act is reconstituted'' (*CW* 5:272–73).

20. To attempt to reintroduce a purity into the concept of difference, one returns it to nondifference and full presence. This movement is fraught with consequences for any attempt opposing itself to an indicative anti-Hegelianism. One escapes from it, apparently, only by conceiving difference outside the determination of Being as presence, outside the alternatives of presence and absence and everything they govern, and only by conceiving difference as original impurity, that is to say as *différance* in the finite economy of the same.

21. Nietzsche again. These texts are well known. Thus, for example, in the wake of Heraclitus: ''And similarly, just as the child and the artist play, the eternally living fire plays, builds up and destroys, in innocence—and this game the *aeon* plays with himself.... The child throws away his toys; but soon he starts again in an innocent frame of mind. As soon however as the child builds he connects, joins and forms lawfully and according to an innate sense of order. Thus only is the world contemplated by the aesthetic man, who has learned from the artist and the genesis of the latter's work, how the struggle of plurality can yet bear within itself law and justice, how the artist stands contemplative above, and working within the work of art, how necessity and play, antagonism and harmony must pair themselves for the procreation of the work of art'' (''Philosophy During the Tragic Age of the Greeks,'' in *Early Greek Philosophy,* p. 108).

| Nine | From Restricted to General Economy |

1. ''My intention is to minimize Hegel's attitude? But it is the opposite that is true! I have wanted to demonstrate the incomparable breadth of his undertaking. To achieve this I could not veil the very slight (and even inevitable) degree of failure. To my mind, it is rather the exceptional assuredness of this undertaking that emerges from my juxtapositions. If he failed, one cannot say that the failure was

the result of an error. The sense of the failure itself differs from the sense of what caused it: the error alone is fortuitous. Hegel's 'failure' must be spoken of in general terms, as one would speak of an authentic movement, pregnant with meaning'' (*Hegel, la mort et le sacrifice* [hereafter *Hegel, la mort*] in *Deucalion* 5 [Neuchâtel, 1955], p. 42).

2. Ibid.

3. "De l'existentialisme au primat de l'économie," *Critique* 19 (Paris, 1947): "It is strange to perceive today what Kierkegaard could not know: that Hegel, like Kierkegaard, experienced the rejection of all subjectivity before the absolute idea. In principle, one would imagine—the rejection being Hegel's—that it was a question of a conceptual opposition; on the contrary. The fact is not deduced from a philosophical text, but from a letter to a friend to whom he confides that for two years he thought he would go mad.... In a sense, Hegel's rapid phrase perhaps has a force that Kierkegaard's long cry does not have. It is not any less within existence—which trembles and exceeds—than this cry," etc.

4. *Le petit,* in *Œuvres complètes* (1970; hereafter *OC*), 2:49.

5. "De l'existentialisme."

6. "Small comic recapitulation. Hegel, I imagine, touched the extreme. He was still young and thought he would go mad. I even imagine that he elaborated the system in order to escape (any kind of conquest, doubtless, is due to a man fleeing a danger). To conclude, Hegel reaches *satisfaction* and turns his back on the extreme. *Supplication is dead within him.* That one should seek salvation is in itself admissible: one continues to live, one cannot be sure, one must continue to supplicate. Hegel gained salvation while still alive and killed supplication, *mutilated himself.* Nothing was left of him but a broomhandle, a modern man. But before mutilating himself, he doubtless touched the extreme and knew supplication: his memory takes him back to the perceived abyss, in order to *annihilate it!* The system is annihilation'' (*L'expérience intérieure* [hereafter *EI;* Paris: Gallimard, 1943], p. 60.

7. On the history of Bataille's reading of Hegel, from the first articles of the *Documents* (1929) to *L'expérience intérieure* (1943), and on the experience of the instruction of Koyré, and above all, Kojève, whose mark dominates visibly, cf. R. Queneau, "Premières confrontations avec Hegel," *Critique,* 195–96. Let us note here and now that at least for Bataille there was no fundamental rupture between Kojève's reading of Hegel, to which he openly subscribed almost totally, and the true instruction of Marxism. We will have to verify this in more than one text. And let us state that, positive or negative, Bataille thought that his appreciation of Hegelianism had to be translated into an appreciation of Marxism. In a bibliography which was to accompany an unpublished *Théorie de la religion,* one can read this in particular: "This work (*Introduction to the Reading of Hegel* by Kojève) is an explication of *The Phenomenology of the Mind.* The ideas that I have developed are all here in substance. It remains to specify the correspondence between Hegelian analysis and this 'theory of religion': the differences between one representation and the other seem to me to be easily reducible.'' "I insist again on underlining the fact that Alexandre Kojève's interpretation does not depart from Marxism in any way: similarly, it is always easy to perceive that the present 'theory' is always rigorously founded on the analysis of economy.''

8. TN. Baillie, the English translator of Hegel's *Phenomenology,* translates *Herrschaft* as "lordship," while Hyppolite, the French translator, translates *Herr* as *maître,* making the "master's" operation *maîtrise. Maîtrise* also has the sense of mastery, of grasp, and Derrida continually plays on this double sense, which is lost in English. The difference between sovereignty and lordship (*maîtrise*) is that sovereignty does not seek to grasp (*maîtriser*) concepts but rigorously to explode them. All citations from Hegel are indicated in the text; and are from *The Phenomenology of the Mind,* trans. J. B. Baillie (New York: Harper Torchbooks, 1967).

9. "A passage from the preface to the *Phenomenology of the Mind* forcefully expresses the necessity of such an attitude. No doubt that this admirable text, from the initial contact, is of 'capital importance,' not only for understanding Hegel, but in every sense: 'Death, as we may call that unreality, is the most terrible thing, and to keep and hold fast what is dead demands the greatest force

of all. Beauty, powerless and helpless, hates understanding, because the latter exacts from it what it cannot perform. But the life of mind is not one that shuns death, and keeps clear of destruction; it endures death and in death maintains its being. It only wins to its truth when it finds itself utterly torn asunder. It is this mighty power, not by being a positive which turns away from the negative, as when we say of anything it is nothing or it is false, and being then done with it, pass off to something else: on the contrary, mind is this power only by looking the negative in the face, and dwelling with it. This dwelling beside it is the magic power that converts the negative into being.' " (*Hegel,* p. 93). Bataille, whom we are quoting here, while referring to the translation [of the *Phenomenology* into French] by Jean Hyppolite, says that he is reproducing a translation by Alexandre Kojève, which he is not doing exactly. If one takes into account that Hyppolite and Kojève had since modified their translations, one has at one's disposal at least five forms of the text, to which could be added the "original," that other lesson.

10. TN. The independence of self-consciousness is the result of the dialectic of the master and slave.

11. "But laughter, here, is the *negative,* in the Hegelian sense." J.-P. Sartre, "Un nouveau mystique, in *Situations I* (Paris: Gallimard, 1947), p. 160. Laughter is not the negative because its *burst* does not *maintain* itself, is neither linked up to itself nor summarized in a discourse: laughs at the *Aufhebung.*

12. *Conférences sur le non-savoir,* in *Tel Quel* 10.

13. TN. Derrida is playing on the idea that *Aufhebung* means to negate and to conserve at the same time. In the *Phenomenology* each step along the way is "lifted up and interiorized," negated and conserved, in the next step. Thus the *Aufhebung* leaves nothing behind, and is the best of speculators because it wastes nothing and profits from everything. Bataille, Derrida is demonstrating, is not a "speculator" because he is concerned precisely with what is left behind, with the excess which the *Aufhebung* excludes because it cannot profit (i.e., make sense) from it.

14. *Hegel,* pp. 32–33. Cf. also, in *L'expérience intérieure* the entire "Post-scriptum au supplice," notably pp. 193ff.

15. Michel Foucault, in fact, speaks of a "nonpositive affirmation," "Préface à la transgression," *Critique,* 195–96, p. 756.

16. "Of the Hegelian trinity, he suppresses the moment of synthesis." Sartre, *Situations I,* p. 144.

17. Cf. Jean Hyppolite, *Logique et existence: Essai sur la logique de Hegel* (Paris: P.U.F.), p. 28.

18. "Post-scriptum au supplice," in *EI,* p. 189.

19. "Only the serious has *a meaning:* play, which no longer has one, is serious only in the extent to which 'the absence of meaning is also a meaning,' but is always lost in the night of an indifferent nonmeaning. Seriousness, death and pain are the basis of its obtuse truth. But the seriousness of death and pain is the servility of thought." ("Post-scriptum," in *EI,* p. 253) The unity of seriousness, meaning, work, servility, discourse, etc., the unity of man, slave and God—such, in Bataille's eyes, is the profound content of (Hegelian) philosophy. Here, we can only refer to the most explicit texts. (A.) *EI,* p. 105: "In this my efforts recommence and undo Hegel's *Phenomenology.* Hegel's construction is a philosophy of work, of the 'project.' Hegelian man—Being and God—is fulfilled in the adequation of the project.... The slave ... after many meanders, acceeds to the summit of the universal. The only obstacle to this way of thinking (which is, moreover, of an unequaled, and in some way inaccessible, profundity) is that man is irreducible to the project: nondiscursive existence, laughter, ecstasy," etc. (B.) *Le coupable,* p. 133: "In elaborating the philosophy of work (this is the *knecht,* the emancipated slave, the worker, who in the *Phenomenology* becomes God), Hegel has suppressed chance—and laughter," etc. (C.) In *Hegel, la mort* especially, Bataille shows through what *sliding*—which, in the speech of sovereignty, will have to be specifically opposed by another sliding—Hegel misses a sovereignty that he "approached as much as he could," and that he misses "for the benefit of servitude." "The sovereignty of Hegel's attitude springs from a movement revealed by *discourse* and which, in the Sage's mind, is never separated from its revelation. It cannot,

therefore, be fully sovereign: the Sage, in effect, cannot fail to subordinate it for the ends of a Wisdom which assumes the completion of discourse . . . He gathered up sovereignty like a weight, which he dropped'' (pp. 41–42).

20. *Conférences sur le non-savoir.*

21. Cf. the ''Discussion sur le péché'' in *Dieu vivant,* 4 (1945), and Pierre Klossowski, ''A propos du simulacre dans la communication de Georges Bataille,'' *Critique,* 195–96.

22. *EI,* pp. 105 and 213.

23. Cf., for example, *EI,* p. 196: ''the sacrificer succumbs . . . and is lost with his victim,'' etc.

24. ''Moreover, sovereignty is the object that always eludes us, that no one has grasped, that no one ever will grasp. . . . In the *Phenomenology of the Mind,* pursuing this dialectic of the *master* (the lord, the sovereign) and the *slave* (the man subjugated to work), which is at the origin of the Communist theory of class struggle, Hegel brings the slave to triumph, but his apparent sovereignty is then only the autonomous will of servitude; for its part, sovereignty has only the kingdom of failure'' (*Genet,* in *La littérature et le mal*).

25. TN. *Erinnerung* is the Hegelian, speculative concept of interiorizing memory. Like *Aufhebung* (cf. note 13 above) it leaves nothing behind. Recognition is the Hegelian category which governs the dialectic of master and slave: it is the master's final recognition of his truth in the slave that permits the *Aufhebung,* the master's interiorizing of the slave, which produces the freedom of self-consciousness. If the master interiorizes servility through speculative concepts, sovereignty must actively forget these concepts; and it must not seek recognition, as does the master, for this inevitably leads to servility.

26. TN. For Plato, Socrates' stature is summarized by the fact that his instruction was oral, that *he did not write.* And Plato always attacks the Sophists, the professional writers, because they make speech inauthentic. Cf. ''La pharmacie de Platon,'' in *La dissémination,* pp. 120ff.

27. Taken outside their general syntax, their writing, certain propositions, in effect, manifest voluntarism, an entire philosophy of the *operating* activity of a subject. Sovereignty is a *practical operation* (cf., for example, the *Conférences sur le non-savoir,* p. 14). But one would not *read* Bataille's text if one did not weave these propositions into the general warp that undoes them by linking them to, or by inscribing them within, themselves. Thus, a page further on: ''And it does not even suffice to say: one cannot speak of the sovereign moment without altering it, without altering it insofar as it is truly sovereign. To the same extent as to speak of it, to *seek* these movements is contradictory. At the moment when we seek something, whatever it is, we do not live in sovereign fashion, we subordinate the present moment to a future moment that will follow it. Perhaps we attain the sovereign moment following our effort, and, in effect, it is possible that an effort is necessary, but between the time of the effort and sovereign time there is necessarily a cut-off, and, one could even say, an abyss.''

28. Sartre's study, cited above, joints its first and second parts with the hinge of this proposition: ''But form is not everything: let us look at the content'' (*Situations I,* p. 142).

29. ''A dislodging, but aware use of words,'' says Sollers (''De grandes irrégularités de langage,'' *Critique,* 195–96).

30. One of the essential themes of Sartre's study (*Un nouveau mystique*) is also the accusation of scientism, joined with that of mysticism. (''Scientism also will falsify M. Bataille's entire thought,'' p. 147).

31. Unknowledge is historical, as Sartre notes (''Unknowledge is essentially historical, since it can be designated only as a certain experience that a certain man had at a certain date,'' p. 140), only on its discursive, economical, subordinated side, which can be seen and, more precisely, can be *designated* only within the reassuring closure of knowledge. The ''edifying narrative''—this is how Sartre qualifies *interior experience* immediately afterward—is, on the contrary, on the side of knowledge, history, and meaning.

32. On the operation which consists in *miming absolute knowledge,* at whose termination ''unknowledge having been attained, absolute knowledge becomes one kind of knowledge among

others,'' cf. pp. 73ff. and 138ff. of *EI*, where important developments are devoted to the Cartesian model (''a solid base on which everything rests'') and the Hegelian model (''circularity'') of knowledge.

33. One would commit a gross error in interpreting these propositions in a ''reactionary'' sense. The consumption of the excess of energy by a determined class is not the destructive consuming of meaning, but the significative reappropriation of a surplus value within the space of restricted economy. From this point of view, sovereignty is absolutely revolutionary. But it is also revolutionary as concerns a revolution which would only reorganize the world of work and would redistribute values within the space of meaning, that is to say, still within restricted economy. This last movement—only slightly perceived, here and there, by Bataille (for example, in *La part maudite*, when he evokes the ''radicalism of Marx'' and the ''revolutionary sense that Marx formulated in a sovereign way'') and most often muddled by conjectural approximations (for example in the fifth part of *La part maudite*)—is rigorously necessary, but as a phase within the strategy of general economy.

34. The writing of sovereignty is neither true nor false, neither truthful nor insincere. It is purely *fictive* in a sense of this word that the classical oppositions of true and false, essence and appearance, lack. It withdraws itself from every theoretical or ethical question. Simultaneously, it offers itself to these questions on its minor side, to which it is united, as Bataille says, in work, discourse and meaning. (''What obliges me to write, I imagine, is the fear of going mad,'' *Sur Nietzsche.*) On this side one can wonder, as easily and legitimately as possible, if Bataille is ''sincere.'' Which Sartre does: ''Here then is an invitation to lose ourselves without forethought, without counterpart, without salvation. Is it sincere?'' (p. 162). Further on: ''For, after all, M. Bataille writes, occupies a position at the Bibliothèque Nationale, reads, makes love, eats'' (p. 163).

35. *Conférences sur le non-savoir*. The Objects of science are, then, ''effects'' of knowledge. Effects of nonmeaning. This is, for example, God, insofar as an object of theology. ''God is also an effect of un-knowledge'' (ibid.).

36. TN. *L'expérience intérieure* was to be part of a projected series to be called *Somme athéologique*.

37. Cf. Meister Eckhart, for example. The negative movement of the discourse on God is only a phase of positive ontotheology. ''God is nameless. . . . If I say God is a being, it is not true: he is a transcendental essence, a superessential nothing'' (*Be ye renewed in the spirit*). This was only a turn or detour of language for ontotheology: ''But when I say God is not being, is superior to being, I do not with that deny him being: I dignify and exalt it in him'' (*Like the morning star*) (Franz Pfeiffer, *Meister Eckhart* [London: John M. Watkins, 1956], pp. 246 and 211).

38. In order to define the point at which he departs from Hegel and Kojève, Bataille specifies what he means by ''conscious mysticism,'' ''beyond classical mysticism'': ''The atheistic mystic, *conscious of himself*, conscious of having to die and to disappear, would live, as Hegel says, *evidently about himself,* 'in absolute rending'; but for Hegel, it was only a question of a phase: as opposed to Hegel, the atheist mystic would never emerge from it, 'contemplating the Negative quite directly,' but never able to transpose it into Being, refusing to do so and maintaining himself in ambiguity'' (*Hegel*).

39. Here, again, the difference counts more than the content of the terms. And these two series of oppositions (major/minor, archaic/classic) should be combined with the series we elaborated above as concerns the poetic (sovereign nonsubordination/insertion/subordination). To archaic sovereignty, ''which indeed seems to have implied a kind of impotency,'' and which, insofar as it is ''authentic'' sovereignty, refuses ''the exercise of power'' (subjugating lordship), Bataille opposes ''the classic idea of sovereignty,'' which ''is linked to the idea of command'' and consequently wields all the attributes which are refused, *under the same word,* to the sovereign operation (free, victorious, self-conscious, acknowledged, etc., subjectivity, which is therefore mediated and turned away from itself, returning to itself for having been turned away from itself by the work of the slave). Now, Bataille demonstrates that the ''major positions'' of sovereignty, as much as the minor ones, can be

"inserted into the sphere of activty" (*Méthode*).

The difference between the major and the minor is therefore only analogous to the difference between the archaic and the classic. And neither the one nor the other must be understood in a classic or minor fashion. The archaic is not the originary or the authentic, as they are determined by philosophical discourse. The major is not opposed to the minor like big to little, high to low. In "Vieille taupe" (Old Mole), (an unpublished article, rejected by *Bifurs*), the oppositions of high to low, and of all the significations in *sur-, super-* (surreal, superman) and in *sub-* (subterranean, etc.), of the imperialist eagle and the proletarian mole, are examined in all the possibilities of their reversals.

40. "Play is nothing if not an open and unreserved challenge to everything opposed to play" (Marginal note in the unpublished "Théorie de la religion," which Bataille also planned to entitle "To die laughing and to laugh at dying")

41. "A gesture ... irreducible to classical logic ... and for which no logic seems to be constituted" says Sollers in *Le toit*, which begins by unmasking, *in their systematicity*, all the forms of pseudotransgression, the social and historical figurations in which can be read the complicity between "the man who lives without protest under the yoke of the law, and the man for whom the law is nothing." In this last case, repression is only "redoubled" (*Le toit: Essai de lecture systématique*, in *Logiques* [Paris: Seuil, 1968], p. 168).

42. Like every discourse, like Hegel's, Bataille's discourse has the form of a structure of interpretations. Each proposition, which is already interpretive in nature, can be interpreted by another proposition. Therefore, if we proceed prudently and all the while remain in Bataille's text, we can detach an interpretation from its reinterpretation and submit it to another interpretation bound to other propositions of the system. Which, without interrupting general systematicity, amounts to recognizing the strong and weak moments in the interpretation of a body of thought by itself, these differences of force keeping to the strategic necessity of finite discourse. Naturally our own interpretive reading has attempted to pass through what *we* have interpreted as the major moments, and has done so in order to bind them together. This "method"—which we name thus within the closure of knowledge—is justified by what we are writing here, in Bataille's wake, about the suspension of the epoch of meaning and truth. Which neither frees nor prohibits us from determining the *rules* of force and of weakness: which are always a function of: (1) the distance from the moment of sovereignty; (2) the misconstruing of the rigorous norms of knowledge.

The greatest force is the force of a writing which, in the most audacious transgression, continues to maintain and to acknowledge the necessity of the system of prohibitions (knowledge, science, philosophy, work, history, etc.). Writing is always traced between these two sides of the limit.

Among the weak moments of Bataille's discourse, certain ones are signaled by the determined unknowledge which is a certain philosophical ignorance. And Sartre justly notes that "he has visibly not understood Heidegger, of whom he often and clumsily speaks" and that then "philosophy avenges itself" (*Situations I*, p. 145). Here, there would be much to say about the reference to Heidegger. We will attempt to do so elsewhere. Let us only note that on this point and several others, Bataille's "faults" reflected the faults which, at that time, marked the reading of Heidegger by "specialized philosophers." To adopt Corbin's translation of *Dasein* as *human-reality* (a monstrosity of unlimited consequences that the first four paragraphs of *Sein und Zeit* had warned against), to use this translation as an element of a discourse, to speak insistently about a "humanism common to Nietzsche and our author [Bataille]," (p. 165) etc.—this, too, was philosophically very *risky* on Sartre's part. Drawing attention to this point in order to illuminate Bataille's text and context, we doubt neither the historic necessity of this *risk*, nor the function of awakening whose price it was, within a conjuncture that is no longer ours. All this merits recognition. Awakening and time have been necessary.

43. TN. *Sens*, in French, means both sense and direction. To lose sense, to lose meaning, is to lose one's way, to lose all sense of direction.

Ten	Sturcture, Sign, and Play
	in the Discourse of
	Human Sciences

1. TN. The reference, in a restricted sense, is to the Freudian theory of neurotic symptoms and of dream interpretation in which a given symbol is understood contradictorily as both the desire to fulfill an impulse and the desire to suppress the impulse. In a general sense the reference is to Derrida's thesis that logic and coherence themselves can only be understood contradictorily, since they presuppose the suppression of *différance*, "writing" in the sense of the general economy. Cf. "La pharmacie de Platon," in *La dissemination*, pp. 125–26, where Derrida uses the Freudian model of dream interpretation in order to clarify the contractions embedded in philosophical coherence.

2. *The Raw and the Cooked*, trans. John and Doreen Wightman (New York: Harper and Row, 1969), p. 14. [Translation somewhat modified.]

3. *The Elementary Structures of Kinship*, trans. James Bell, John von Sturmer, and Rodney Needham (Boston: Beacon Press, 1969), p. 8.

4. Ibid., p. 3.

5. *The Savage Mind* (London: George Weidenfeld and Nicolson; Chicago: The University of Chicago Press, 1966), p. 247.

6. Ibid., p. 17.

7. *The Raw and the Cooked*, p. 2.

8. Ibid., pp. 5–6.

9. Ibid., p. 12.

10. Ibid., pp. 17–18.

11. Ibid., pp. 7–8.

12. TN. This double sense of supplement—to supply something which is missing, or to supply something additional—is at the center of Derrida's deconstruction of traditional linguistics in *De la grammatologie*. In a chapter entitled "The Violence of the Letter: From Lévi-Strauss to Rousseau" (pp. 149ff.), Derrida expands the analysis of Lévi-Strauss begun in this essay in order further to clarify the ways in which the contradictions of traditional logic "program" the most modern conceptual apparatuses of linguistics and the social sciences.

13. "Introduction à l'oeuvre de Marcel Mauss," in Marcel Mauss, *Sociologie et anthropologie* (Paris: P.U.F., 1950), p. xlix.

14. Ibid., pp. xlix–1.

15. George Charbonnier, *Entretiens avec Claude Lévi-Strauss* (Paris: Plon, 1961).

16. *Race and History* (Paris: Unesco Publications, 1958).

17. "Introduction à l'oeuvre de Marcel Mauss," p. xlvi.

18. TN. The reference is to *Tristes tropiques*, trans. John Russell (London: Hutchinson and Co., 1961).

Eleven	Ellipsis

1. This is the title of the third volume of the *Livre des questions* (1965). The second volume, the *Livre de Yukel*, appeared in 1964. Cf. chap. 3 above, "Edmond Jabès and the Question of the Book."

2. TN. The exit from the identical into the same recalls the "leap out of metaphysics" into the question of difference, which is also the question of the same, as elaborated by Heidegger in *Identity and Difference*.

3. TN. The eternal return is the Nietzschean conception of the same.

4. Jean Catesson, "Journal non-intime et points cardinaux," *Measures*, no. 4, October 1937.

Sources

one   "Force et signification." *Critique,* nos. 193–94, June–July 1963.

two   "Cogito et l'histoire de la folie." Lecture delivered 4 March 1963 at the Collège Philosophique and published in *Revue de métaphysique et de morale,* 1964, nos. 3 and 4.

three   "Edmond Jabès et la question du livre." *Critique,* no. 201, January 1964.

four   "Violence et métaphysique: Essai sur la pensée d'Emmanuel Levinas." *Revue de métaphysique et de morale,* 1964, nos. 3 and 4.

five   " 'Genèse et structure' et la phénoménologie." Lecture delivered 1959 at Cerisy-la-Salle and published in *Genèse et structure,* edited by Gandillac, Goldmann and Piaget. The Hague: Mouton, 1964.

six   "La parole soufflée." *Tel Quel,* no. 20, winter 1965.

seven   "Freud et la scène de l'écriture." Lecture delivered at the Institut de Psychanalyse and published in *Tel Quel,* no. 26, summer 1966.

eight   "Le théâtre de la cruauté et la clôture de la représentation." Lecture delivered at the Artaud colloquium, International Festival of University Theater, Parma, April 1966, and published in *Critique,* no. 230, July 1966.

nine   "De l'économie restreinte à l'économie générale: Un hegelianisme sans réserve." *L'arc,* May 1967.

ten   "La structure, le signe et le jeu dans le discours des sciences humaines." Lecture delivered 21 October 1966 at the International Colloquium on Critical Languages and the Sciences of Man, The Johns Hopkins University, Baltimore.

eleven "L'ellipse." First published in *L'écriture et la différence,* 1967.